RESILIENCE BY DESIGN

HOW TO SURVIVE AND THRIVE IN A COMPLEX AND TURBULENT WORLD

IAN SNAPE | MIKE WEEKS

WILEY

STRESS IS A
GLOBAL EPIDEMIC

As part of its 2019 Global Emotions Report, Gallup asked 151,000 people in 143 countries about their stress levels.

The day before the polling was carried out, 35% of people globally said they experienced "a lot of stress."

The highest reported stress by country was Greece at 59%, with the US ranking in the top 10 at 55%, with Uganda also at 55%.

Clearly, there is much more to being stressed than geography, poverty, or war.

Library of Congress Cataloging-in-Publication Data

Names: Snape, Ian, 1968- author. | Weeks, Mike
  (Trainer), author.
Title: Resilience by design : how to survive and thrive
  in a complex and turbulent world / Ian Snape, Mike
  Weeks.
Description: Hoboken, New Jersey : Wiley, [2022] |
  Includes index.
Identifiers: LCCN 2021033032 (print) | LCCN
  2021033033 (ebook) | ISBN 9781119794936
  (paperback) | ISBN 9781119794981 (adobe pdf) |
  ISBN 9781119795063 (epub)
Subjects: LCSH: Resilience (Personality trait) | Stress
  (Psychology) | Job stress.
Classification:LCCBF698.35.R47S6292022(print)|
  LCC BF698.35.R47 (ebook) | DDC 155.2/4--dc23
LC record available at https://lccn.loc.gov/2021033032
LC ebook record available at https://lccn.loc.
  gov/2021033033

Cover Design: Bel Ramos
Cover Illustrations: Tim Ulewicz
Printed and bound by CPI Group (UK) Ltd, Croydon,
CR0 4YY

C115830_151021

If stress is the global epidemic of the twenty-first century, then resilience is the cure.

Resilience is the ability to prepare for, respond to, and adapt to incremental changes; challenging, difficult, and disruptive situations; and major upheaval or catastrophes.

Resilient people make sense of their external world in ways that are highly resourceful, both for themselves and for others.

CONTENTS

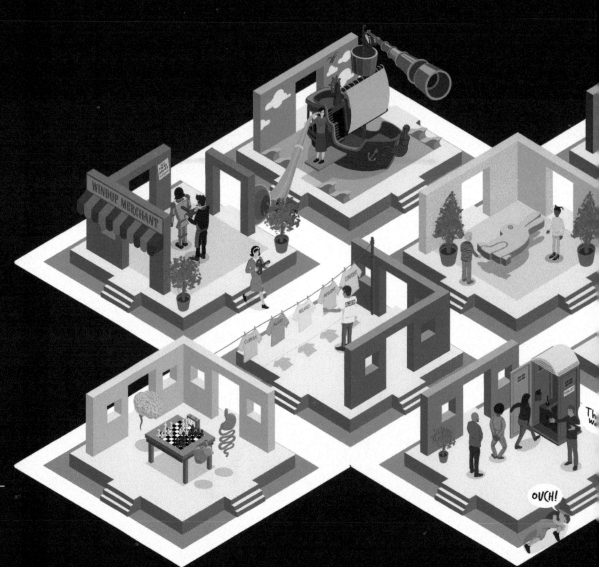

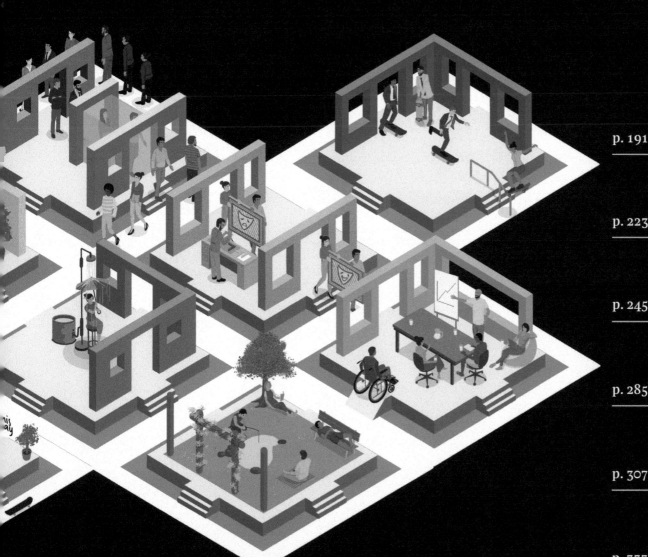

DEDICATED TO

Lizzie, Atticus, and Aurelius

&

Bean, Iggy, and Obe

—————————

*Without question, our resilience is grounded
in the loving support of our families.*

ABOUT THE AUTHORS

IAN SNAPE

Dr. Ian Snape is former research leader and executive at the Australian Antarctic Division. He has led teams on 14 polar expeditions to both polar regions.

A fan of the Harry Potter books, he's the real-life Professor Snape, previously holding Professorial Fellowships at the University of Melbourne and Macquarie University. He is the author of more than 100 academic papers across a wide range of scientific disciplines.

In a parallel life, just like Snape from Hogwarts, he's a master in defense against the dark arts, holding black belts in Taekwondo and Hapkido. He is also a flow junkie, a passionate ski mountaineer, a climber, and a competitive sailor.

Using the techniques in this book, he coaches and trains CEOs, olympic athletes, and frontline professionals.

MIKE WEEKS

Mike Weeks is a former free solo climber and adventurer. He began coaching in 2004, famously working on screen with Jack Osbourne in the globally broadcast *Jack Osbourne: Adrenaline Junkie*.

After a brief flirtation with celebrity, Mike began training and coaching elite athletes, members of the UK special forces, and frontline workers, including medics responding to humanitarian disasters. In 2010, he was placed in charge of developing a mental health clinic and program for Sean Penn's JPHRO, which supported over 50,000 displaced Haitians following the catastrophic earthquake. He's also provided resilience and recovery training across the USA, in Peru, the Philippines, and Ukraine.

Mike currently leads sovereign-security resilience initiatives with the Indonesian government, to combat illegal fishing and trafficking, as well as clean energy transition.

In 2014, Ian and Mike were introduced by their shared friend and mentor John Grinder. Realizing their parallel interests and experience in training frontline professionals, they formed Frontline Mind. Mike focused on developing the company's creative and media arm, and Ian focused on science, leadership, and program design.

OUR MISSION:

"To enable individuals, teams, and organizations to survive and thrive in a complex, turbulent world."

To do this, we created a state-of-the-art online learning platform. We aimed for a fusion of science, art, and effective learning design. This book mirrors that program.

Though we live in different countries, we continue to train teams together, seeking new opportunities to learn and challenge each other. Our relationship goes beyond business. We are like brothers; our families have become one, and we regularly adventure together in the outdoors.

ABOUT THIS BOOK

As humans, it can sometimes seem that we're flawed by quirks of evolution, each seemingly destined to experience a lifelong rollercoaster of ups and downs, joys and sorrows, gains and losses, health and disease, stress and resilience.

One popular Eastern philosophy goes as far as saying:

"All life is suffering."

We disagree!

Suffering may be the experience for some people, sometimes, but our view, backed by scientific evidence, is that we can create a better life and become more resilient to life's ups and downs. We are not predestined to suffer, or in fact predestined for anything. We each have agency, and we can craft and shape our continually evolving sense of identity, lifestyle, and the contexts we inhabit.

We agree that people are experiencing unprecedented pressure to respond to rapid change, increasing resource demands, and uncertainty. Reported cases of stress, burnout, anxiety, depression, and a multitude of connected illnesses are on a steady rise in most of the modern world. However, as we will reveal, we always have a choice in how we respond to pressures, demands, and uncertainty.

For millions of people, learning how to be resilient isn't just a benefit for the constantly shifting demands of their work. Resilience can improve every element of their lives. With the world changing so quickly around us, this is no longer just nice to have. It's absolutely essential if we are to survive and thrive in a complex, turbulent world.

We've given talks to, trained, and coached thousands of people around the world, including during humanitarian disasters, in the extremes of Antarctica, and in the jungles of the Amazon. We've helped people develop resilience everywhere from the slums of Haiti to the polished board rooms of major corporations.

Across these varied domains, we've modeled, studied, and interviewed individuals who stand out. We call these people the resilient elite. They range from mountain guides and Olympians, special-forces soldiers, mental health nurses, correctional officers and first responders, to entrepreneurs and scientists. The resilient elite are also hidden in plain sight. They are the single mums and dads bringing up disabled children with very little external support, or the elder-care workers who deal with grief and loss on a daily basis and somehow manage to leave this behind when they step through their front door.

One fact we discovered again and again:

There is no such thing as a stressful situation.

How well we survive and thrive is entirely down to how we perceive ourselves and the world around us. Our resilience depends on our ability to access the behavioral patterns that have enabled our species to sense, respond, adapt, and thrive through both feast and famine, calm and chaos.

Resilience by Design is the world's most detailed and evidence-based how-to manual for resilience. It bridges the gap between neuroscience theory and practical techniques that can be used every day. We wrote it for the people we care about, the people we love, and the people we have yet to meet who want to change their lives for the better. We wrote it because, right now, more than ever, millions of people are living in uncertainty and need a guide for the unknown paths ahead. Whether you're a formal leader in an organization or community, or an informal one in a family or social setting, you can use the techniques we cover in this book to simultaneously develop resilience for yourself and to help those around you. Every input into the complex system that is our world affects all of the connected parts, often in unpredictable ways. You'll find that, by developing personal resilience, you'll become a catalyst for positive change in all the contexts in which you play a small or a large part. By becoming resilient, we can positively influence our families, friends, work colleagues, and even new acquaintances, to become more resilient as well.

As you read these pages, you'll learn how to perceive the world differently, how to think and act differently at work and across other situations. If you want to bring resilience to a challenging home life, or if you want to excel in whatever field you choose, this book will help. This book can be read from end to end, or you can thumb through the book, dipping in here and there for a story that catches your eye, exploring some of our research, or experimenting with an activity, or adopting time-tested techniques.

OUR APPROACH IS:

Practitioner-led. Our priorities, program design, and the structure of this book reflect what resilient practitioners actually do when operating under pressure or in a crisis.

Theory-backed. We present the scientific findings from neuroscience, psychology, complexity theory, neurolinguistics, cognitive science, and philosophy, where these fields help to make sense or explain what practitioners actually do. Rather than leading with theory, we lead with practical advice. This is a conscious choice. We believe that much of the published theory on resilience is disconnected from real-world application.

Evidence-based. The techniques we present are tried and tested, and we have tracked evidence for efficacy in individuals, teams, and organizations.

By using the techniques we'll cover in this book for as little as five minutes per day, you'll be able to develop entirely new thinking skills. By practicing these skills, you'll find that they will arise reflexively in situations that you might have previously responded to with a stress response, or with anxiety, or confusion.

No matter where you presently are between stress and resilience, it's our intention to inspire you and the people you are connected with to take personal responsibility for your life and your choices. It is only when we take responsibility that we can begin working toward living our best life, which is adaptable to all circumstances.

We invite you to take a deep breath, forget everything you think you know about stress, switch to a state of curiosity, and allow us to show you how to develop your own elite level resilience — by design.

FOR MORE INFORMATION ABOUT RESILIENCE TRAINING:

info@frontlinemind.com
frontlinemind.com

ACKNOWLEDGMENTS

This book would never have been written if not for the influence, teachings, and insights of our shared friends and mentors, John Grinder and Carmen Bostic St. Clair. Both of us have shared experiences rock climbing and adventuring with John, and we acknowledge him as the catalyst in both of our careers as coaches and trainers. Carmen and John's work forms the backbone of this book.

We also found that the resilient elite operate adaptively in response to context in a way that is well described by the Cynefin framework, developed by Dave Snowden. We gratefully acknowledge Dave, Sonja Blignaut, Zhen Goh, and Michael Cheveldave at Cognitive Edge for generously sharing their ideas, for challenging and mentoring us, and then partnering with us to co-create online training resources.

John Grinder and Dave Snowden both draw heavily on original ideas from the late anthropologist Gregory Bateson. Possibly more than any academic of his generation, or the generation before him, Bateson understood the nature of mind, systems, complexity, and the importance of relationships in our place on earth. His writings underpin their work and ours.

Penny Tompkins and James Lawley have mentored and supported Ian to develop a deep appreciation of metaphor through their original work and David Grove's Clean Language. Their artistry is beyond words.

In a world of reductionist thinking, those experts who can grasp the complexity of life stand out. Our writing, training, and choices in life have been greatly impacted and improved by workshops and publications by the following authors: Ian McGilchrist (*The Master and His Emissary*);

Nassim Nicholas Taleb (*The Black Swan, Antifragile, and Skin in the Game*); Norman Doidge (*The Brain That Changes Itself* and *The Brain's Way of Healing*); and Gerd Gigerenzer (*Gut Feelings* and *Risk Savvy*).

A special thanks to Gary Kuehn and a number of other mountain guides, some sadly no longer with us. He was the first person Ian modeled to unpack tacit decision-making and leadership in complex, high-risk domains. For three years, Gary allowed Ian to literally follow in his ski tracks through crevasse fields, dodging avalanche-prone terrain to the ends of civilization into a war zone in the Middle East chasing first descents. And to John Grinder again, for giving Ian the skills to know when to model and when to hold back enough to stay alive, avert disaster, or rescue others when things went bad.

Thanks to Scott Coleman for discussions, research, and editing; Bailey Murzecki-Hince for a brilliant job in research and bibliography. The book has benefited immensely from discussions, editorial and technical reviews by many people: Bryan Szabo, Robert Holmes, Sonja Blignaut, Zhen Goh, Catherine Viney, Chet Richards, Robert Kirk, Penny Tompkins, Mike Radburn, Prof. Siobhan Harpur, Dr. Greg Swartz, and Dr. Lizzie Elliott. Greg Hince, Dorian Broomhall, Jared Dubey, Nick Mitchell, and Mel Murzecki-Hince provided essential background support in our adjacent ventures and kept the light on in our business ventures.

Thanks to our agent, Roger Freet at Folio Literary Management, for his endless good cheer, business acumen, and guidance. Finally, this publication would not be possible without the support and trust from our brilliant team at Wiley Publishing, namely Shannon Vargo, Deborah Schindlar, and Sally Baker.

TIM AND BEL

Tim Ulewicz and Bel Ramos have been central to the development of our brand. They have also been central in the creation of this book.

Tim is a full-time illustrator at Frontline Mind. Based in Bristol, England, he is a top-level break dancer and graffiti artist. He adds the "cool" to our company and this book.

Bel is a graphic designer based in Hobart and has been responsible for the design and the overall feel of this book.

SOURCE ATTRIBUTION

We have taken every effort to reference our sources. We cited 462 scientific papers, 94 books, and 84 miscellaneous publications to both respect other people's ideas and in the hope that our book acts as a conduit to further learning. Where we have discovered an idea presented in a book that is coherent with our synthesis and is itself derived from earlier work, we have tracked down the original research and cross-checked the primary evidence. Where practical, we have referenced both primary and secondary sources. If we have missed an original source, we apologise. Please send us a correction and we will clean-up our referencing in the 2nd edition.

DISCLAIMER

The ideas and activities presented in this book are designed to create more choices for you. This includes the choice to continue doing whatever you would have done without reading this book. The choices you make are entirely your own, and we take no responsibility for any outcome, adverse consequences, distress, or injury that may result from the application of the patterns of resilience presented here.

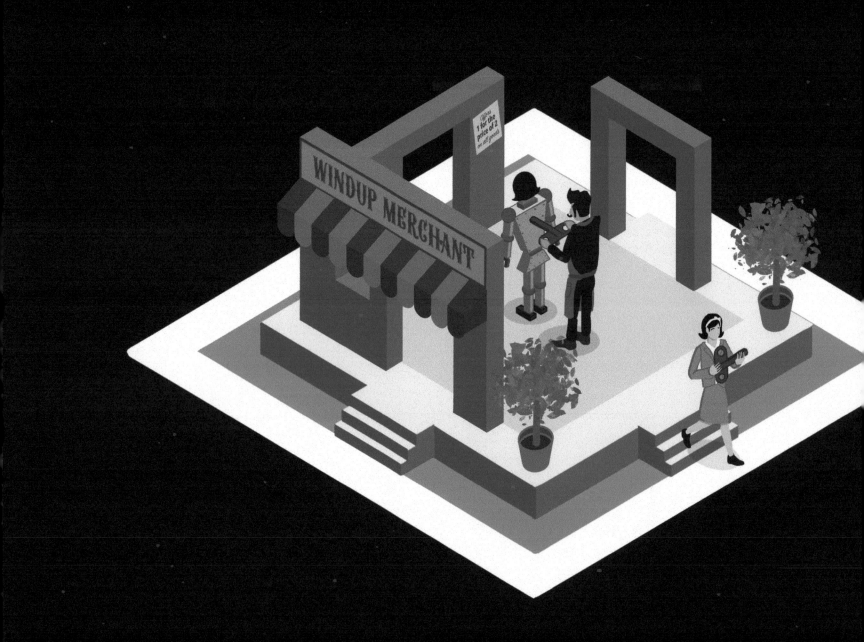

RESILIENCE

STRESSED OR CONFUSED?

In the first half of the 20th century, the researcher and medical doctor Hans Salye brought to popular use the term "stress" as a "biologic response."[1–3] Since then, the original concept and meaning of stress has mutated.[1,4,5]

We often misuse the word "stress" in the context of both our health and our relationship with the external world, especially our immediate environment.

Stress often describes the **cause** or specific environment, such as the workplace or traffic jams on the motorway. For example, "it's a stressful workplace" or "the traffic on the motorway is stressful."

Stress is used to describe the **affect**, the mechanism of injury, or the process of doing. For example, "he winds me up," or "the traffic is doing me in."

The World Health Organization has a simple and precise definition of workplace stress:

*"Workplace stress is the **response** people may experience when presented with work demands and pressures that are not matched to their knowledge and abilities and which challenge their ability to cope."*[6]

Stress then is a response to pressure and demands — just one of a range of possible responses available to us. Unfortunately, the relationship between the demands and pressures of the workplace or any situation and the incidence of stress has been linked through causation.

Stress is also used to describe the **effect**, the felt state of being. For example, "I feel like I'm going to explode!"

THE INSIDE-OUT UPSIDE-DOWN VIEW OF WORKPLACE STRESS

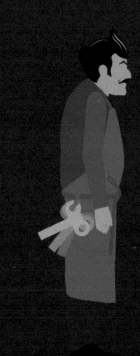

WINDUP MERCHANT

When people talk about stress, they often assume a direct, causal relationship between the external context and a person's internal response. For example, Medibank[7] describes how tight deadlines or job insecurity *cause* stress.

This kind of thinking permeates the scientific literature on stress. Studies have linked the number of deaths firefighters witness to incidences of PTSD.[8] Burnout syndrome has been linked causally to Intensive Care Unit workplaces.[9,10] The list goes on and on. We are told that events from persistent abuse, exposure to death and violence, working with trauma and suffering, through to bullying or unrealistic workloads cause stress.[11–15]

This is the outside-in view of stress.

Thinking in this way creates victims by placing the blame on external factors that we're told are *sources* of stress. This ignores the role of personal choice in

a largely unconscious creative process of responding to external stimuli.

We look at stress differently. We view stress inside-out and upside-down. People create felt states of being, and then they call these emotional states stress. This stress is not external; it is internal, a response that is generated based on our unique perception of the world.

The term "stress" is inappropriately applied to both the cause or environment, and affect or mechanism, and it is also used in a highly ambiguous way to describe a variety of states that some people create unconsciously to cope with challenging environments.

Some people, especially those who believe stress is bad and is caused by their external environment, create a state that might be characterized by tightness in the chest, restriction of blood vessels, high blood pressure, and down the track, hypertension, cardiovascular disease, and premature death.[16–25]

Others use the term "stress" to describe states of heightened response to challenge that include the opposite physiological characteristics. The terms "distress" and "eustress" have been used to describe these responses, although in detail everyone creates "stress" in unique or idiosyncratic ways.

Indeed, people respond in many different ways to the same environment or situation, often without the label "stress." Some people are able to cope with all sorts of challenges. Some people even cope well with bullying, threats to physical safety, or exposure to potentially traumatic events such as death or extreme human suffering. However, as the challenges or risks go up, so does the *probability* that more and more normal people will experience coping difficulties in environments for which they are ill-equipped.

In these circumstances, many people respond with distress as their otherwise resilient state fails to cope, hence the correlation between risk and stress.

In many cases, there is a strong correlation between stress and adverse life events or workplace risk factors; however, this relationship is not causative. Most importantly, people are able to adapt and learn from adversity, and resilience can improve naturally through experience or through training.

CORRELATION IS NOT CAUSATION

If we temporarily accept the view that resilience in a population of people follows a "normal" or Gaussian distribution, we would have three groups of people (sadly, experts use these sorts of statistics to define what is "normal" or "not normal," sometimes with adverse consequences for anyone that is different in some way).

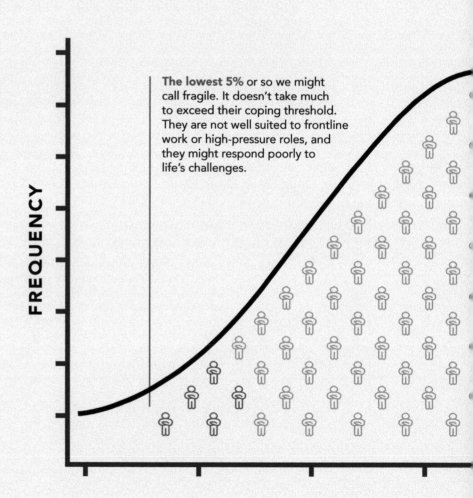

The lowest 5% or so we might call fragile. It doesn't take much to exceed their coping threshold. They are not well suited to frontline work or high-pressure roles, and they might respond poorly to life's challenges.

FREQUENCY

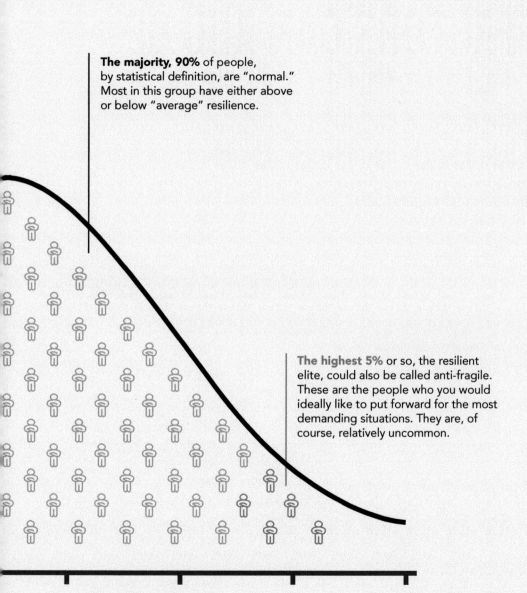

The majority, 90% of people, by statistical definition, are "normal." Most in this group have either above or below "average" resilience.

The highest 5% or so, the resilient elite, could also be called anti-fragile. These are the people who you would ideally like to put forward for the most demanding situations. They are, of course, relatively uncommon.

RESILIENCE

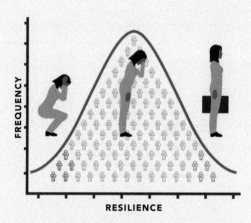

FREQUENCY

RESILIENCE

It's important to remember that resilience is not fixed. Many people go through periods when they are more or less resilient.

LIFESTYLE RISK FACTORS CAN ADD UP

Multiple lifestyle risk factors can easily add up in ways that challenge resilience.

The workplace is one context that commonly overwhelms resilience strategies, and very few organizations effectively screen for resilience. This often leads to a mismatch, where the demands, pressures, risks, and threats exceed the "normal" or "average" employee's ability to cope.[6]

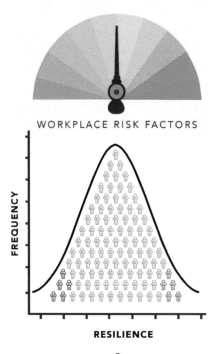

WORKPLACE RISK FACTORS

FREQUENCY

RESILIENCE

Some common workplace risk factors include:

- Overwhelming workload[26–38]
- Insufficient resources to do the job
- Bullying
- Threats to physical well-being
- Poorly defined KPI targets
- Lack of transparency
- Unsocial rosters
- Excessive overtime

Collectively these workplace risk factors can easily add up.

Nearly half of frontline employees report being depressed, anxious, stressed, or having PTSD.[39–44] These are mostly "normal" people who are operating in an environment where their current ability to cope has been exceeded.

RISK FACTORS ROOM

OVERWHELM

ILL-DEFINED KPI TARGETS

INSUFFICIENT RESOURCES TO DO THE JOB

POOR TRANSPARENCY

UNSOCIAL ROSTERS

EXCESSIVE OVERTIME

BULLYING

THREAT TO PHYSICAL WELLBEING

Workplace risk factors

RESILIENT PEOPLE CREATE HEALTHY WORKPLACES AND LIFESTYLES

In our view, it is best to restrict the term "stress" to the description of an internal state of response to the external world. The term is misleading when used to describe either the external environment as a source or cause of stress, or the imagined causal link between stimulus and response.

Continuing to use the workplace as an example, if there were a cause-effect relationship between workplace and stress, it would more likely be an upside-down one. Stressed-out people create high-risk workplaces; resilient people create healthy and productive ones.

It is better to think of states such as stress and the broader concept of personal resilience as embodied responses occurring in complex systems. Schools, workplaces, shopping malls, and even homes are examples of complex systems that change as a consequence of feedback based on our interaction with them.

We can take two approaches, preferably simultaneously, to bust the stress epidemic and develop resilience:

1. Train every individual to become more resilient in their responses, recognizing that this is an inside-out process. In this way the new "normal" becomes skewed toward resilient.

2. Reduce lifestyle and workplace risk factors, such as financial overcommitment or exposure to poor management practices, thereby lowering the threshold required for personal resilience.

Importantly, resilient people who choose their emotional states are in the best possible position to create a lifestyle that supports their intentions and supports others around them to do the same.

RESILIENCE BY DESIGN

Throughout this book, we direct attention from unresourceful states like distress to the concept of resilience.

Personal resilience is the ability to prepare for, respond to, and adapt to change. This could be incremental change, challenges, difficulties, or disruptions, as well as dramatic upheaval or catastrophe.

Resilient people make sense of their external world in ways that are resourceful to them. They perceive differently from those who "stress" over similar situations. Provided that the response is properly calibrated, stress, anxiety, fear, or any other state can sometimes be appropriate at the right intensity in specific situations.

- If stress is a signal to take action, and we do take action, it serves us well.
- If anxiety alerts us to prepare for the future, and we do prepare, it serves us well.
- If fear warns us of a threat, and we respond with appropriate caution, it serves us well.

Any one of these states can be overdone, though, resulting in paralysis, or down the track, burnout, ill health, and early death.

Our challenge is to develop context-appropriate states with an intensity that matches the needs of the moment. When we give states an emotional label or, worse, a diagnosis, all we are doing is communicating with others in a form of shorthand. Whether or how we are understood by others is always contingent on their own experiences.

Resilient people have access to a wide range of states, opening up the possibility for an equally wide range of responses. The more possible responses you can draw on, the greater the chances that one of them will meet the challenges and risks of the situation you encounter.

Confidence to the point of arrogance, or overdone stoic attitudes such as toughing it out no matter what, can end up with the result of catastrophic failure.

Resilience by Design unlocks the creative process of personal resilience. To support the reader in doing this, we present research-backed, practical material in what we hope is an engaging and thought-provoking format.

Keywords that are commonly used to describe states of resilience are...flow, confident, in control, good stress, edgy, calm, excited, connected, and even "bitchy."

HAPPINESS IS NOT ESSENTIAL FOR RESILIENCE AND HIGH PERFORMANCE

Ian: You won through the first four rounds. What happened in the fifth?

Carmen: I didn't do my usual mental preparation routine.

Ian: What were you thinking that you didn't prepare the same way?

Carmen: I felt good...

Ian: Is "feeling good" an important part of your high-performance state?

long pause

Carmen: No, when I fight at my best, I don't feel good, **I feel bitchy**.

— Carmen Marton, three-time Olympian and 2013 Taekwondo World Champion

THE FOUR CHOICES MODEL

To enable people to better appreciate where they are placing attention in their response to their environment, whether professional, relational, or social, we created the Four Choices Model.

1. STAY STRESSED

The first choice is to stay stressed.

Choosing to do nothing about stress is choosing to remain stressed. It is a legitimate option, albeit one that has risks. Stress is linked to six of the top ten leading causes of death.[46] Blaming external circumstances and choosing not to accept personal responsibility for our well-being is akin to praying to win the lottery without buying a ticket.

We also occasionally meet people who have strong secondary gains for remaining in states of acute or chronic stress. For example, they might be receiving support in the form of workers' compensation or perhaps help from their family. Remaining in a state of stress may actually benefit them.

Often these responses are entirely unconscious. Do not confuse such responses with conscious manipulation and feigned ill health for personal gain.

2. DEVELOP RESILIENCE

The second choice is to develop resilience, which gives us access to a wide range of resourceful states, including flow, excitement, confidence, calm, and a feeling of being fully present. It might even mean temporary anger or frustration, or a determination to force a change.

3. CHANGE THE NATURE OF THE ENVIRONMENT YOU ARE IN

The third choice is to change your external environment. In the workplace, this can be done by constructively reducing risk factors such as unrealistic workloads or a poor relationship with your manager. In your community, this could mean getting involved with local youth initiatives to reduce crime, or planting communal gardens. If you have already developed resilience, this option becomes easier, as those with resilience often have increased agency, which allows them to better shape their environments.

4. LEAVE

The fourth choice is to change the external environment by getting out of it. Many people quickly discover new options and possibilities when they operate from a position of resilience, and leaving is one highly effective strategy.

Do not confuse leaving with quitting. Taking personal responsibility for our own health and well-being, even if it means a drastic change to where you work or live, is very important for resilience.

Sometimes the last resistance we encounter here is a belief that the situation a person finds themselves in is "not fair." Being bullied is a good example of this. The choice then comes down to pragmatics, such as balancing the likelihood of constructive change or winning a legal case, with the consequences of prolonged stress, a massive legal bill, and the potential downsides of change, such as less pay in a new job, or swapping familiarity for uncertainty and a new adventure if you relocate.

FAILURE TO BOUNCE

DOMINIC BAKER

Dominic Baker is the newly appointed CEO at Cricket Tasmania. Three months prior to this interview, Dom was off work, burned out with "nothing left in his resilience bucket." As part of his road to recovery he trained in the techniques covered in this book.

I've always viewed myself as the person who can fix what others cannot. The bigger the challenge, the better. And yet I got myself to a level of burnout where I had to acknowledge it was going to become unfixable. I was like a ball that had gone flat and no longer bounced back.

I asked myself, do I change my environment altogether, or like many people, do I stay trapped and stressed?

Some people run their resilience buckets so low that they become empty, after which you'll see major mental health issues arise. Before that happens, it's important to self-examine in an honest way.

For me, exhaustion set in, constant second-guessing, anxiety, and panic that came with not being able to succeed. My body operated at a heightened defensive level for far too long. I stopped spending quality time with my family and friends, isolating myself from my family because I didn't want to put them through what I'd gone through that day. I never wanted to talk about work when I went home. It was bad enough going through it the first time, let alone a second time with my wife.

I didn't sleep or exercise. I did nothing to stay resilient. I thought I could fight through it all, even though the signs were there that it wouldn't end well.

When I removed the blinders, so many opportunities opened up to me. It's remarkable how quickly the human body and brain can recover from situations of high stress and low resilience; remarkable how struggling to get out of bed to face a new day can become rising with new energy to face the day's challenges.

By taking a mental health program and simply changing my breathing, my confidence was restored. I no longer had the feeling like someone was standing on my chest all day.

Just learning the ability to breathe correctly and center myself — the clarity that came from that is unbelievable.

I think that people often feel uncomfortable in the workplace to talk about their mental state. But it's important to work out how to put air back into the ball so you can bounce back once again.

I took six weeks off, and I needed every day of it. Time off allowed me to think, to really hit the ground running when I came back. I went straight back into an environment that really hadn't changed a lot. What had changed really was me, not the environment.

I needed that six weeks to ensure that I was ready to cope, that I had enough coping mechanisms that I was well practiced and well versed and confident with those. It gave me a completely different outlook when I went back into the exact same situation.

"I gave myself a target to be out within a year, and I think I was out within three weeks — into a new job that I love."

ACTIVITY

RESILIENT AT MY BEST

When uncovering how people do "resilient at their best," we use a questioning process adapted from clean language. The syntax is a bit quirky, AND it avoids negations with "but," AND it avoids the imposition of leading questions. It can be applied individually or with teams of up to twelve people.

If you wish to use this process with your own teams or family, sit in a semicircle. The process works best when it includes a facilitator to scribe and ask developing questions.

HERE ARE TWO EXAMPLES OF UNCOVERING "RESILIENT AT MY BEST" USING CLEAN QUESTIONS:

Step 1.

When you're resilient at your best, that's like what?

It's like I'm on a bushwalk. There's movement, a sense of going somewhere with people around.

Step 2.

And when **there's movement, a sense of going somewhere**, and you are on **a bushwalk**, is there anything else about **bushwalk**?

It's fun, energizing and I'm comfortable not knowing what's coming up.

Step 3.

And when it's **fun and energizing** what might we see or hear?

I'm upright [shows posture], and moving [shows gestures], and engaging with others.

Step 1.

When you're resilient at your best, that's like what?

It's like a cat, relaxing.

I can picture myself letting things go at the end of the day, leaving other people's issues with them. Being able to be independent and confident like a cat. Making my own choices, being able to switch off.

Step 2.

And when you **leave other people's issues with them**, and **picture yourself letting things go at the end of the day** is there anything else about **letting things go**?

I don't need to fix everything, I don't need to fix other people's problems. I'm accepting, knowing that people are the expert of their own lives.

Step 3.

And when **accepting**, what kind of **accepting** is that?

It's freedom!

Step 4.

And when you **are accepting and have freedom**, what might we see or hear?

It's like I'm a ball, big and happy [shows posture] and I can breathe [shows breathing].

ACTIVITY

AND WHAT SUPPORT DO YOU NEED?

Step 2.

And when **you are on that journey with signposts, with the right people,** what kind of **right people** are those?

They are open to discussing where we are, and where we might be heading. They are respectful, and they let me rest when I need to, and we are all in this journey together.

Step 1.

And when resilient at your best, and for you to be **like you're on a bushwalk, with movement, a sense of going somewhere with people around,** and it's **fun, energizing, and you're comfortable not knowing what's coming up,** what support do you need?

I need to know roughly where I'm going, I need some signposts. I need to keep on top of my nutrition, and rest. And I need to have the right people on the journey with me.

Step 3.

And when **the right people are respectful, when you are all in this journey together, and there are signposts,** what might we see or hear?

You would see us all working together, and there would be times when I'm resting, and times when you would hear us discussing which way to go.

Step 1.

And when resilient at your best, and for you to be **like a cat, relaxing** where you **let things go at the end of the day, leaving other people's issues with them** and where you **make your own choices, and are able to switch off**, where **you're accepting,** and you have **freedom,** what support do you need?

I need time alone, with planned time in nature. I need my immediate loved ones, and the support of my colleagues.

Step 2.

And when you **need time alone, planned time in nature, immediate loved ones, and the support from your colleagues**, is there anything else about that **support from your colleagues?**

It's knowing they have my back, and that we can resolve conflict quickly. There is an openness and calm as we resolve differences together.

Step 3.

And when you have that support **[gestures to list]** what might we see or hear?

You would see us all talking together calmly. Or you would see me spending quiet time by myself, and you might not hear very much at all.

MAKE SPACE TO LEARN

"Between stimulus and response, there is a space. In that space is our power to choose our response. In our response lies our growth and our freedom."

— Stephen Covey[47]

Sometimes, we are able to create ample space and time between stimulus and our response. In those situations, we can think through options and develop alternatives. However, in an increasingly fast-paced, complex, and turbulent world, we also need to learn in a way that trains our unconscious or intuitive, reflexive responses.

The commonly presented view is that either rational or intuitive responses are best. We challenge such binary, black/white, yes/no categorizations throughout this book. We take the view that many resilient responses are more nuanced — often a constructive blend of both rational and intuitive modes.

Importantly, constructive doesn't necessarily mean harmony. Sometimes it pays to hesitate, to experience conflict, at least briefly, when there is a tension between two different systems of thinking. We also challenge binary views of the external world. It is seldom black and white; rather, it is colored with a rich pallet.

Resilience, then, is not a static trait. It is an active and forever-evolving process of questioning, discovery, and learning. It is a process of recalibration of our internal responses to the shifting patterns in an ever-changing external world.

We don't doubt that some aspects of resilience are innate — part of a long or short evolutionary trajectory that we inherited from our parents. Our focus is more on the epigenetic and behavioral choices that are available to us as we develop our own agency. At each fork in the road, we have an opportunity to shape ourselves and our surroundings in ways that are resourceful to us.

Sometimes, the space between stimulus and a necessary response is a matter of a fraction of a second. Even in these microscopic interstices, we can design or prepare responses and position choices ahead of time.

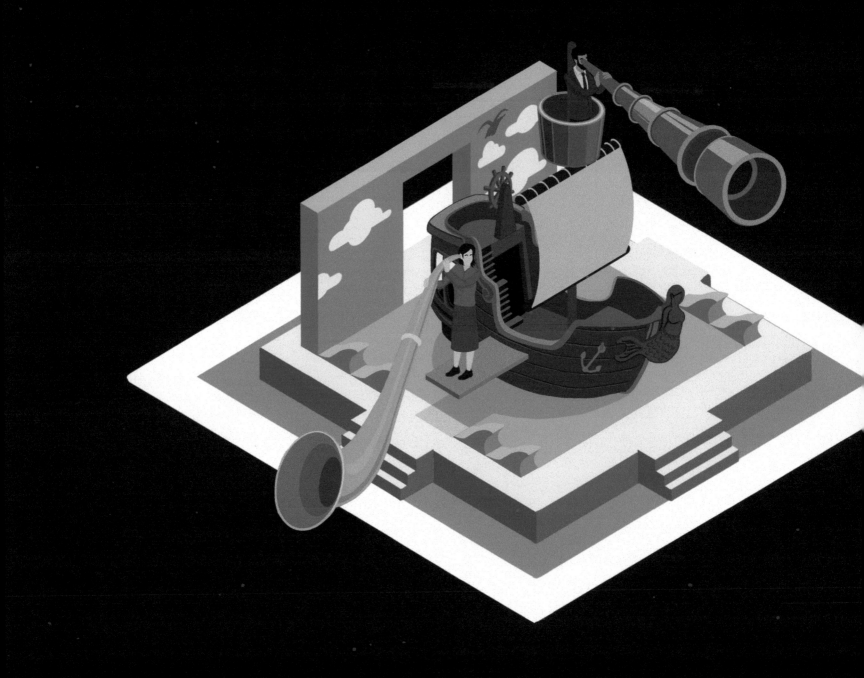

SENSEMAKING

LEARNING TO NAVIGATE

Evolution has provided us with a pre-programmed ability to navigate and make sense of our world.

All animals, humans included, have access to an immense and fast-flowing stream of sensory information about the world we inhabit. We have evolved sensing systems that selectively filter this information in ways that offer survival advantages. This focus on survival comes at a cost. Our sense-making works with incomplete data, so it cannot always be trusted.

This sensing system kicks in (sorry mums, pun intended!) long before we are born. The baby in the womb knows its mother's voice and can learn and form memory traces that are detectable after birth.[1] By the age of one month, babies blink when something moves toward their eye, and by the age of one year, children can construct a visual world and navigate through it, even sensing what is edible, and not so edible.

As we become more experienced at sensing, our calibration improves. We begin to detect patterns earlier even when the signals are quite weak. This pattern detection gives us more time to evaluate and respond.

In the distant past, this might have helped us detect a predator in the thick grass of the African Savannah against a backdrop of blades and stalks blowing in the wind. For some, predator detection is still relevant; for most of us, a more common use might be noting the subtle movements, and sometimes not so subtle movements, of a hesitant driver who is about to change lanes without signalling.

Learning of this kind happens unconsciously without being formally taught. As Donald Hoffman puts it, "Parents don't sit down with their kids and explain how to use motion and stereo to construct depth, or how to carve the visual world into objects and actions."[2] Indeed, most parents don't know how they do this themselves. Children sense-make as a matter of course.

Our innate biological programming enables all of us to learn through experience.

This form of learning gives an important clue how to change patterns of behavior and, importantly for this book, develop resilience – by design.

One challenge that arises as a consequence of sensemaking and learning is that every human has a unique interpretation or re-presentation of reality. What we call our "maps," the way we plot the outerworld in our innerworld, are all different. Sometimes these differences are minor, and sometimes they differ in almost every feature.

TO UNDERSTAND THIS BETTER, HERE IS A SIMPLE EXERCISE

The next time you go on a journey with your family or friends, ask everyone to draw a map of the route they have just been on. Ask them to include as many observations as they can remember.

If someone was hungry, they might recall bakeries; if the driver was watching the fuel gauge, they might notice petrol stations;

if someone was bored, they might recall a very long tortuous road.

The journey has far too many potential points of interest to plot everything. We filter out everything that doesn't have some bearing on our inner reality, with a bias toward salience (information that is important to us).

For resilience, it is important to appreciate that more detailed maps of reality are not necessarily more useful. After all, there are good reasons that we have evolved to filter out impossibly detailed streams of input: if we could not filter in this way, we would become overwhelmed with superfluous data, unable to detect or respond to crucial patterns in life — like a crouched lion or a hesitant driver.

THE CASE AGAINST REALITY

The late anthropologist Gregory Bateson argued that it is impossible to know what any actual territory (reality) is. We rely exclusively on our senses. Though our eyes, ears, and other sense organs report back to us adequately, they give us an imperfect map of reality.

For Bateson the usefulness of a map is not necessarily its literal truthfulness. For a map to be useful, it simply needs a structure that matches the structure of the territory.

"We say the map is different from the territory. But what is the territory? Operationally, somebody went out with a retina or a measuring stick and made representations which were then put on paper. What is on the paper map is a representation of what was in the retinal representation of the man who made the map; and as you push the question back, what you find is an infinite regress, an infinite series of maps. The territory never gets in at all. Always, the process of representation will filter it out so that the mental world is only maps of maps, ad infinitum."

— Gregory Bateson[3]

In *The Case Against Reality*, cognitive scientist Donald Hoffman argues that there is not even a benefit to having the structure of the map match the structure of reality. For Hoffman, fitness beats truth.[4]

Linking mathematical models and game theory to Darwin's theory of natural selection, Hoffman argues that our perceptions evolved to detect patterns that convey evolutionary advantage, and having maps that are truer to life would be a disadvantage in an evolutionary sense.

From the perspective of resilience, those who strive to ground their beliefs in evidence don't appear to be immune to stress. They possibly don't even have any evolutionary advantage over those prone to magical thinking, like superstitions, divine protection or astrology.

Ignorance, so they say, is bliss!

"Taking the red pill" has become a popular metaphor for the adoption of a free-thinking attitude based on evidence.

No matter how challenging the conclusions are to accept, the red pill demands that we accept what the evidence tells us.

In the case of sensemaking and resilience, the red pill that we are inviting you to swallow is the realization that we can never know absolute reality. We can never know "truth" with certainty. All we have are approximations that may or may not be useful.

This book does not focus on the search for objective truths. Instead, we explore techniques that create perceptions and responses that are resilient and useful.

"This is your last chance. After this there is no turning back. You take the blue pill: the story ends, you wake up in your bed and believe whatever you want to believe. You take the red pill: you stay in Wonderland and I show you how deep the rabbit hole goes."

— Morpheus, *The Matrix*

WEIGHING UP PERCEPTIONS

BENEFITS

Our senses are programmed to detect patterns. They do this by filtering out whatever does not fit into the pattern.

How we code the information our senses detect is subjective, not objective. As such, we can manipulate it for our benefit. We can, if we wish, change our coding, making subtle adjustments to the way that memories are formed and how we attribute meaning to past events.

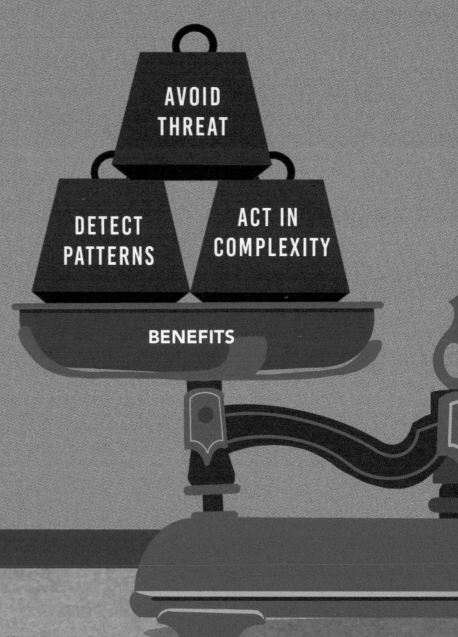

COST

Being able to quickly detect patterns comes with a cost: we don't see what we are not looking for. This is called inattentional blindness, and it is what illusionists use to deceive us.

Ironically, the more expert we become at something, the more prone we are to inattentional blindness. Our focus becomes narrower, and we tune out more and more. We forget how to scan for novelty.

INATTENTIONAL BLINDNESS

When we are developing resilience, it is important to recognize that inattentional blindness leaves us open to missing change or novel differences. Improving how we perceive the world can lead to better situational assessment and more choice in our emotional states and the decisions we make.

Improved calibration of our outer and inner worlds also allows us to detect patterns when they are still early or weak signals. This gives us more time to create choices in the gap between stimulus and response.

FILTERING THROUGH THE SENSES

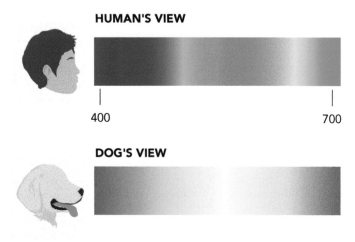

HUMAN'S VIEW

400   700

DOG'S VIEW

To illustrate some of our inherent biases, consider the visual spectrum.

For seeing, there is literally more than meets the eye. We can see in a very narrow bandwidth of the light spectrum — between about 400 and 700 nm in the visible spectrum. This immediately yields a very specific representation of the world around us in trichromatic shades of red, green, and blue.

Dogs, by comparison, are thought to be dichromatic. They see the world very differently. What they lack in colour resolution, they make up for in low light sensitivity. They can see six times better than we can in the dark.

Our visual system is also used to create internal representations of the past or future as we remember, visualize, imagine, hallucinate, or fantasize. These images can be moving or still, 2D or 3D, color or black and white, or vary in many subtle ways not unlike the incredible flexibility offered by a desktop video editing suite.

CONSIDER THE IMAGE BELOW

1. What do you see?
2. What do you infer from what you see?
3. What story might you tell for this illustration?

NOW CONSIDER THIS IMAGE:

1. What do you see?

2. What do you infer from what you see?

3. What story might you tell for this illustration?

When you look again now, the scene looks very different. The scene has been sprayed with luminol, a chemical that fluoresces when in contact with blood and illuminated with UV light. The picture now tells a dramatically different story.

Cna yuo *raelyl* trsut yuor sesnes?

WE SEE WHAT WE EXPECT TO SEE

Depth and motion are constructed from shadow, intraposition, and space cues, but there's more than meets the eye. Cultural or belief bias is a kind of feedback that can also filter our perceptions and contribute to inattentional blindness.

Modified after Anon[5]

Australians were asked to describe the picture here. The most common response was:

"It's a family in a room with a dog...(or sometimes, with a dog that looks like a kangaroo!)."

When the same question was asked in Africa,[5] or framed in Australia as being set in Africa, the response was more commonly:

"It's a family sitting under a tree, and there is a woman with a box on her head."

The stories and inferences about this family scene vary wildly. Some people make inferences about the family dynamics, such as who likes who and how the people are related. Others point to clues that suggest something about the family's socioeconomic status.

We have demonstrated that the visual system constructs a version of reality that is mostly useful to us. It can't take in everything at once, so it filters in ways that are strongly influenced at the cellular level in the human eye, as well as by our cultural, social, and economic context.

One of the best examples of inattentional blindness is the Monkey Business Illusion.

The original illusion, created by Daniel Simons and Christopher Chabris, has two groups of people, some dressed in white, some in black, passing basketballs back and forth whilst moving randomly. Observers are tasked to count how many times the participants in white pass the ball.[6]

Engrossed in the task of counting, about half of those given these directions fail to notice that somebody in a gorilla suit walks into the circle and pounds their chest while facing the camera before walking off. The gorilla is on screen for nearly nine seconds.

In a follow-up study, the same researchers explored whether those who know an unexpected event is likely to occur are any better at noticing other unexpected events. The second video again uses white and black clothed players moving randomly, with the same rules and a chest-thumping gorilla.

Only 17% of those who were familiar with the original gorilla video noticed one or both of the other unexpected events, like the curtains changing color, or someone stepping out, compared with 29% of those who were unfamiliar with the original gorilla video.

The study demonstrates that, even when we are primed to the possibility of an unexpected event, this does not substantially enhance our ability to recognize them when they occur. We only see what we are looking for.

MORE MONKEY BUSINESS

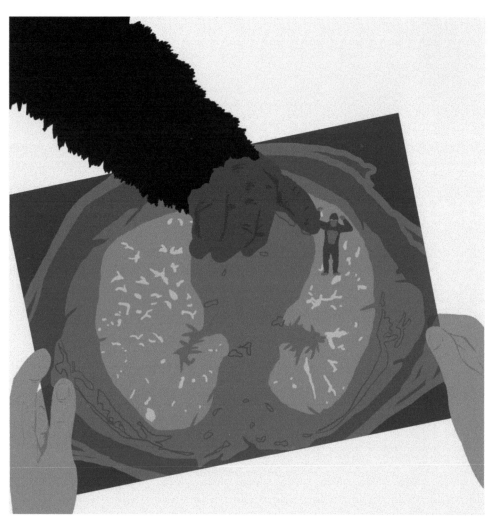

"Working with the reality of inattentional blindness is part of the core science of better sense-making in complex systems."

— Dave Snowden

In an extension of the Monkey Business Illusion, additional experiments have tracked inattentional blindness into frontline work domains. Researchers asked 24 radiologists, expert observers of x-ray images, to perform a lung nodule detection task.[7] A gorilla 48 times larger than the average nodule was inserted in one of the images.

83% of radiologists did not see the gorilla. Eye-tracking revealed the majority of those who missed the gorilla looked directly at it.

The implications for inattentional blindness in healthcare are enormous. Experts of all specializations risk missing unexpected illnesses the more attuned they become to the patterns they expect to see.

In a different example, it's possible that inattentional blindness led to false imprisonment of a Boston police officer.

At 2.00am on January 25, 1995, Officer Kenny Conley chased a shooting suspect who climbed a chain-link fence to escape. Michael Cox, an undercover officer, had arrived at the scene moments earlier. In the dark, other officers mistook the arriving officer for the fleeing suspect, brutally assaulting him from behind.

In his statement, Officer Conley said that he ran right past the place where Cox was being attacked, but he claimed not to have seen the incident.

The prosecution successfully argued that Officer Conley must have seen the incident and was therefore lying to protect his comrades. Conley was convicted of perjury and obstruction of justice and was sentenced to 34 months in jail.

Chabris and Simons explored this scenario using principles illustrated by the Monkey Business Illusion. They simulated the Boston incident by having someone run after an actor along a route near which three other actors staged a fight.[8]

At night, 65% of subjects did not notice the fight; during the day 44% failed to notice.

It is apparent from the Monkey Business experiments that we literally don't see what we don't expect to see.

PAIN IS REAL AND ALL IN THE (EMBODIED) MIND

Where inattentional blindness in the visual system is one unintended consequence of pattern detection for survival, felt sensations can also be overdone or underdone as a signal for threat.

At times when it could be useful, we often fail to pay attention to appropriate sensations such as those we might describe as emotion or pain. Conversely, we also experience intense emotions (such as fear or anxiety) or chronic pain when there is no injury or objective threat.

SO WHAT IS GOING ON HERE?

The pervasive myth about pain says that when the body is injured, special pain receptors convey pain messages to the brain. In fact, pain is entirely biopsychosocial and is best described as a threat signal.

Moseley and Butler describe pain as a perceptual inference that tends to err on the side of caution.[9] For example, phantom limb pain occurs in over two-thirds of all people who lose a limb. Pain from the missing limb can be so severe that some sufferers contemplate suicide. The pain is the mind's attempt to protect a limb it remembers having.

Dr. Vilayanur Ramachandran famously performed an experiment with amputees who had phantom limb pain. He had participants place their hand in a mirrored box that created a reflection that made it look like the amputee still had two intact hands.[10] The amputee knew that the reflection of his or her hand was an illusion, but part of the mind accepts that the reflected hand is real. For those suffering from phantom limb pain, opening and stretching the reflected hand often relieves cramps and pain in the phantom limb.

Pain, and even pain relief, are entirely matters of perception.

SELF-CALIBRATION

An essential component of resilience is the ability to modulate perception of our bodily sensations, including pain or emotions. We call this self-calibration, and we all use it. Without self-calibration we would miss the signal of hunger and the correlating need to eat; we would not know when to sleep in response to the signal of fatigue.

Consider for a moment the last time you experienced pain or severe discomfort. Maybe it was something you ate that disagreed with you, or perhaps it was a headache that immobilized you after a long day staring at a screen. What was your response? Did you try to deaden the pain with medication? If so, you have potentially sacrificed an opportunity to develop your self-calibration. You received the signal, but you didn't listen to what that signal was telling you.

Conversely, you might listen too carefully. Since pain is a response to a perceived threat, if the perception is skewed, the response may also be skewed as well.

People often experience pain that relates to the threat from a physical injury that healed many years previously. The threat signal has become "stuck." The memory of the injury is enough to bring the associated sensations flooding back.

When experiencing pain or discomfort without an immediate and obvious cause, ask yourself the following question: **"If this pain was directing me to change something, what would that be?"**

In the case of the stomachache, pain might be telling you to stop eating so much junk food; headache may be a signal to get more rest and recovery, or it might be telling you to improve or remove a relationship. There is an endless range of perceived threats that our pain signals could be alerting us to. Popping your painkiller of choice lowers the volume of an important message. We suggesting listening first before dampening or switching off signals.

In *Explain Pain*, Dr. David Butler and Prof. Lorimer Moseley literally explain the mechanism by which pain acts as a signal for perceived threat, and people's pain response is diminished.[11] Related studies describe effective treatment for complex regional pain and phantom limb pain using Graded Motor Imagery.[12] This process retrains the brain to identify left and right limbs using motor imagery and a mirror box, like Ramachandran used for phantom limb pain.

By training the embodied mind to recalibrate, it is possible to reduce pain. In addition to quantifiable reductions in the perception of pain and improved quality of life, self-calibration can also produce bioplastic changes in neurology, such as cortical reorganization.[13-15] Such approaches contrast with the often-poor efficacy and high risks of addiction and overdose associated with attempting to medicate pain away.

Just like medication can be inappropriately applied to treat pain, so too can mindfulness when it is applied to work-related stress. This is illustrated by the account of Leanne in the *Ladybird Book of Mindfulness*:[16]

"Leanne has been staring at this beautiful tree for five hours.

She was meant to be in the office. Tomorrow she will be fired.

In this way, mindfulness has solved her work-related stress."

ACTIVITY

HOW LONG DOES THE NOW LAST?

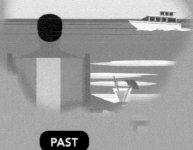

PAST

"Mindfulness is the quality of being present and fully engaged with whatever we're doing at the moment — free from distraction or judgment, and aware of our thoughts and feelings without getting caught up in them."

— Headspace

What we call mindfulness is a widespread and enduring philosophy that is at least 3,500 years old. At its core, mindfulness is an appreciation of the benefits of being fully aware in the moment.

Mindfulness, yoga, breath work, tantric practice, meditation, prayer, qi gong, and a host of other practices all aim to appreciate the benefits of mindfulness, being fully present in the moment, and what author Eckhart Tolle calls "The Power of Now."[17]

So what exactly is "the now" and how long does it last?

What is the other stuff that is "not the now"?

We invite you to take part in a simple thought experiment.

Step 1.

Remember a time and place from your past when you enjoyed doing an activity you are passionate about.

Immerse yourself in that memory, reliving the moment as if you were really there.

See events through your eyes. Inhabit the memory rather than looking on as an observer.

Are you remembering in color? Are the colors true to life?

Focus on the sounds. Are there voices? Become aware of sounds both near and far. Are there any internal sounds? Do you hear your own inner voice running a commentary, or is there inner quiet?

Experience the sense of movement in your body. How do you feel? How is your breathing?

What can you smell? What can you taste?

Now, return to the present.

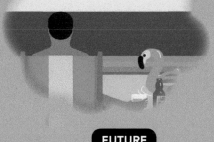

FUTURE

Step 3.

Now compare the two experiences.

For most people there is no discernible difference. Neither is any more "real" than the other. For the minority of people who do experience some small difference between the past memory and future created experience (for which we now have a memory!), it usually only takes a few minutes of coaching to match the experiences precisely.

Past and future experiences are practically identical. Most of us can separate the remembered past and the imagined future in some way.

What then, is "the now"?

Neuroscientists have measured the time it takes for the senses to rattle around the body and brain into consciousness: it's perhaps a few hundred milliseconds (around half a second).[18-20]

So, let's assume then that being in the now is a fleetingly brief experience, which almost immediately becomes memory.

Step 2.

Get up and move around. Shake that memory out of your body by jumping up and down. Vigorous movement for ten seconds or so is usually enough.

Now direct your attention to a time in the future when you could enjoy a similar experience to the one you were remembering.

Create an imagined experience which is *similar*, but not identical, to the previous memory.

Deeply immerse yourself in this created experience. As before, check that the images, sounds, body sensations, smells, and tastes are all present.

Now, return to the present.

Get up, move around and, once more, shake that created memory out of the body.

Where is your a

Being in the now is to experience that which is fleeting — no sooner experienced than it is gone, passing into the realm of memory.

Once an experience passes into memory, it can be replayed or modified, and we can create immersive experiences that are practically identical, or radically different, to past reference experiences.

Memory is malleable, and experiences can be re-experienced from different perspectives, and we can also change the meaning we attribute to such sensory-based experiences.

We live entirely in a created or recreated experience of "reality."

attention now?

This being so, there is no excuse for not having a resourceful experience, moment by moment. Emotions like happiness are 100% created internally and have zero causation from events in the external world. As people discover their own innate creative process for how they experience the past, present, and future, performance naturally lifts as they discover more choice.

By all means, be "in the now," and also remember that, using the same techniques, you can immerse yourself in the future. By vividly imagining a possible future and engaging all the embodied senses, peak performance can be rehearsed authentically. When the future arrives, you'll be ready for its demands.

If recollection of past experiences is debilitating today, you can also access or re-imprint those memories in more useful ways for the purpose of learning and creating the life you most want to inhabit.

MEMORY AND THE SENSES

If you've witnessed a disaster or potentially traumatic event, you'll know there could be advantages in being able to forget the experience or only recall aspects of it that are salient and required for the purposes of learning.

Memories can be debilitating if they invoke involuntarily felt sensations. As an example, some people experiencing a traumatic stress response can remember events as if they are full-color movies with surround sound, linked to the same (or different) dysfunctional felt sensations. It is literally like they are reliving the experience over and over again as vividly, or even more vividly, than they felt the first time.

Instead they might choose to remember the traumatic event differently. It could be as a movie in black and white with no sound. This typically lessens the emotional impact.

By changing *how* memory presents itself, we can change how we respond to it.

MIKE'S EXPERIENCE

In 2016, my then two-year-old son nearly drowned. My neighbor's teenage kids had taken him into their play group, only to become distracted by television. The teenagers failed to notice when my son wandered outside where he fell into their unfenced backyard pool.

Whilst I spoke with my neighbours at their front door, my four-year old son alerted me that his brother had wandered out, alone, to the pool. My heart pounding, I raced through the neighbor's house (past four teenagers watching TV) to find my child underwater and fighting for his life.

After receiving the all-clear from the hospital, I relived the event far too vividly, including possible worst-case scenarios: "What if my four-year old had not alerted me?"

The memory recurred spontaneously with extremely strong sensations of fear in my stomach and chest, signaling that I should act, even hours after the fact. Realizing that a pattern was establishing itself, I reconstructed my memory of the event,

changing it from a full-color movie to an animated black and white, single line, pencil drawing. Years later, this is still how I recall what happened that day.

That change of memory structure immediately lessened the sensations, whilst retaining enough of the memory and discomfort to remind me to be careful about whom I leave my children with.

Years later, both my sons are addicted to the ocean through surfing and bodyboarding. Whilst I retain an alert-to-risk signal that is useful, it rarely interferes with the joy of seeing my boys in the water.

The importance of self-calibration, a fully embodied awareness of how we experience and respond to external events in the moment, or in the past, underpins how to create personal resilience.

MICRO-NARRATIVE

THEY WENT THIS WAY

"In this line of work, bad decisions cost lives."

RON COLBURN

Chief Ron Colburn (U.S. Border Patrol – Retired) currently serves as the president of the Border Patrol Foundation, a 501(c)(3) nonprofit organization. Ron has one of the most extensive backgrounds in border security in the world today, having served for over 31 years in critical operational positions in the field with the U.S. Border Patrol, at the headquarters of U.S. Customs and Border Protection, and at the White House Homeland Security Council.

I've been alone on a dark trail and heard just a light boot scuff on a rock. That's all I hear, and because my senses are completely with the experience, I begin to assess, "Okay, that sounds like it's maybe another 20 to 40 meters or yards down the trail for me, so I still have time to listen to see what I'm dealing with here." Then I'll start hearing the crunch of more footsteps. If they're moving very slowly and very tactically, I assume these will be bad guys. This might be a point man, armed with a rifle or a pistol. It's essential to be aware and sensitized to the fact that I must not stand out in the middle of the road or trail, or turn on my flashlight and go, hey, everybody, you're all under arrest. Because doing that will likely get me shot in the face.

Over the years, smugglers have gotten pretty tricky about how they hide their trails. They bring a roll of carpet, walk across the road, roll the carpet back and go on. We've caught them with the leaf blowers where they blow out the dust or sand behind their trail and they will tie the hooves of cattle to their feet and walk, thinking that it will trick us. They walk backwards thinking that somehow that would fool us. There's a number of novel ways that they try to disguise their illegal activity.

What they don't realize is that anything occurring between the lawful port of entry on the ground and in the desert is going to be pretty much illegal, unless of course you have an open range for cattle running and activities like that. We get some legitimate agriculture and cowboys working the area but everyone else is likely to be there illegally.

If you're seeing footprints, especially large groups walking north from the border with Mexico, then you can assume that something or someone is breaking the law either smuggling in narcotics or human trafficking.

The art of man tracking is really evidence gathering. Forensics in its simplest form. The skillset comes from the experience of the tracker, and of course his or her vision and ability to interpret or make sense of what they're seeing on the earth, on the ground, usually a disturbance of some sort. It can be very subtle like discoloration. As a person is walking, they may kick over a rock that has been there for decades, shone on with UV and sun-derived infrared light which tends to bleach the rock on the top.

If the rock is kicked over it'll be darker on the bottom. That will catch the tracker's eye, as well as the shadows. When a footprint or boot print of a horse is in deep sand, the angle of the sun can show the shadow from far away.

I love the old movies and cowboy shows where they're looking at a branch about shoulder height that's bent one way, and they say, "They went this way." Unless somebody actually walks into a bush, which at night they sometimes do by accident, you rarely see something like that as an indicator. It's going to be at the ground level where there are indications of someone passing through a particular area.

Smugglers often toe out as they walk, which hints that they may be carrying heavy loads. When they have 10 people with 40 pounds [each] of marijuana on their backs, you may have a trailing guy with a gun and a point guy with a gun. Or you may have 30 people, 10 of who are women and one's carrying a baby. If the woman's walking up front with the guide and you don't have good night vision you might think that person is carrying something other than a baby, such as a bundle of drugs or a weapon. I've jumped out on groups like that in the middle of the night, and on more than one occasion had people instantly pass out from the shock or lose control of their bladders.

During my time as a border patrol agent, I was in a lot of survival fights and I got hospitalized half a dozen times, but thankfully never killed anyone. It gets tough out there, especially when you work alone. It's why we're always sensing and interpreting our environment so that we can make rapid decisions.

In this line of work, bad decisions cost lives.

KNOW THYSELF

Dating back to 300 BC and inscribed in the Temple of Apollo at Delphi are the words "Know Thyself." From at least as far back as the ancient Greeks, people have understood the importance of self-knowledge and self-calibration as a foundation for learning.

Post Greek philosophy, neuroscience is exploring the same territory, providing important insights into how we make sense of the world around us. We can use these insights in a practical way to extend our sensemaking calibration range, such as by training breathing and heart rate variability to support our response to pressure or challenge.[21,22] We can also learn to filter information differently to overcome cognitive biases, and we can re-experience memories in more useful ways like Mike did with the near drowning of his son.[23] We can literally improve how we make sense of the world moment by moment.

Most people have five prominent senses: sight, hearing, touch, taste, and smell. What is up for debate are the less-well-understood aspects of sensing such as proprioception (the sense that helps us locate our bodies in physical space), our sense of movement, and even our ability to detect electromagnetic fields. As another practical example, Ian spent six months wandering the world wearing a magnetic sense belt, a compass of sorts that sends a signal to the body to develop a better intuitive felt understanding of direction and space.[24]

After receiving sensory information, we create a corresponding system of internal representations of our experience (visual, auditory, kinaesthetic, gustatory, and olfactory, and other less well-defined representations such as space and time). These are known as modalities, and these re-presentations can be a re-creation or memory of an experience we have already had, or they can be entirely new imagined experiences.

Traumatic memories show us how the senses can co-create experience through what we call "cross-modal association." People vividly recall images, sounds, sensations, and even smells and taste, activating a felt sensation that can be so strong that it is debilitating.

This is very much like a synaesthesia — a neurological trait that results in a linking of senses that aren't normally recognized as being connected. The stimulation of one sense causes an involuntary reaction in one or more of the other senses. For example, someone may hear colour or see sound, or experience numbers and letters with colours.

Mike was able to remap his memory of his son's near drowning through a simple process of changing the structure of his memories. He identified that the vividness of the memory was driving the fear sensation that arose, so he swapped full-color images to pencil-lined drawings.

One caution, though, regarding the Know Thyself movement: all too often, explorations of self-discovery result in people adopting a fixed view of their identity, and an associated removal of choice. So-called personality profiling tends to create pigeonholes for people.

Men are not from Mars, women are not from Venus, and so called Myers-Briggs personality types have no more scientific foundations than astrology. All personality profiles are based on behavior, often without reference to context (or from patterns of vague language designed to manipulate people). Behavior can be easily changed, and so too can our sense of identity. It can be as metaphorically and literally as easy as changing our clothes, especially if we wear a uniform that is linked to a role, such as a police officer, a yoga instructor, or even a flamboyant rock star.

Just like "⚤- the Artist formerly known as Prince," or references to Mars and Venus, metaphors can subtly create or remove choice in our behavior. They can either limit or delimit who we define ourselves to be.

METAPHORS ARE A

BRI

BETWEEN THE CONSCIOUS

DGE

AND THE UNCONSCIOUS

CROSSING THE BRIDGE

The process of perceiving begins when we receive information through specific sensing cells. It is then transmitted via our neural network in an already highly compressed way that is filtered by our previous experiences, values, desires, beliefs, fears, and our culture. In this way, our sensing is transformed and mapped into unconscious meaning even before we have conscious awareness of it. Carmen Bostic St. Clair and John Grinder call this "First Access."[25]

Much of what could be available to us in First Access is further transformed into the creative realm of metaphor, again often before we become consciously aware, and well before any interpretation or naming of experience has taken place.

We know this to be the case for resilience, for example, through the interviews we have conducted with frontline professionals and extreme athletes. Their strategies and embodied thinking patterns are invariably hidden in metaphor (where one pattern of behavior is expressed in terms of another) and symbolic representations and movements.

These self-generated metaphors reflect autonomic or unconscious pattern detection and response. To understand or unpack the early stages of this response process requires an understanding of metaphors.

Metaphor is a pervasive yet largely hidden part of experience and communication. In fact, we use metaphors approximately six times every minute when we are speaking, mostly "under the radar" of our conscious attention.[26] The closer we look, the more we can penetrate the mystery. To borrow a metaphor from Louis Pasteur, "the veil is getting thinner."

Our minds use metaphors to make sense of the world.[27] For instance, when we're faced with an abstract or difficult concept, "we can wrap our heads around it" by referring to a simpler concept, to something we already get. The source of the metaphor is usually something tangible or that we can experience bodily and directly. We map this more straightforward concept onto the abstract one. Through this process, we can make sense of an almost impossibly complex world.

"Life is a journey" is another common metaphor in which we use the concrete familiar experience and attributes of a journey to help understand the more abstract concept "life." The metaphor of a journey is expressed in common phrases like "I'm on the right path," "I'm at a crossroad," or "I'm stopping to smell the roses."

In their book *Metaphors in Mind*, Penny Tompkins and James Lawley note that metaphor is about capturing the essential nature of an experience. This is not limited to verbal expressions. A metaphor can include anything that is symbolic for a person. For example, it might be non-verbal behavior, an image, an object, a painting, or an artistic activity like sculpting or dancing.

METAPHORS GENERATE AND REGENERATE MEANING

There are striking similarities between metaphors across cultures and languages. Since people throughout the world use similar metaphors, and since these tend to be based on concrete or sensory

"Once we have a metaphor for a concept, we both perceive and act in accordance with the metaphor"

— Williams & Bargh[28]

experiences, it makes sense that the cross-concept mapping that happens during metaphor might have a neural basis. How and where these paths cross may be linked to the brain's sensory centers.[28]

This prediction is supported by some fascinating recent studies. In one study, people were first given a coffee to hold and then introduced to a stranger. They consistently rated the newcomer as "warmer" if the coffee they were holding was hot rather than iced: the sensation of physical warmth affected their perception of metaphorical warmth.[28]

Our brains make no clear distinction between literal and metaphoric concepts; and indeed, MRI scans show that both are processed in the same neurological areas.[29] The brain, it seems, is big on neural reuse.

In some ways, metaphors are an extension of our sensemaking process, where we selectively pay attention to information relating to pattern detection, whilst reducing the overwhelming volume of experience, keeping only what is most

noteworthy. There is a downside: because metaphors describe one experience in terms of another, they specify and constrain our ways of thinking about the original experience.

Having a workplace metaphor of "It's dog eat dog" will lead to very different views, feelings, actions, and outcomes than "I'm running with my pack." These two examples provide a clue to how metaphors can influence perceptions of our external world and our internal responses. Metaphors underlie and are predictive of our beliefs, and they can generate and regenerate meaning.[30]

When Isadora Duncan, the creator of modern dance, was asked to explain one of her performances, she said, "If I could tell you what it meant, there would be no point in dancing it."

This highlights the slippery nature of metaphors. When we cross the bridge of metaphor, we lose fidelity along the way. Our intentions are not always clear. Meaning is open to interpretation. Duncan wasn't willing to articulate what

her metaphor stood for, but it wasn't just stubbornness on her part. She was using her dance to describe something that cannot be expressed with literal language. Like our minds, she needed metaphor to make sense of something incredibly complex.

As we use individual words and narrative, we impose a further compression on the richness of human experience as our brain tries to interpret the patterns around us and then explain what choices we have made. Precisely where our attention is at any given moment can be revealed through hidden patterns in language, our tonality, our physiology, our behaviors, and the metaphors we live by.[31]

Before turning the page, consider this simple sentence: "The cat plays with a ball of string."

THE CAT PLAYS WITH A BALL OF STRING

1. What kind of cat did you imagine?

2. What kind of ball of string did you imagine?

3. How was the cat playing with the string?

4. And, when your cat plays with that ball of string, what would you like to have happen?

WAS THE CAT YOU IMAGINED ANYTHING LIKE OURS?

Not only do people interpret the meaning of words very differently based on their own experiences, there is often an underlying personal intent. We each have an unstated idea of "what we would like to have happen." We each have our own unique answers. We see a different cat, a different ball of string, a different form of play, and, most importantly, we each have our own ideas about what we would like to have happen. How we answer the questions above is based on our experiences, contexts, values, and even on what temperature our coffee is when we are asked the question.

The act of capturing meaning and sharing intention in symbols and writing is not as objective as we would like to believe. Consider the ambiguity in the following sentence: The man watches the woman with binoculars. There are two possible meanings. Which one did you latch onto immediately? Was the man using binoculars to watch the woman, or was the woman using the binoculars (and being watched by the man while doing so)?[27]

It all hinges on the simple preposition *with*. If even a simple sentence like this has pitfalls, imagine how much more challenging it is to communicate exactly what we intend when we act as narrators, tellers of our own stories. This becomes even more difficult when our intentions are not clear even to ourselves.

Metaphors are at the heart of *Resilience by Design*. We can use them to assist people to move from one perception to another: where they might start by describing how stress is crushing them, they can flip the script with the aid of metaphor. They can reframe their experience to something more resilient. Rather than talking about being crushed, they can talk about being able to "bounce back."

Using the power of language and metaphor to reframe perceptions and change the nature of memory is one important key to developing resilience.

SMASHING
NARRATIVE

The language we use and the stories we tell about ourselves and others distort memory, change the nature of experience, and can influence all aspects of life. As we know from studies of split-brain patients, the left side of the brain makes up stories to explain the multi-modal inputs from our senses and forms of thinking that involve our whole embodied mind.[32,33]

The language our minds use to frame these stories can change our experience. Here's just one example: German researchers explored whether the choice of gender influences perception of objects. They created a list of 24 objects that have opposite genders in Spanish and German and asked a group of native Spanish speakers, and a group of native German speakers, who also spoke English to generate three adjectives for each noun on the list.[34]

The researchers found that object gender influenced the choice of descriptive words and perceptions. The word "bridge" is feminine in German and masculine in Spanish.

German speakers described bridges as beautiful, elegant, fragile, pretty, and slender, while Spanish speakers said they were big, dangerous, strong, sturdy, and towering.

Being aware that language can influence meaning in subtle ways is an important foundation for developing resilience, particularly when others might benefit from manipulating us or we are communicating or responding to challenging events.

Language even influences the very nature of memory. In a famous study by Elizabeth Loftus and John Palmer, students were asked to estimate the speed of a simulated traffic accident. The students were asked, "How fast were the cars traveling," with a variation in the verb that expressed the impact (smashed, collided, bumped, hit, or contacted). The estimated speed varied by more than 30% depending on which verb was used.[35]

Smashed	Collided	Bumped	Hit	Contacted
40.8 mph	39.3 mph	38.1 mph	34 mph	31.8 mph

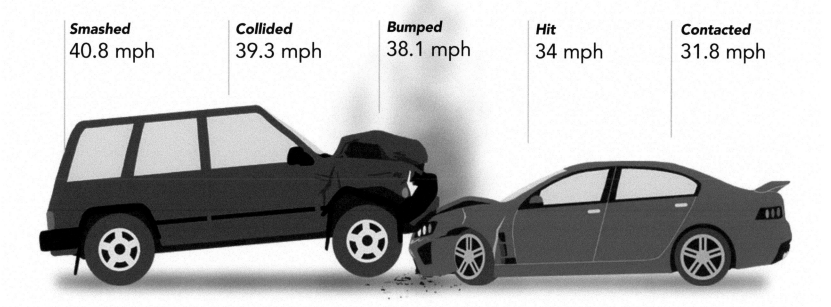

In a follow-up experiment, 150 participants were shown a short clip of a car accident and then asked questions about it. One group of 50 were asked how fast the cars were going when they *smashed*. A different group of 50 were asked how fast the cars were going when they *hit each other*. A third group of 50 were not asked questions about speed.

One week later, the participants were asked ten questions about the scene they had witnessed. They were asked if they had noticed any broken glass. When the word *smashed* was included in the question, participants were more likely to report seeing broken glass, even though no broken glass was present in the clip.[35]

Memory is fragile and easily distorted. How we trigger recall, including the words we use, can shape what we remember.

This has important implications for police interviews and eyewitness accounts, or for anybody who is concerned with accurate reporting. Even though someone might believe they are telling the truth, their memory can be faulty, or people can be easily led to believe something that did not happen. By extension, there are profound implications for ourselves and our work mates as we use language and stories to communicate on a daily basis, often introducing ambiguity, or leading others to create images or narratives that can influence them and us in unforeseen ways.

Our takeaway message: Be careful with your imagined interpretation of a narrative. Narratives invariably feature greatly compressed information; when you decompress this information in your mind, you might be distorting it. What you hold in your mind might be miles away from what someone else is trying to communicate.

To discover someone else's version of reality, ask questions like: What sort of cat? What kind of ball of string? What kind of play? Ask them to be specific.

IS THIS REALLY YOUR LAST CHANCE?

The way we make sense of the world around us has likely evolved in a fitness-beats-truth way.

Humans have highly developed minds that compress information, creating opportunities to act quickly from complexity. We know that:

- We selectively sense reality to detect patterns that we expect to discover.
- We filter information through the senses with an intent to survive.
- We change representations of images, sounds, smell, taste, and feelings into symbols and metaphors.
- We then use words and narrative to compress experience still further into a literal and metaphoric form that can be communicated over great distances.
- And we introduce bias as an unintended consequence of pattern detection, as well as deleting important information during sensemaking and communication.

By considering how the sensemaking process transforms sensory inputs into experiences and then uses those experiences to aid in decision-making, we are given a number of choice points that can help us create resilience — by design.

Humans create states of pain, usually in response to perceived threats, but our perceptions aren't entirely reliable. We don't see the gorilla in the room unless we are looking for it — and even if we are looking for it, we're probably missing something else!

Like pain, our emotions and experiences are real, but also created in the embodied mind.

We started this chapter with a quote from Morpheus from the film *The Matrix*.

"This is your last chance. After this there is no turning back. You take the blue pill: the story ends, you wake up in your bed and believe whatever you want to believe. You take the red pill: you stay in Wonderland and I show you how deep the rabbit hole goes."

If you think that taking the red pill will lead to a truer experience of reality, then please read this chapter again. And remember the twists and turns in the two matrix sequels.

We're all for an evidence-based approach to life, where we use science and facts rather than faith and magic to inform decision-making. The blue pill also represents much more than fantasy. It's a pill that holds the promise for more spirit, flavor, creativity, and richness of life.

Ultimately none of us will ever know absolute reality.

It's only likely that some of us will live in a closer or more useful approximation of reality than others.

So, if you think there are only two choices, the red pill or the blue pill, think again.

Take the red pill, or take the blue pill, or take no pill, or, like the Gorilla that only some people can see, take them both together.

Maybe by doing so you will break some unresourceful decision-making patterns, which in turn can lead to more resilient ways of being and whole new ways of thinking.

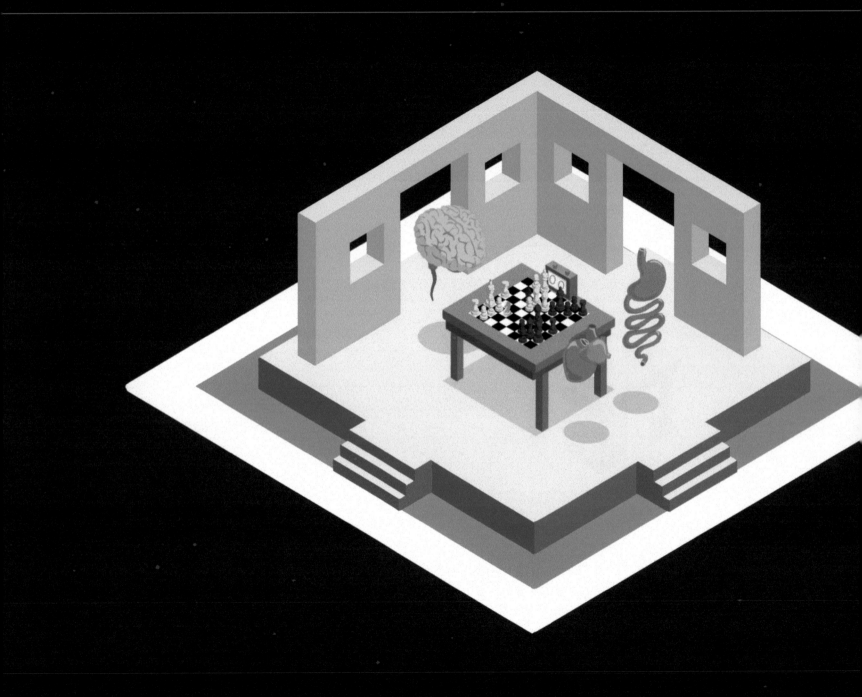

THINKING

YOUR OPERATING SYSTEM IS READY TO UPDATE — PLEASE PLUG IN!

At the heart of resilience is the ability to make good decisions so that we can take appropriate action in the world.

Thinking...everyone does it, but what exactly is it?

Thinking is much more than our internal self-talk. It is an embodied process involving reorganizing the senses out of necessity, curiosity, and for purpose.[1-3]

Thinking precedes and is the process that leads to states, ideas, decisions, responses, and actions. The vast majority of our thinking occurs beneath conscious awareness, never surfacing to our conscious attention.[4,5]

Much of our thinking occurs in the head brain, with its densely packed neurons and glial cells, although the gut (enteric) brain and heart (cardiac) brain also feature prominently.[6]

Where our unique form of distributed thinking starts and ends is not well defined. Indeed, aspects of our thinking might not even be within what is considered human, as recent studies demonstrate how the human microbiome influences our thoughts. Trillions of microscopic bacteria, viruses, and parasites that live in our gut communicate with the head brain via the vagus nerve in ways that appear to influence our thoughts and emotional states.[7,8]

Metaphors and icons that represent the mind commonly focus on the head, and often involve cogs or computer circuits. The implication contained in these representations is that we are hard-wired. However, recent discoveries in neuroplasticity reveal that our thinking and behaviors are more soft-wired.[9] An operating system that automatically connects to the internet might be a better metaphor than cogs and circuity, though even this only gets us part of the way there. Robert Logan, a researcher in physics and media ecology, argues that even advanced artificial intelligence lacks our creative ability to manipulate and restructure internal representations and, ultimately, our inner and outer worlds.[2]

In much the same way that software updates need to keep pace with a rapidly changing environment, we also need to update our thinking and behaviors. For a handrail on how to do that, by design, we begin by looking at how humans learn.

THE LEGACY OF H.M.

The most famous human subject in neuroscience is Henry Molaison.[10,11] Henry, known as HM in the literature before his death in 2008 at the age of 82, suffered from severe epileptic seizures that doctors linked to a childhood bicycle accident. By the age of 27, the seizures were so severe that Henry could no longer work or lead a normal life. In 1953, Henry agreed to experimental brain surgery in an attempt to reduce the impact of the seizures.

Henry's neurosurgeon, William Scoville, removed significant portions of Henry's hippocampi, areas that we now know are needed to form new memories.[11–13]

Henry's epilepsy did improve, but he lost the ability to form new declarative memories — the ability to recall something and describe it. His working and procedural memory, though, remained intact. He was able to remember much of his life before his surgery, and he could still walk and talk. He could remember information like a string of numbers or a name for brief moments, but he could not commit them to his long-term memory.

Recognizing the extent of Henry's memory impairment, Scoville asked Brenda Milner, a cognitive neuroscientist, for help. Milner and her student, Suzanne Corkin, studied HM for more than 30 years. His case contributed a lot of new information to how we view memory, learning, and the role of regional functional specialization in the brain.[13-17]

In 1962, Milner demonstrated that Henry could learn certain tasks without knowing that he was learning them. He was able to repeat learned tasks without being able to recall when or how he had learned them. Henry could, for instance, draw between the parallel lines of a 5-point star while he watched his hand in the mirror. Despite having no conscious recollection of having ever done the exercise before, Henry gradually got better and better at this challenging task, even commenting to Brenda that the task was "easier than I thought it would be."[17,18]

There are several important implications of this study. For the first time, Milner and Corkin were able to show that the hippocampus plays an important role in the creation of long-term explicit memories. Henry was able to learn new physical skills using motor learning, which accesses very different parts of the brain. They showed that we can learn in different ways, and we can acquire new patterns of behavior without even realizing that this is what we're doing.[10,12]

Later research in the 1990s and early 2000s found similar abilities for the unconscious uptake of new experience through what became known as mirror neurons.

MONKEY SEE, MONKEY DO

In the 1990s, an Italian neurophysiology team made a discovery which would later be heralded by some as the most important neuroscience findings of the twentieth century.[19,20]

The researchers implanted electrodes in the brains of macaque monkeys and then studied their brain activity while the monkeys were engaged in motor activities like holding and lifting objects.[21,22]

During a break from the research, one of the scientists reached toward an object of some kind. A monitor buzzed to alert him that motor activity was firing in the brain of one of his research subjects. The macaque's brain had lit up in the area that showed activity when it gestured or lifted an object. However, the monkey hadn't moved. It was simply sitting, watching the human move his hand.

This moment of scientific serendipity opened entirely new avenues of research into a particular class of brain cells, now known as mirror neurons. Mirror neurons are present in human brains and also in the brains of other primates. Subsequent studies have provided strong evidence that mirror neurons are responsible for transforming what we see into knowledge of both the intention of another's actions, as well as learning the viewed act for ourselves.[20] No verbal instruction is required, just observation of the action, which gives the phrase "monkey see, monkey do" a whole new and scientifically backed foundation.[23]

Vilayanur Ramachandran, a neuroscientist from the University of California, has gone so far as to suggest that mirror neurons shaped the beginnings of modern culture and civilization. Skills such as tool use, fire and shelter building, language, and the ability to read or interpret another's intentions all developed very quickly, possibly as a result of a sudden emergence of this system that allows us to learn and intuit quickly from observation.[24]

Instruction manuals or handy tips wouldn't be of any use to us as kids because language and its meaning arrive much later than our immediate need for basic behaviors. Long before we learn to understand written or verbal instructions, our neurology soaks up a multitude of experiences: states that we often label in later life as emotions, and movement patterns and behaviors that, when repeated, become habits.

Just as we can copy desirable behaviors, such as walking, smiling, and lifting a spoon to our mouths, we can also paint undesirable traits onto the canvas of our neurology.

Those sudden and unexpected states that we might call fear, anxiety, anger, jealousy, or procrastination, and even poor states of health, can be copied from others when we are not paying attention to their acquisition.

There are many practical applications for what we've learned about mirror neurons. We can, for instance, become alert to what we might be inadvertently learning from those around us, and we can design learning experiences so that we are ideally positioned to learn from those who perform well in areas in which we might like to improve our own performance.

Of key importance, as we learned from Henry Molaison, words and language are not necessary for certain types of learning or even for thinking more generally. Indeed, they might be positively unhelpful. As we'll see, internal self-talk is one of the most commonly reported ways of undermining personal resilience.

LEFT BRAIN INTERPRETER

There is no doubt that acquisition of language was transformational in human evolution. Language enabled us to capture and then communicate ideas. We could pass knowledge down through generations and, through translation, across cultures.

However, language, and in particular the inner voice that we sometimes refer to as self-talk or inner dialogue, is not always as it might seem.[25]

Michael Gazzaniga's research into inner dialogue illustrates this point.[26] Until recently, many patients who experienced debilitating epileptic seizures underwent what is called split-brain surgery. In the operation, the corpus callosum that divides the left and right hemispheres of the brain is severed to prevent epileptic cascades.

Surprisingly, patients who undergo this procedure appear to function quite well, and the dysfunction that such surgery introduces is quite subtle. Gazzaniga was exploring some of these subtle changes when he stumbled upon a feature he called the left-brain interpreter.[26–29]

In his experiment, Gazzaniga flashed two pictures at a patient for just a moment, with images separated for each eye. To understand what happened next, we need to know that when light enters the eye it crosses at the

optic chiasm, with images entering the right eye projected into the left side of the brain, and vice versa. While we know that key aspects of language are processed in the right hemisphere, the primary language centers are dominant in the left side of the brain.[26-30]

Because the patient's hemispheres were separated, each hemisphere saw different images. A picture of a chicken claw was flashed to the left hemisphere, and a snow scene with a shed unrelated to chickens was flashed to the right hemisphere. When asked to select pairs of related images, the left hand selected a snow shovel and the right hand, the picture of a chicken.[26,27]

When asked why he made that selection, the patient replied, "Oh, that's simple. The chicken claw goes with the chicken, and you need a shovel to clean out the chicken shed."[26]

The left brain, responsible for processing language, had not seen the snow, but it had seen the chicken. To help explain the choice of the shovel, it created a narrative that worked with information it had on hand.

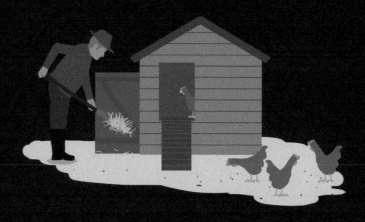

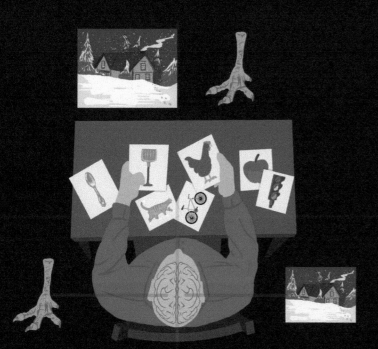

Gazzaniga called this process the left brain interpreter, and it's not limited to those with surgically separated hemispheres.[25] One important role of the left brain is to provide a rational and word-based explanation of our thinking. We explain sensemaking and especially unconscious thinking through the left brain interpreter. Just like external narrative, internal narrative can provide a feedback loop that shapes our recollection of past events and how we engage with the present.

One way to manage unwanted and intrusive commentary by the left brain interpreter is by the use of the body scan, tongue drop, and box breathing method. Through these simple and resourceful techniques, we can train ourselves to switch off our inner dialogue and tune into or out of other thinking.

TONGUE DROP

A colleague of ours, Leon Taylor, was once a competitive diver. At the 2004 Olympic Games in Athens, he won a silver medal for Great Britain in the synchronized 10-meter diving event.

If you watch videos of Leon walking from the back of the diving board to the edge of it, you'll see an interesting and subtle change to his physiology a second or so before he dives.[31]

Just before Leon's muscles spring into action, his tongue pushes forward out of his mouth in a fixed position. When Leon was asked to recall and describe this point in his dive sequence, he said: "This is when there is no internal dialogue. Everything goes quiet."

Leon isn't the only person who uses tongue position to enhance performance. Athletes in a wide range of fields use this technique, and it's common in meditation practices, which seek ways to quiet the mind. When researching for this book, we interviewed special forces snipers, martial artists, musicians, and writers. Many of them told us that, when they are seeking sharp focus or clarity, they lower their tongue into the base of the mouth.

The Mayo Clinic has studied the benefits of allowing the tongue to relax. The researchers found that simple habitual postures including certain tongue positions can add to the background sensory and physiological load that increase sympathetic arousal. Advice to lightly place the tongue *up* on the palate of the mouth to increase relaxation has been shown to actually increase muscle tension. Letting the tongue *drop* into the floor of the mouth does the opposite. It reduces tension in the muscles of the temple and around the hyoid bone in the throat, supporting parasympathetic activation.[32]

The tongue drop also increases heart rate variability (the variation in time between heartbeats). Higher variability between heartbeats is usually associated with a strong ability to tolerate physiological strain or recover from prior accumulated stress.[32,33]

Dr. John Grinder, a linguist and modeler of human behavior, posits that when we engage in self-talk (internal dialogue), the tongue replicates the movements of speech with micro muscle-movements. We might not be speaking, but we're still using the organs of speech.

By preventing the movement of the tongue in contexts where internal dialogue is not useful, we can reduce and often entirely eliminate self-talk for as long as the tongue is stable. We also find that deliberate practice leads to enhanced access to inner quiet. With enough time and practice, we don't even need to consciously activate the technique. It becomes automatic.

Try the tongue drop now. Notice how the inner chatter stops. You can use the tongue drop in any context where internal dialogue is undermining your performance. Use it whenever you need inner quiet time. We regularly receive feedback from clients who have used the tongue drop as part of their nighttime routine to help them fall asleep.

When combined with the body scan and box breathing, the tongue drop technique can support a resilient state in any context.

TO USE THE TONGUE DROP:

Step 1.

Gently and firmly push the tongue down into the lower jaw, touching the tip of the tongue below the lower gum line.

Step 2.

Hold this position, focusing your attention on limiting any movement in the tongue.

Step 3.

Appreciate some freedom from your internal chatter!

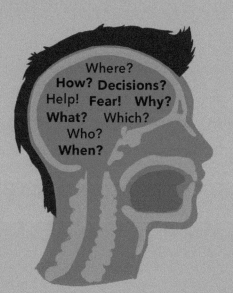

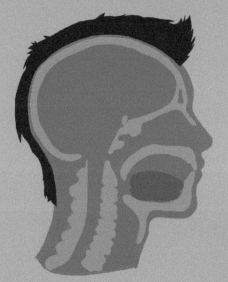

MULTIPLE BRAINS

Another big piece of the neuroscience puzzle concerns the presence and function of our "other" brains.

Humans have at least three brains. The head or cephalic brain is joined by the gut or enteric brain, and there's also the heart or cardiac brain. All of these organs meet the formal definition of a brain.[6,34]

Each has:

1. Large numbers of sensory and motor neurons. The head brain, which most people think of as THE brain, has around 86 billion neurons, the gut brain has around 200–500 million neurons, and the heart brain has between 30 and 120 thousand neurons.[35-37]

2. Support cells such as glial cells.

3. The ability to perceive, assimilate, store information, and learn.

4. The ability to mediate complex reflexes.

5. The ability to produce neurotransmitters.

Together, these brains form an important part of our neurology that we call the embodied mind.[38,39]

Of key importance from the perspective of thinking and decision-making is the recognition that much of our thinking is distributed, occurs beneath conscious awareness, and involves all the senses.

We most commonly become aware of signals from the embodied mind in the form of physical sensations, some of which we call emotions. Images, symbols, and metaphors, as well as dreams, also sometimes rise to conscious attention. Metaphors are often hidden in plain sight in the sentences we use in everyday life. Sayings such as "I knew it in my gut," or "It was a decision of the heart" are obvious examples of metaphors that suggest a form of thinking that is not of the head.[39]

Unfortunately, much of the sensing and thinking from our other brains remains buried or ignored by certain features of the left hemisphere of the head brain. In fact, as Prof. Iain McGilchrist notes in *The Master and His Emissary: The Divided Brain and the Making of the Western World*, one of the left hemisphere's functions appears to be the reduction and categorization of information. It compresses and sorts information rather than integrating and appreciating it in its entirety. This is particularly prevalent in Western society, less so in Eastern culture.[25,40]

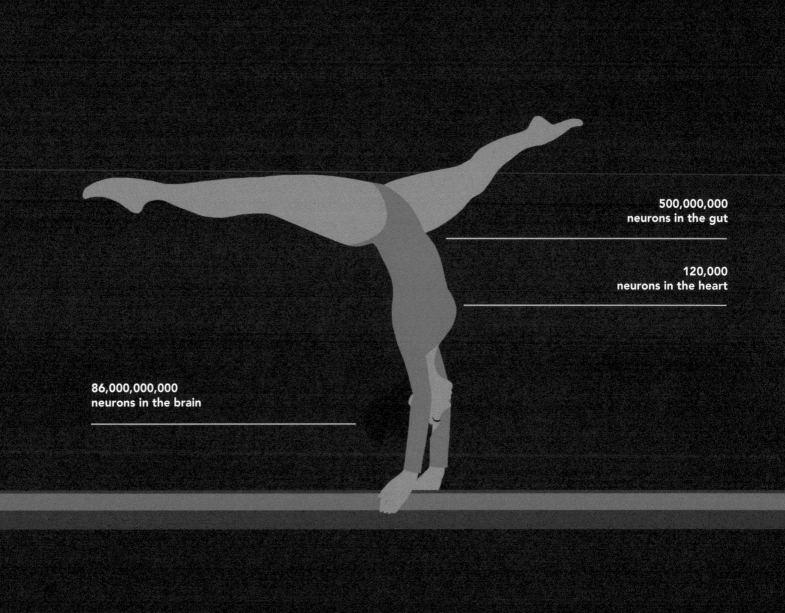

500,000,000
neurons in the gut

120,000
neurons in the heart

86,000,000,000
neurons in the brain

THINKING AND THE DIVIDED BRAIN(S)

In the introduction to his book, Prof. Iain McGilchrist uses a story attributed to Nietzsche* to illustrate the impact of the divided human brain.[25] The story goes something like this...

"There was once a wise spiritual master, who was the ruler of a small but prosperous domain, and who was known for his selfless devotion to his people. As the people flourished and grew in number, the bounds of his small domain spread, and with it the need to trust implicitly the emissaries he sent to ensure the safety of its ever more distant parts.

It was not just that it was impossible for him personally to order all that needed to be dealt with: as he wisely saw, he needed to keep his distance from, and remain ignorant of, such concerns. And so he nurtured and trained carefully his emissaries, in order that they could be trusted.

Eventually, however, his cleverest and most ambitious vizier, the one he trusted most to do his work, began to see himself as the master, and used his position to advance his own wealth and influence. He saw his master's temperance and forbearance as weakness, not wisdom, and on his missions on the master's behalf, adopted his mantle as his own — the emissary became contemptuous of his master. And so it came about that the master was usurped, the people were duped, the

domain became a tyranny, and eventually it collapsed in ruins."

Stories like this are as old as humanity itself. They resonate far from the sphere of political history. McGilchrist argues that something similar is taking place inside ourselves — in our brains. The master and emissary are, respectively, the right and left hemispheres of the brain. The hemispheres should cooperate, but they are in a state of conflict.

The hemispheric battles are recorded in the history of philosophy, with major losses and victories marked in the history of Western culture.

At present, our civilization finds itself in the hands of the emissary (the left hemisphere). Gifted though the left hemisphere may be, it behaves like the ambitious regional bureaucrat. It has its own interests at heart.

Meanwhile, the master (the right hemisphere) is led away in chains. His wisdom gave the people peace and security, and now he has been betrayed by the emissary.

One of the dominant functions of the left hemisphere includes a need to reduce complexity into parts.[25,41,42] This reductionist trait is often supported by a confidence (or delusion). It knows (or thinks it knows) that what is being reduced is all that is needed to be accounted for, where the whole is only the sum of its parts.

Consider, for example, a flower. The left hemisphere sees the flower, but it does not see the ecosystem that has produced it — the earth that it came from, the air and sunshine it integrated into its cells, the relationships it has with pollinating insects, the temperature that dictates its lifespan, and endless other factors. These are all boiled away when we focus purely on the flower as a thing.

In Ikebana, the ancient Japanese art of flower arranging, when a cut flower is placed into an arrangement, it is not simply viewed as a showcase for the flower. Rather, it is an art form that appreciates the relationship between the flowers and the whole. Everything is considered: the field depth, the relative size of each individual flower, the empty space between the flowers, and the space (context) in which the flowers stand.

Ikebana is just one representation of how the right hemisphere tracks for inclusiveness, curiosity, novelty, beauty, and difference in the world.[25,41,42]

If we do not intentionally interrupt the dominance of the left hemisphere, we may continue to reduce experiences, categorizing and labeling as we go. Oversimplified reductions pigeonhole our thinking.

Like a Japanese flower arranger, we could consider each part, the relationship between the parts, and the context.

Throughout this book, we will be inviting you to consider the little things that work together to create the whole. We'll be asking you to consider context and relationships. Like the Japanese flower arranger, we want you to consider how complex systems can be managed and understood without attempting to oversimplify them.

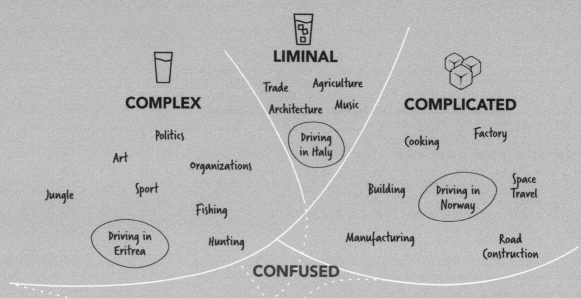

COMPLEX

LIMINAL

COMPLICATED

Trade   Agriculture

Architecture   Music

Politics   Factory

Art   Driving in Italy   Cooking

organizations   Space Travel

Jungle   Sport   Building   Driving in Norway

Fishing

Driving in Eritrea   Manufacturing   Road Construction

Hunting

CONFUSED

CHAOTIC   CLEAR

THINKING ABOUT THINKING CAN BE COMPLICATED...AND EVEN COMPLEX!

"I do not underestimate the importance of the left hemisphere's contribution to all that humankind has achieved, and to all that we are, in the everyday sense of the word; in fact it is because I value it, that I say that it has to find its proper place, so as to fulfill its critically important role. It is a wonderful servant, but a very poor master."

— Prof. Iain McGilchrist[43]

We do not intend to give you the impression that the left hemisphere is the problem child of the right. As McGilchrist makes clear, both hemispheres serve important roles. By applying each hemisphere to the challenges suited to it, we can improve our thinking capability.

Humans are animals that specialize in thinking, and our extraordinary cognitive powers have enabled us to undertake remarkable tasks.[44]

We have arranged some of these remarkable tasks in part of the Cynefin framework. From complexity science, Professor Dave Snowden has developed a sensemaking framework, called Cynefin, a Welsh word that means "habitat" or "place of our multiple belongings."[45]

In the Cynefin framework, the boundary between complex and complicated is called liminal, meaning a state of transition.[46] The domains in Cynefin are best thought of as phases rather than gradations, and liminal conditions contain elements of both types of systems, like a mix of ice and water. In the case of water, liquid water is a complex medium with eddies and currents (complex patterns). By contrast, ice is ordered with structure. A mix of ice and water contains both systems.

This metaphor serves us well as we address the imbalance that McGilchrist highlights between the master and his emissary. Our goal is to match the best mode of thinking in a way that meets the challenges of context.

With many exceptions, rational thinking is often best applied in the complicated domain (like fixing a problem in a factory); intuitive thinking is often best suited to complex systems (like surviving in a jungle). Liminal highlights that some systems have elements of both complex and complicated. In these conditions, both modes of thinking are ideally deployed simultaneously.

We suspect that the liminal transition between complex and complicated is critically important for personal resilience. It is very much a place of "and," not either/or modes of thinking and acting.

The Cynefin sensemaking framework allows for the same system to be experienced differently by different people. Similarly, systems can be radically different depending on the location, climate conditions, and cultural norms. To illustrate the relationship between context and different ways of thinking and acting, consider driving in different countries.

Driving in Eritrea involves pattern detection and rules of thumb that help you navigate poor roads, the random presence of animals, and erratic traffic flow. Drivers seldom follow the rules, and the death rate is 24.1/100K people per year.[47]

Compare Eritrea with a country like Norway, where the roads are good, the cows are contained in paddocks, and the rules are followed closely. In Norway, rules of thumb aren't much help. What does help is knowing the rules precisely and following them. Thanks to the ordered nature of the system, and adherence to the rules, the death rate on Norwegian roads is only around 3.8/100K per year.[47]

Italy, with death rates around 6.1/100k per year, is somewhere in between Eritrea and Norway.[47] In Italy, drivers must rely on a combination of formal rules and idiosyncratic but understandable patterns of rule-breaking. You can, for instance, expect quite a lot of tailgating and light-jumping.

For global drivers, different modes of thinking and action are appropriate in different contexts. Importantly, sticking to the rules appropriate to Norway will quickly get you killed in Eritrea. We assume Norwegiens find it challenging to drive in Eritrea, and vice versa!

ADAPTATION AND THE NEUROPLASTICITY ADVANTAGE

Fortunately, we can all learn to drive in conditions as diverse as Eritrea, Norway, and even London...

While Eritrea challenges drivers to remain agile to potholes, cows, and poor adherence to road-rules, navigating London by car presents an entirely different challenge. London and its roads have built up over more than 2,000 years, with little in the way of integrated project planning.

The labyrinth of roads, roundabouts, one-way streets, narrow laneways, and perpetual roadworks all combine to make the job of the London cabbie much more complex than it might appear to some.

To earn their licenses, would-be black-cab drivers spend several years driving around the city on mopeds, memorizing the intricate network of 25,000 streets, including, for example, all the tourist hotspots within a 10-kilometer radius of Charing Cross train station.

This apprenticeship is unique to London taxi licensing. Typically 50–60% of trainees fail to qualify. The cognitive demand of such a herculean memory task literally changes the brains of the successful candidates.

Using functional magnetic resonance imaging, neuroscientists Eleanor Maguire and Katherine Woollett of University College London discovered that London taxi drivers developed more gray matter in their posterior hippocampi as they underwent training. Interestingly, the successful trainees did not perform better on all tests of memory, and in some cases performed worse than non-taxi drivers in other aspects of visual memory.[48]

It seems that an enlarged hippocampus posterior (rear) occurs at the expense of its anterior (front), creating a cognitive-talents trade-off. This process of changing the brain is called neuroplasticity.

In his 2007 blockbuster book *The Brain That Changes Itself*, Dr. Norman Doidge brought the concept of neuroplasticity to popular attention. Scientists long believed that brain structure was largely fixed early in life, until its eventual decline with old age. More recently, researchers have been looking at cases of individuals who cured themselves of Parkinson's, overcame severe learning disabilities, and recovered from brain problems previously thought to be incurable. Many people have discovered the lifelong potential for recovery, learning, and cognitive well-being.

"Unlearning is hard, because once circuits are established in the brain, they are notoriously difficult to change because neuroplasticity is competitive."

– Dr. Norman Doidge[50]

However...

"Neuroplasticity isn't all good news; it renders our brains not only more resourceful but also more vulnerable to outside influences. Neuroplasticity has the power to produce more flexible but also more rigid behaviors — the plastic paradox."[49]

Brain plasticity has been likened to creating a rut by driving a vehicle over a field again and again. The tires create a rut that becomes difficult to break out from. Our minds do something similar. Our attention is naturally drawn toward the well-worn path, where the going is easier. Our thoughts want to follow these ruts. As the saying goes, "Neurons that fire together wire together."

The metaphor of ruts in a field also explains why it's so difficult to replace undesirable behaviors with new ones. As Doidge puts it, "It was always a mystery in conventional learning theory as to why it is so much harder to unlearn something than learn it."

To get out of the rut, we have to learn a new approach that supersedes and overprints the previous pattern. Our approach recognizes this important distinction and focuses on providing better and more-attractive alternatives to conventional ways of thinking and acting. It's less about stopping the problematic thought pattern or behavior than about finding a better and more-useful approach, and then repeating the new pattern to create new pathways, or new ruts even, using our metaphor of driving across a field.

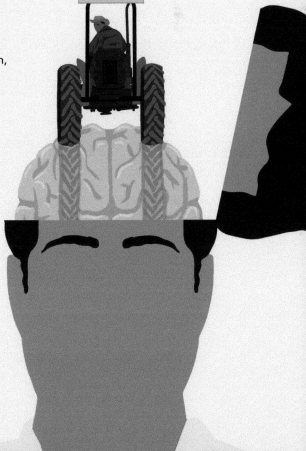

OLD DOGS CAN LEARN NEW TRICKS

As we age, there is a tendency for cognitive decline with a decrease in our ability to think with clarity, maintain attention, remember accurately, and respond quickly. However, common, age-related degradation is not a given. Recent studies demonstrate that neuroplasticity operates throughout life. It turns out that old dogs *can* learn new tricks.[9]

To do this, we need to be prepared to think like children, with curiosity, creativity, and fearlessness. In the most watched TED Talk of all time, Sir Ken Robinson, education advisor to the British Government, said this about children:

"Kids will take a chance. If they don't know, they'll have a go. They're not frightened of being wrong...if you're not prepared to be wrong, you'll never come up with anything original...And by the time they get to be adults, most kids have lost that capacity. They have become frightened of being wrong. And we run our companies like this. We stigmatize mistakes. And we're now running national education systems where mistakes are the worst thing you can make. And the result is that we are educating people out of their creative capacities."[51]

Curiosity, creativity, and motivation combine to create a learning environment in which the neuroplastic brain can thrive.[9]

Even the most unpleasant experiences like persistent or chronic pain are amenable to change through our thinking. As Prof. Lorimer Mosely, a clinical scientist who specializes in pain, says:

"Bioplasticity got you into this situation and bioplasticity can get you out again."[52]

The same plastic potential applies to congenital cognitive disability, traumatic brain injury, stroke, or conditions such as PTSD, depression, or anxiety that might have been practiced for a long time. It is possible to retrain the brain and our whole neurology.[9,49,53,54]

The same is also true for all patterns of behavior.

Our brains, like the sleeping old dog by the fire, can lose their motivation to take on new information or learn new tricks if we don't challenge them with novelty. Behavioral neuroscientist Edward Taub calls this "learned non-use." When, for instance, a stroke has substantially weakened one limb, the weak limb's movement is suppressed due to preference for the stronger limb. The weak limb may have the potential for rehabilitation, but this potential is never realized because it is easier to rely entirely upon the stronger limb.[9,55,56]

The principle of learned non-use applies to any behavior, and it can critically undermine personal resilience. It is extremely easy to get sucked into unhealthy convenience, to lean too heavily on our support systems, or to convince ourselves that we are utterly helpless.

To maximize the benefits of neuroplastic potential we need to continually challenge our thinking.

The highest-performing learners challenge themselves. They operate brimming with intent and curiosity. They are, of course, children!

IF WE LEARN LIKE CHILDREN, WE PROBABLY NEED TO SLEEP LIKE CHILDREN

Just like children, we need plenty of sleep and rest to think and learn effectively. Sleep contributes to plastic change by allowing learning to be consolidated. Plastic change occurs in both REM and non-REM sleep.[49,57] Some changes in thinking are instantaneous, and we might be able to establish new patterns remarkably quickly. Others might take many months of diligent practice, repetition, and gradually increasing challenge. Whether fast or slow, these changes will only take place in a well-rested mind.

Canadian neuroscientist and educator Barbara Arrowsmith-Young gradually changed her capabilities over many months of practice through deliberate brain training exercises such as card identification games. She outlines her personal journey and the methods she developed to overcome her own congenital cognitive disability in *The Woman Who Changed Her Brain: Unlocking the Extraordinary Potential of the Human Mind*.[49,53]

One standout attribute in her story is her incredibly high intrinsic motivation. Intrinsic motivation is a key feature of being able to place and hold attention. It also provides the neural basis for "purpose" in many of the measures of resilience.[58]

There are many small life changes that we can make to maximize our neuroplastic potential. By minimizing practicing unwanted behaviors, making measurable progress toward learning new skills, and seeking rewarding change, we can all improve our overall brain health. Importantly, skills which involve multiple senses simultaneously prove more challenging and ultimately most beneficial for the brain.[9]

People skills, such as rapport, appear to require special attention, so connecting and communicating with others can also promote brain plasticity.[9]

Throughout this book, we encourage you to think in ways that engage conscious/explicit AND unconscious/implicit strategies in ways that will improve neuroplasticity. One deliberate approach involves using models that can help you develop new or faster approaches to sensing and thinking to give you an advantage in just about every form of decision-making and action.

MICRO-NARRATIVE

FIGURING IT OUT

ANDREA PLACE

is a professionally licensed firefighter/paramedic within the state of Minnesota. She has a Bachelor of Fire Sciences and is a Nationally Registered Paramedic with 15 years of experience. She is married and has three young children.

I've been a firefighter for fourteen years and yet it still amazes that when I get off the truck without a hood or a helmet on, people act with surprise and often say out loud, "There's a woman firefighter!" Moms especially point it out to their kids, "Look, honey, she's an actual female firefighter."

When I first started as a medic with the busier service, I would go out in a jump vehicle, an SUV, from which I would get dropped to a call, mostly for medical incidents. My partner would leave me and disappear to run another call until the engine got to us. I would be in an inner city apartment complex with my gear and my bag but other than that, I was on my own. For me, that was a big eye opener as to what our job entailed.

Being young, I was a little naive and not necessarily aware of all the evils of the world at that point. There were situations such as walking into an apartment where there are guns sitting on the table and I have to say to myself, oh, I'm aware that's over there, but I'm just going to get on with my work over here.

In those situations and when I go on calls, I don't think about my husband or my kids. I may get the phone call from my husband saying that the kids are being monsters, and that's really the only time I allow myself to think about home life. It's a coping mechanism because I know the dangers and I don't want to have that weighing down on me when I'm supposed to be doing a job.

One deeply memorable call was to a thirteen-month-old baby girl who was killed by her father.

He beat her and put her back in her crib. We worked to save her and worked her even though we knew she had gone. I have a very hard time leaving a kid and not trying everything in my abilities to bring her back.

"When I'm at my best, I'm positive and upbeat and I feel like I can conquer the world."

For a long time I dealt with that event by smoking and drinking. Then I found out I was three months pregnant with my son. So on top of the strain of work events like that, and others, I had the emotions and hormones of a pregnant women and God-knows-what-else going on in my body!

It begins to mount up unless you do something about it.

I've often wished there was some way to talk about the more extreme calls, or to feel comfortable discussing it, because inevitably in a firehouse no one wants to admit that something is bothering them. Most of us refuse to talk about what we go through because it may make us look like we're weak, especially as a female. But there are times when I have wanted an outlet to talk to somebody[6], just as long as it's not in a forced manner.

That murdered baby incident simmered in me for a long time before it actually made its outward show. I had failed to realize the effect it had and I was acting differently at home.

Eventually my husband called me out on it and said, "You need to figure this out." So, I did a lot of soul searching and changing of habits and not bringing my work home with me. I got healthy and focused on what needed to be changed. In the past I would have smoked cigarettes and sipped Jameson in the corner. But you can't function at your best if you do that and it's important to find ways to switch off, relax at home. Simple changes make a big difference. No electronic devices or TV in the bedroom. A long wind-down period, including reading books before sleep. I never watch the news. I don't want that negativity on my mind. I ate junk food in my early days and had brain fog. Now I pay attention to eating healthy food; I like to run to burn off some of the feelings of stress from the day. It all helps toward performing better. When I'm at my best, I'm positive and upbeat and I feel like I can conquer the world. I come in and have a positive attitude and I don't let anything bring me down.

Sometimes I come to work and I have this feeling, it's gonna be a good day, and when I go out on calls and have a smile on my face, nothing gets to me.

OODA LOOP[58]

The military strategist Colonel John Boyd (the inspiration for Maverik, played by Tom Cruise in *Top Gun*) created the oddly named OODA Loop. OODA is an acronym for Observe–Orient–Decide–Act.[59]

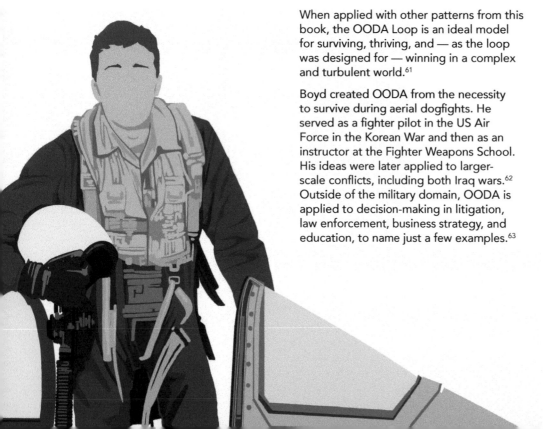

When applied with other patterns from this book, the OODA Loop is an ideal model for surviving, thriving, and — as the loop was designed for — winning in a complex and turbulent world.[61]

Boyd created OODA from the necessity to survive during aerial dogfights. He served as a fighter pilot in the US Air Force in the Korean War and then as an instructor at the Fighter Weapons School. His ideas were later applied to larger-scale conflicts, including both Iraq wars.[62] Outside of the military domain, OODA is applied to decision-making in litigation, law enforcement, business strategy, and education, to name just a few examples.[63]

OODA describes naturally occurring and mostly unconscious recurring decision-making cycles. A person or a group first observes, then orients, decides, and, finally, acts. After the action, there is feedback, and the loop starts again with improved or recalibrated observation.

If we accept that our individual and collective views of the world are, at best, a useful, albeit partially complete map of reality and, at worst, an impractical map that bears little resemblance to reality or survival advantage, OODA can help us create more salient maps based on the inputs and evidence that we feed into the loop.

OBSERVE   ORIENT   DECIDE   ACT

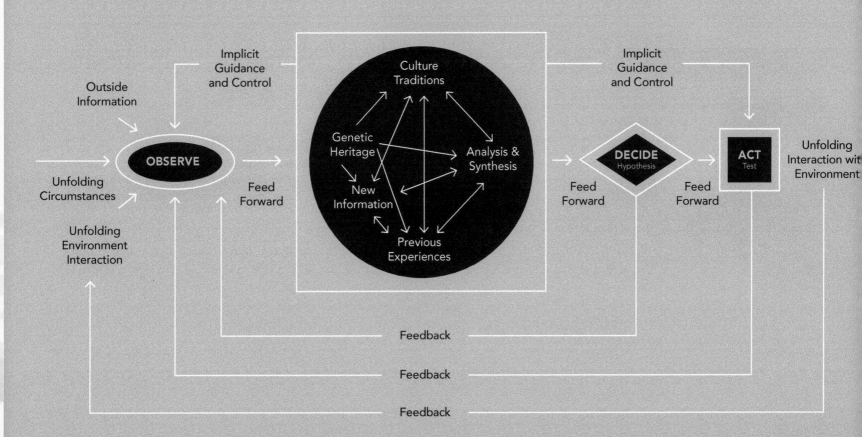

REMEMBER TO LOOP

OBSERVE

Before we can approach a decision, we must first gather salient information. This could include data, test results, well-developed models, narratives, or conversations, and perhaps most importantly, it can also include observations of other people — particularly patterns of behavior.

It is essential to realize that even so-called objective information will have issues of bias and uncertainty. We should place all information on a spectrum of reliability, understanding that evidence is never complete and is constantly evolving. Inevitably, we are filtering for the signal amongst all the noise and, rather than more and more data, it is important to know what to pay attention to and what to ignore. We recommend adopting an observer or third person position and paying close attention to patterns.

ORIENT

This step offers the most leverage to successfully use the OODA Loop, creating choice in the gap between stimulus and response. It is the step that challenges bias and identifies patterns and new opportunities. It is also important to identify what type of system we are operating in, which in turn allows an approach to decisions and actions that are coherent or appropriate for that system. For example, is rapid action the best response to chaos, or is a more cautious probe to detect complex patterns needed? Do we have enough information, or does a complicated situation need expert analysis?

Orientation can be greatly improved by understanding our own biases and preferences for action. Although it is notoriously difficult to sidestep biases such as inattentional blindness, simply being aware, curious, and open to being wrong is often enough to trigger a deliberate shift in how we orient.

DECIDE

Decision time! We have four options:

Option 1: An implicit or unconscious loop back to Observation. This could be an authentic unconscious move, intuitively knowing that more information is needed before making a decision, or it could be paralysis and dithering in a negative feedback loop, only observing what fits your biases.

Option 3: A conscious decision to cycle back to Observe for more information. It helps to know what sort of information you need and potentially where to look. Perhaps seek insight from people with alternative views, challenge accepted norms, deliberately make implicit knowledge explicit, or consciously task your unconscious to direct you where to go next.

ACT

When we act, we trigger the opportunity for feedback. This is the evidence for the success or failure of this particular loop. Action is our opportunity to test our understanding of the system and interaction with the environment. This provides insight back into Observe, starting the loop anew.

Many actions trigger both desired and undesired effects, often including second- or third-order effects, or even a cascade of unintended consequences, especially in complex unpredictable systems.

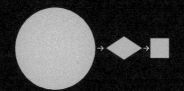

Option 2: An implicit unconscious move to action. High-quality instinctual moves of this type are ideally suited to fast-paced, complex, or chaotic systems, where it is usually more effective to use intuition and rules-of-thumb and to trust the signals that arise in the moment rather than attempting to apply step-by-step, rational thinking to work it out.

Option 4. We understand enough to make a decision and to act based on what we have learned during observation and orientation.

Notice in Decide, in particular, that OODA is not linear. It is made of several choice points and multiple loops.

LET'S NOT 00-00-00

From Act, notice that there are two feedback loops. One, the "Unfolding Interaction with Environment," is about the outcome of your chosen Action. In this feedback loop between Act and Observe, we encourage an identification of the intention/purpose for the Action. This is also a good time to check that the consequences are acceptable.

The other Feedback loop offers the opportunity to review your thought process. This should be evaluated separately from the resulting outcome. For example, you might have received a positive outcome but still notice flaws in your application of OODA, or your application might be immaculate and you still received a negative outcome.

To illustrate this, imagine a poker game. The odds tell you to go all-in. Yet, when you do, you lose. That doesn't mean it was necessarily a bad decision or action. You played the odds and lost. It happens to the best of us.

However, in the feedback review, you'll want to check more than the formal odds. What were the non-verbal cues that the player across from you was sending in your direction? This is an example where a feedback cycle can help calibrate the more subtle weak signals — such as the "tell" of your opponent for example.

In such a situation, you might just have a hunch, that niggling feeling, that even though the odds are in your favor, you sense that she is holding something special. That hunch is a signal from your unconscious. Though you don't consciously realize it, you've picked up on one of your opponent's non-verbal cues.

OODA provides a model for improving how we think and act in the world. It includes multiple feedback and feedforward loops, and it uses both implicit and explicit moves between sensing, deciding, acting, and reviewing. Fast and efficient use of OODA results in better decision-making and a competitive advantage. It also offers a mechanism for review and overhaul of any aspect of your life.

One common trap has been identified by David Ullman in his paper, 'OO-OO-OO!' The Sound of a Broken OODA Loop." All too often, teams or individuals get stuck in the decision-making stage creating an OO-OO-OO — the stuttering sound of a broken OODA loop (say it out loud; it's the sound of someone dithering!).

Indecision costs far too many people and organizations time and resources. At best, they lose their competitive advantage; at worst they get wiped out.[63]

THINKING IN HIERARCHIES

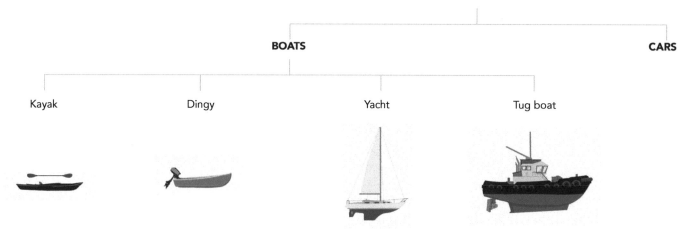

FORMS OF TRANSPORT

BOATS   **CARS**

Kayak   Dingy   Yacht   Tug boat

Consider two very different hierarchies (after Bostic St. Clair and Grinder):[64]

The first involves logical levels with three rules.

1. Is an example or type of _____.

2. There are decreasing examples as you move down in levels.

3. All examples are not required to make coherent sense of the set they belong to.

So, for "boat," members of that set include kayak, dingy, yacht, and tug.

Depending on your interest in boats, higher-level sets could include:

Forms of transport, Things that float, or Objects made by engineers

Note that there are fewer examples of "Boats" than there are "Forms of transport" because of the inclusive nature of the subset "Boat" within the set "Forms of transport."

If a tug boat was omitted from the set of examples, the set would still make coherent sense.

One of the best ways to improve the way we think and OODA loop is to learn how to systematically move attention up, down, and sideways, tracking from fine details to the big picture and back again, and identifying what belongs together and what does not.

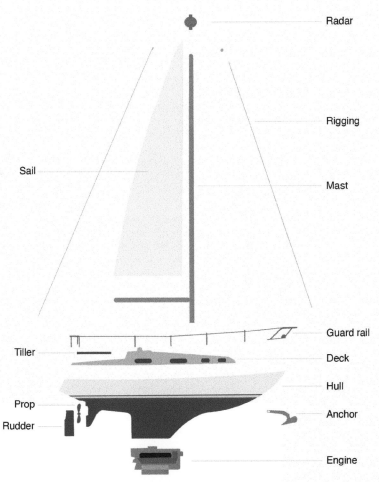

Radar

Rigging

Sail

Mast

Guard rail

Tiller

Deck

Prop

Hull

Rudder

Anchor

Engine

By contrast with a logical levels hierarchy, consider a parts-whole relationship.

In this hierarchy, the rules of membership are:

1. Is made up of _____

2. There are increasing members as you move down the levels.

3. All examples make the whole.

In the case of "boat," boat is made up of hull, mast, sails, wheel, etc. Hull is made of planks, nails, glue, varnish, etc.

Higher-level sets could include flotilla, but there are few options going up the levels.

Note that there are more examples of parts than there are equivalents of "flotilla."

If hull is omitted from the set, critically, there is a part missing from "boat" and it would not make coherent sense.

Clearly these hierarchies are very different, and the distinction goes some way to explaining why so many conversations seem to be at cross purposes. Imagine an engineer heading into technical problems with a widget in the factory while discussing global business development needs with her CEO; or a parent discussing the impact on the community of a teenager's rule breaking, while the teenager is only interested in fitting in with their rebellious friends. In these examples a certain amount of step-by-step pacing is required to get all parties on the same level.

Moving attention around these patterns is also useful for resilience because it allows us to analyze and discover choices and connections in different logical ways. These hierarchies also help explain or unpack deductive, inductive, and abductive thinking.

DEDUCTIVE, INDUCTIVE, AND ABDUCTIVE THINKING

Thinking patterns can go down, up, or sideways in either or both types of hierarchies.

DEDUCTIVE THINKING

Deduction is broadly analogous to rational or conscious thinking. It is a reductionist process, heading down in logical levels, or focusing on parts in parts-whole hierarchies.

Deduction starts out with a general statement or hypothesis. It then examines the possibilities until it arrives at what seems like a logical conclusion. Importantly, each logical step supports the next. The theory, if correct, will be supported by a string of connected and logically supported observations.

In deductive reasoning, if something is true of a set in general, it is also true for all members of that set.

For example: "Birds are warm-blooded egg-laying vertebrate animals with feathers, wings, and a beak. Typically, they can fly" (note the option to not fly...which is handy for penguins).

House martins, eagles, and swans (and penguins) all meet the set requirements, therefore they are birds. Note too that they are examples of the logical set "Bird."

Deductive conclusions are certain, provided that all of the underlying presuppositions are true.

However, deductive thinking, even when applied correctly, can still arrive at an incorrect generalization. For instance, Europeans used to believe that all swans were white. Every available piece of evidence suggested that this was true — until Dutch explorers landed in Western Australia in 1697 and saw black swans.[65,66]

INDUCTIVE THINKING

Induction tends to move upwards. Rather than breaking information down into small pieces, it puts the pieces together, making connections. Induction begins with observations (sensing) and, detecting a pattern, forms a theory. While deduction moves from the general to the specific, induction moves from the specific to the general.

Induction often involves jumps of intuition or unconscious pattern recognition.

The famous example of induction gone wrong is Taleb's story of the inductivist turkey who gets fed every day of its life and develops the assumption, with increasing confidence, that every day will be the same. The pattern repeats with regularity, confirming their theory. The turkey is brimming with confidence until the farmer appears in the doorway holding an axe in his hand.[67]

ABDUCTIVE THINKING

Abduction has elements of both deductive and inductive thinking. Professor Robert Logan sees abductive thinking as the thinking pattern that separates humans from other animals and, at least for now, from artificial intelligence.[2]

When we track its movements, we can see that abduction involves a series of steps up logical levels, across to adjacent or distant logical types, then back down to similar logical levels where pattern recognition and insight occurs. This is then reversed or transported back to our current context, where it can be repurposed and adapted (in science, this is called exaptation-adaptation).

For example, let's say we wanted to move away from petroleum engines in "Boats"; we could go up to "Other forms of transport," across to "Cars," then down into "Hydrogen cars" or "Battery cars." We could then bring this idea back to "Boats," seeking ways to adapt or modify hydrogen- or battery-powered engines to make them appropriate for boats. This example is actually happening thanks to partnerships between car makers and boat engine manufacturers.

In science, there is a constant interplay between theory-based deductive thinking and observation-based inductive thinking. Of course thinking patterns can also wander around in loops or move up, down or sideways in random fashion. When combined with abduction, these patterns form the basis of creativity and innovation. Most major scientific breakthroughs involve abductive thinking — a flash of inspiration, or that aha! moment. The surprising nature of such discoveries is because, until that aha! moment when the connection is made, the many steps and scanning across domains happens unconsciously. Sometimes it can be as straightforward as up, across, down, and back, or it can occur as many exploratory loops.

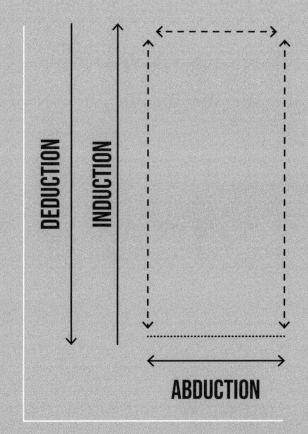

Generality
High Logical Levels
Intentions
Holistic

DEDUCTION
INDUCTION

Specificity
Low Logical Levels
Outcomes
Parts

ABDUCTION

Domain
Logical Type

ACTIVITY

CREATIVITY EXERCISE

HOW TO ENHANCE AND TRAIN CREATIVE THINKING.

Step 1.

FRAME THE CONTEXT.

Identify the problem you are trying to solve or the gap between the present and a future desired outcome.

Choose a space on the floor, and in this space, use all your senses to experience the problem or imagine the outcome.

Step out of the context and move away from it. Shake/move your body long enough to change state.

Step 2.

Play a flowstate game. You can use the alphabet chart — you can find instructions in Chapter 10 — Flow. You might not need to play a game. Juggling or slacklining might work for you. There are many examples of activities that quickly induce flow.

Step 3.

Enhance the state for creativity by thinking in metaphors, logical levels, and parts-whole relationships.

Choose any random object that appeals to you in the moment. Now challenge yourself to quickly find as many uses as possible for this object. Speed is important. Be sure to go up, down, and sideways in logical levels. A coach or collaborator can be helpful here too.

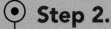

Hmmm...

Step 4.

Step back into the context with your new state for creativity. At first, allow thoughts and ideas to emerge without internal narrative interruptions.

YOU CAN THEN ASK YOURSELF SPECIFIC QUESTIONS:

- What are some of the ways that I can achieve my outcome?
- What would my outcome be if the barriers were removed?
- What is the first step that will start me along the pathway to the changes that I want?
- What will the next step be after that?

AN EXAMPLE OF STEP 3 USING A COAT HANGER:

What are all the uses you can think of for a coat hanger? Be as creative and imaginative as you can: **hanging clothes, TV aerial, earring, nose pick, back scratcher, etc. If I bend it like this, it could be a bookend, or, if I bent it like this, it could be an arrow.**

What else could you do to it? **I could melt it and turn it into a ball, I could freeze it and use it to chill drinks, etc.**

And what could you do if you had lots of coat hangers? **Hang lots of clothes, create a mural, build a fence, etc.**

And if you could reduce the coat hanger into parts, how could you do that, and what could you do with the parts? **I could snip it into bits and make steel pins, I could blow it up and use the fragments to make a picture, etc.**

And coat hangers are an example of what? **Things to hang clothes.**

And what other things can be used to hang clothes? **Clothes racks, the floor of my teenage daughter's room, doors, tree branches, etc.**

And doors, what are some of the other uses for doors? **Keeping a draft out, filling a hole in a wall, providing security, etc.**

And what are the other parts of a door? **Hinges, screws, panels, windows, etc.**

And if you have all of those things — how could you use them all? **I could build houses, make an art form, sell them at the market, make a catapult, etc.**

FROM INTERNAL CONFLICT TO TEAMWORK

Just like any teamwork, it's wonderful when we have cognitive congruence, when different modes or sources of thinking are in agreement or alignment. And just like teamwork there is a danger if this is forced or pursued to excess.

Often, the rational and intuitive forms of thinking are presented as either one OR the other, often with a bias or preference.[25,68,69] Rather than viewing it as a contest between rational and intuitive thinking modes, pitting them against each other, it is better to improve the dynamic relationship between them.

When we foster a "team" within ourselves, this removes any master/servant relationship.

The concept of team also removes a potentially unhealthy drive for perfect alignment or false harmony. When both modes of thinking are cooperating, it doesn't mean that they will be in perfect agreement. They might present very different insights simultaneously. Highly successful and resilient teams tolerate and even nurture constructive conflict and difference of opinion.

This team approach extends our sensing capability both inward and outward. It allows us to take a positive frame on other people's incongruence with a sense of curiosity. Using the metaphor of parts, it's possible that one part of us or them has an intention that is at odds with a different part.

For example, we might commit to spend more time at the gym to get fit and then find ourselves stuck at the office because we need to keep the boss happy. Alternatively, deductive reasoning might lead us to believe one course of action is the best way to go, while inductive or abductive pattern recognition might be joining dots in a way that sends a weak or even strong signal, cautioning against that course.

Recognizing conflicts in ourselves and others can greatly help us extend our thinking. Connecting and engaging with others can also help discover solutions to difficult problems or a tricky bind, such as how to get both time at the gym and meet the needs of a demanding boss.

However, remembering the cautionary tale of the master and his emissary, we apply an important rule of thumb. If in doubt, listen to the master. Go with your intuition. And then, close the OODA loop based on the evidence from Action. The idea is to train for better unconscious decision-making, and to train for a more nuanced conscious or rational exploration of complexity and patterns. Ideally, this also creates deep respect and trust within ourselves and with others.

The more we practice this respectful collaboration, with internal checking of different ways of experiencing and of thinking, the faster we can learn and the better we become at decision-making in complex or fluid situations. This team approach to sensing and decision-making also extends outward to include others, which in turn can help us to learn faster and respond in faster and better OODA loops.

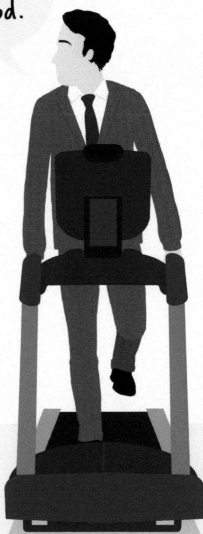

IF YOU'RE GOING TO BE A TURKEY, BE A WILD TURKEY

The saying "Don't be a turkey" means don't be stupid like the inductivist turkey. Like so much fake news, the inductivist turkey observes and, thanks to confirmation bias, only sees the evidence that reinforces what it already suspects or wants to be true.

If we extend the metaphor to a deductivist turkey, he might observe that every day the farmer opens the gate and fills up the feeding tray, providing on average 426 grains of feed per bird with a standard deviation of 8.2%. Over the course of his life, the deductivist turkey also amasses several theories related to turkey cultural dynamics regarding feeding. He concludes, with 95% confidence, that the best place to be to maximize access to grains (in the 10th percentile) is to park-out right next to the bird feeder at feeding time.

Being the fattest bird, he's slowest and first to die at Christmas/Thanksgiving, with the inductivist turkey next in line.

The abductionist turkey meanwhile has heard the compelling evidence from her inductivist sister. She is fascinated by the theories and supporting observations

from her deductionist brother, but she is far more concerned by what happens to the chickens every six weeks or so in the adjacent cage.

The abductionist turkey observes that chickens are also fed every day, just like the turkeys. Every six weeks, though, the chickens are stretched out on a chopping block and slaughtered. She's seen this happen twice now. It's still too soon to confirm a pattern with any confidence, but she has a visceral reaction every time she hears cleaver and wood meet with a "thunk." There's a heavy feeling in her gut. She has a sense that this bodes poorly for turkeys.

She only has two points of observation. This is nothing compared to the daily observations that her inductivist brother has used to support his theory.

She gets his inductive narrative. It *is* compelling, and she *wants* it to be true, but her mirror neurons fire whenever she sees the chickens stretched out on that block. She feels their terror, and she is more than a little confused by the mismatch between her left brain interpreter that's saying the shovel is to clean out the chicken shed.

What?

Her gut instinct, that heavy feeling in the pit of her stomach, led by her enteric brain, is sending out distress signals: GET OUT OF THIS CAGE, OR YOU WILL BE NEXT!

She sees that the ducks that fly overhead land on the lake. They seem to spend a lot of the day searching for food. This is clearly not as easy or predictable as her life in the cage, but hey, they are free, and what is that flying business all about?

In fact, it's clearly a complex world out there, and she really has no way of predicting what might happen outside the cage.

So the abductionist turkey hatches a plot to escape.

She observes that, as the farmer enters the pen, all the other turkeys swarm around the feeder. She resists the impulse to join them, breaking out of group think. Instead of rushing forward to the feeder, she steps back, observes, and orients herself. She notices that while the farmer is feeding the turkeys, the gate behind him remains open.

The rational part of her wants more information before she makes a final decision. She feels like she's caught in an OO-OO-OO trap. Decision made: she is going to fly the coop.

For the rest of the week, she models the ducks and practices flapping her wings. It's not exactly elegant flight, and the cage is not an ideal practice ground, but by using her mirror neurons and embodied rehearsal drills she manages to dramatically increase her speed over ground.

She also practices tongue drop. The last thing she needs when committed to the break-out is more gobble, gobble, gobble from the left brain interpreter.

When her brothers are busy talking turkey, she uses embodied rehearsal in a feedforward OODA loop to practice dropping into flow and flapping for freedom. She uses everything she knows about neuroplasticity to completely retrain her brain. She resists joining the gang around the feeder. Instead, she focuses on flapping out of that gate in a state of flow with maximum preparedness for what might happen next.

When her moment comes, she executes her plan flawlessly — no conscious thinking required. She drops into flow, and uses "implicit guidance and control" to reach the Act step in OODA. She narrowly makes it through the open gate, surprises herself

how much height she makes with a hasty flap over the farmer's dog (didn't/couldn't have anticipated that one!), and she escapes to freedom.

Though her initial plan was to stay with the ducks down by the lake, she pivots to a new plan when she sees a wild turkey on the edge of the woods. She follows him and discovers a whole community of free-spirited birds roaming amongst the trees. Like her, they seem to accept that sometimes you have to act with imperfect information to survive and thrive in a complex, turbulent world.

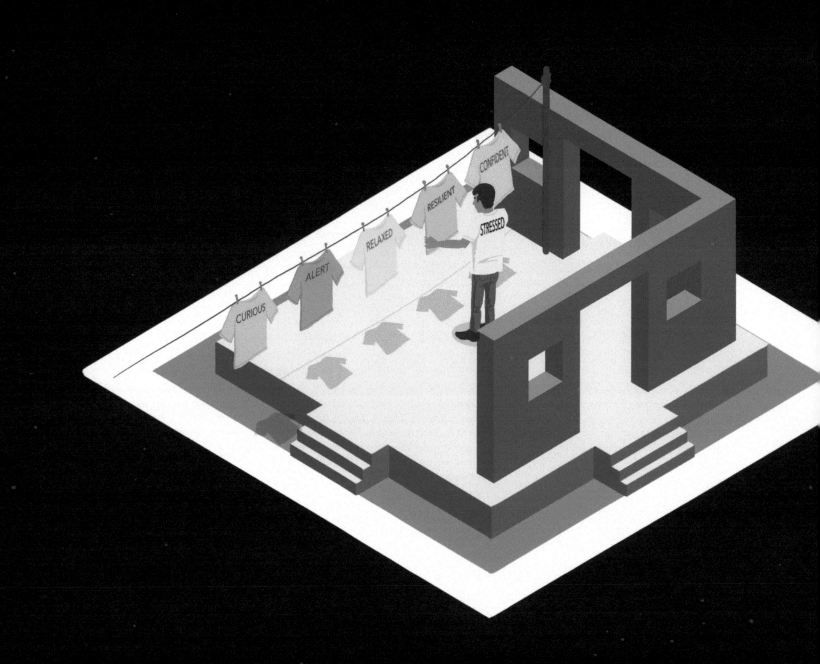

STATE

FROM SOLID STATE TO DIGITAL

In Western culture, we assign a lot of importance to sensations we label as emotions. This usually relates to the dominant feeling that we might experience in a particular moment in time or context.

Emotions are not objects, though. They are words that describe sensory experiences that are often complex, varied, intricate in detail, and abstract in concept. There are common themes in the expression and description of frequently reported emotions, such as anger, anxiety, sadness, and of course stress. For example, anger is often described as "hot" and "emanating from the chest," but we have also heard anger described as "cold" and "it's behind my eyes." The label might be the same, but at the fine scale of individually created experiences, there are countless differences.[1,2]

This is especially important to remember when we start to unpack the emotional state called stress. Stress means different things to different people.

Sadly (contradiction intended), stress and other emotions can and do rule the day-to-day lives of many people. Happily (!), emotions, or more precisely states, do not just happen to us.

We use the word *state* to describe everything that we experience in a given moment in time.

If you ask someone how they are feeling, they will often describe their experience with a single emotional label, such as angry, anxious, or happy. When we ask them to describe their state in more detail, we often find multiple emotions jostling for attention. There might also be sensations that have not been named. Words are not always able to adequately describe what is being experienced.

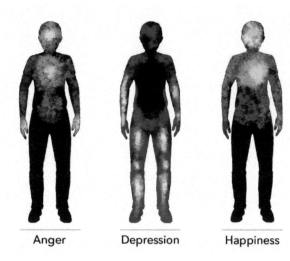

Anger   Depression   Happiness

Lauri Nummenmaa and her colleagues have mapped the subjective human feeling space. Illustration after their original research.[2]

By reconnecting with the full richness of human experience, we can start to create a wide range of choices in the states we create in the gap between stimulus and response. Choice includes whether we describe states with an emotional label, as well as being able to modulate intensity. A bit like a radio, we can switch states on and off, we can change the volume, and we can change the station.

To explain how to do this, we artificially divide "state" into four interconnected systems that are points of leverage for change. These are physiological, neurological, biochemical, and the microbial. Like all complex biological systems, changes in any of these will invariably feed back and influence the others, which in turn influences our state as a whole.

MICROBIAL SYSTEM

The human microbiome comprises trillions of microbes we have (or should have) living in symbiosis with us. Sometimes, there are less mutually beneficial living arrangements. Mostly, these reside in the gut, though microbes in the skin, eyes, and mouth are also important.

PHYSIOLOGICAL SYSTEM

This is our physical disposition, including our posture, breathing, and movement. It also includes external and internal sensations.

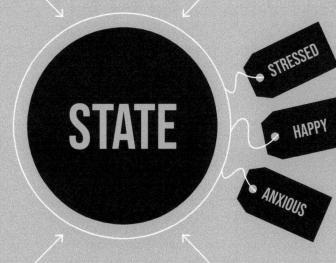

STATE

STRESSED

HAPPY

ANXIOUS

BIOCHEMICAL SYSTEM

This is the internal chemical environment, including blood sugar, hormones, neurotransmitters, as well as prescription and self-medicated drugs and alcohol.

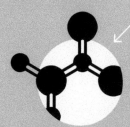

NEUROLOGICAL SYSTEM

This is our nervous system, including the head brain, spinal cord, and peripheral nerves, which collectively forms our extended and embodied sensing and thinking system.

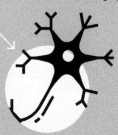

BODYSCAN

Interoception is the ability to perceive
the internal state of our body.

Interoception is essential for emotional regulation, learning, and decision-making. It is, of course, also crucial for the fulfilling of biological needs, such as the urge to eat or rest. It does not always reflect reality; we often experience sensations that are not true. We might, for example, respond to hearing about an insect infestation by feeling itchy or having crawling sensations on our skin.

Body scanning is a process we can use to check in with our internal and surface felt sensations. It can help improve sensitivity or calibration to our internal states.

Research has confirmed that humans can improve their self-calibration of somatic (body) signals, meaning that the more we practice body scanning, the more accurately we can detect our sensations and interpret the intent of our signals.[2–4]

When used either in isolation or alongside other techniques that you will learn in later chapters, the body scan can help direct attention to where we are holding excess muscular tension, which is a common symptom in self-reported states of stress.

Body scanning can also improve the conscious awareness of signals arising from our unconscious, such as the "gut instinct" that tells us we are in danger (noting that many people's signal for danger is nowhere near the gut).

HOW TO BODY SCAN

By learning how to use body scans, we can improve decision-making, reduce pain, change movement patterns, or reduce stress, anxiety, and trauma. In the first example here, we focus on reducing stress. Later, we integrate scanning into an exploration of the structure of thinking and state.

To reduce a state of stress in the moment, we will begin by directing you to bring full attention to all areas of your body in a systematic way, first finding, and then releasing, tension.

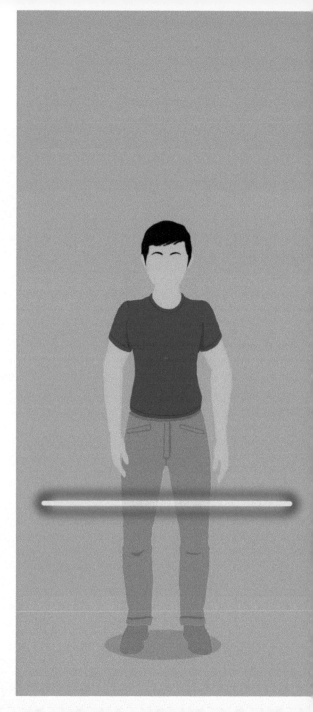

Step 1.

Become completely aware of your body position, be it sitting, standing, or lying down.

Step 2.

Imagine a beam of horizontal light that is a little wider than you are. This is your scanner. Like a photocopier scans the page, this will scan your body.

Step 3.

Scan your body up and down. Starting at your toes, imagine the beam of light moving up your body to the crown of your head, then back down to your toes.

Step 4.

Whenever you locate muscular tension, slow the scanner down and bring your complete attention to that area of your body. Pay close attention to your facial muscles and shoulders.

Step 5.

Consciously release the tension you've located with the scanner by relaxing the affected muscles as fully as possible. You may wish to shake or move these muscles around to get them fully loosened.

Step 6.

Continue to run the scanner up and down your body until there are no more tension-filled trouble areas.

With practice this process can be used very quickly as required in the moment. You might like to start practicing with a challenging conversation, or perhaps when you are dealing with children who are testing boundaries. When you start to feel comfortable with the process, you can start applying it in high-stakes situations.

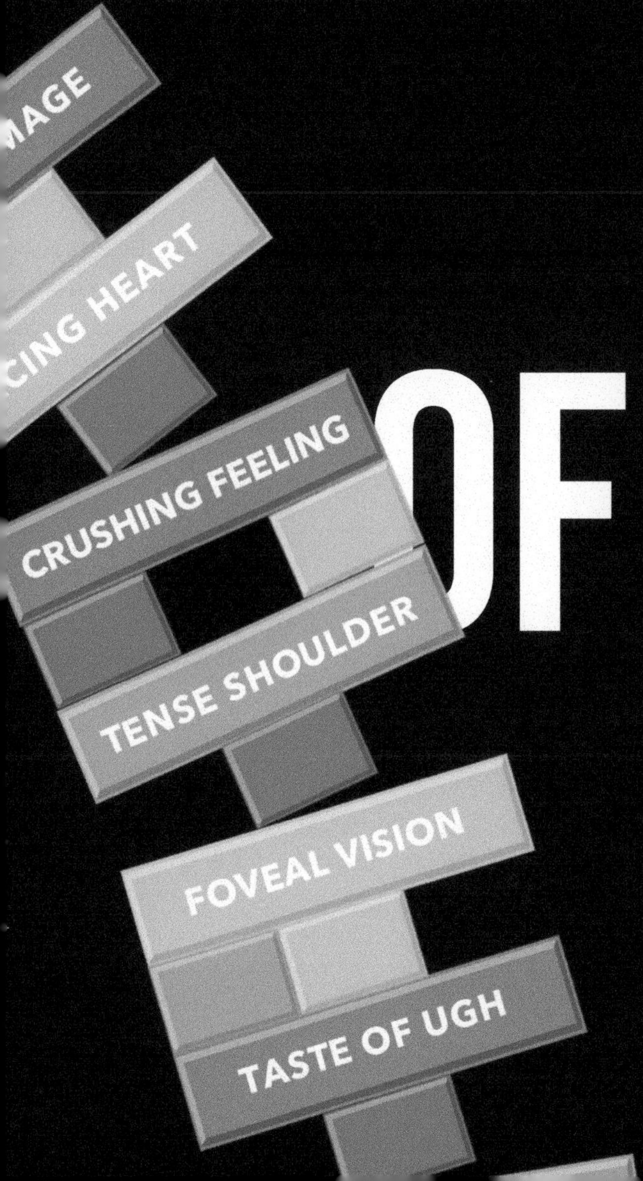

MAGE

CING HEART

CRUSHING FEELING

TENSE SHOULDER

FOVEAL VISION

TASTE OF UGH

OF THOUGHTS

ACTIVITY

EXPLORING THE STRUCTURE OF THOUGHTS

Building on the body scan process, we're going to explore the relationship between thinking and state. To begin, think of a person whom you dislike. Choose a mild example.

Step 1.

See and hear this person as if they're really in your personal space, right now. Do this for at least 20 seconds before continuing.

As you think of the person, did you experience a sensation of some kind in your body?

Most people describe felt sensations that confirm, or signal, "dislike." Common words are tension, heaviness, agitation, a sense of "away from." There are no right or wrong answers. The variety is nearly endless.

Step 2.

Next, take a moment to consider how this internal representation is structured. What are the pieces you put together to assemble the whole?

VISUALS

Was the image of the person you saw larger than life, life size, or smaller than life?

At what distance to you did the disliked person's image arise? Were they near or far?

Was the person's image in color or black and white?

Was it moving or still?

Was the image 3D or 2D?

Was it sharp or out of focus?

Most importantly, were you in the image with the person or were you looking at them through your own eyes ?

SOUNDS

What sounds do you associate with this person?

Were they speaking?

If so, at what volume level?

What were they saying?

FELT SENSATIONS AND SMELL AND TASTE

Fire up that scanner again. When you imagine the person, what does the scanner pick up? What felt sensations are associated with the images and sounds?

Run the scanner slowly. Take time exploring how your body is reacting and producing sensations. Are there any smells or tastes? What do these tell you?

Step 3.

CHANGING THE NATURE OF EXPERIENCE

Now take 30 seconds or so to forget the person. Move around so that you break the state you just experienced. A few deep breaths and motorboating your lips can help speed this up.

Now we invite you to play a little Jenga-style game with the structure of your thoughts. The idea is to change the blocks, remove some, replace them with others, and see what happens. Does the state collapse, or does a new related structure and experience emerge? For each change you introduce, run a quick body scan to check for differences. Remember too that you can always return the Jenga pieces back to how they were before.

START BY CHANGING THE IMAGE QUALITY

Think of that same person again, only this time, change the colors. If you originally recalled them in vibrant colors, change the image to black and white, or vice versa.

If the image was large, shrink it down to size. If it was moving, make the image static. Play with the distance, or change the image from 2D to 3D or vice versa.

Most importantly, if you were seeing and hearing that person as if looking at them in real space and time, change the image so that you are observing yourself observing them.

CHANGE SOUND QUALITY

If sounds were loud, turn down the volume. If they were not making any sound, add some pleasant background noises.

WHAT OTHER ELEMENTS CAN YOU IDENTIFY AND CONSCIOUSLY CHANGE?

The purpose here is to intentionally manipulate the way we structure our memories and thoughts. We are exploring, noticing what happens when we make changes to that structure. You might like to restore the structure back to "dislike" or choose something different.

When working with clients who are recovering from trauma, we've found that one or two structural changes to a memory can completely shift a traumatic stress response that has persisted for months or even years.

How we think about the past, present, and future is interconnected with aspects of our state and vice-versa. For example, image quality or sound volume can alter breathing patterns; or we could take stimulants that make our heart race, and our thoughts and narrative can match that faster tempo; simultaneously, this might be subtly influencing our gut microbiome and digestion.

Learning how the senses influence our thinking and experiences can provide leverage that will help us choose our states to support resilience and high performance. The structure of our thinking and the combination of senses we use doesn't have to be a teetering stack of Jenga blocks. It can, through design, be remade in stable and resilient ways.

I CHOOSE

MY OWN

THOUGHTS

WE DON'T CATCH EMOTIONS LIKE WE CATCH FLU

We often hear people connect emotions to identity:

I am depressed.
I am anxious.
I am stressed.

They might also imply that the state is pervasive and binary, as if a switch has been turned on. It's as though they've caught an emotion, just like they might catch the flu.

I have anxiety.
I have depression.

Sometimes, there is a form that has been pathologized:

I have Anxiety or Depression, sometimes with a capital letter denoting a formal diagnosis or condition.

When you have the flu, you have it 24/7 until you recover. The same is rarely true for states or diagnosed "mood disorders," even when they're highly generalized.

Treatment by "mood medications" often supports this presupposition, with chemicals delivered 24/7, presumably in the hope of correcting or restoring some sort of chemical imbalance in the brain. There is rarely direct evidence of any chemical imbalance for a patient, or even indirect evidence for such an imbalance from a population of people; the chemical imbalance theory is a marketing myth.[4,5]

Chemical dependency is not what we want. Instead, we want to:

* Reverse attention from a fixation with the problem to times and places (context) we do not experience the problem state.
* Identify the outcome, not just the remedy (we discuss this distinction in Chapter 8).
* Learn to modulate the intensity of emotions/states in a way that is analogue (along a continuum), as well as the binary (on/off) option.

The idea that emotions are an analogue state is easy to demonstrate. Consider all the times you have experienced what you call happiness. Notice the difference between the happiness that is like a quiet joy of contentment, versus the happiness that is like an almost overwhelming feeling you might have experienced during periods of intense excitement. We can all dial the intensity or volume of states/emotions up and down to suit the context. With practice, this becomes automatic.

CAROLYN'S STORY, IN HER OWN WORDS

In 2013, my community of Dunalley in Tasmania was destroyed by bushfires. I worked in state government at the time, and I was redeployed to help with community recovery. After a year or so, I found myself struggling. I was diagnosed with several mental health conditions.

Although initial talk was about recovery and returning to prior capacity, my journey evolved to have a focus on a new sense of purpose and resilience through recovery coaching and artwork.

After a poor experience following an attempted return to work, I found myself trapped in a workers' compensation system, facing the prospect of being medicated for anxiety and depression.

I explained somewhat naively to Ian, my coach, that I had depression and had been prescribed antidepressants. He challenged me: "What, did you catch it like the flu?"

"Eh?" I said, not fully understanding the question.

"Seriously, are you depressed 24/7, like being ill with the flu?" he replied.

After explaining more about the implication of what I said, he asked me to keep a diary. Each day, I would record the intensity of depression between 0 (none) and 10 (the most intense feeling of depression I had ever experienced). He then set me an activity to do every day. He called this "The Walk of the Senses."[6]

My task was to walk the same route every day through my local bushland, paying attention to only one of my senses at a time — what I could see, what I could hear, what I felt on my skin, what I could smell and taste.

Then I had to record how depressed I was when reflecting on the walk.

When I paid attention to my senses during my walks, I experienced no depression. And as I mapped my attention in 15-minute blocks of time through the days, I discovered that I only experienced depression when I thought about going back to work in a team that I found threatening.

Eventually, I made the choice to leave. I got out of working for the government, and I am now thriving as an artist creating children's books.

I never did take the medication.

ACTIVITY

ANALOGUE EMOTIONS

SAFETY FIRST

Please take personal responsibility for your own safety in this exercise. If you doubt you can engage safely, move on to the next section. You may be ready to return to this exercise by the time you finish this book, either alone or with the guidance of an experienced coach.

Identify a context in your life where you are highly resourceful, and you feel safe. Choose a space on the floor. This will be your safe zone. Either imagine a boundary or identify the boundaries of this zone with post-it notes or with lines drawn on the floor with dry-erase markers. This space will be your anchor or sanctuary if you need to escape to take a break. The space or note becomes an "anchor" for a lifeline of sorts.

Step into the safe location and recall a time when you were at your most resourceful and re-experience the resourceful state for 5–10 seconds. Step out, and shake that state off.

Step back in and recall the same resourceful state. Step out one more time and shake it off. Now step back in with no conscious recall. Test that your state shifts to the resourceful state that you have anchored to that space.

If, at any point, you get a signal that the following activity is too much, or if you feel that your attention is heading down a path you'd rather leave unexplored, step back into your safe space and redirect your attention to your anchored memory.

Step 1.

Visualize a line on the floor a few meters away from your safe location. If you can, actually label marks along the line that represent equal increments between 0 and 10. You can use post-it notes again.

Step 2.

Choose a state that you recognize, have given an emotional label to, and which you would like to explore. Anxious, depressed, angry, or frustrated are common examples. On the scale on the floor, 0 represents none of that emotion, and 10 represents the maximum of that emotion that you can imagine.

Remember a time and place, a context, when you experienced this emotion. Ask yourself: What was the positive intention (the intended benefit) of having this?

Place yourself at the appropriate point on the line that corresponds to the intensity you felt. Make sure that you are facing the 10 end of the line. Now immerse or fully associate yourself into the context you identified that was connected to the emotion. Run the body scan process to understand how and where in your body you create that state at that intensity.

3   4   5   6   7   8   9   10

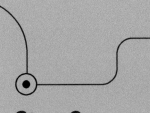

Step 3.

Be alert to any changes as you next learn to modulate the intensity of the felt sensations. For example, as you move up and down the line, metaphors and images might change as well as the felt sensation.

Paying particular attention to the sensations in the body, take a step along the line upwards in intensity. If you started at a 6, what is it like at 7? If it is not too unpleasant, step up again to an 8.

Step 4.

Now go backwards down the line, back to where you started. Recalibrate with a body scan.

Now take another step backwards. If you started at 6, go to 5. Continue stepping backwards, down the scale. You might get to zero, or there might be a residual threshold where you detect a strong resistance to letting go.

Step 5.

Practice moving up and down the line and identifying the subtle differences in the body as you do so. At somewhere like a 6, feel the difference between 6 and 6.5, then 6.1. Finally, experience subtle changes from leaning forward and backwards along the line, sensing small increases and decreases in intensity.

Step 6.

Step off the line. Shake the state out completely.

Notice how much variation there was. What changed? Where did it change? You can probe further with questions like these:

  What kind of [sensation]?

  Then what happens when [sensation] does that?

  Where does [sensation] come from?

If there was a resistance to switching the state off completely, for example, perhaps you could only lower the intensity to a 2, ask yourself questions like these:

  Is that lower limit the most useful state for the context?

  Is that sufficient and useful as a signal for action?

  Would a different state entirely be more appropriate to meet the positive intentions?

BELIEFS ABOUT STRESS

In her popular TED talk, Prof. Kelly McGonigal describes *How to make stress your friend.*

The research that Prof. McGonigal refers to is a paper published in 2012 led by Abiola Keller: "Does the Perception That Stress Affects Health Matter? The Association with Health and Mortality."[7,8]

In the paper, Keller concludes:

"High amounts of stress and the perception that stress impacts health are each associated with poor health and mental health. 33.7% of nearly 186 million (n=28,753) US adults perceived that stress affected their health a lot or to some extent [...] Those who reported a lot of stress and that stress impacted their health a lot had a 43% increased risk of premature death."

Notwithstanding the confusion generated by introducing causation, where stress causes a physiological response like heart pounding (reflecting a position where stress is seen as an outside agent), there is a dangerous presupposition (highlighted) — that if you feel stressed it is only bad for you if you believe it to be.

We acknowledge that forming a strong belief about something can activate either the placebo effect (make yourself well) or the nocebo effect (make yourself ill).

> *"Stress. It makes your heart pound, your breathing quicken and your forehead sweat. But while stress has been made into a public health enemy, new research suggests that stress may only be bad for you if you believe that to be the case."*

— Prof. Kelly McGonigal[8]

The 43% of people who died a premature death — amounting to more than 20,000 deaths a year in the United States alone — most likely died through inaction, not their beliefs (which Keller refers to as *perceptions* — an important distinction) about stress.

It is highly likely that the people who self-identified as being stressed, who also perceived that stress was bad for them, calibrated that they were stressed with the form of stress that is associated with ill health. They then failed to act. This inaction brought about their premature death.

Those who self-identified as being stressed, who perceived that stress was *not* bad for them, were in fact describing a different state entirely.

We propose that if you calibrate being stressed, and it is the sort of stress associated with tightness in the chest, vaso-constriction, high blood pressure, or any other warning signs that are idiosyncratic to you, you should pay attention. Rather than ignoring this sign, respond to it. Take action to change either your state or your context.

We suggest starting with adjusting your state so that it can be more resourceful. We usually begin with adjustments to posture and breathing to create a platform that is primed for resilience.

LET'S GET PHYSIOLOGICAL

If you want to get any joy out of being depressed...

Sometimes the solution is far simpler than we realize.

One of our favorite insights comes from Charlie Brown. In one of many insightful cartoons, Charlie Brown demonstrates to his friend Patty the relationship between posture and depressed.

In a sequence that could play out in a water cooler conversation anywhere, Charlie Brown ends with a deep insight: "If you're going to get any joy out of being depressed you've got to stand like this."

Other common sayings such as "stiff upper lip," "shoulders back," or "take a deep breath and let it go" all recognize that positive changes are possible through adjusting through small or large physiological changes.

There is a key relationship between posture and emotions.

Professor Amy Cuddy's TED talk on power posing is one of the most watched lectures of all time.[9] In her talk, she says that posture influences perception. Expansive and open postures, she says, correlate with feelings of power.[10]

Subsequent studies have supported some of her claims, although other studies were not able to reproduce evidence for her claims that there is an associated biochemical change.[11-14] This is not to say these claims are false; an inability to replicate findings might be due to a weak scientific design. We suspect a strong link between physiology and biochemistry, so we look forward to more research in this area.

Today's visit to the one-stop crisis center is as bittersweet as any other day. I love seeing the incredible people who work here, ceaselessly providing a glimmer of humanity for the most needy in our world.

What I don't love is the rising feeling of anticipation for what I will be confronted with.

I'm told about the first case and I immediately have to swallow my emotions rather than become reactive.

The first patient summary goes as follows: Raped by a family member, most likely an uncle/stepfather/brother. As soon as the pregnancy showed, the mother flew into panic and beat the daughter, probably in the hope of causing a miscarriage, but mostly trying to conceal the abuse.

When no miscarriage could be provoked, the daughter was dumped outside a public hospital. The girl, beaten unconscious, delivers her son, far too many months premature.

The boy is immediately adopted out whilst the emergency staff dealing with the beaten girl prepare her for a life alone, now that her family has disowned her.

The girl's age: 14 years.

THE PAIN OF INNOCENTS

The reports go on: A 12-year-old who is five months pregnant… a 5-year-old who has been raped…Endless battered women, victims of trafficking, sex slaves, dowry victims, women scarred beyond recognition from acid attacks. Countless victims of incest...all here seeking help and safety, and often slipping into a spiral of depression and hopelessness.

Over a year, this place will receive thousands of women and children, desperately hoping for essential care, for a short while at least. For many of them, the future outside of the center holds more of the same of what got them here. The cycle seems to never end.

I look at the women who run this place, knowing that they live each minute engulfed in the pains of innocents.

Here, there's no place to hide from the glaring cruelness of mankind. And in the tired yet still sparkling eyes of this team, I see the best that humanity has to offer.

I feel humbled and inspired by their dedication to help others. The compassion that drives so many acts of kindness seems to come from a place that can only be sourced amongst such need.

Even with my training and resilience, I feel the weight of guilt, responsibility, and the need to act.

I shift my attention again, take some deep rhythmic breaths, and say out loud, "What can I do to help?"

The staff that I'm here to support all smile and nod. They're incredibly grateful for the extra support.

Because for them, the work never ends.

"Even with my training and resilience, I feel the weight of guilt, responsibility, and the need to act."

SUNITA TOOR

has a multidisciplinary background in sociology, psychology, and philosophy, with a PhD in law. Her main expertise is working with female offenders and vulnerable victims as well as governments, NGOs, and police officers in developing policies and training to respond to the needs of the vulnerable.

CHAIN OF EXCELLENCE

The *Chain of Excellence* is a useful change sequence that places state as the key leverage point for behavior and performance.[15] The chain recognizes that state is linked to physiological disposition, which in turn is linked by the critical act of breathing.

You may have heard someone say, "Just take a deep breath, and you'll be fine."

High performance is reflected in many spiritual and martial art practices as a way into an enhanced posture, altered states, and even, some allege, enlightenment.

The four links in the Chain of Excellence offer us a reminder of the foundations of personal resilience and performance.

Breathing is a leverage point for physiological change. Effective breathing comes from good posture, and, at the same time, effective breathing can also be used to create good posture.

State is a term used to describe the rich experience of sensing, thinking, and decision-making. Leverage to change state can be found in any of four interconnected systems: neurological, physiological, biochemical, and microbial. By changing state, we affect performance or behavior.

Physiology is an essential element for resilient states. By changing physiology through breathing, posture, or movement, we can adjust state.

Performance or behavior, specifically the high performance associated with resilience under pressure, are the patterns of actions, words, and relationships with the external world.

For many people, manipulation of breathing is the simplest leverage point leading to a corresponding shift in physiology and onward through the chain.

HERE IS A SIMPLE EXERCISE

Whilst sitting, take a deep breath and hold it in whilst squeezing/tightening your muscles in as many places as possible. Keep holding the tension in your muscles until you can't hold your breath any longer.

Notice the sensations in your body.

Next take another deep breath and hold. This time relax your muscles completely (run your body scanner as you do so).

When you feel the need to breathe, notice the sensations in your body. And then breathe!

Finally, stay with the relaxed posture (no tensing) and take a deep breath. Hold it for ten seconds, then exhale slowly and take another deep breath, holding it for another ten seconds.

Do this for as long as you want.

Again, notice the sensations in your body.

Many presenters use the *Chain of Excellence* to prepare them to speak in front of large crowds. If you observe great presenters, pay close attention to their breathing. It is almost always deep and even. Their posture is relaxed and upright, and their overall state is one that is appropriate for the content being presented.

Inexperienced or anxious presenters will often breathe too fast, catch words in their throats, fidget, and hunch over. They have a state that is more suitable to a teenager asking someone out on a first date!

When we work with people who want to fine-tune their performance for presentations, or ANY type of performance, we first bring attention to the state needed to deliver specific skills and behaviors most effectively.

If in doubt, remember that it all starts with breathing. At the very least, remember to breathe in... AND out...

HIGH-PERFORMANCE BREATHING

Scientists are only just beginning to understand the mechanisms and benefits of deliberate breathwork, whereas breathing techniques in yoga (pranayama) were developed by the yogis of India around 6,000 years ago.

FIGHT OR FLIGHT

When the sympathetic nervous system is activated, heart rate increases as you move into a heightened state of alertness. Highly aroused states of this kind are also called the fight-or-flight response. Because they increase strength, speed, and attention, these aroused states can be extremely resourceful in emergencies.

All mammals activate a sympathetic response when they sense danger. When the threat passes, they typically revert back to a relaxed alert state. Although other animals are not immune from trauma and can clearly remember past events, humans seem to ruminate, replaying the past in their minds over and over to an unprecedented extent. Unresourceful thoughts extend the sympathetic response, as we practice the states we name as worry, stress, and anxiety.

This aroused state can save our lives in a pinch, but it is excessive for most day-to-day tasks. When we spend too much time in this overactivated state, we can experience burnout, severe health problems, and early mortality.

In everyday situations, such as driving in traffic, picking up groceries at a busy supermarket, getting the kids ready for bed, or walking into the office, it is essential to have the choice to tone down the intensity of the sympathetic

nervous system. Also, it is important to be able to activate our parasympathetic nervous system, the state of reduced heart rate associated with calm, recovery, creativity, and general restoration.

It may be that, by intentionally slowing breathing, we are modeling breathing of the kind that naturally occurs during a relaxed parasympathetic state. Have you ever seen somebody anxious or stressed who is breathing slowly and rhythmically? Probably not.

There are dozens of different breathing patterns available for use, for a wide range of purposes and in a wide range of contexts. Be aware, though, that some are contraindicated for some medical conditions or extreme activities, such as hyperventilation before breath-hold diving. If you have any respiratory conditions, consult with your physician before attempting any of the following breathing patterns.

The breathing patterns we highlight here have a reasonable evidence base. We also provide a simple process that will help you discover your own ideal breathing for performance. As with all exercises, if you feel unwell or get a signal that the breathing pattern is not for you, stop and recalibrate.

Box breathing is one way to induce a slow rhythmic breathing pattern that quickly and naturally reduces overly heightened states. Although there is little supporting evidence in the scientific literature, we know from our own application and widespread anecdotal accounts that box breathing helps those who practice it.

"Many people will never be bothered by air pollution because they don't stop talking long enough to take a deep breath."

— Vikrant Parsai

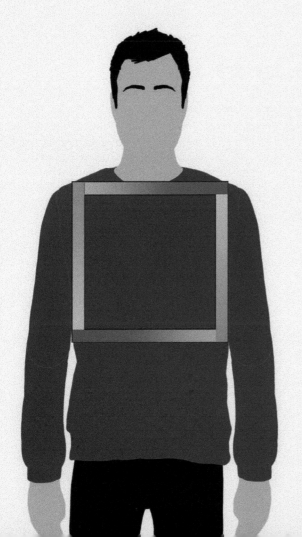

BOX BREATHING

Box breathing takes its name from the neatly balanced phase durations. The simple and effective 4, 4, 4, 4 pattern is the same one that Navy Seals use during training exercises.[16]

- Inhale through your nose, counting to four as you do so.
- Hold for four counts.
- Exhale through your mouth, counting to four.
- Hold the empty exhaled position for four counts.
- Repeat

To get the most out of box breathing, practice it for a few minutes every day. Through regular practice, it will become an unconscious, reflexive response.

WORKING WITH THE SIGNAL TO BREATHE

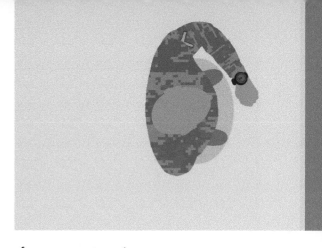

Some breathing patterns aim to correct for hyperventilation, while others access these hyperventilated states.[17-19]

Practitioners of Buteyko, named after Russian physician Konstantin Buteyko, claim that his breathing pattern can treat illnesses such as asthma through a combination of nasal breathing, reduced breathing, and relaxation.[17,20] A 2020 Cochrane review found benefit from such breathing exercises with only a moderate to very low certainty, but many still swear by the method.[21]

The Wim Hof method and the breath hold techniques developed for freediving are two other widely used breathing patterns. Both techniques use breath training and deliberate interoception. For improved freediving, apnea breath hold training uses facial immersion to activate the diving reflex, also known as the diving response and the mammalian diving reflex, which preferentially distributes oxygen to the heart and brain. It also involves carefully calibrating a progressively more intense signal to breathe as subjects learn to tolerate more and more CO_2-buildup (the trigger to breathe). The Wim Hoff method

also uses gradual cold exposure in a similar way to challenge tolerance.[22]

Both techniques can help us build resilience for challenges anywhere in life.

THE ICEMAN

The Wim Hoff method is named after the extreme-cold athlete known as the Iceman.

The purported benefits of the Wim Hoff method include:

- Increased energy
- Better sleep
- Improved performance
- Reduced stress
- Greater cold tolerance
- Faster recovery
- Stronger immune system

With 20 world records, there is no doubt that Hoff is extraordinary. The question is, can others achieve similar results by following his method?

The answer appears to be yes. In one remarkable study, researchers compared the responses of two groups of people

after exposure to an intravenous administration of E. coli endotoxin.[23] One group was trained by Hoff, the other wasn't.

The results demonstrated that Hoff's training techniques improved both the autonomic nervous system and the immune system. The trained volunteers saw increased epinephrine levels, which in turn led to increased production of anti-inflammatory mediators and subsequent dampening of the proinflammatory cytokine response.

The implication is that we can all greatly improve our resilience by learning to breathe well whilst engaging deliberately with our inner world under conditions of gradual exposure to cold. This feature of gradual exposure to challenge, like extreme cold, is important for resilience more generally.

Importantly, it would seem that breath regulation has effects far beyond subjective experiences such as improved mood.[24] In aquatic environments, this can mean the difference between pass and fail in a pool test, or even life and death.

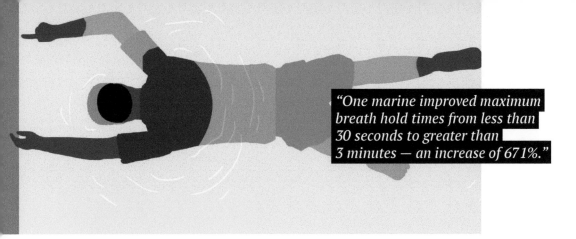

"One marine improved maximum breath hold times from less than 30 seconds to greater than 3 minutes — an increase of 671%."

MARINE RESILIENCE

In a pilot study with the US Marine Corps, Marines were trained by the authors of this book, using a combination of breath hold techniques, relaxation, and perception changes. The result was significantly increased water survivability.[25]

Reconnaissance Marines are elite operators trained to work at the interface between land and water. They found that an unacceptably high percentage of aspiring Recon Marines were failing the pool tests. In the words of one of their instructors, "Water is a great leveller."

A number of features of standard military training inadvertently encouraged low breath hold times. Trainees were entering the underwater swim phase in a highly aroused (increased oxygen use) state. The training was viewed as a "stress test," rather than a "relaxation test." Many also falsely believed that the signal to breathe indicates low oxygen, whereas in fact it indicates a build-up of CO_2.

In the pilot study, each Marine was taught how to enter the pool in a deeply relaxed state whilst still remaining operational. We used three main relaxation techniques: body scan, tongue drop, and third position observation (we'll return to this later), as well as a freediving breath hold protocol.

With as little as a few hours of aquatic survival training, all the marines improved their static breath hold capability.

- Over the course of 5 days, the average breath hold improved by 147%.
- One marine improved maximum breath hold times from less than 30 seconds to greater than 3 minutes — an increase of 671%.
- For one recruit who failed a fully clothed underwater swim test, distance improved 140% after approximately five minutes of coaching.

The breathing methods in this chapter create very different effects and are used for different intentions.

For instance, the Wim Hoff method should never be used in any context in which passing out could have negative or dire consequences, such as freediving or driving a vehicle. Apnea and freediving techniques are typically safe when trained under expert supervision; however, even experienced freedivers have been known to pass out underwater and only survive thanks to a quick-thinking and quick-acting diving partner.

We have found, over and again, that there's an optimal breathing pattern for every need. We encourage you to safely explore the ranges of your own breathing.

To begin discovering what works best for you, ask this question of yourself in any context, and develop the answer:

For you to be resilient and performing at your best, your breathing will be like what?

SOLAR PANEL

We previously established that deliberate breathing influences body posture and performance. Conversely, we can change our breathing by making deliberate changes to our posture. Changing our physiology is a simple way to shift into a high-performance state. Learning to calibrate and adjust our physiological disposition can help us activate, stabilize, and sustain high-performance states.

Daniel Moore, a New Zealand-based performance coach, specializes in helping people recover from trauma and persistent pain. He's also an osteopath who uses gentle movements to correct misalignment and release trapped emotions. Moore uses a simple metaphor to help people understand the power of near-perfect postural alignment: the solar panel.

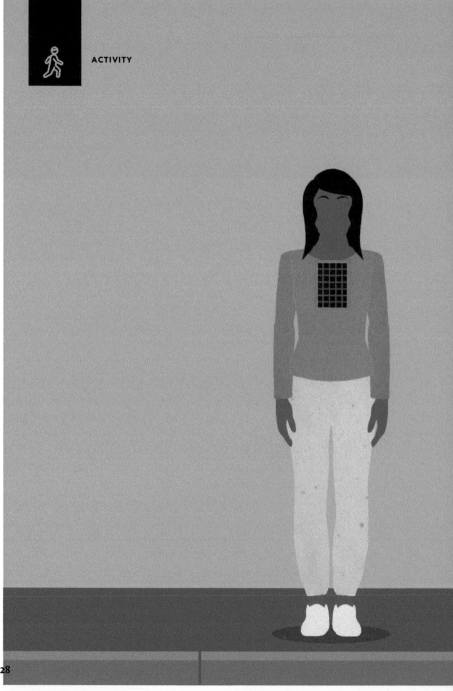

HERE'S HOW YOU CAN INSTALL YOUR OWN SOLAR PANEL:

Imagine that you have a solar panel balanced on your sternum. Adjust your posture so that the solar panel tilts to catch the sun's rays.

Notice how your shoulders fall into natural alignment with your ears and hips.

Notice how your breathing becomes relaxed and easy.

Notice the absence of tension across your shoulders.

Once your solar panel is activated, walk around a bit. Notice how it feels.

Finally, break the state. Shake it off and see what it feels like going back to your normal posture. Notice the differences.

We ask coaching clients to simply practice this and observe the incredible changes that flow on from having great posture and natural breathing. In some cases, years of depression or persistent anxiety melt away.

The next time you're entering a situation where you experience tension, take a moment to activate your solar panel. Perhaps run a quick body scan, and notice the subtle shift in your perception of what is ahead.

"The idea popped into my head around a solar panel based on Iron Man, because I'd seen Iron Man have this wonderful device in his chest that energized him. It just evolved from there until it got to the point where the description was the simple shift or lift of the sternal angle in the most subtle and gentle way you can to get the maximum amount of change. The trick is to do it big, and notice that that's probably too much. Then go back to not doing it."

— Daniel Moore

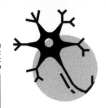

NERVOUS SYSTEM

When we think of what we think with, the brain is usually the first thing that comes to mind.

This is only partially accurate, though. We think and experience with more than just our brains. We think with our entire nervous system.

Our brains and peripheral nervous systems allow us to contemplate multiple universes, eternity, quantum physics, the nature of reality, gods, philosophy, paradoxes, and an endless degree of complexities, known and currently unknown. It provides the possibility to enlighten or equally, to delude — depending on how we use it.

Our nervous system also ensures that, as we hold ideas and concepts in mind, we feel related sensations. We don't just feel our thinking, our feelings ARE our thinking, as much as images, or internal sounds and self talk.

Knowing that our brain and nervous system is connected to, and influenced by, other bodily systems really matters, because we think and exist as a whole system that is more than the sum of its parts.

THERE ARE TWO COMMONLY HELD MYTHS THAT WE REJECT:

The first is that thinking occurs in the head brain. Evidence indicates that thought is only a distributed function involving the head brain and also, as a minimum, the gut and heart brains.[26-30]

Cognition is a better and more general term that encompasses what is commonly considered to be thinking. We have used the common term "thinking" throughout to challenge common usage of the term, and to avoid academic jargon as much as possible. In this respect we view that thinking, following the so-called 4E view of cognition (Embodied, Embedded, Enacted, and Extended), is an integral part of an internal ecosystem nested in the broader ecosystem of the outside world.

The second commonly held myth is that thinking occurs only in the auditory channel through self-talk. In fact, we know the left brain interpreter is merely providing a best-fit explanation for decisions that have already been made elsewhere in the broader cognitive network. Thinking involves all the senses. Often our best decision-making occurs when we can shut down internal self-talk using techniques like the tongue drop or by accessing flowstate. This allows for the other senses to play a more significant role in thinking.

In our experience, so-called rational thinking expressed through self-talk is overrated for many applications of resilience, especially in high-pressure, complex situations in which risk is high.

BIOCHEMISTRY

"A living cell requires energy not only for all of its functions, but also for maintenance of its structure. Treating humans without the concept of energy is treating dead matter."

— Albert Szent-Györgyi (Nobel Prize winner for medicine)

Biochemistry influences state. If you want evidence, just look at a drug addict going cold turkey, or, to use a less dramatic example, the effects experienced by those trying to remove sugar, nicotine, or caffeine from their diets.

Nutrition is critical for energy and well-being. Too much, too little, or the wrong types of either food or drink can result in poor health outcomes. These can have knock-on effects, influencing how we feel in often subtle or sometimes dramatic ways.

Possibly the most widespread impact on resilience and well-being in modern times is associated with our diet. Nutritious food and clean drinking water have given way to diets crammed with processed foods and sweetened drinks. Relying on packaged or processed foods means a high intake of refined carbohydrates and unhealthy trans fats.

Excessive carbohydrate consumption leads to addiction, insulin resistance, and metabolic syndrome (a cluster of physiological and biochemical conditions including high blood pressure, high blood sugar, excess belly fat, and abnormal cholesterol levels — all linked to cardiovascular disease and diabetes).[31-33] Clearly, metabolic syndrome also has a profound effect on resilience.

Life requires energy, and we need to make sure we're eating enough to power our curiosity, exploration, and deep engagement. However, some foods disrupt energy and metabolism, resulting in a pronounced feeling of lethargy after mealtime. High-glycemic carbohydrates can have a fast-acting influence on state — usually an initial rush of energy followed by a crash (the lazy afternoon carb coma). A meal high in carbohydrates triggers a spike in insulin, which in turn makes more tryptophan and serotonin. These chemicals initially make you feel good, just before making you feel drowsy.[34]

There is no such thing as a universally perfect nutrition plan; as the saying goes,

"One man's meat is another man's poison." An athlete who trains twice a day requires an entirely different amount and ratio of carbohydrates, fats, and proteins than an elderly person whose only exercise is a walk around the block with the dog. Those losing weight require a different nutritional approach to those needing to gain it. We encourage people to (safely) experiment with what works for them, and remember that nutritional needs can change daily and seasonally.

THE COST OF PROGRESS

Though we may be light years ahead of our ancestors technologically speaking, our biology hasn't changed much over the centuries. Our cells still use nutrients and make energy. We have *slowly* evolved in the way that we utilize nutritious food, and we need to be careful of unforeseen downsides if we *suddenly and radically* depart from traditional ways of eating. The consequence can be catastrophic for resilience and well-being.

A simple and functional rule of thumb is to eat only what grows, runs, swims, or flies in the field, orchard, river, ocean, or sky.

If you choose to eat manufactured, chemically laden products, don't be too surprised if you find changing state to be a challenge. You might need all of your focus to figure out what to do with the toxic burden you have ingested.

Consuming quality food enables us to convert the sun's energy, stored in plant and animal cells, directly into our own energy needs, and there are important linkages between nutrition, sunlight, and well-being.

One key relationship involves a complex interaction between food, sunlight, resilience, cardiovascular disease, and mortality.[35-41]

LET THERE BE LIGHT

Seasonal Affective Disorder (SAD) is well known in high-latitude countries, where a reduction in sunlight in winter accompanies a tendency to stay indoors to avoid inclement weather.[35] SAD shares many symptom traits with depression, including low energy, lethargy, poor sleep, and loss of appetite. There is also a significant increase in mortality through cardiovascular disease during the winter months — a pattern that is not seen in equatorial countries.[42-44]

SAD correlates with Vitamin D deficiency. Vitamin D is produced by exposure to UV-A in sunlight.[45] Many SAD sufferers try to manage their symptoms with Vitamin D supplements, but these seem to have little positive benefit.[46-48]

Given the widespread concerns surrounding skin cancer, Dr. Paul Mason, a practicing physician and researcher from Sydney, asks the all-important question: "How do we get more [of what we need] from sun exposure while minimizing the risk of skin cancer?"

Although Mason cautions that people have varying sensitivity and risk factors for cancer, the answer appears to be to maximize skin exposure to sunlight at those times of day when the UV-A can penetrate the earth's atmosphere, but when UV-B is preferentially filtered and is at a minimum. At high latitudes, this means getting out when the sun is low in the morning and evening, and in winter.[49, 50] As they say, "Only mad dogs and Englishmen go out in the midday sun."

If your state varies with seasonal rhythms, or if there are daily fluctuations, regular doses of sunlight might help.

THE HUMAN MICROBIOME

Unless you've been living in a cave for the last decade or so, you have probably heard or read about the human microbiome — the microscopic organisms living symbiotically (or in many cases, dysbiotically) inside us and on our skin.

What we've learned is that a sterile environment isn't as good for us as once thought. If you *have* been living in a cave, you probably have more diverse and resilient microbiota inhabiting your insides than someone who lives in a regularly scrubbed and sanitized modern apartment.[51]

A diverse microbiome comprises bacteria, fungi, parasites, and viruses that are collectively responsible for essential metabolic activities such as food digestion, as well as the production of biologically active chemicals like serotonin.[51-53] The neurotransmitter serotonin is often referred to as the "feel good hormone," and recent studies implicate microbes in the production of 95% of our serotonin. Serotonin is also the chemical at the center of highly contentious medicines called Selective Serotonin Reuptake Inhibitors (SSRI) — common antidepressants.

If you still believe, as many do, that thinking is something that happens exclusively in the head, you might be surprised to learn that we are now finding evidence that gut microbiota play an important role in the development of brain function and in the pathology of stress-related diseases and neurodevelopmental disorders.[54,55]

A number of studies support the existence of a brain-gut-microbiome axis, in which microbes communicate with the central nervous system through the hormonal (endocrine) system, nervous system, and various immune signals.[52,56] With bacteria in our gut playing such an important interconnected role, imbalances in these bacteria will likely influence our states.[52,54] Conversely, what is known as stress-induced enteric dysfunction might increase risk for "mental illness" via a negative feedback loop.[55,57]

As further evidence of the powerful link between microbiome and state, we might consider the relationship between microbes and autism spectrum disorder.

People with behaviors that meet the criteria for inclusion on the autism spectrum have risen rapidly in the past few decades (in the United States from 1 in 150 to 1 in 54), more than can be attributed to wider testing and broadened diagnostic criteria.[58] To the surprise of many, the gut microbiome appears to have a relationship with some of the symptoms associated with autism. A 2019 study demonstrated long-term beneficial effects for children diagnosed with autism through a revolutionary fecal transplant technique. Improvements in gut health and reductions in autism symptoms appear to persist two years after treatment with a 45% reduction in core symptoms related to language, social interaction, and behavior.[59]

It is possible that overuse of antibiotics and antimicrobials is implicated in at least some of the rising numbers of autism diagnoses.[60,61] Although antibiotics are one of humanity's greatest medical achievements, the effect of overuse on the microbiome can have long-term consequences.[62,63]

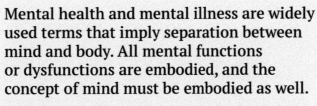

More broadly, we seem too dependent on the idea of the magical pill that can cure everything. In the 1950s, when mood-altering medications exploded in popularity, we started to suppress undesired states like depression, anxiety, or stress with medications, preferring the quick fix to more difficult but less intrusive interventions. Today, many are attempting to reverse this trend. Holistic approaches are back in favor, with human health and well-being viewed as components of a larger ecosystem, with each part affecting all the others.[64]

Perhaps, if there is a magic pill for persistent mental illness or neurological conditions, it won't be a pill at all. It may turn out to be a holistic approach to health with the microbiome at its center.

Mental health and mental illness are widely used terms that imply separation between mind and body. All mental functions or dysfunctions are embodied, and the concept of mind must be embodied as well.

Perhaps we also need to extend the concept of mind and what it is to be human to include the microbiome.

ACTIVITY

EMBODIED VISUALIZATION

We use the term "embodied visualization" to place emphasis on the engagement of all the senses, especially felt sensations and movement. There is a distinction between visualizing ourselves *over there* acting out an event, and visualizing the scene around us as the actor — experiencing it through our eyes and all our senses, just as we would any other embodied experience.

Research has shown that embodied visualization can enhance learning in activities like golf, basketball, playing the piano, rock climbing, teaching, or giving keynote speeches.[65-69]

HERE ARE STEP-BY-STEP DIRECTIONS FOR EMBODIED VISUALIZATION:

Step 1.

Identify a future event you want to prepare for.

For example, you might have an upcoming public speaking event, and you might want to be highly engaging, to be in an optimal state, and to manage your speaking time well.

Step 2.

Identify the feedback you would like to receive. What kind of feedback would indicate success? In particular, what would you see, hear, and feel?

This might be people in the crowd leaning in and listening carefully to what you're saying. It might include a building of confidence as you realize your message is being well received. It might also include more distant benefits — perhaps a broader network, or more work for your business.

Imagine seeing and hearing as if the audience is really there in the context in the space around you.

Step 3.

Step into the context from First Position (your own point of view). What do you see and hear? Engage with the context by moving through the actions you will take during the real version of this future event. Check that your state is suitable for the task and use the *Chain of Excellence* to fine-tune. You can choose to move through the actions (in this example, presenting) using macro- or micro-movements. The benefit to micro-movements is that you can practice in this way in public without attracting attention to yourself.

If visualizing yourself speaking in front of a crowd, you might imagine hearing your own voice and the noise of the crowd. You might feel a podium under your hands, or you might feel yourself holding a microphone. Internally, you might be feeling an increased state of confidence or noting your steady heart rate as you perform under pressure.

Using this approach, you can completely embody the experience of delivering a speech to a large audience without even leaving your home.

Step 4.

If you only practice for when things go well, you might be underprepared for the uncertainties of real life. A few pressure tests, using plausible scenarios, will help you prepare in case things don't go according to plan. You can create these yourself, or you can work with a partner who plays the role of the saboteur.

Imagine being back presenting to the audience, completely embodying what it would be like to deliver your speech. Unexpectedly, someone in the front row yawns and slumps forward. They've fallen asleep! How do you respond? The microphone suddenly cuts out, or the slides don't work. What do you do?

Step 5.

Take a step back, away from the context you have visually and auditorily created and shake off the state. Physically shake out while you're getting comfortable with this technique. Notice the difference between your state in this re-created context and your state in the present.

We recommend you use this embodied visualization technique again and again until it becomes second nature and until you can utilize it in any situation where you want to improve your performance.

YOUR STATE OF *is* MIND

The concept of mind is embodied, inseparable from the fleshy stuff from our toes to the top of our heads that we identify as belonging to us. The body and multiple organs that meet the definition of a brain, as well as our peripheral nervous system and even the microorganisms that reside in and on us, all influence our sensing, thinking, and decision-making.

For the purpose of acting in the world and understanding how we can develop resilience, we have artificially compartmentalised state into four interconnected systems:

- Physiological
- Neurological
- Biochemical
- Microbial

It is important to remember to reintegrate these and consider again the whole person. They are no more separate from each other than the mind could be extracted from the body.

Another important point to consider is that the process of naming states (or anything for that matter) is often a dangerous oversimplification.

We note there is an important relationship between posture and state, although research on the subject has yielded ambiguous results.[70,13,14] This may be the result of a focus on "power posing," where the term "power" might mean different things to different people.

In the same way that Kelly McGonigal's beliefs about stress are confounded by idiosyncratic experiences of stress and differences in meaning attributed to names for states, so too it is possible that "expert" notions of what a power pose constitutes is an imposition that is simply not correlated with how most people experience a sense of power. For example, the Shaolin Monks are reputed for their incredible power and martial arts prowess, but you don't see them power posing like Wonder Woman.[9]

Studies of the extreme temperature athlete Wim Hoff reveal the interconnectedness of the different elements of state and provide a counterexample that demonstrates the positive intention for the so-called stress response.

Although the autonomic nervous system and our immune system were long regarded as systems that could not be voluntarily influenced, Hoff demonstrates that practicing techniques involving attention and breathing whilst sitting in a bath of cold water can induce biochemical changes that influence the immune system in a beneficial and highly resilient way. The Wim Hoff method, famed for busting stress and promoting resilience, can, perhaps paradoxically, induce an increase in so-called stress hormones as part of an enhanced state of healing.

Clearly, not all notions of stress are bad for you.

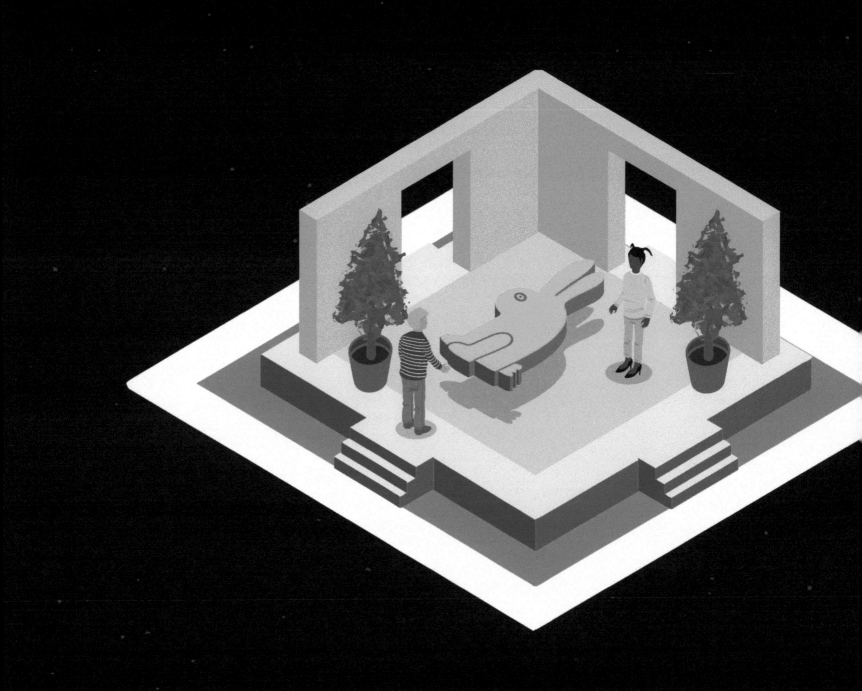

PERSPECTIVES

PLACING ATTENTION

The choice to move between different perspectives is a skill practiced by people who are resilient.

Where, when, and how we place our attention, with respect to ourselves, others, and the context in which we are interacting, will influence our thinking, our behaviors, our performance, and our overall quality of experience in work, play, and day-to-day life.

People began deliberately using and developing the three different perceptual positions (self, other, and observer) long before anyone was writing about these distinctions: from yogis going into the inner realm of self-awareness (first position); to aboriginal hunters, occupying the persona of their prey to encode animal movement patterns into their body and improve predictive capability (second position); to shamans soaring above the

grounded world in the totem of an eagle or hawk to gather insight for guidance in tribal decision-making (third position).

The vast majority of us shift perspectives to some extent every day without conscious awareness. Individually, though, there are considerable differences in how deeply or frequently people switch perspectives. Most people who are untrained do not have clean, distinct access to each perceptual position. Rather, they inhabit blended states that incorporate elements of all three.

FIRST POSITION

"From my standpoint."

"See it through my eyes."

"If you were in my situation."

First position or first person is the perceptual position of ourselves. It involves seeing, hearing, feeling, smelling, and tasting through our own eyes, ears, mouth, nose, and body. It also includes experiencing the world through our filters in the form of our knowledge, beliefs, values, aversions, preferences, and motivations.

Very young children frequently inhabit first position. It is sometimes called an egocentric viewpoint or "self-immersed perspective" in psychology.[1–5]

From a first position, people refer to themselves in a two-person conversation as "I." This is obvious of course, though the distinction is useful when developing and distinguishing second and third positions.

Individuals often associate first position with a variety of personal metaphors. If you're asking somebody to see something from your standpoint, through your eyes, or as though they were in your situation, you're speaking from first position.

High-quality embodied thinking from first position is central to resilience, performance, and well-being.[6–8]

We can enhance our first person capabilities; this can, however, be overdone.

Blind people can learn to echolocate

There are many incredible examples of sensory adaptation and enhancement from a deep appreciation of first-person experience. Blind people have been able to remap sound into images using echolocation like that used by bats and dolphins; elite athletes, freedivers, and high-altitude mountaineers have been able to slow their heart rates through conscious effort, allowing them to survive and thrive in extreme environments.[9-13]

There are studies that tentatively suggest that humans may even have latent abilities to detect pheromones such as those released during fear and arousal. We've long assumed that only animals can do this, but recent cutting-edge research is suggesting otherwise.[14-17]

From first position, we have the opportunity to share our own experiences through rich storytelling, "and then I turned the light on..."

We cannot begin to develop resilience until we possess both a healthy awareness of ourselves and our needs and an ability to communicate with others. However, we must be prepared to step out of this perspective. If we immerse ourselves too completely in first position, we become egoists. We disregard the feelings, needs, and positions of others. Solely operating from first position leads to a lack of situational awareness. It's not possible to read the room when we are convinced that ours is the only perspective that matters.

We've all experienced this when we try to come to an agreement with somebody who is being selfish. They are steadfast in their positions, and rather than communicating with you, they just wait for their turn to speak (or worse, they don't wait and interrupt!). They rarely listen to or appreciate other perspectives. This is what happens when we overdo first position.[18-20]

SECOND POSITION

Second position (also known as simulation or subjective perspective-taking) is when we assume the perceptual position of another person, animal, or thing.[21-23]

An approximation of second position can be obtained by matching the breathing, posture, and movements of another person. We can then start to consider how the other person sees things by looking through their eyes, hearing through their ears, speaking with their voice, and feeling just as they might feel.

To deepen the experience, we can follow their attention, subtly mirror their actions, imitating their way of responding to the world. The deeper we go, the more we start to get a sense of not just what they see, but also how they filter their experience of the world. This can help us understand how their beliefs, values, and motivations might be influencing their perspective.

Examples of second position include the deep connections often experienced between some mothers and daughters, or between identical twins. You can see it as well in aboriginal and African dances where the dancer inhabits the animal prior to the hunt. Method acting also works with second position; the actor goes beyond mimicry to take on the role completely, to *become* the character. This is also how any apprentice learns a trade: by closely observing and imitating that tacit knowledge of an expert until they themselves become the expert.

From second position, imagine seeing yourself through someone else's eyes. The "you" in second position would refer to yourself "over there" in an imagined two-person conversation. When you say "I" in the second position, this refers to the person whose perspective you are inhabiting.

Many people describe second position through a variety of metaphors. You might tell somebody that you want to walk a mile in their shoes or see the world through their eyes. If you are trying to see what they see or experience what they experience, you are inhabiting the second position.

We know from research on mirror neurons that most people are wired to experience movement patterns, and, by extension, the emotional experiences of others.[22,24,25] Humans, primates, and possibly other animals access second position naturally from an early age. It is the fundamental way that we learn as children, before consciousness and a Victorian approach to education gets in the way of natural inductive learning.[26-28]

This ability to create an experience as if we are in another person's shoes is regarded as an element of individual and collective intelligence that influences our ability to learn. For example, in a study of late-primary to early-secondary school students, those with the ability to assess and describe another person's point of view were found to have a higher academic performance than those who lacked these social perspective-taking skills.[29,30]

Shared second position is at the heart of rapport, having empathy for others, and people skills that lead to effective teamwork and social cooperation.[29]

However, as with first position, striking the right balance is crucial. Second position can be underdeveloped, and it can also be overdeveloped and overutilized.

People who have behaviors characteristic of the autism spectrum label have difficulty establishing rapport. They also often have difficulties with empathy, imitation, pretend play, and social interaction.[31-33] The neuroscientist Vilayanur Ramachandran argues that their mirror neuron circuits are functioning differently, and there is an "almost perfect fit" in expected behavioral traits if mirror neurons are implicated.[34]

When second position is overdone, we can become overly concerned with what others think. Some people are unable to make decisions for themselves; they agonize endlessly about the opinions of other people.

In the film *My Left Foot*, Daniel Day Lewis, playing paralytic Christie Brown, refused to leave his wheelchair between scenes. He wanted to truly experience the problems associated with the condition. His refusal to break from character earned him an Oscar, but it also earned him broken ribs from his continually hunched position in the wheelchair. [35]

Professionally, second position is often overdone in the therapeutic and social care industries. Frontline professionals frequently come home from work having vicariously lived through the trials, tribulations, and traumatic responses of their patients and clients. This can lead to burnout and, potentially, a secondary traumatic stress response.[36–39]

"**To walk a mile in your shoes.**"

"**To see it through their eyes.**"

"**If I were you.**"

THIRD POSITION

Third position is sometimes referred to as the meta, director, or observer position.[21] In this position, the observer clearly perceives the world as if they are positioned away from both first and second positions. They are not a participant. They are an observer.

"Step back for a moment."

"Take a bird's-eye view."

"Be a fly on the wall."

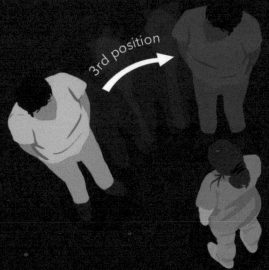

3rd position

In third position, we are interested and curious, observing ourselves as one of the actors in the context under consideration. In cognitive psychology, this is referred to as a self-distanced perspective.[2]

Examples of people who frequent third position include emergency medical staff and soldiers, where too much first or second position would get in the way of doing the job. Scientists often like to think that they operate from this position of relative objectivity and curiosity with enough distance to recognize and avoid their own biases. Some scientists do a reasonable job of this, though many appear to operate from a defensive first position. Others are able to move between the different perspectives with relative ease. For example, Einstein is famous for his second-position experience, during which he felt like he left his body and inhabited a particle of light traveling as a wave. Later, he demonstrated a clear ability to speak from third position when discussing science, philosophy, and politics.[40]

From third position, people often refer to themselves "over there" as "he/she," or if with another person in a conversation, as "they."

Many people describe accessing a version of third position through a variety of metaphors. You might hear phrases like "take a step back," "get a bird's-eye view," or "observe like a fly on the wall." What is implicit in these metaphors is an awareness of the importance of space in perception and sensemaking. Our location is relative to other locations we could occupy and to the people or objects that also occupy the space around us. This relative positioning, especially distance, is important.

How we perceive or create the perception of distance is integral to the way that we detect and react to patterns of movement, especially those that could be associated with threat. For example, we have a different unconscious response to a lion running at a distance than to that of snake-like movement near our feet — both creatures could potentially be a threat, but the distance informs our response.

The micro-changes we make by moving around in any environment help us literally change our perspective, looking from new angles at past, present, or future events. This is why the metaphor of stepping back is so common in narratives of resilience. By becoming deliberately distant to the idea we are contemplating, we can access more abstract future-focused thinking.

Using a third-person pronoun when reflecting on something we ourselves have done can help create distance. It allows us to become less emotionally engaged and more objective.[36]

There are similar benefits when applied to recalled memories that are persistent and unresourceful. First-person recall of a potentially traumatic event, with all the senses firing in first position, is a very different experience than recalling the event in third position from an imagined distance. If the memory activates an unresourceful state, we might want to replay it as though it were an old black-and-white movie, with the TV at a distance and the sound turned down low.[29,30,41,42]

We can also use technology to create a sense of distance. One technique for a robust and low-risk debrief process for challenging situations or critical incidents is to debrief to yourself using the video function on your phone. Then watch the video of yourself from a clean third-person perspective, listening and noting the non-verbal patterns of the person (you) in the video. Participants invariably learn something new when they do this, and they often are quick to identify what they can do to recover.

As with first and second positions, it is possible to overdo it with third position. Common examples include some doctors, scientists, and engineers who are perceived as being too logical and cold. Some frontline emergency professionals often need an exceptionally robust third position to deal with a continual stream of trauma patients. The danger is that they become too detached from their patients, and start to treat them impersonally like a number or a diagnostic label. They too need to learn to move in *and out of* this detached position. If they don't, they may struggle to empathize with the people who need their help. Worst of all, they may carry the "clinical" third position into their personal lives, becoming cold and distant with loved ones.

All the positions are important, and there are times when we can benefit from one or other position as a "clean" experience, meaning with no trace of the other two positions. In this respect, third position is a good cleanser for the switch between first and second positions.

ACTIVITY

DEVELOPING FIRST POSITION

Conducting a body scan whilst immersed in the present is one example of how to develop first position present. Another activity is the walk of the senses. Both of these processes are described in detail in Chapter 4 — State.

When you are in first position, you can sense the world in the moment. This is "being in the now." You can also recall past events or create imagined future scenarios from first position. We illustrate these distinctions here.

When you recall past events or create imagined future scenarios from first position, you would not see yourself standing separately, "over there" somewhere. That would be a view from third position. You would see the scene as if through your eyes. You can still use the body scan to calibrate or develop awareness of the sensations in the body whilst having a first position experience in the past or future.

A fully immersive first position experience of an imagined future scenario aims to create a rich appreciation of what might happen and how we might respond. It allows us to imagine, test, calibrate, and connect with what is important to us. We can also consider possible risks or prepare to mitigate potential downsides. Again, we can use the body scan to question and connect with felt sensations and embodied signals.

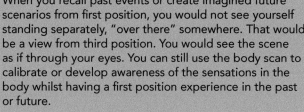

DEVELOPING SECOND POSITION

When you are in second position, you can experience the world *as if* through another's senses. It is also possible to imagine being an animal or object, like Einstein did with a particle of light.

Second position can be used in real time in the present, or, through recall, you can inhabit second position in events from your past or in an imagined future scenario. The example we provide here is of a present context.

Step 1.

Identify a person whose experience you want to better understand. This could be your partner or a potential employer, or it might be a friend you are having a dispute with, or your daughter who is sitting at home waiting for you to return from a late night at work.

Step 2.

Quieten your inner dialogue. It often helps to use the tongue drop method we described earlier.

Step 3.

Imagine yourself floating into their body. You see through their eyes and hear with their ears. Breathe in rhythm with the person you are being. Replicate their movements and gestures in your own body with micro muscle movements. If they move their right arm, you activate a movement in your right arm, just enough to get a sense of the movement patterns.

Step 4.

Repeat this micro muscle movement copying, replicating the other person's body movements, such as their head tilts and facial expressions, bringing these movements into your body. Feel what they might feel. Inhabit this created version of the person for long enough that you get a taste of their experience in this context. If there is internal dialogue in this position, it is your imagined creation of their internal commentary. You might imagine an internal commentary about that person, over there, that looks like you!

People are often surprised at the ideas and intuitions that arise when they use second position in this way.

Step 5.

After you experience second position, shake the experience out of your body and return fully to first position, to being fully yourself, back in the present moment.

A light warning: Before you start modeling someone else using second position, set an intention to only pick up their experience temporarily. Bring none of their undesirable habits or patterns of behavior with you when you return to the first position.

DEVELOPING THIRD POSITION

When you are in third person, you will experience situations, other people, or even an imagined view of yourself from a perspective that is different than if you were in the scene. As with first and second positions, third can be applied in real time, to a replay of past events, or to an imagined future scenario.

Step 1.

We deliberately impose a state of curiosity, with an intention for impartial observation without judgment. Inferences/ interpretations and consideration of intent and impact are ideally delayed, at least initially, while we are gathering information from this observer position.

Choose a context you would like to observe as an impartial third party. This could be an interaction between you and your partner, an interaction with a potential employer, a dispute with a friend, or getting a perspective on your current work situation.

Our illustration depicts someone still in first position at this step.

Step 2a.

This is the move to third position. Step away from where you were so that you can look back at a projected hologram of how you were in that context.

If doing this for a past or future situation, the same applies. Step back and look at where you were previously in first.

Be sure to shake out any sensations you might have carried with you. Adopt the posture and attitude of a curious impartial observer.

I can see a guy over there hunched over his desk, I note that everyone else has gone home

Step 3.

As an option, some people find it helpful to offer third-position insights formally to the person, over there, who looks like them. Notice that our language here maintains a separation between third and first, as the third person presents their findings to the projected first-position self. Some do this out loud. We use a process like this for giving performance feedback.

Shake out and return to first position, taking with you new insights and options.

Most people report that this detached but curious position is ideal for recalling challenging interactions.

Step 2b.

Check that the third person position you have created does not have the sensations or intentions of first position. If it does, step back again, or even multiple times, looking in on the observer, or the observer observing the observer, etc. Most people experience a significant change the first time they step back for a second time in this way. It "cleans up" the third position. In a clean third position, observations become more evidence based.

look at that poor guy there working late...

I need to triage! I am going to prioritize right now.

WHERE'S MARY?

JILL ROBINSON

is an experienced graduate nurse with 30 years senior operational management experience. She has lead multidisciplinary teams across a wide variety of adult health and social care environments, hospitals, and residential and nursing facilities.

One thing I have learned from thirty-five years of nursing is that it's pointless trying to convince someone with dementia that what they're experiencing are hallucinations. In their world they are absolutely real and the question becomes how flexible can I become to work effectively with someone in that state?

"Where's Mary?" "What time is it?" like a stuck record — on and on she went, hour after hour, relentless. And yet it had all started so well — the family home was warm and comfortable, homely and inviting.

My replies were relaxed and measured, carefully spoken with thought and compassion "Mary's gone to a wedding today, I'm looking after you." "It's 8 o' clock, breakfast time, why don't you sit down?" Less than a minute later, "Where's Mary? What time is it?" And with that she got up and made for the door. This two-question plaintive monologue continued minute by painful minute, hour after hour. Gradually I could hear my voice rising both in volume and pitch, my shoulders stiffened and raised until they were touching my ears, and my neck disappeared. My answers became shorter and more angry "I've told you already…sit down…stop it!" My world shrank until all I could hear was that voice and those questions.

I tried everything: TV, reading the newspaper, sitting in the garden, making tea, nothing worked …."Where's Mary?" "What time is it?" I could feel my blood begin to boil. My head was pounding, I was sweating, my breathing shallow and quick. How much more of this could I take?

It had seemed like such an easy job — one day as a nurse to someone living with the experience of dementia, whilst the family went to a wedding. That day felt like a life sentence — never-ending torture.

Then I walked away into the living room — just for a minute, to break the constant pattern of her desperate questions and my increasingly abrupt answers. Wondering what would happen if I left her alone? Dare I ring the agency and feign sickness — anything to find a way out of this.

In that moment of quiet I took a deep breath and slowly let it out, then another and then a third. I could feel my heart slow a little and was able to lift my head and take in my surroundings. There on the piano was an old photograph of a beautiful young woman, vibrant, laughing, long wavy

brown hair, holding hands, sitting at the same piano with a little girl who was about 6 years old. Elsie came into the room, and for the first time I noticed her rubbing her hands together – wringing them continuously, her walk was a pace up and down back and forth, back and forth, looking intently out of the window into the distance down the road. For a split second I was Elsie and in that instant I knew what Elsie was doing — she was waiting for Mary, who was late and should have been home. Once again the plaintive cry went up: "Where's Mary? What time is it? " I picked the photo up and pointed to the little girl with a quizzical look. Her face crumpled and she sobbed "Mary... Mary ...where is my Mary? Why isn't she home yet?" and with that she rushed again to look out of the window. Mary was her daughter — not the 60-year-old daughter who was at a wedding; she was Mary, the 6-year-old daughter who

hadn't come home from school and was overdue...maybe even lost...I steadied my voice, looked directly into Elsie's eyes and firmly and convincingly asserted, "Oh Elsie, you remember, don't you...she is having tea with her friend and will be home in time for bed tonight." Elsie stopped, and looked perplexed before nodding knowingly and saying, "Ahhh." The pacing, hand wringing, and questions ceased and in that blessed moment of relief I asked "I wonder if you would be kind enough to show me how to play the piano — I hear you are very talented and it will make our day pass so easily."

The next hour or more was spent listening as Elsie played old tunes, sometimes singing along, fully absorbed in the activity. That's when I knew I would survive that day.

MAKING THE MOST OF DIFFERENT PERSPECTIVES

Ideally, we would all have the choice to access clean and distinctly separate first, second, and third perceptual experiences on command or unconsciously as we need them. When exploring and developing these skills for the first time, it usually requires deliberate conscious practice. After a short period of time, the different perspectives will start to emerge reflexively.

Once you can cleanly switch positions in different contexts using the steps we outline in the training activity, you can get creative with how and where you apply the practice. For example:

Use second position to capture the movement patterns of competitors in sport by modeling from video replay. Just watch a comparison of Kobe Bryant and Michael Jordan for an example of pattern replication.[43] Of course, this application can be generalized to performance in any domain.

Use third position in a critical incident, operational debrief. Invite your team to stand behind a window, looking outward as they replay what happened. Look and gesture in the direction of the event, even if it was a long way away. Insist that the first responders all remain in third position as

they identify how operational procedures could be improved. It is well established that reviewing such experiences from a self-distanced (third) rather than a self-immersed (first) position reduces the risk of trauma. This can also help lower arterial blood pressure and improve heart rate reactivity.[44]

Use first position body scanning to tackle unspecified food allergies. Learn to sense which foods might be implicated in the allergic reaction you are having by scanning yourself as you wander around the supermarket. Scan again after eating safe amounts, learning to detect more and more subtle signs of what is edible for you. Keep a detailed diary to exclude whatever is not working for you. Research suggests that we might have a remarkable untapped potential to fine-tune our own dietary regime, especially for detecting nutritional deficiencies.[45-47] We know people who are allergic to nuts who can walk into a kitchen that had prepared satay sauce (using peanuts) three days prior, feel the faintest tingle on their lips, and know that there is danger.

The applications are unlimited, and you'll soon start to experience some of the benefits of this practice. Technology can help us with some of this work.

We can learn to recognize subtle shifts in first-position states by using heart rate variability monitors, which can be combined with synchronicity analytics to compare heart rate or movement synchronicity between two people or a person with an animal. EEG and heart rate monitors can help us train third position viewing of traumatic or otherwise painful memories.[48-51]

The ability to move between the three positions is akin to flowstate. Those trained to access flow states often report that, when in flow, they can effortlessly access first, second, and third position in an instant. Time slows and distorts in these states, and there are perceptual shifts as well. Some report hearing their own heartbeat; others are hyper-aware of their movements or body position, or the experience of others. Some even report seeing themselves vividly from outside their bodies.

The potential use for these different perspectives is unlimited. We can all naturally take differing perceptual positions to one degree or another, and learning to do so by design can be a truly transformative experience.

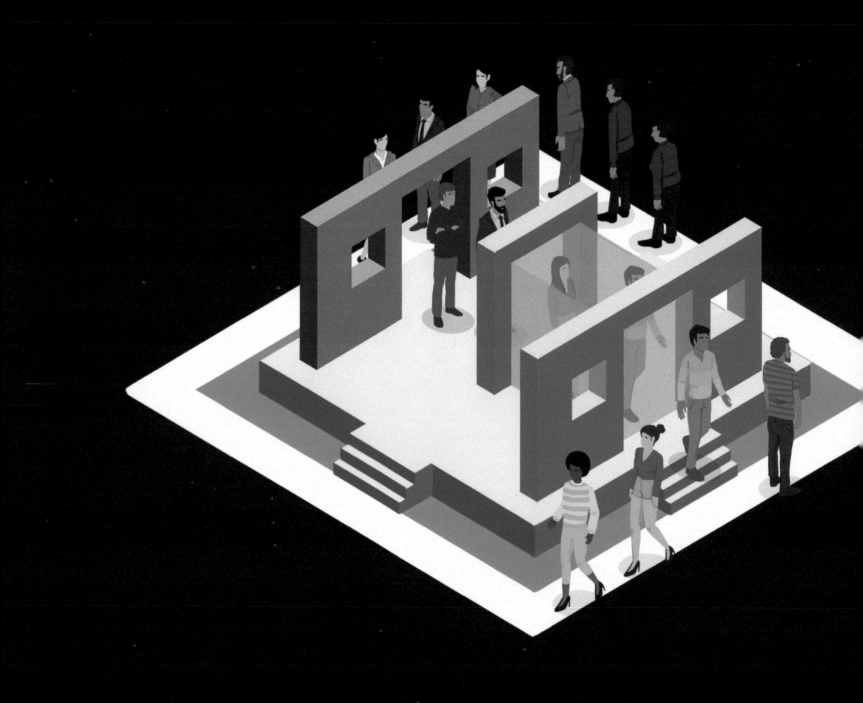

CONTEXT

PIG IN MUD, OR FISH OUT OF WATER?

The saying "as happy as a pig in mud" (or something less savory) refers to the experience of being perfectly at home in one's preferred habitat. "A fish out of water" describes the opposite, perhaps evoking the image of a fish gasping for air, slowly dying.

Our relationship with context, meaning the different environments and situations we find ourselves in moment by moment, is critical for resilience.

How we frame or describe our context is not a straightforward process. It is fraught with ambiguity, unconscious bias, and differences of perception. Descriptions of context are often highly compressed representations of what's important to us. It's easy to think of context as a limited number of features, such as location, people, and what you're doing at the time.

However we choose to frame context, the boundary is always one of perception. Take the contextual elements of place, for instance. Depending on the breadth of your perspective, you might be thinking about your workplace, or you might be thinking about your community, your town, your state, your country, etc. Place, weather, culture, politics, the economy, and interactions such as conflicts all interweave to make context an opaque and constantly shifting concept. How we frame this concept influences how we assign meaning to the world we inhabit.

The people who are a part of any given context all have relationships beyond their relationship with you. They have their own beliefs and values, and they have equally complex interactions with their world, your world, and the one we all share.

It used to be said that everyone is connected by six degrees of separation.[1] In 2016, Facebook calculated that it was 3.57 degrees of separation, and this number is getting lower and lower with each passing day. The internet and social media are breaking down physical, social, and political borders, sidestepping the limitations of distance.[2]

Taking into account all the different elements and interconnectedness to frame a universally accepted or agreed-upon frame for a particular context would be impossible and unhelpful. We have to limit what we notice and what we ignore, what we include and what we exclude, within the contextual frames we apply.

We've emphasised frequently in this book that resilience is the ability to choose effective responses to events in the complex, turbulent world around us, *as well* as shaping or designing that world. Whether we like it or not, we live in a dynamic relationship with a world where the only certainty is change and death (and, in most countries, taxes).

Most of how context can influence us, and how we influence it, goes unnoticed. It is beneath our conscious awareness. When we appreciate how it influences us, and how we can influence it, we can bring an entirely new sense of agency into our lives.

The place to start developing this dynamic relationship is with situational awareness. Salience, knowing what is important, is key. Imagine for a moment, it's the evening and you are walking past some street cafes and bars. There are cars, chatter, music playing, the chink of glasses, maybe a hundred people on the street. Everyone seems relaxed. Across the street, a man holding a brown paper bag stumbles. He looks up in your direction, and then crosses the street toward you. Your context just changed as the earliest signs of a new pattern just emerged.

We don't yet know what might happen. If the man genuinely poses a threat, then almost certainly our interaction will shape the outcome to some extent. In this instance, we noticed a change in context very early, so we have many choices available to us. We can cross the street, back up, meet the conflict head on, seek the company of others, etc. Imagine instead we miss these signs, and only notice the man when he stumbles into us. There is less time to decide how to respond and far fewer choices.

In another example of salience, many people report work-related stress. Is the stress signal they're receiving related to the whole company and its mission and culture, or is the problem more localized, to perhaps the team dynamics, the manager, or the project? Perhaps the stress response is related to travel requirements, location, unsociable work hours, or even just poor coffee.

Getting specific and defining what is important to pay attention to in context can help us fine-tune our situational awareness, which in turn can guide how we best respond to our environment. Seeking specificity can also help with identifying what we might change and how.

This doesn't mean we can control everything. There can still be factors we have little or no agency over. Instead of trying to control the uncontrollable, we want to know how to best respond to context in a way that acknowledges the *type* of system we are concerned with, which can then inform how best to act.

CYNEFIN
FRAMEWORK
(PRONOUNCED KUH-NEV-IN)

Cynefin, developed by Professor Dave Snowden and his collaborators, is a framework to aid sensemaking. Cynefin is a Welsh word which has no literal translation into English. The closest approximation would be "a place of your multiple belongings." [3,4]

Cynefin recognizes that our sense of who we are, the types of actions we take, and the roles we fill will change depending on the context. The Cynefin framework acknowledges multiple perspectives, and it allows us to respond to context in ways that suit the system and our role in it.

Cynefin has five domains. At the center of the framework is the Confused domain; surrounding this are Clear, Complicated, Complex, and Chaotic. Each domain has certain characteristics and a different way to make sense of the situation and respond. The framework accommodates uncertainty in a way that ensures we do not become paralyzed with indecision. It allows us to respond in ways that appreciate the differences between ordered systems and the unpredictable nature of complexity and chaos.

COMPLEX
PROBE - SENSE - RESPOND

COMPLICATED
SENSE - ANALYZE - RESPOND

CONFUSED

CHAOTIC
ACT - SENSE - RESPOND

CLEAR
SENSE - CATEGORIZE - RESPOND

This represents a fold, or a cliff, which is easy to fall over, but difficult to return from.

In both the Clear and Complicated domains, there is a direct relationship between cause and effect; the same event can happen again, repeating itself, and not by accident. In Clear, most people can see what the cause-and-effect relationship is. Nobody disputes it. In Clear we can "sense-categorize-respond." For example, imagine landing in a foreign country and renting a car. As soon as you sit in the driver's seat, you sense and categorize. Though it differs across countries, you know which side of the road you should drive on, and how to respond.

The Clear domain is very important. We see value in the application of detailed planning and rigid control systems in both professional and recreational contexts. Unfortunately, people often underestimate the cost of creating such order. Consider what the epic cost would have been to attempt getting all UK drivers to switch from the left side of the road to the right, to align with Europe only 30 km away. Or worse yet, all of mainland Europe to switch to the left side just like the Brits!

Attempts to force people into the Clear domain, when in fact the situation is more Complicated or Complex, risks a collapse into Chaos. This is why the boundary between Clear and Chaotic is shown as a fold or a cliff, which is easy to fall over, but difficult to return from.

We can observe this in companies that have fallen over the metaphorical cliff. Companies such as Kodak, which became complacent and failed to innovate from film to digital. If we fail to invest in our personal development, we too may take a similar tumble.

In the Complicated domain, while there is also a linear, repeatable relationship between cause and effect, these relationships are only really self-evident to experts. From the expert perspective, such situations might appear to be in the Clear domain. Experts will know how to investigate or analyze complicated problems.

Decision-making in the complicated domain follows a "sense-analyze-respond" pattern. I gather incoming data, analyze it, and this informs me what to do, or tells me who to call, to tell me what to do.

A major mistake is to attempt imposing a single solution (best practice) in a complicated situation where some degree of nuance or expert understanding is required. For example, a doctor who is expected to prescribe a drug for certain symptoms, rather than assessing personal, social, or economic factors.

IT'S CLEAR THAT THIS IS A DUCK

WHEN EXPERTS DISAGREE, AND THERE'S MORE THAN ONE WAY TO SKIN A CAT, IT GETS COMPLICATED.

FROM CONFUSION TO CYNEFIN

I CAN SEE THE PATTERN, IT'S COMPLEX

The boundary between Complicated and Complex is an important one. On the Complicated side of the boundary, we can trust somebody with appropriate training and qualifications to make accurate predictions. In the Complex side, we need to take a different approach, beginning with widening our understanding of what constitutes expertise. In the Complex domain, experts can become particularly susceptible to inattentional blindness. **If we are to account for the unexpected, we need to seek diverse insights.** Experts might miss the obvious — just like they do with the gorilla in the X-ray images.[5]

For personal resilience, this could mean asking others to share their perspective. An example could be if someone is struggling with a complex business problem and you are the expert. It might be that a solution could emerge by talking with someone unrelated to your field of expertise whose experience in a completely different domain unlocks the door you've been knocking at for ages.

In the Complex domain, there is no linear relationship between cause and effect. We can only understand a complex context by acting in it. Action produces evidence (feedback), which then illuminates patterns that support multiple contradictory hypotheses. Instead of gambling on one solution, we test these hypotheses, often simultaneously.

Decision-making in a complex domain is "probe-sense-respond." This is best approached with multiple small probes, like testing where to plant a tree in a rocky garden before actually committing to digging a big enough hole.

In a medical example, perhaps a patient complains to their doctor about a sore back. She or he may benefit from a change of diet, or from exercising or examining their undesirable states or lifestyle choices. They might try massage or seek professional help from a movement or postural specialist. These probes are intended to uncover the relationships between factors, rather than focusing on a single approach, such as surgery in the example of back pain.

In the Complex domain, every action changes the context in unexpected ways and the only certainty is that every choice/action will produce some unintended consequences. Making use of safe-to-fail experiments

or probes can reduce risk and increase our ability to recognize and seize upon unexpected opportunities, potentially saving time and resources in the process.

In the Complex domain, abductive thinking comes into its own. Because the complex domain is never predictable in a linear way, intuition or gut feelings are often more reliable guides than rational analysis. We often use heuristics or rules-of-thumb to guide our decision-making in the moment.

Heuristics are also important for acting in Chaos, which is characterized by the absence of any effective constraints, such as the panicked movement of people in a busy train station if there is a fire and smoke. People would not be constrained by the usual orderly way of moving between platforms, or follow the dominant left or right side of the stairs protocol.

If chaos arises accidentally, it's a crisis. We need to "act-sense-respond." The priority is to rapidly create some form of constraint that will allow us to manage the situation. A well-known heuristic first response to fire is "Get down low, and go! go! go!" This deliberately constrains behavioral

choice. In crisis situations, we must be open to sensing and adjusting to potential changes in the occuring events. The first rule, though, is to act and do so quickly. In the midst of a crisis, command and control work well.

Chaos can also be used deliberately to break established patterns and force change. An example might be radical restructure of an organization. We have to remember that Chaos takes energy to maintain and is always temporary in nature. Patterns soon begin to emerge. In the case of the radical shake-up of a company, new tribes and patterns of working — often inherited from existing systems — establish themselves quickly.

Confusion, in the middle of the framework, is often a starting point for sensemaking, or a place to revisit during change. Being aware enough to identify that you are confused is generally desirable, though staying confused for a long time is generally not. Naivety to confusion has upsides and downsides — ignorance is bliss, as they say; alternatively, you are heading for a potentially unpleasant "learning opportunity."

WHAT'S YOUR PREFERRED HABITAT?

There is a tendency to assess contexts according to our personal preferences for action.

Bureaucrats like clear order, and they tend to assess problems as a failure of process. Scientists and engineers like to derive answers from complicated challenges. However, if the challenge proves insurmountable, they tend to blame failure on a lack of time or resources that may have enabled them to thoroughly investigate the issue. Politicians are pretty good at navigating the complex. They detect what is important to voters, often adapting their values and policies to get elected. Dictators love a crisis. When people are confused or scared, they look for certainty. Dictators seize upon the opportunities presented to them in the moment to grant themselves absolute power to tell everybody else what to do.

Most of us have a natural habitat where we're comfortable — our "happy place." The same is true of domains. We can make short trips into other domains as part of our extended "foraging" zone; and there are certain domains that we might

sense to be completely "inhospitable." It is important to clarify in which domains you prefer to operate, so you can work on developing tactics that will expand your operational comfort zone.

CONSIDER THESE HOLIDAYS:

In the Clear domain, you could book yourself a Contiki tour. These are highly organized, guided tours. Expert guides create a detailed itinerary and organize every step along the way. Planes, trains, and automobiles are scheduled with military precision down to the minute. Even where and what you'll eat has been predetermined. These are perfect for vacationers who want to turn up, switch off, and be guided. For others, a tour like this would be like a prison sentence.

In the Complicated domain, you might plan a family holiday to Europe. Over three weeks of sightseeing, you design plans to get from city to city, and you will probably plan the accommodation ahead of arrival. Most people won't book the restaurants or cafés, and much of the sightseeing can be spontaneous whilst moving from one

tourist hotspot to the next. You can hire a guide, consult with one, or you can find your own way.

A Complex holiday might involve a ten-week backcountry ski trip in the European Alps (we're projecting our own fantasies here). You book a campervan to provide a greater degree of freedom. The Alps usually have good snow coverage between mid-January and late March. But chasing powder requires considerable agility and a willingness to probe-sense-respond (literally in the case of snowpack prone to avalanche). In this case, a campervan allows maximum freedom to follow the best weather and snow and to always be on site for fresh tracks.

It is very difficult to consistently plan for chaos, remembering that chaos is temporary in nature and highly energy demanding to maintain. Many thousands of travelers (and holiday companies) experienced chaos to their holiday plans when Covid-19 hit in 2020. There were rolling travel restrictions, borders opening and closing, lockdowns, and constant uncertainty.

CONSIDER THESE HOLIDAYS:

- Contiki tour.
- Family holiday to Europe.
- 10 week trip to Europe by campervan.
- Pamplona - Bulls.

Contrast this unplanned chaos with a planned dive into chaos. The Spanish town of Pamplona sells out of hotel rooms many months in advance of its world-famous running of the bulls. The trip might start with planning, but once the bell tolls signaling the release of six thousand-pound raging bulls with sharp horns, the context becomes one of pure life and death chaos.

SOMETIMES WE COMPROMISE ON OUR PREFERRED HABITAT FOR OTHER BENEFITS

Let's build on the metaphor of preferred habitat, extended foraging, and the concept of an inhospitable zone. We'll do this using an example of work environments.

The benefits of factory work or a career in a fast-food restaurant include the security of a regular wage, predictable hours, and well-structured work environments. Such jobs often have a good social scene. They provide security, and they make personal budgeting and planning possible. The downsides include inflexible schedules

and repetitive work, often with no ability to influence procedure or offer creative input.

Many people enjoy these sorts of jobs, especially the social aspects, whilst others tolerate them for some other benefit. They might, for instance, use the steady paycheck to help fund their education, or it might be for the sake of their children's education. By contrast, the extreme uncertainty of a start-up enterprise might be viewed by those seeking security as inhospitable, a last option to provide income if they can't land a regular job.

Others thrive in the chaos and confusion of starting a small business, for short periods of time at least. For the most part, entrepreneurship is about detecting patterns or trends of buying behavior. Those who are unable to navigate out of chaos, confusion, and high uncertainty into more orderly ways of operating will usually run out of money, good will, or energy. Many entrepreneurs understand complexity. They identify a need in the market and with trial and error they find a product or service that satisfies that need. Many still fail to execute well because they

don't enjoy the disciplined part of creating and executing on a business plan. They never move into the sort of profitability that comes from order. The smart entrepreneurs hire people who love to do work in orderly domains.

Many people talk about stressful environments without recognizing the elements they are responding to with a self-produced state of stress. Often it's a mismatch between preferred habitat and the nature of uncertainty in the context they find themselves in.

We encourage you to carefully consider preferences for action and what makes up your habitats. A key component of resilience is the ability to thrive in the extended foraging zone and, for a time at least, survive in the inhospitable zone. When you find yourself outside your comfort zone, it is crucial to understand your intention for being there. You can then begin looking at options to get out, back to that happy place.

NO ONE CAN MANAGE TIME — WE CAN ONLY MANAGE ATTENTION

There is an old Russian proverb:

If you chase two rabbits at once, you won't catch either of them.

When we divide our focus, we often divide the quality of our work as well. If we want to be effective, it mostly requires focusing on one task at a time.

However for every proverb there's a counterexample. We also say:

You can't see the forest for the trees.

If we focus too intently, we can miss the broader context and opportunities. It's possible that these contradictory sayings have a good neural basis, reflecting two opposite ends of the spectrum between hyper- and hypo-attention.

At one extreme, hyper-attention is the dedicated focus on a single activity at the expense of other demands. The potential downside of overdone focus could include a loss of flexibility, as one example. When overly focused, we might miss urgent deadlines, or we might have poor situational awareness, and our relationships might suffer.

Those with hyper-attention exhibit some of the behaviors that are associated with Autism Spectrum Disorder. When applied in the right context though, such abilities can be incredibly productive.

At the other extreme, hypo-attention is working with multiple activities that simultaneously receive a small portion of our dedicated conscious attention. This can enable incredible creativity, with multiple interconnected ideas spinning out in rapid succession.

Often, hypo-attention occurs at the expense of timely individual task completion. Tasks can get abandoned half-done. There can be an overwhelming sense of busyness with little to show for the effort. Those who are prone to hypo-attention may demonstrate some of the behaviors associated with Attention Deficit Hyperactivity Disorder. Like states of hyper-attention, such abilities can be incredibly valuable when applied in an appropriate context.

Managing attention, just like most behaviors, is context- or task-specific. There are some contexts when having choice to access either hypo- or hyper-

attention states can be highly useful. Consider, for example, a bomb disposal expert. Every fiber of their being is concentrated on cutting the correct wires. High-pressure moments like this are not the time to be thinking about the state of global politics, calling home to check what's for dinner, or scribbling down some notes for an idea you've just had for a book you'd like to write one day.

At the other end of the spectrum is the multitasking required by a school teacher, managing a school outing. Safety, kids, roads, buses, lunch boxes, phone calls from parents, filling in learning outcomes to meet some government-imposed performance benchmarking, all the while thinking in the back of their mind about grabbing a quiet moment to check in on little Jilly, who's struggling with issues at home.

NEURODIVERSE AND NEUROTYPICALS CAN LEARN FROM EACH OTHER

In much the same way that people have preferred habits and extended foraging zones, so too they have different attentional preferences. Fortunately,

employers are increasingly appreciating the value of neurodiversity. When putting attention into workplace design and the principles of reasonable adjustment, it's possible, at least to some extent, to match preferences to needs.

The challenge and the opportunity are in developing choice where there is a mismatch between personal preferences and organizational needs. For those who naturally operate well at one extreme or another, resilience is about gradually learning processes or "fast hacks" that allow them to be attentive in new ways. For "neurotypicals," there is much that can be learned from people with exceptional focus or creative unfocus. In fact, there is a danger in not developing distinctly different modes of working. The middle ground of attention is often highly ineffective.

Possibly more than at any other time in history, people report being overwhelmed at work, a problem that seemingly arises from a never-ending pattern of interruptions.[6-8] No matter where you prefer to sit on the attentional spectrum, these constant interruptions disrupt productivity and creativity.

Many modern industries involve a large amount of what management guru Peter Drucker called "knowledge work" — non-routine problem-solving that requires a combination of deductive, inductive, and abductive thinking. Knowledge work requires a high cognitive load, which is easily disrupted by the *wrong sort* of distractions. An incoming email, a ringing phone, or a social media notification is enough to knock people out of flow. However, the right sort of distractions can constructively overload conscious overthinking in a way that allows more creative ideas to emerge.

Interruptions can also hinder the efficiency of routine work. Being interrupted has become such a common feature of the modern working environment that poor workflow is the norm rather than the exception.

Rejecting this as a given, we can deliberately manage our attention with strategies and boundaries, to create an appropriate environment for efficiently engaging in a wide range of tasks and attentional preferences.

Many people work best on obvious or routine tasks if they focus on moving through their workload one task at a time — the classic daily tick list. This is what we call *task mode*. For creative tasks or more complex knowledge work, many people benefit by engaging in several challenges in parallel, switching between them in a state of high cognitive load. We call this *creative mode*.

Of course, most people will need to switch between modes, sometimes day to day, and sometimes inside of a single day.

Some high performers have highly idiosyncratic ways of optimizing state and managing their environment. It is important to recognize there is no single solution that works for everyone. Idiosyncrasies such as our circadian rhythms, family situations, or even the proximity to our favorite barista can all influence when, where, and how you can best batch or sequence different activities. We (Ian and Mike) like to switch between the extremes of task and creative modes by changing locations. Each time we switch, we mix in a little downtime: a quick power nap, a meal, or even checking our email.

OPTIMIZING FOR TASK MODE

Planning tasks so that you can focus attention on them one by one can provide a notable increase in productivity.

Here is our list of other factors that support productivity:

1. MANAGE YOUR SPACE AND TIME.

Manage other people's expectations. Be bold, close the door, and hang a Do Not Disturb sign on the handle.

Limit all non-essential stimuli. Keep only essential materials nearby.

Use a timer to keep to a set schedule.

Turn phones to flight mode and place them out of sight.

Buy a wristwatch or a desk clock. Train yourself to look at the clock rather than your phone.

Design your working space for elegance and simplicity. Think *monk in a cave*.

2. CREATE STIMULATION AND MOTIVATION.

Use a reminder (a photo, drawing, quote, etc.) of your desired outcome.

Avoid last-minute completion deadlines (and the stress that often drives them) by making routine tasks competitive for yourself well ahead of time.

Order your tasks. Rack 'em and stack 'em. Set a stopwatch, wind yourself up, and go!

3. USE BATCH PROCESSING.

Identify batches of work ahead of time (either the night before or first thing in the morning) so you can efficiently batch with similar tasks. For example, travel reconciliations, returning phone calls, or photographing receipts.

Block attention from all incoming channels of distraction (emails, phones, text alerts, etc.), until after the block of batch processing is complete.

Be disciplined and assign specific times of the day for checking communication channels.

Researchers have compared groups of people based on their tendency to multitask and their belief that multitasking helps their performance. They found that those who both regularly multitask and assume that it boosts their performance were actually worse at multitasking than those who like to do a single task at a time. They also found that multitasking leads to more errors and that it takes significantly more time to get tasks completed if you switch between them.[9-11]

If the tasks are complicated, time and error penalties increase, which can add up to a loss of 40% of total daily productivity.

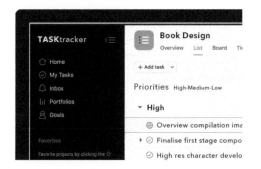

4. FIRST, DO WHAT'S IMPORTANT.

In the morning or the night before, identify the most important task you need to accomplish. Before you move on to anything else, complete that task.

5. CONCENTRATE YOUR TIME.

Using a timer, experiment with ideal focus periods. Start between 20 and 90 minutes at a time. Identify what works best for you.

6. TAKE "KNOW-NOTHING" BREAKS.

Pushing hard on linear task efficiency can be tiring. Move around. If you're having trouble clearing your head, use the tongue drop and box breathing techniques.

OPTIMIZING FOR CREATIVE MODE

Professor Allan Snyder from the University of Sydney conducted experiments that show when the left hemisphere of the brain is inhibited, the right hemisphere is able to increase creative problem-solving abilities, often to a remarkable degree. [12,13]

If you want access to the right hemisphere's creative problem-solving abilities, multitask, splitting your conscious attention between several different tasks or projects. With the conscious mind fully occupied, your unconscious will be free to work in the background.

We recommend experimenting with how many and what type of parallel tasks work for you. Everybody's different. Professor Dave Snowden, who uses this technique, likes around ten to a dozen projects running in parallel; Ian likes to limit it to around four of them.

1. CHECK AND OPTIMIZE STATE.

Run a body scan, checking you have energy levels set for creative activity. Sleep, eat, exercise, power nap, meditate, or work out — whatever you need to support your unique creative process.

2. SET YOUR INTENTIONS.

Even if you're unsure what the outcome will be, know your intention. Through internal dialogue, you can directly ask your unconscious mind for help with some simple self-talk. It could be something like: "Hey unconscious, I really want to solve this problem, and I would appreciate your support." We know of many high-performing creatives who do this before going to sleep or meditating.

3. ESTABLISH AN OPTIMAL ENVIRONMENT.

Figure out your ideal setting to get the right stimuli. Members of our team use ear protectors to ensure access to quiet, or they take a walk in nature.

We have an entire wall painted as a whiteboard that we use to collaborate visually as a team. Or we create mind maps in a virtual shared environment.

We've coached professional writers who have written entire books whilst walking on treadmills, with their laptops in front of them at a pace of 2 miles per hour, per chapter!

4. ACCESS FLOW.

Once you've set your intention, there are multiple options for accessing flowstate. You can play flowstate games, or you can set up a series of challenging parallel tasks. Quite a few people find success by starting with somewhere in the range of three to five simultaneous tasks.

Alternatively, do anything that helps you access flow: ride your bike, walk a slackline, juggle flaming torches, roller skate backwards whilst reciting prime numbers — the possibilities are endless. The purpose is to get the left hemisphere and internal dialogue out of the way.

5. CAPTURE IT FAST.

In creative mode, it's rarely important to have a polished project. Instead, stay with the flow and let ideas arise and bubble over. Ideas are easy to reshape and adapt once they are drawn or written, or have been articulated in some form.

If you find yourself daydreaming, this may be exactly what is needed. For creative processing, allow yourself to daydream. You may find the opportunity to step sideways in a quirky new direction. Let your imagination roam without borders until you access a free flow of ideas and then let it roam some more.

Ensure you set a timer, or make an arrangement with another person to pull you out of your creative zone after an agreed period. There is a difference between constructive daydreaming and procrastination.

RAT PARK

Maybe just...
one more
sip?

Though they are frequent subjects in laboratory studies, rats and mice are not humans. Whenever we see studies involving rats or mice, we apply a healthy dollop of skepticism. That said, no chapter on context could omit mention of the famous Rat Park experiments, which examined the role of habitat on drug addiction. The experiments match our own experiences helping people beat addictions.

The central question that drug addiction researchers wanted to know, and still want to know after more than 40 years of experimentation, *is what is the neural mechanism by which addiction occurs*? Understanding this is widely regarded (erroneously) as the first step toward breaking the deadly cycle of this enormous problem. The problem with animal experiments, though, is the influence of environment or context.[14-15]

Bruce Alexander and a team of Canadian researchers wanted to explore the question. They had a hunch that social isolation and environmental enrichment played a significant role in addiction. They took a rather novel approach. Rather than isolating their test subjects in tiny cages with little to no stimulation or enrichment, they created Rat Park, a veritable Disneyland for their rodent research assistants.

In the park, rats could freely move around a space 200 times bigger than typical lab cages. They could interact socially in a mixed-sex colony; they had varied food, water, balls, and wheels for play; there were even places for a little procreation here and there.

They also added a feature you definitely wouldn't find at Disneyland: the rats had unlimited access to morphine (the precursor to heroin and other derivatives that are abused).[16-20]

They kept some of the rats in smaller cages and gave them identical access to the morphine. Some rats lived in isolation in Rat Prison for the duration of the study, some enjoyed Rat Park for the entire time. Some started off in prison and were let into Rat Park after 65 days, and some in Rat Park were rounded up by the whitecoats and sent to prison after enjoying the park for 65 days (surely not the retirement they had hoped for).

The prison rats drank a stunning 19 times more morphine solution than males living in Rat Park. The park rats tried a little tipple of morphine here and there but otherwise mostly ignored it. The females in Rat Park tried the morphine more than males, but on the whole, all of the park rats preferred tap water.

When the Canadian Senate convened to discuss Canada's opiate epidemic, Alexander discussed his findings with the senators. He focused on one of the more interesting aspects of his study. Rats that were raised in cages and then transferred to the park ignored the morphine solution in its stronger form, but they fell for more diluted morphine mixtures, especially as the sugar content rose. [21]

Alexander concluded that they wanted this sweet mixture of sugar and morphine, but only when the drug's effects did not disrupt their normal social behavior. Being socially connected in a stimulating environment was more

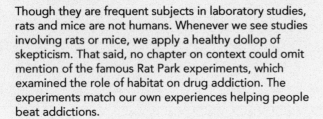

Urgh Man, I'm
WAAAASTED!

rewarding to the rats than getting high. This changed the dominant narrative of addiction.[22]

It is now recognized that social isolation and environmental characteristics are important factors in drug addiction. Alexander argues that drug abuse is a way to cope with chronic distress. It's more of a response to our environment than any intrinsic neuropharmacological dependence.[16,20]

Follow-up studies have successfully replicated the concepts behind Rat Park. Although some details have not been reproduced, the emerging weight of evidence supports the idea that, when given the choice between opiates and social interaction, rats choose the latter, preferring abstinence to addiction.[23-30] The search for neural mechanisms that cause addiction continues. So far, nothing has turned up that has significantly impacted clinical treatment, and there is far more success by changing the context to create more choices for people to find their own way out of addiction.[15,31]

In 2018, 46,802 Americans died from opioid overdoses.[32]

In 2015 tobacco and alcohol use cost the human population more than a quarter of a billion disability-adjusted life years, with illicit drugs costing further tens of millions.[33]

IF RATS CAN CHOOSE, SO CAN WE

We know that drug abuse is less about neurochemical addiction than it is about relief from distress.

All drugs, whether opiates, alcohol, cigarettes, or prescription medications offer some form of positive benefit.

Sometimes, like the rats in Rat Park, addicts realize how much more the drug is taking than it is giving, and this provides enough motivation to stop. Unfortunately, rates of drug abuse, the cycle of abuse and abstinence, and the frequently fatal end to this cycle, all indicate that this is insufficient.

A successful intervention needs to create conditions where the positively intended benefits, such as relief from distress, are provided by something other than narcotics.

Some of the other benefits of drug use we have uncovered in interviews with clients include:

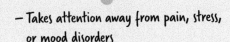

- Takes attention away from pain, stress, or mood disorders
- Relieves boredom
- Gives a feel-good high
- Shared social experience
- Helps cope with the pressures of work
- It's easier to go along with friends and family than buck their expectations.
- Confidence booster
- Helps forget painful memories
- It's cool/counterculture, and a part of identity.
- Enables creativity
- Quiets destructive self-talk

These forms of relief are virtually identical for other addictions, such as overeating, gambling, adrenaline sports, or sex.

One important reason that treatments commonly fail to break addiction is that they're often viewed as complicated problems to be solved, rather than complex patterns of behavior that are embedded within context.

In the reductionist approach, there is a focus on the problem. Addiction is viewed as a behavior to "stop doing." However, nothing is provided to fill the hole in the addict's life. They have no equivalent alternative that meets the underlying benefit of the addictive behavior. Treating practitioners are viewed as experts that identify causation and prescribe a treatment (or incarceration). This sets up a problem-remedy loop. Addicts stop for a while, but don't get their intentions met (like relief from distress), and they're back to their old habit again. Until they can identify an outcome and a pathway to that outcome, they are stuck in the vicious cycle, with an external locus of agency that relies on experts to somehow get them out.

In a holistic approach, the addict is viewed as the expert of their own ecosystem dynamics. Other perspectives (expert or otherwise) may or may not be useful. The approach recognizes that the problem is complex. Addiction is seen as a pattern that provides a combination of benefits and painful consequences for the individual and others embedded within a wider context, such as family or community.

In much the same way that individuals usually have agency to change their workplace environments, the addict has a choice to change their context.

If you are attempting to break the cycle of addiction, we recommend a two-pronged approach:

Develop resilient strategies that provide more positive forms of relief from distress, social isolation, boredom, etc.

AND

Either manage the context or remove yourself from it.

Unlike rats in cages (or, for that matter, in parks), most of us have the power to either change our context or remove ourselves entirely. This is not to say such a transition will be easy or without risk. For instance, it could involve severing ties with family and friends and developing new social networks. That's hard enough for people without addiction issues.

Importantly, hoping to identify and fix a single cause of addiction is an error. Instead, we need to very carefully design constraints (barriers and that make drug taking more difficult) and attractors (viable alternatives to addiction). This approach can be applied by ourselves or by society more generally.

Constraints, such as incarceration, are the most common way of managing drug addiction, and they are rarely as effective as identifying attractors. The so-called War on Drugs has failed.[34] Incarceration rates for taking drugs are at an all-time high.

THE FAILED WAR ON DRUGS

Around the world, there are roughly 11 million people in prison at any given time.[34-37] Many of these are addicts:

- Around half of prisoners take illicit drugs behind bars.
- Restricted access to illicit drugs means they often take more dangerous drugs, also administering them in more dangerous ways, such as injection.
- Recidivism rates (reoffending on release) are commonly 30–40% and as high as 70% in some jurisdictions, with drug offenses being the commonest form of recidivism.

Prisons are clearly not places for rehabilitation — quite the opposite. Drug-taking behavior in prisons makes sense in the context of Rat Park. The addict is seeking relief from distress, and what could be more distressing than imprisonment?

Instead of a poor and overly simplified solution (incarceration) to a complex problem, we need a health focus on well-being with environmental enrichment and strong social connection to networks that extend into communities. It is critical to offer alternatives to reimmersion back into a drug-culture.

Evidence shows that a focus on the threat of incarceration to dissuade drug-taking has failed in the same way that prohibition in 1930s America failed to reduce alcohol consumption.

By contrast, decriminalization of drugs (for users, not dealers) can lead to a decline in addiction, overdose mortality, transmissible diseases like HIV and hepatitis, and casual use.[38] Fatalities from drug overdose in the United States where incarceration is used as a deterrent are around 312 per million.[39] In Portugal, where drugs are treated as a social health issue, only 6 people per million die from drug overdoses each year. [38]

The evidence-based approach that works for all kinds of addictions recognizes that individuals are embedded in complex environments. We can both choose how we respond to context and also shape context to be more favorable to us. We can also change context entirely, although sometimes we might need to gradually transition into and out of challenging habitats.

ON THE INSIDE

NIYAH SMITH

is a British musician, producer, songwriter, engineer, consultant, artist manager, A&R manager, events manager, and entrepreneur. He co-founded Richouse Entertainment, and is the marketing consultant at Hot Money Digital. Smith is best known for managing Shauna Shadae and Jade Silvia.

I originally grew up in Hackney, London. It was the slums back then and rough, a ghetto, and you just didn't want to live there, unlike now. There were a lot of drugs and violence, a lot of…. what you wouldn't want your children to see.

I grew up mostly just me and my mum. Dad's been there, but not been there, if that makes sense? I have an older brother but the generation gap was too big for us to spend much time together.

Being in the wrong crowd meant that, of course, something would come around and that's how I ended up going to prison in 2012. It wasn't like I was even doing so many bad things in life. Prior to going to prison I never had any convictions. I was playing a lot of tennis. I used to study hard, but my friends were gang members and I got caught up in that crossfire during that time, which made me learn a massive, massive lesson.

They wanted me to come on a long journey, they didn't tell me what it was about. Turned out they were getting a firearm and had that in the car. Nobody wants to admit it was theirs, of course. So four of us ended up going down for it based on joint enterprise. The firearm was actually in the vehicle rather than in anyone's possession, but we still all went to prison.

I was 19. When you've grown up with friends, you just don't grass. If you did, you'd lose everyone. I would still pick the route that I did. I went to prison for nearly five years. That's better than being known as a grass for 10, 15, or 20 years, you're always going to be known as that. So it's something that I would never do.

I never had problems in prison. A lot of people have fights every week, ending up in "the block," which is where you don't have any privileges, no TV and restricted movements around the prison. In nearly five years I had no problems, because I just wanted to get on with it. I knew I was away, I was not getting out and I just felt like the best thing to do is make the most or my time.

A TV, on the outside, you barely even watch it. But in prison it's like gold. You don't want to lose it. Imagine sitting in your room with no phone and no TV for 23 hours a day, with no family or outside friends.

Upon arriving I said to myself, you're here, you're going to be here for the next four years. It's now up to you how you adapt to your current situation without driving yourself mad. The quick way to become depressed is wake every day and say, "Oh, I'm in prison, I can't wait to get out!" Better to say, "Okay cool, I'm in prison, but what can I do? What milestones can I set myself? What targets can I set for three months' time, like getting qualified on a course?" It's no different to the outside. Set yourself goals, do lots of different courses, and keep busy and don't become depressed about being inside. Small things, like not having a phone or being able to call someone, that's hard at first. You realize how much you've lost. I've had a phone for years and then it's just gone!

You never get a second chance to make a first impression. I'm a very calm, humble, respectful person. I don't pretend to be the dog's bollocks, I'm not a gangster, I'm not a wannabe rich person. That all made for

"You never know how much freedom you've got until you lose it. Freedom is priceless."

an easy run. Prison is very territorial. People come in their first week and get into a fight or they come and make a bad reputation immediately. Some say, just keep yourself to yourself and don't speak to anyone, just do your own thing, but that's hard to do.

You're not in a working environment where you go to an office from 9:00 AM to 5:00 PM, and have 20 desks with your other colleagues and may not have to talk to each other. With prison, you're pretty much amongst the same people all the time. Eventually you're going to start having conversations, because that's what you do.

In prison I obtained a Heavy Goods Vehicle driving license. As much as I wanted to go straight into music, I needed to pay the bills whilst I was on my music course. The music industry is no easy run. You might not make any money from it for the first three to five years. Within two weeks of getting out, I had a paying job as a driver. I was then able to juggle both work and my music career.

I used my time inside to learn a lot about the technical sides of management, copyrights and record and publishing deals, and radio and press and PR and so forth. I'm fortunate to have a record label job, but I still do the driving work, three, four nights a week.

I manage two female artists. One I signed to the record label that I work for, and the other I manage and take care of her calendar, emails, sorting the studio, the mixing, the mastering, the radio plugin, photography, shooting the videos, marketing the videos. Some artists want to get on radio, but don't know how. Some want to get to another artist to collaborate, but don't know how, some people want to get into the magazines, but they don't know. I play the role for all of that.

I was inside for nearly five years. In the same amount of time from now, I want to be a head of Artists and Repertoire of a major label record department. I'll be overseeing all artists' releases across the label, which I think is realistic. I've done

a lot of case studies of people who I look up to, who are very good friends of mine in the industry.

Coming from where I come from, there's not always success stories — not from Hackney! We had no money, no real support from my father's side. For me to have been where I've been, to where I am now, I felt like it's even more rewarding than someone who has had a decent upbringing, who has had both parents around, who wasn't brought up in a ghetto.

I feel like it's more rewarding, even for someone like me who has been through all of that, we can call it trauma in a way, depends how you want to perceive it... And yeah, so for me, I just feel like it's even doubly rewarding. Some people around my area don't even make it to age 25. I'm blessed to be where I live, have a family, have a great job, and a future.

You never know how much freedom you've got until you lose it. Freedom is priceless.

LEAVE YOUR BAGGAGE AT THE DOORSTEP

Carryover (also known as spillover)[40] is like finishing a cup of coffee and using the unwashed mug in a wine tasting. The subtleties of the wine will be overwhelmed by the strong flavor of the coffee, quite possibly until inebriation.

Carryover is what we're referencing when we say we have arrived in a relationship with baggage. States, behaviors, expectations, and experiences in one context are carried into another where they clearly don't belong.[41-43]

Some people never put down their baggage. They carry it from relationship to relationship, from context to context. Perhaps the most common carryover refers to the transfer from a work context to a family context, although the reverse also occurs.

Examples of carryover include constantly checking in at work instead of being present for important family events; being preoccupied with a hobby or interest at the expense of relationships; or ruminating on a conflict from work in a way that interferes with our sleep. This is particularly problematic for frontline workers, who frequently bring hyper-aroused or hyper-vigilant states across contextual boundaries.

Of course, carryover isn't only a negative effect. Getting a raise, promotion, or positive feedback at work can all support happiness, which could be carried into an otherwise unhappy home life.[44-47] Or take the case of the hyper-vigilant off-duty law enforcement officer who, when out with friends, correctly detects the very earliest patterns of threat from a potential mugger.

For long-term resilience and well-being, choice over the state we experience in different contexts is key. Preventing carryover is the first step in preventing crossover — where one person's negative response to a work situation is picked up by their intimate partners. Your anxiety, stress, or burnout becomes their anxiety, stress, or burnout.[41-43,48,49]

Crossover is particularly likely when the individual pays extremely close attention to the feelings of others, in what we would describe as an overdone second position. Such crossover is sometimes incorrectly described as a kind of contagion.[48] This is a poor metaphor for what is happening. Emotional transference is not like a virus, and it cannot be caught like the flu. A simple step out to third person/observer position, or even something as minor as a subtle shift in posture, can be enough to allow someone else's emotional transmission to pass you by.

Regardless of how others might respond to our carryover states, we can make life easier for them by selecting how we place our attention to manage the transition between contexts.

Similar to a palate cleanser between different-tasting food or drink, we offer a way to move between different contexts, using what we call the doorstep pattern.

For many people, the doorstep is the natural transition point between contexts. It doesn't have to be a doorstep, though. You can choose any location or anchor. It might be the locker room at work or at the gym. It might be a time signal, perhaps when the bell goes off signaling the end of a shift. It might be your after-work shower, or it might be the moment when you change from your uniform into regular clothes. Some people use the doorstep pattern when they step on to public transport or when they mount their bicycle to pedal home. Others use it just before they pick up the kids. The doorstep in these instances is just a metaphor. Create the doorstep wherever you choose.

When crossing these transitional thresholds, your aim is to consciously or unconsciously switch from one role or identity into another: from police officer to mother; from wife to business partner; from friend to colleague; from activist to father, etc.

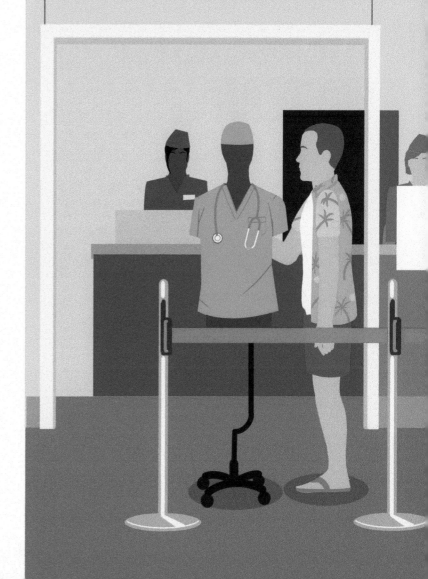

Left Baggage

ACTIVITY

THE DOORSTEP PATTERN

Initially, the doorstep process may take a few minutes to establish. The idea is to embed a routine that, with practice, will enable you to make smooth transitions almost instantaneously and with no conscious effort. Some of the steps are described in more detail in Chapter 4 — State.

Begin by identifying which transition you would like to clean up. Where or what is your version of the doorstep?

Step 1.

BODY SCAN:

Locate problematic elements of state, such as tension or poor posture, that are associated with your response to the outgoing context, such as work.

Relax, shake it out, and let go.

Notice where you are carrying tension. Loosen that part of your body.

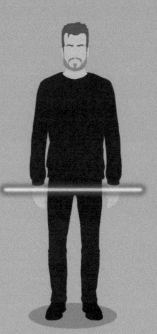

Step 2.

BOX BREATHING:

Repeat until your breathing is regular and posture is relaxed.

You can box breathe whilst body scanning. Keep using it until you have switched off the outgoing state.

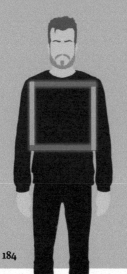

Step 3a.

OBSERVE AND CHECK:

Step back and go into a third position. See yourself standing on the threshold.

From this observing position, ask: **Is he/she ready to cross the threshold and transition into this new context?** If the answer is yes, go to **Step 4**.

If elements of the old state persist, such as tension or lingering thoughts, ask: **What resources does he/she need to cross that threshold?**

Is there an open loop of some kind? Is there unfinished business? Is there a task you have to complete before fully transitioning? If so, either do it or commit to do it at a specified time.

You might need more time to process or decompress events. A walk or some physical activity might help.

Step 3b.

RESPOND TO SIGNALS:

Sometimes, there is a lingering, nagging sensation. This can be the result of a recurring pattern at work that is bothering you, or someone may have cut across your values. It might be a deeper question like *what's it all for?*

These nagging sensations are often signals that we need a dramatic change, perhaps a new career, or a change in our personal lives. Pay particularly close attention to when and how these signals manifest. You may need to commit to a significant change before a clean transition into the new context becomes possible.

Step 4.

ENTER YOUR NEW CONTEXT:

Take one final observation from the third position. You might have dropped off the old state, but have you picked up a new one? Are you ready for what's coming next?

You might choose to deliberately build a new state that is ready for action in the next context.

Finally, step back into first position. Cross the threshold.

INTERCONNECTEDNESS

While the doorstep pattern can help you drop *your* baggage, it can be challenging to get others to do the same.

We know from the research into mirror neurons that humans are biologically predisposed to match the states/emotions and actions of others. Most people who empathize with the struggles of others will know what this crossover effect, in the moment, is like.

Lifestyle choices, including whom you partner with, whether you marry, where you live, and whom you associate with, can all influence our lives either profoundly or subtly. For the most part, these are complex interactions that influence us, but they never cause us to behave in a particular way. We have a choice of how we respond, provided we are aware of what's happening.

This depends upon situational awareness, which is a state of alertness to what is salient in context at a moment in time, what is emerging, and what might be on the horizon.

Ideally, of course, we would make predictions and then prepare for what the future will bring. Sometimes we can do a reasonably good job with prediction, but in complex systems, there is always uncertainty and feedback from our interaction in the system.

The 2020 Global Risks Report by the World Economic Forum (WEF) begins by noting how interconnected risks are being felt:

"The growing palpability of shared economic, environmental and societal risks signals that the horizon has shortened for preventing — or even mitigating — some of the direst consequences of global risks. It is sobering that in the face of this development, when the challenges before us demand immediate collective action, fractures within the global community appear to only be widening."[50]

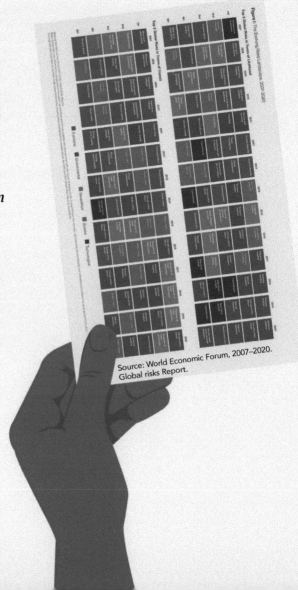

Source: World Economic Forum, 2007–2020. Global risks Report.

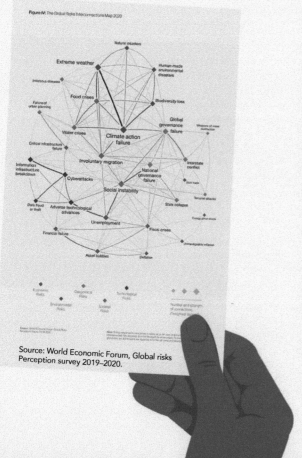

Figure IV: The Global Risks Interconnections Map 2020

Source: World Economic Forum, Global risks Perception survey 2019–2020.

For 2020, the authors identified *climate action failure* linking to *extreme weather* as the most critical and impactful possibility. The dominant trend in their risk analysis between 2007 and 2020 is from economic and societal risks such as *pandemics* and *chronic disease* in the years 2007–2010, to *environmental risks* with *weapons of mass destruction* and *water crises* in the years 2017–2020.

You'll notice a glaring error in this projected trend. The risk of a global outbreak like Covid-19 didn't even crack the top five in recent years. It's not that pandemics aren't considered in the report; they just weren't expected to be as problematic as other issues in 2020.

This reflects a critical weakness in using the likelihood-consequences approach to forecast risk for complex global systems. We simply cannot predict the future in such a way. In the words of Taleb:

"I know that history is going to be dominated by an improbable event, I just don't know what that event will be."[51]

The *Global Risks Report* also highlights that we, as individuals, are embedded in context. At the local level there is much we can do to create or influence the environment around us, especially the people we associate with, where we work, and how we recreate.

Those hyper-local contexts are themselves embedded in regional, national, and global systems. Our choices, actions, interactions, relationships, place of being, and every process and thing that we include in our life are deeply connected and have an impact.

Small changes can become larger ones as they radiate outwards. Context is connected to context ad infinitum.

The Covid-19 pandemic highlights that we cannot predict the future with certainty. Given this uncertainty, we should not prepare *exclusively* for one risk or another. In addition to preparing for the possible risks, we need to prepare in a generic way for plausible risks. This is one of the benefits of developing resilience throughout life.

IT'S A JUNGLE OUT THERE

It's perhaps not surprising that so many metaphors for risk, opportunity, and change come from nature. The idea of natural selection and biological evolution has been known since 1859, when Darwin brought the idea to the attention of the world in his best-selling book, *On the Origin of Species.*[52]

Perhaps less well known is the application of selection to non-reproducing, higher-level systems including ecosystems or societies. Natural selection can be based solely on differential persistence involving biotic as well as abiotic self-replicating patterns. Ecosystem examples include coral reefs, rainforests, and savannahs. Societal examples include agricultural systems, dominant belief systems, culture, and economies.[53] However, unlike systems in nature that evolve through random mutation and serendipity, humans have a unique capability to imagine the future and influence or design our environments.

Unfortunately, many people wander aimlessly through life, oblivious to evolution of all sorts, and with no sense of personal responsibility or ownership of the future they help to create.

In the cautionary tale of *Animal Farm*, written by George Orwell in 1945, farm animals rebel against their unkind human masters. They initially create a society based on equality and freedom. However, the ideals of the rebellion are betrayed, and step by incremental step, the farm slides into a form of dictatorship.

The fable reflects events leading up to the Russian Revolution of 1917 and then on into the Stalinist era of the Soviet Union. The metaphor transcends left or right politics, alerting us to the perils of collective inaction. There are early signals of manipulation and unwanted change, but the animals ignore these weak signals.

Like Orwell, we urge caution and alertness to context. Our environment can slowly change around us. Ignore these signals and you may one day find yourself trapped. Something that started as a preferred habitat might evolve into an environment that is far from benign.

Other animal metaphors also serve us well in situational assessment of context.

The metaphor of the black swan came to popular attention via Nassim Taleb, whose book *Black Swan: The Impact of the Highly Improbable* was a smash success when it was released in 2007. He named the book after a common phrase given to us by the Roman poet Juvenal in the second century AD: "A good friend," he said, "is as rare as a black swan."

By the seventeenth century, the black swan was a stand-in for something that was virtually impossible. Nobody in the West had ever seen a black swan, so it was assumed that they simply didn't exist. This misconception was dispelled in 1697 when Dutch explorers became the first Europeans to see black swans in Western Australia.[54] Thanks to Taleb, the black swan is now a stand-in, not for the impossible, but rather for the unexpected. He argues in favor of preparation for the unexpected.

"To make a decision you need to focus on the consequences (which you can know) rather than the probability (which you can't know)."[51]

Some people have mistakenly described Covid-19 as a black swan event. Others rightly identify that Pandemics have recurred throughout human history with devastating consequences. Some argue that pandemics are more like the elephant in the room. Another animal metaphor for risk, meaning that there is an obvious problem or difficult situation that people do not want to acknowledge.

Then there is the more recent metaphor of a gray rhino. Michele Wucker coined the term and is the author of *The Gray Rhino: How to Recognize and Act on the Obvious Dangers We Ignore*.[55] The metaphor alludes to the large obvious event that's coming right at you.

"The gray rhino is a metaphor designed to help us pay fresh attention to what's obvious and ideally to create the kind of emotional connection that people had with black swan. The black swan did a great job in getting people to realize that they couldn't predict everything, but it has been misused and people have used it as a cop-out. 'Oh, nobody saw it coming!'

The gray rhino is more dynamic. It's a metaphor for missing the big, obvious event that's coming at us. And the important part is that it provides choices: either you get trampled, or you get out of the way, or you hop on the back of the rhino and use the crisis as an opportunity."[56]

It goes without saying, failing to respond to a charging rhino is not a resilient strategy.

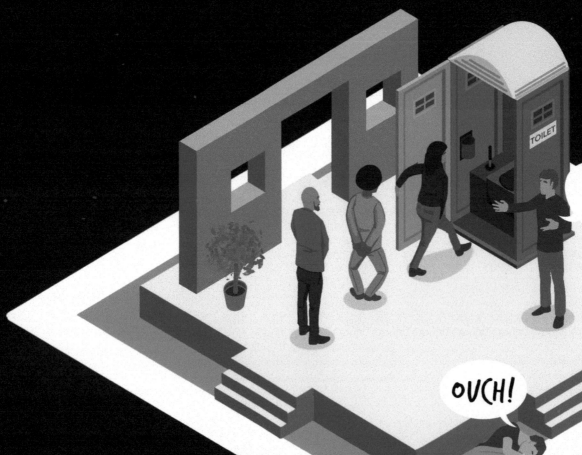

SIGNALS

DOT DOT DOT DASH DASH DASH DOT DOT DOT

"Brains evolved many millions of years after bodies did, to support bodies. Once bodies had brains, they changed so body and brain could interact and adapt to each other. Not only does the brain send signals to the body to influence it; the body sends signals to the brain to affect it as well, and thus there is a constant, two-way communication between them."[1]

— Dr. Norman Doidge

We develop and expand the concept of signaling between brain and body in line with the 4E Concept of Cognition, where mind is:

- **Embodied** throughout the whole person
- **Embedded** in context
- **Enacted,** by shaping and being shaped, through a dynamic interaction with the world
- **Extended** into our physical and social environment[2,3]

From our expanded description of mind, it's clear there is more than just two-way communication between brain and body. There is no "and." Rather, there are embodied brains (multiple) that are deeply connected to our peripheral nervous system and to our microbiome, even beyond what is usually considered *human* or part of us.

It is important to appreciate that signaling involves involuntary expressions through the senses — especially felt sensations and movements. These often come in the form of symbolic representations, that usually go unnoticed by the conscious "us," although sometimes they are apparent to others who are observant!

Like learning any new, unfamiliar language, signals can at first appear confusing or difficult to understand. Like the bad joke of the English tourist abroad, we must remember that speaking louder does not make communication between two different cultures and languages any clearer.

Pain and stress are prime examples of signals that are easily misunderstood, and both are known to shout louder and louder when ignored.

A DISTRESS SIGNAL IS INTERNATIONALLY RECOGNIZED AS A CALL FOR HELP

In Chapter 4, we discussed Professor Kelly McGonigal's famous lecture, in which she suggested that Americans die prematurely, not from stress itself, but from the belief that stress is bad for you.[4,5]

Acknowledging this possibility, we present a more obvious interpretation: the people in the study McGonigal cited failed to act on a clear signal that was in fact inherently harmful when ignored. However, we agree that beliefs can induce either the placebo effect (make yourself well) or the nocebo effect (make yourself ill). Both placebo and nocebo effects are mediated by diverse neurophysiological processes that are activated by signaling consciously and unconsciously held beliefs. Placebo/nocebo effects are far more than individual self-reports or perceptions such as pain or mood (not to denigrate these important states).[6–9]

Researchers have found that the placebo/nocebo involves a wide range of physiological, biochemical, and microbial processes. Multiple brain systems, neurochemicals such as naturally produced opioids and dopamine, as well as other epigenetic factors that can essentially activate or block our predisposition for wellness or illness, are all implicated. Placebo has been shown to improve life expectancy in those suffering from cardiovascular disease; it can also be seen in autonomic responses through electroencephalogram monitoring (EEG) of the brain; it's been documented in immunosuppression/enhancement through neuroendocrine biochemical changes; it can increase or decrease inflammation, as well as improve heart-rate variability after experiences of stress.[10-17]

The important point in all of this is that activating the placebo or nocebo occurs through a form of communication that is not straightforward or literal. It's not as simple as just asking the placebo to get on with the job, although that might be a useful start. In addition, a two-way translation needs to take place, between one form of communication and another. The placebo effect needs to be activated at the unconscious level of state, with the neurological, physiological, biochemical, and microbiological systems engaged in the self-healing process.

The statement that "the belief that stress is bad for you and could lead to premature death" is plausible. However, this needs to be considered alongside the more obvious interpretation that stress is a signal to pay attention and take action.

In structured interviews, we've discovered that people experience stress in vastly different ways and in response to a wide range of stimuli. At its simplest reduction, most people can innately tell whether the state they describe as stress is "good-stress" (eustress), or "bad stress" (distress).

Persistent distress is the type of stress associated with cardiovascular constriction, high blood pressure, and increased heart rate. It is frequently associated with cardiovascular disease such as stroke, heart attack, and a host of other illnesses. Many of these conditions lead to early death.[18-20]

Distress might be a reasonably well-adapted, short-term response to threat (though there are preferable states, such as flow), but it is ultimately a signal to act.

Sadly, many people ignore these signals — even when these internal distress calls are being picked up by those around them. Some go to extreme lengths to tune these signals out — even to the point of medicating them away.

It's like sticking your head in the sand whilst firing a distress flare. Others can see what you cannot.

DON'T MADICATE THE MESSENGER

The danger when attempting to use pharmaceuticals or other mood-altering chemicals to manage states like stress, anxiety, or depression is that they dampen a well-intended signal. They may temporarily remove the unpleasant feelings, but they do nothing to address the multiple relational factors that make up an individual's life.

The distress signals that we're describing here are transmitted from the unconscious, and we need to use all our senses to receive and interpret such messages. We can't do that when the signals are suppressed or ignored. We especially can't pick up on these signals when we're in a drug-induced fog.

Other side effects can also be significant, and, while there is evidence for the efficacy of prescription medications, this evidence is strongly biased in favor of those who profit from selling pharmaceutical remedies.[21,22]

In his book *Bad Pharma*, Ben Goldacre describes several studies that evaluate the efficacy of drugs based on whether they were independently undertaken or sponsored by drug companies. From thousands of trials and hundreds of drugs, Goldacre documents systematic reporting bias, missing data, statistical jiggery-pokery, and collusion on a global scale.

The impact of over-prescribing could be even more insidious. In *Anatomy of an Epidemic: Magic Bullets, Psychiatric Drugs, and the Astonishing Rise of Mental Illness in America*, Robert Whitaker documents how, since the psychiatric pharmaceutical revolution in the 1950s, mental illness has become more prevalent, not less. How can this be? With all the advances in modern medicine, shouldn't mental health in Western countries be significantly better than it was before these advances?

Whitaker believes that modern psychiatric drugs are doing more harm than good. He argues they exacerbate rather than alleviate a wide range of conditions including mood disorders such as stress, trauma, and anxiety. His concern is that these medications are causing changes in the brain in ways that one-off or episodic and potentially manageable disorders become chronic and severe disabilities. In some cases, he notes, suicide rates and severe harm have risen.

Whitaker coins a new term for the drug-induced, systemic decline in mental well-being in countries like America: madication. His play on words seems to be supported by a study published in the Harvard Data Science Review in 2019. Using a statistical surveillance methodology of medical claims from 2003–2014 for over 150 million

people who consumed 922 different drugs, the review tracked the association between prescription medication and 43,978 suicidal events in America. They found that ten commonly prescribed drugs including alprazolam (common trade name Xanax, used to treat anxiety and panic attacks), butalbital, hydrocodone (opiod used to treat pain), and codeine/promethazine mixtures were strongly correlated with suicide risk. [23]

Whilst the study methodology was unable to determine causation, the large population and powerful dataset supports other studies, as well as abundant anecdotal evidence, that lead us to the same conclusion: drugs prescribed to treat stress, anxiety, depression, and trauma often make matters worse.[21,22,24]

Even relatively innocuous self-administered medications, like over-the-counter paracetamol (acetaminophen), can subtly change the way we receive and respond to signals that are critical for incorporating felt sensations into consideration of risk or well-being. A 2020 study using three double-blind, placebo-controlled experiments found that paracetamol increased risk-taking behavior.[25] This makes sense when we consider what we know about signals. If pain is associated with a strong signal away from perceived threat (the pain), and we reduce our capacity

to experience pain signals, then *any* decision-making that may have significant downside consequences could also be influenced.

Similar studies have begun looking at the effects of caffeine on decision-making, especially where people are consuming high-caffeine, high-sugar energy drinks.[26,27]

Food, medications, and other drugs can block the signaling between different parts of the body, disrupting the entire embodied thinking process. Our embodied sense of concern or alertness to risk has been described as being like a "faint whisper of emotion."[28] Or, as we prefer to describe it, without attaching an emotional label, a "weak signal."

If you are taking medications to remove unpleasant states or conditions like chronic stress, anxiety, or trauma, and if these medications are not working well for you, be careful transitioning off them, as they can induce a rebound effect. Work carefully with your treating practitioner to gradually taper, and use your own internal self-calibration and signals to guide your withdrawal, always with an appreciation for what positive intent the drugs were satisfying and how that same intent can be satisfied with lifestyle choices that have less downside than drugs.[29-32]

THAT FEELING INSIDE

Sensory signals have provided life-saving information throughout the evolution of our species.[28,33] Disrupting the signals that alert us to risk — signals we evolved long ago to safeguard us from predators on the African plains — should come with an obvious warning.

It's evident to most that drugs and alcohol lower or even obliterate our ability to make reasonable decisions, which is why driving under the influence of drugs and alcohol is banned in most countries. The social impact of impaired decision-making associated with drugs and alcohol is well established, with crime and domestic violence sitting at the top of the list of undesired consequences.[34-37]

These sorts of impairments are obvious. However, many of us miss the more subtle effects of what we ingest. We're being warned about these effects, but the signals are often weak. This means we need to develop a more nuanced awareness of signals, and/or amplify the signal.

We invite you to recall a *pleasant* experience from your past.

Take a moment to immerse yourself in the memory. See and hear this memory as though you were back in the experience, inhabiting your body and perspective. Spend at least thirty seconds in this first-position recall.

How was it?

We invited you to inhabit a pleasant memory from your past. As you associated with that memory, accompanying sensations, or signals of "pleasant" would have likely made themselves known to your conscious awareness. It is these sensations that inform us the experience has a pleasant value of some kind and that we might desire to seek more of it.

We can see how, if we recall a mildly unpleasant memory, the signals will be different. Rather than drawing us back for more, the message is more likely to be: stay away.

Our unconscious is constantly sending messages to direct us toward what we need and away from threats.

Some signals are obvious and self-evident, others more subtle or idiosyncratic.

TIRED OR BORED?

Tiredness is usually an obvious sign that we need to rest or sleep. The signals might be heavy eyelids, excessive blinking, dry eyes, heavy shoulders, and, of course, yawning.

Hunger, when not confused with other signals, such as boredom, thirst, or loneliness, is a signal that our body requires fuel.

When feeling cold, the signal is clear. We are being exposed to external elements that are lowering our body temperature, so we should either wrap up or get indoors.

Boredom could be a signal that we're not being challenged or utilizing our skill set in some way, or that we've become habitually overstimulated, like a kid who needs a screen to sit still long enough to eat a few mouthfuls of dinner.

The importance of noticing and appreciating our signals cannot be overstated.

Stick your head underwater. You'll almost immediately start receiving a signal to breathe. The longer you remain underwater, the more difficult it becomes to ignore this signal. It's our way of trying to survive. Other signals are doing something similar, and yet, we ignore so many of them.

If you've ever asked someone if they're hungry, only to see them look at their watch to know if it's lunchtime, then you've probably seen someone out of tune with their internal signal system. Hunger has nothing to do with a set time in your schedule; it's a signal that tells of a biological need.

What signals do you ignore?

Take a minute to note down three contexts in which you have ignored signals, then identify the positive and negative consequences that come with ignoring each of them.

When we act upon or override signals there are invariably both positive and negative consequences. For instance, you may be dog-tired and desperate for bed, but you know that, if you push aside those signals of exhaustion for another hour, you will be able to complete the task, ease pressure from tomorrow's workload, and go to bed with a signal of satisfaction.

Context: Sports Injury

Ignored Signal: that niggle in my calf, that I just knew at the time, meant I should rest

- Consequence: I tore my achilles

+ Consequence: I didn't complain to my coach who expected me to train

Context: I got robbed

Ignored Signal: "Suspicion" … I felt a tingle in my spine

- Consequence: Lost a little money to a con man

+ Consequence: I avoided offending him, based on a poorly defined feeling I had

Context: I've put on weight

Ignored Signal: "Hunger"

- Consequence: I became ravenous and binged on food when I took breaks from long periods of work

+ Consequence: I finished my project by pushing on through

You might wake up each morning dreading the thought of arriving at the office. You push these feelings aside because you know that bills have to be paid. Perhaps putting up with the job is better than the fear of insecurity from being out of work, so you accept and keep the dread until you can find an alternative job.

This assumes that you acknowledge the signal and comprehend its intent. Many people sleepwalk through life, oblivious to the various well-intended signals that are generated within us every day.

WHEN THERE'S NO LINE IN THE SAND?

A line in the sand is a metaphor for a boundary or threshold that is clear and obvious. If you cross *this* boundary, then *that* will happen. As an example, in many monogamous relationships, having an affair is a line in the sand. If the line is crossed, then the consequence is an end to the relationship.

Many more relationships break down, not from a single act of infidelity but rather many factors combining in some way. In complex situations such as these, decision-making is often more intuitive than rational.

"An intuition is neither caprice nor a sixth sense but a form of unconscious intelligence."

— Gerd Gigerenzer

In *Gut Feelings: The Intelligence of the Unconscious*, Professor Gerd Gigerenzer explains that intuition is actually our unconscious embodied thinking responding to complex patterns in the external world.[38]

Intuition enables us to respond when urgency and/or complexity require more than logic and analytical thinking. Our unconscious recognizes the need and sends us a signal that we typically call intuition. Often the pattern is not explicit, and the message is rarely precise. Instead, responses are often heuristic (also known as rules-of-thumb) that allow us to respond quickly to patterns in our environment. Fight, flight, or freeze are widely studied examples that many animals use.

We might, for instance, experience a strong "no/don't do it" signal when, walking alone at night, we turn down a dark alley to take a shortcut.

Not all dark alleys are dangerous places with criminals lurking in the shadows. If we analyzed data from all dark alleys the world over, the numbers would probably be on the side of such places being mostly safe. We're probably safe stepping off a well-lit road, but our intuition suggests otherwise in this *type* of context.

In the world of real consequences, not one analyzed minutely with the help of charts and graphs, a simple heuristic could be, "Don't be alone in a dark alley where escape is difficult." Arriving at this conclusion could be rational and conscious as you step away from the light. What is more likely, though, is an uneasy signal, possibly triggering you to go back the way you came until you feel safe again.

Neither approach is 100% reliable. However, the benefit of rapid, unconscious pattern detection is that many patterns can be compared, either to direct experience or vicariously to patterns in other people's narratives. This enables an ability to scan broadly and quickly for both risks and opportunities.

Returning to our walk home at night, imagine routinely taking that short cut with no adverse consequences.

One day, a surprise signal arises that tells you to avoid a path you have traveled many times before. Maybe your unconscious has detected a subtle change in shadow, or maybe some barely perceptible sound has registered just beneath your conscious perception. Ignore these signals at your peril, especially when the downside of avoiding the shortcut is is probably just a few extra minutes walking in the evening air.

Intuition is especially useful for making decisions when you have a lot of domain-specific experience. A novice skier in the backcountry can't rely on their intuition to keep them out of the path of avalanches. The unconscious needs experience before it can compare patterns in the environment and make relatively accurate predictions based on these patterns. Put a mountain guide with 30+ years of experience on an avalanche-prone mountain and most decisions will be made intuitively, with a side of logic or analysis. In high-risk scenarios when intuition is overridden by logic, the results are often fatal. It's far too easy to talk ourselves out of a hunch with logical arguments, especially when we consciously want something, like getting to the top.

Trust your gut, or your heart, or your big toe for that matter.

We commonly hear or read that the gut or heart is the source of intuitive signals. This might fit with evidence of the gut-heart-brain axis, but in no way are those regions a sole origin or locci for the expression of intuition.

Intuitive signals can arise as physiological sensations anywhere: sounds, images, tastes, smells, or some combination of these, can all be signals from the unconscious. They can be very clear signals (binary yes/no), or they can be less certain. However signals arise, and however distinct they are, it's beneficial to pay attention to what they're telling us.

ACTIVITY

IF YOU'RE NOT QUITE FEELING IT...START WITH YES, NO, OR MAYBE

Step 1.

Find a comfortable spot to sit, away from distractions.

Begin to self-calibrate. Run a full body scan. Release any tension you find.

Breathe in a way that enables relaxation to deepen.

Once you have accessed a relaxed state, identify a scenario (real or imagined) in which you are certain you would receive a strong "no" response. For instance, you might imagine reaching out to stroke a dangerous animal, or you could imagine a child or a loved one approaching a coiled venomous snake.

Step 2.

See and hear as if you are in that context for a few moments. Pay close attention to that choice point, just before you act, where that unconsciously generated signal for "no" is clear to you.

It's important here to ensure the signal is involuntary. You are not trying to consciously force a signal where you think it should arise.

Notice where the "no" signal is in your body. Is it a felt signal, or is it coming to you through another sensory channel? It could be a combination of one or more sensory channels.

Step 3.

Upon identifying the signal and location, touch that part of the body and acknowledge it consciously. A verbal thank you sent from the conscious to the unconscious can help to stabilize the signal.

Stand up, move around, and turn the signal off. Return your attention to the present.

Step 4.

Now repeat the same sequence to generate a "yes" signal. As before, begin with a body scan and breathing. Follow this by identifying a context (real or imagined) in which you know you would have received a strong "yes" signal.

Notice where and how that "yes" signal arises. Touch that part of your body and thank your unconscious for providing the signal.

Step 5.

Stand up, move around, shake your body and return your attention to the present. Repeat the same pattern for "maybe." Maybe is often shorthand for, "I need more information to know how to act."

Step 6.

Once you have identified your involuntary signals, such as muscular movement, feeling, sound, or change in vision, it is important to test that it is involuntary by attempting to re-create the same signal with your conscious intent.

Let's say, for example, your finger moves in a certain way, or you feel a sensation in your chest. Can you consciously repeat the same movement with the same quality of sensation? If you can, this is not a true unconscious signal. Repeat the original steps to elicit a signal that cannot be consciously replicated.

If you cannot make the sensation happen again consciously, you have a verifiable signal. Many people report that they can consciously replicate a movement or response, but importantly, they can tell that it feels different somehow. When that happens, you know you have your signal.

Sometimes the signal is clear: it's either a yes or a no. How easy (and boring!) life would be if all decisions were either yes or no.

WHO LIVES AND WHO DIES IN THE DEATH ZONE?

Climbing Everest is a common metaphor for an almost impossibly difficult task, and for good reason. Most climbers undertake a minimum of six months of regular training. They then spend a further six to eight weeks acclimating themselves to the altitude at Everest base camp.

For some, climbing Everest is about bragging rights. For others, it's the culmination of a lifetime of climbing. To stand on top of the world's tallest mountain can give a person a lifetime of conversations at cocktail parties, but in the Death Zone above 8,000m, adventure stories can quickly turn into horror stories.

On the 10th of May, 1996, eight people died near the summit of Mt. Everest. It was, at the time, the worst accident in the long history of Everest attempts.

The post-incident review identified several cognitive biases that created a cascading series of poor decisions. When you're in the Death Zone, biases can turn deadly. In the 1996 Everest disaster, experienced guides decided to push for the summit even though they knew a storm was coming and that they had passed their return deadline of 2:00 p.m. Many summited two or more hours after the agreed safety turnaround limit.

They pushed on because a number of cognitive biases combined to override prepared decisions that were rationally calculated ahead of time. We assume as well that a number of climbers also overrode their implicit signals to turn back. Eight climbers never returned.

Whether we are planning an Everest ascent or not, we can learn from their mistakes. Many of the same biases are highly relevant to the risks each of us face every day.

The risks of burnout, debilitating trauma, and, in extreme cases, suicide are tangible for anyone who pushes on past their limits or past their turn-around point. What we call the Everest Pattern plays out in countless domains — from romantic relationships to running a business, from investing in the stock market to scaling work projects, from political views and affiliations to high-risk adventures.

The Everest Pattern is different from a line in the sand. Where a line in the sand is for a single criteria, the Everest Pattern is focused on sensing in a continually evolving, dynamic situation, tuning into the external environment and our own internally generated signals.

COGNITIVE BIASES OVERRIDE SIGNALS

SUNK COST

The investment of money (usually in the range of $50–100k) and preparation time for an Everest ascent are enormous. For most climbers, the final push to the summit is a gruelling 15 hours. Many are forced to turn back only a few hundred meters before the summit. When we feel we have invested a great deal in something, we are more inclined to ignore other signals. Examples of a sunk cost could be an investment in education or career, or time spent mentoring someone or developing a work relationship.

Recognize sunk costs and use embodied visualization to rehearse letting it all go.

PEER PRESSURE AND IDENTITY

Peer pressure, the overt and sometimes covert expectation that you "should" get to the top is common in elite sports. It is also common in frontline work, where peer expectations are linked to being a hero. This becomes particularly dangerous when it becomes part of the narrative we tell ourselves about who we are. "I'm not a quitter" or "I'm a winner" can work well in some circumstances and not so well in others. Wrapping up what we do for a living with our sense of identity can be perilous if that involves being a hero against impossible odds.

Identify peer pressure and identity expectations; reframe with a get-out clause.

COMPETITION

In the Everest disaster, two rival guide companies were vying for king of the hill status. Every climber who reached the summit would add to the brand's reputation, so guides were encouraged to do all they could to get climbers to the peak. When it is not safe to fail, safety becomes secondary. Our signals and our fears are both pushed to one side. In everyday life, we sometimes find ourselves competing with others based on status or material wealth. Or we compete with ourselves to a set of internal values.

Be alert to competitiveness; balance the reward against the downside consequences.

The cognitive biases involved in the Everest disaster can teach us valuable lessons about decision-making and resilience.

FAME AND FORTUNE

For many, climbing Everest is no longer about a romantic ideal of adventure in the high peak. Those who have made it to the peak are often rewarded financially with sponsorships or lucrative slots on the talking circuit. We regularly meet professionals who have trapped themselves in a routine of excessive overtime to fund their lifestyles. Whether it's global fame and fortune or recognition in our own sphere of influence, our ego can easily lead us into dangerous territory.

Be aware of your ego and aspirations; know what price you are prepared to pay.

CONFUSION UNDER PRESSURE

In the Death Zone above 8,000m, humans are essentially slowly dying from hypoxia and extreme cold. Thinking becomes muddled, or, as the Everest mountaineer Tim McCartney-Snape describes it: "thoughts become slippery." In many intense situations, and especially in the midst of novel experiences, we need clear unconscious signals for when we cannot rationally think our way through the situation.

Well-established turn-around points and safety rules-of-thumb are helpful, but they cannot replace a clear signal for "no" that has identified a threatening pattern in complex situations.

THE "I'M NEARLY THERE" DELUSION

Sometimes, we think the peak is so close that it is achievable. We tell ourselves that it's just over the next rise, and then just over the one after that. Ignoring signals because you think you are nearly there can be a serious error. This could be the point just before your partner leaves you because of excessive work, the point where your kids greet the dog with more enthusiasm than you when you come home, or it could be the signal to take a break before exhaustion and burnout.

If you are considering pushing yourself to or beyond your limits, remember the Everest climbers. Their cognitive biases overrode their signals to back off and to get out of the death zone. Tragically and unnecessarily, they died. Make sure you don't do the same.

ACTIVITY

THE EVEREST PATTERN

The Everest Pattern will help you develop decision-making for complex, high-risk situations. It involves sensing the external world for salient information about risk, and then relating your signals to the consequences associated with your choices and actions. You will literally see, hear, and especially feel when it's time to turn back, take a rest, or quit.

The Everest Pattern can be applied to a single intense event or to the cumulative risk of sustained high-pace activity. Remember that we're exploring the consequences of *plausible* events, not trying to determine the likelihood of any particular event occurring.

Step 1.

SET UP AND CONTEXT

On the floor, create a line that has two endpoints. At one end of the line is 0 (no risk); at the other end is 10 (extreme risk).

Unlike analogue emotions we described earlier, this line represents the risk environment, not your internal reponses. We're developing the dynamic relationship between internal signals and external patterns (evidence) that are associated with risk.

To begin, think of a task, project, or situation that concerns you.

Step 2.

ORIENT YOURSELF

Move to a point that *feels* appropriate for the current degree of risk the task, project, or situation holds. If it's just an idea at this stage, with no commitment yet, you're at zero. If you are already up to your eyeballs in a nightmare situation, you might be at an 8!

Get a sense of your state at this point. You can use body scanning to help. If you are above zero risk, what are the consequences that most concern you? You might already be receiving a signal at this point that means *no! stop! get out!*

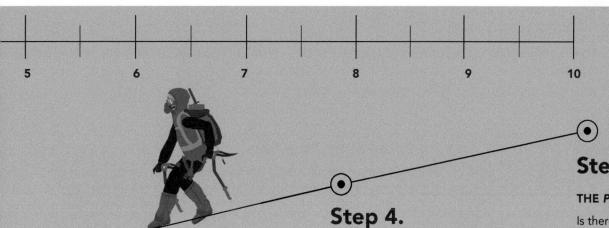

5 6 7 8 9 10

Step 3.

LAST POINT OF TURN AROUND

Move your body to 10 at the extreme end of the line. Identify the worst-case scenario. In the case of climbing Everest, this would likely be death, or worse. In less extreme circumstances than Everest, it might be exhaustion, burnout, or having to remortgage your house.

Using your bodily sensing to lead (in other words, don't overthink it), step down the line from the worst-case scenario *until just before* the accumulation of risk factors means that the worst-case scenario is likely to happen.

What is the external evidence that alerts you to this? You are unpacking here what your unconscious identified. In the case of Everest, it could be your location at 2 p.m., how many people are around you, the pattern of clouds, or even how heavy your legs feel.

If the worst case scenario is not acceptable to you, this is your *last point* to turn around.

Step 4.

EXPLORE SIGNALS AND RISK

Moving further down the line, what level of risk is acceptable to you? Are you prepared to take it to the absolute limit, risking a slide into that worst-case scenario? How far along with the project or situation are you prepared to go? Be aware of your intentions and plausible consequences at every stage.

Connect to your signals. At a critical point, you should experience a shift from *yes* or *maybe*, to a clear *no*. This might be the same as the last turn-around point you identified in Step 2, or it might be at a point with a lot less risk.

Once you have identified the signal for *no*, explore this boundary further. Where is your attention? What happens to the internal signal *just before* the risk reaches this level? Is the change like a switch? Or is it something that has built up, like a light that gets brighter and brighter? How will you know it is time to turn back?

Adjust the intensity of the signal if you need to so that even if your rational thinking becomes confused, you get a clear unambiguous message to turn back.

Step 5.

THE *PLAUSIBLE* UNEXPECTED

Is there anything else that might change the risk profile? For example, on Everest you might have a 2 p.m. turn-around time, but what if you *already* have gear failure? What if there is overcrowding? That turn-around time might need to be revised, or even removed as a useful trigger for action.

Imagine a number of *plausible* scenarios, moving your body up and down the line as you do so. You could imagine being days away from a summit bid, without a cloud in the sky, and yet you realize that, with your team moving too slowly, the risk of a summit bid is already unacceptable.

It's time to manage expectations. In the case of Everest, you could choose a different peak entirely. For a project that is plagued by ever-increasing sunk costs, it could be insistence of demonstrated progress at a fixed cost.

Ultimately, it's not necessarily the specific factors that we identify ahead of time that we are concerned with. We are training ourselves to detect and respond to patterns that we might not have thought of.

After using this process on a live task, project, or situation, there is an opportunity to refine and revise your perceptions and signals, like an after-action review.

IS THAT OTHER GUY OKAY?

TIM MACARTNEY-SNAPE

Tim Macartney-Snape AM is an adventurer, author, and entrepreneur. On 3 October 1984, Macartney-Snape and Greg Mortimer were the first Australians to reach the summit of Mount Everest. He is also the co-founder of the Sea to Summit, an adventure gear company.

I love being in the mountains. I just love the environment. The aesthetic appeal is enormous. At the same time, it's an unstable place to be. As you go higher, as the terrain gets more vertical, it gets more unstable and there's more chance of you falling, or it falling on you. So I've always had a strong sense of what could happen.

Another part of the appeal for me is the challenge and continually striving to be good at what I do. I get a deep sense of satisfaction from being organized and efficient. Some of the people I have climbed with over the years are incredibly disorganized and are, or rather they were, more suited to solo climbing. The disorganized climber attitude will bring you undone in the end, and they're better off not having others around them.

We need a certain amount of good fortune in adventurous situations and when you get a lucky break, you've got to make the most of it. You've also got to be aware of the risk and be prepared to retreat. I think I've naturally tried to understand where I am in the context of what I'm doing. In the mountains the main context is survival.

I've backed off many, many times because I sensed that the situation just wasn't right. There's a feeling, a signal, that gut instinct, whatever you want to call it.

It's been described before, there's a phenomenon, especially when you get exhausted you feel your brain is splitting in two. It feels like there's another presence and it's not quite connected to you. That presence feels like it's a wiser you, or a guardian. I've thought a lot about it, and I reckon that it's your subconscious being allowed out because the conscious part of your brain is compromised by the lack of oxygen.

You're starting to shut down. The brain shuts down and you can feel your thoughts become slippery. At altitude, you start to lose the ability to direct your thinking. It goes all over the place, your mind starts drifting. You have to actually work consciously to reign it in.

That other presence, though, is sort of watching over you. It's not directly saying, do this, do that, but it's sort of nudging you, subtly making suggestions about what you ought to be doing and not doing. The conscious brain is the one with awareness that I'm here to get to the summit, and then another part of you is going well, that's all well and good but, what about the weather? What about that snow slope? What about your partner?

This other part is just behind me. It's as if it was just outside of me, on my shoulder, but you know it's not. It's funny, I've stopped to get my water bottle out of my jacket and you have a drink and you go to hand it to this other interesting, imagined self. I mean, that's how weird it gets at altitude. You've actually looked around to see if that other guy is okay. And of course that person's not there. He's you.

That other entity is a very comforting presence. It gives you confidence. And then from that confidence comes strength because you know, we've got this under control, we can do it.

I've climbed with people that are very good technically. They are great at breaking things down, or fixing a machine; but they're hopeless for actually getting a feel for a mountain or the outdoors. It's important to have empathy with your environment, tapping into what's really going on. All the senses come alive when that happens. It's like I know I'm in a soon to be dangerous thunderstorm situation, because I can smell and taste it.

I've been on some very bold ambitious first attempts with experienced teams and there's been a unanimous decision to turn back. That happened with an attempt on a new route up K2 led by Doug Scott in 1987. The conditions that season just didn't feel right and despite very generous sponsorship we decided to abandon the expedition. Other teams weren't so lucky, and some climbers didn't make it back that year.

On other occasions, like last season when I was guiding in Nepal, I had a bad feeling about the weather just before the summit. Some people were keen to keep going, but we turned back and were lucky to make it to low ground before a two-day blizzard hit that wasn't forecast. That would have made it extremely difficult to descend safely.

"In the mountains, you have to trust your instincts and be organized. Part of the joy of being in the mountains is the uncertainty of it all, that, and the natural beauty and the opportunity to spend time with wonderful people that I get to adventure with."

BEYOND EVEREST INTO HYPER-STATE

Where we use the Everest Pattern to improve decisions in complex, high-risk situations, we can adapt the process to re-calibrate states like stress, hyper-vigilance, and anxiety that are disproportionately intense for the evidence-based risk.

It's about adjusting the volume of signals or states to match the environment. If you are at home in a quiet room, there's no need for full volume to hear music. If you're on the subway in rush hour, you might need to turn it up. States/signals are similar. Hyper-vigilance is an example of the volume being turned up too high. It is a common situation in law enforcement.

We provide (with permission) a story of one such officer's path to recovery.

TIM'S STORY

Tim Coy spent more than a decade in Tasmania's Risdon Prison managing inmates in the maximum security unit. In 2009, a riot broke out. He operated above his full capacity for more than nine hours. He burned out, and over the subsequent days, he fell in a heap. Coy spent many months off work with severe ill health.

At one point, his wife joked to him, "Don't you dare commit suicide or I'll kill you myself."

As we worked through his trauma and started the recovery process, we identified that he was living in an extreme state of hyper-vigilance. Even when sitting in a coffee shop, he would keep his back to the wall, scanning the room and watching the entrance, constantly expecting the worst. On the risk line, regardless of context, he was constantly vigilant at an 8 out of 10 intensity.

By training him to develop a nuanced understanding of the felt sensations in his body, he was able to dial down

hyper-vigilance to appropriate-vigilance. So, when he was in the coffee shop, where the risk was 3 rather than 8, he learned to reduce the intensity of his state to 3 out of 10 vigilance to match the risk in the context.

Some contexts were less, and some were more, especially where there was a high chance of meeting inmates he had previously managed who were now roaming free in the community.

By helping him understand the intention for vigilance, he was able to recalibrate his state to better match the shifting context of threat. Simply numbing hyper-vigilance, for example by medication, would have left him vulnerable to very real risks.

Coy returned to work and, after a short period, he was promoted into a supervisory position at the women's prison. He later transitioned into a role as a well-being officer and established a peer support program for correctional officers.

The pattern of hyper-vigilance is a common one for law enforcement officers. Far too many of them overdo the protective state. The result is burnout and problems managing relationships with family and friends. However, this doesn't mean that they should have the same kind of vigilance as, say, a school teacher or an accountant. Their roles demand vigilance, and it needs to be context appropriate. Attempting to remove vigilance and return experienced law enforcement or correctional staff to the population "normal" is doomed to failure and potentially exposes them to harm.

Always respect the positive intention for the signal, even if there is some degree of discomfort or pain.

PAIN IS A SIGNAL

"When you learn about pain you will hurt less."[39]

— David Butler and Lorimer Mosely

When injury occurs, our neurology assesses the damaged region, taking into account what actions might be able to either prevent or minimize further damage.

If we consider the intense pain that occurs when breaking a bone, and how, when the limb is stabilized or we remain perfectly still, the pain is mostly absent, we can begin to appreciate what's really going on with pain. When movement takes place at an injured site, our neurology sends a signal of discomfort or pain to prevent further damage. Our neurology creates a *subjective* localized pain experience in the region of the injury. This is not intended as a punishment.[1]

If pain was *objective*, caused, for example, by damage to nerve endings, then localized sensations such as acute pain arising from a break or cut would be constant, irrespective of stabilization. Conversely, people in war zones have lost limbs and reported feeling no pain at all until much later.[40] In this example, a pain signal to remain still is overridden, because the embodied mind has determined that being mobile offers a better chance of survival.

As David Butler and Lorimer Mosely say in *Explain Pain*, simply learning about pain is often enough to hurt less. As we say, pain is both real and all in the (embodied) mind.[39]

Acute pain provides an immediate signal to our system to alert us to danger. It usually passes quickly.

Chronic pain is complex and often evolves from acute pain episodes. It's like the metaphor of ruts in a field that we used to describe the neuroplastic paradox. Repeating the experience of pain quickly creates new ruts (painful neural pathways that are difficult to overprint) long after the sense of threat has been removed.

Often, there is also another intention. For example, a sore back from an injury lifting something at work could quickly become associated with a generalized sense of threat at work. Butler and Mosely argue that chronic pain is usually psychosocial and subjective. For back and knee pain, consider for a moment the research reported in *Surgery, the Ultimate Placebo* by orthopedic surgeon Professor Ian Harris. In sham surgeries, when a patient is cut open but with no musculoskeletal

corrections, Harris describes that 74% of placebo surgeries provide a benefit and about half worked as well as the real surgery.[41,42]

Accepting that pain is a signal for threat has profound implications for the millions of people who live with chronic pain. The challenge is to teach our unconscious that it can experience something different once the expectation of further damage has passed, whilst simultaneously addressing the psychosocial intentions for pain that are symbolically, not literally, related to injury.

LEARNED PAIN

Psychiatrist and pain specialist Michael Moskowitz turned to pain research as a way to help him understand his own experience with chronic pain (the result of a number of accidents).

Moskowitz describes chronic pain as "learned pain." "The body's alarm system is stuck in the on position, because the person has been unable to remedy the cause of an acute pain, and the central nervous system has become damaged. Once chronicity sets in, the pain is much more difficult to treat."

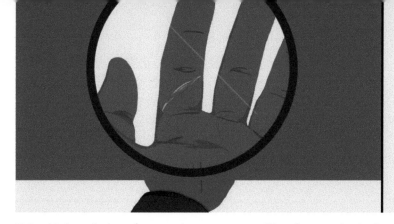

Using his knowledge of neuroscience, Moskowitz developed an approach that could effectively resolve chronic pain in clients, many of whom had given up hopes of ever finding a solution.

He first provides his pain patients with an understanding of the brain's neuroplastic capabilities. In this respect, he follows a process similar to the one Butler and Moseley outline in *Explain Pain*.[39]

Embodied visualization techniques are especially important. They can help people imagine and literally reshape neural pathways. Through pattern interruption and attention training, we can change the structure of the brain in the areas related to experiencing pain.[43] Embodied visualization can also help introduce new movement patterns where there might otherwise be a reluctance to risk a pain response.

Moskowitz uses the acronym MIRROR to outline his system. To be consistent with the terminology we have been using in this book, we have adapted Moskowitz's acronym.[43] Though we describe them slightly differently, the six essential elements remain the same.

Like all neuroplastic change, especially when attempting to overprint deeply ingrained patterns that have been practiced for a long time, it is important to do each of the following:

M: Be highly **motivated**, with a strong sense of personal responsibility and agency.

I: Recognize a positive **intention**, and identify a desired outcome — something other than the simple remedy of *not pain*. Check, is there a current intent, or is the intent no longer relevant to today's context?

R: Pursue new patterns with **relentless** determination, even if it is sometimes uncomfortable or difficult to focus.

R: Respect the value of the signal system, and develop a reliable relationship with our unconscious selves.

O: Embrace **opportunities** afforded by the pain signal to practice new patterns.

R: Restore the embodied mind so that it is once more an effective team with a normal or even super-normal resilience.

MIRROR provides a handrail that helps patients take an active role in their treatment, as opposed to a passive dependency on expert advice or prescription. In much the same way that we can learn to recalibrate states/emotions such as hyper-vigilance, we can use MIRROR and related techniques to retrain our neurology to interpret pain differently.

In tackling hyper-vigilance, Tim Coy recalibrated his state so that it matched the context. We can recalibrate our experience of pain in a similar way. Using something as simple as a magnifying glass, a team led by Lorimer Mosely showed that the subjective experience of pain can be increased if our view of an injured site is magnified, or reduced if our view is distanced.[44] Similarly, by using a real mirror (not the acronym), we can use images of pain-free parts of the body to convince our minds that there is in fact no objective pain.[45-47]

All of these approaches, using mirrors and MIRROR, as well as explaining pain, are ways to recalibrate signals that are no longer serving us well.

WHEN THE SIGNAL GETS JAMMED

We have made the case in this chapter that the senses provide us with signals. Until we develop the habit of enquiring what the intention is for the signal, it is easy to fail to notice the important ones or to respond to them inappropriately.

When placed in context, signals are either:

1. A historical remnant that is no longer useful

2. Still relevant today

AN HISTORICAL REMNANT

Imagine an old-timer in the Morse code office. He tapped out an SOS signal seventy years ago when he was a young man. Someone forgot to let the old guy know the signal was received and the threat was responded to ages ago. He's been frantically tapping out that distress code all day long ever since. Dot dot dot dash dash dash dot dot dot, day in, day out, year in, year out.

Chronic pain is often like the old guy who has been sending that SOS signal for decades. The threat that the pain was originally a response to has long since disappeared, but that message hasn't gotten back through. If we want him to stop sending the signal, we need to send a signal of our own back to him, telling him that the threat has been assessed and dealt with.

To uncover which of the two options applies, you can use yes, no, or maybe signals to provide a two-way communication between the conscious and unconscious. In the case of an historic signal that is no longer useful, this can lead to immediate and lasting pain relief.

In other cases of historic signaling, patterns of persistent pain and maladaptive behavioral response are more ingrained. Signals like pain are especially prone to the neuroplastic paradox — that ability to form a competitive pathway that becomes stronger and stronger the more we try to not have the problem. From the perspective of our neurology, focusing on not having pain is much the same as focusing on having pain. Our attention is still on pain. Just like any problem-remedy loop, the more we practice, the more strongly wired our neurology becomes to support having the problem.

In the case of well-established habits, like the metaphor we use of driving in a rut in a field, it takes deliberate practice to establish new pathways. Depending on how deep these ruts are, it can take

anywhere from a few weeks to six months to overprint the rut.[1,43,48]

In many ways, pain and other unpleasant signals or states are very similar. They are positively intended, but sometimes dramatically overdone and practiced long after the context has changed. This is part of the problem with the diagnostic term Post-Traumatic Stress Disorder (PTSD). The term "Post" presupposes that the traumatic response is in relation to the past. This is sometimes the case, and in our experience, treatment is incredibly fast and effective. One or two coaching sessions usually leads to asymptomatic recovery. More often though, the signal is more complex.

STILL RELEVANT TODAY

Unfortunately, when applied to frontline personnel or people still living with the potential (or perceived) threat of re-experiencing a traumatic event, the "Post" in PTSD is misleading. The well-intended "to keep me safe" signal is not addressed, so the response is no longer just about a past event or events. It is very much in the present.

There might, for instance, be an unconsciously perceived risk of return to active duty when there has been no reduction in organizational risk factors. If risks remain the same, then new coping skills are required so that the person can return to the context and be safe. In the absence of either a reduction in risk or improved coping skills, the signal sticks around as the best way to ensure safety.

Typically, a traumatic stress response isn't "disordered" either. It may result in disordered and deeply impactful effects throughout life, but the signal itself is usually ordered.[49] It would be better to abandon the diagnostic term PTSD and instead refer to people as "experiencing a traumatic stress response."

When states like trauma, pain, or hyper-vigilance are related to a contemporary perception of threat, medication or attempts to remove the state without addressing the underlying concern are problematic. They either do the patient a disservice by leaving them vulnerable, or they simply fail because the person wants to keep the genuine benefit of the state, which is to keep them safe.

THE ANSWER IS OFTEN HIDDEN IN PLAIN SIGHT

By working in the symbolic realm, we can conduct a nuanced exploration of states/signals. There is invariably some sort of symbolic representation. Often, the metaphors we use for pain involve conflict, weapons, and damage.[50,51] For example, if we have walked a long way, and our feet are sore, we might say, "My feet are killing me." This sets up an internal conflict within ourselves that is at odds with the Respect step in the MIRROR process.

By developing embodied metaphors we are often able to gather great insight and new ways of responding to signals. In an exploration of pain and metaphors, Marian Way recounts how one of her clients described neck pain:

"My bad neck is like two rough pebbles grinding together, with bits chipping off."[52]

By asking, "And what would those pebbles like to have happen?" Marion helped the client realize that the rough pebbles wanted liquid. "This meant that movement was needed." Way's client hadn't been moving her neck, and by unpacking the metaphor, she came to understand the signal's intention. When she started moving her neck, she said she felt better.

Importantly, Way helped her client move from a focus on the problem (pain) to a focus on the outcome. In this case, movement and feeling better.

The process Marion Way used was developed by David Grove, a psychotherapist from New Zealand. In the 1980s, when Grove was working with veterans to help them resolve trauma, he noticed that they invariably described their experience in metaphors. By paying attention to the metaphors his patients were using, he helped them access a deeper level of experience that revealed the structure of their embodied thinking and the patterns that shaped their lives. The process is highly effective in resolving pain, trauma, or even problems in business.[53-57]

By working with our own metaphors, we can improve communication and build trust between the conscious and unconscious aspects of mind, sometimes even when we are asleep.

DREAM ON

It's not just in our waking hours that we experience signals or nuanced ideas and communication from the unconscious. As any vivid dreamer can tell you, the dream state is a rich sensory experience. For some, dreams are delightful, imaginative, and insightful; for others, they can be terrifying. In nightmares, vivid recollections are twisted, and the signals for help become grotesque distortions of our waking reality.

At the time of writing this book, the world is in the grip of the Covid-19 pandemic. In the journal *Dreaming*, four studies have revealed how the pandemic has entered into people's dreams. One study reports that 20% of dreams had explicit references to Covid-19. Those who have suffered due to either job loss or illness report dreams that are more vivid than usual.[58-61]

The dream world is a reflection of the day-to-day one, and, by learning how to make use of the dream state, we can benefit from its processing power to help us make sense of external chaos.

When we dream, our brain's visual areas become more active than when we're awake. Our prefrontal cortex, which handles executive functions such as logic, language, and applying appropriateness and social constraints, is less active, so thoughts from the day that are taken into our sleep time go through a different sensory system. This system, rather than using language and logic, uses symbols and images.[62]

If applying calibration to the intent behind our felt signals and state to inform our choices is an important first step, uncovering and usefully interpreting the unconscious metaphors we live by is the second step. Then the third

step is learning to engage with and make use of our dream world. This brings us full circle, back to some of the earliest activities of shamans and dream weavers, who helped guide our ancient forebears through the underlying patterns present in dreams and visions.

Fortunately, we can add the insights of empirical science to the tools of the shaman and the mystic, and there's less need for crystal ball woo-woo.

If your unconscious is providing you with troubling or perplexing dreams, we encourage you to ask yourself: *What is the intention for this? How can I satisfy that intention during the daytime?* You might also, quite literally, sleep on it for the answer!

Remember that dreams are symbolic; rather than trying to understand them literally, think of them as metaphors that express one thing in terms of another.

Imagine, for instance, that you are struggling with a decision whether to leave a workplace you hate, but that pays well. You're going to sleep each night with unanswered questions. Do you accept a new job that's both fun and meaningful if it means a big pay cut? Late that night, you wake from a dream. You were stumbling through a dark wood, with vines trapping and tripping your every move, and then you enter a bright clearing. You suddenly find yourself boarding a boat to a new city with bright lights. The message is obvious. Especially if you wake with a sense of excitement about the prospect of a new job, and a sense of dread about the old.

Everything we encounter during the day can manifest in our dreams. Our dream state is often strongly influenced by our media diet.

A study of more than 1,000 Turkish residents found that, the more violent media content they reported consuming, the more violent their dreams became.[63] Researchers found the same link with sexual media. A media diet rich in pornography leads to an increase in sexual dreams. Media immersion doesn't stop when we put down our phones, shut our laptops, or turn off our televisions. It continues even in our sleep, and it has a profound effect on us.

Is it any wonder that people often report feeling exhausted even after sleeping all night?

We don't have to be passive observers of our dreams, though. We can use dream states to help us process waking experiences or solve thorny problems. Many people report discovering solutions to problems; others who go to sleep conflicted receive strong signals that help them get off the fence of indecision. Both of us (Ian and Mike) use dream time to access our unconscious capabilities. We will set a specific challenge prior to sleep, and ask our unconscious to find a solution.[64] We both utilize the first hour or so of the day as an opportunity to capture our nighttime creativity.

Einstein's Theory of Relativity came to him in a dream about cows getting zapped by an electric fence. In his dream, Einstein saw the cows jump at the same time as the fence gave them an electric shock. But a farmer standing at the other end of the field saw them jump one by one.

In his dream, Einstein argued with the farmer about their different versions of reality. When Einstein woke, it was with a new insight. The events looked different from the two perspectives because the light took longer to reach the farmer at the other end of the field. This insight led to the Theory of Relativity, one of the most famous scientific discoveries of the twentieth century.[65]

If we accept that unconscious communication arises in our sensory channels as both direct sensations such as hunger and as less obvious forms like symbolism and metaphor, then dreaming provides a privileged nighttime extension of our capacity to understand both ourselves and our context.

The thinking we do while we sleep can help us identify what else we may need to do to remain resilient during our waking hours.

Mooving right along.

HOW TO RESPOND WHEN...

Meds are fake news
Placebo is real
Pain is in the mind
Thinking is in the body
And
The best answer is maybe.

Courtesy of the internet, we all have incredible access to more information than at any other time in history. And yet, the wise are more confused than ever, and the confused are more certain than they should be.

In complex situations, signals, intuition, or direct communication from the unconscious are our best choices. Unconscious detection of chaos or emerging patterns provides insight that can be matched to heuristic guidance. These are simple rules that can help navigate uncertainty until more evidence becomes available that might confirm or refute the wisdom of a particular course of action.

Responding to weak signals, either external or internal ones, will give us more time to decide. There are also usually more choices early on than waiting until events escalate or your signals are screaming at you.

Signals or intuitions are not prescient, though. They can be wrong. Heuristics can be wrong. Wise folks know when they are confused; they know how to determine the context they are in and how to respond. Sometimes, the answer is clear. Sometimes, the best course of action is to be decisive and act, even if the outcome is uncertain. Sometimes, the best answer is "maybe." Sometimes, we need to probe the external situation or our internal unconscious to gather more information.

Such internal information might be in the form of symbols. Metaphors and signals are more figurative than literal. Often, they are irreducible. In the same way that great art cannot be reduced to the descriptive label pinned beneath the frame, so too our patterns of unconscious sensing, thinking, decision-making, and communication might retain elements of mystery and ambiguity.

How dull life would be if everything in it were entirely known, certain, and written perfectly across the page. Or worse, what if there were no signals, no felt sensations, no symbols or metaphors or dreams; and life was like sleepwalking in a Madicated stupor.

Are your beliefs about stress killing you?

If you have activated your nocebo effect, reframe your beliefs to support the placebo and make yourself well.

To cut through the confusion, sometimes it's as simple as Occam's razor.

Also called the law of economy, Occam's razor is a principle named after thirteenth-century English philosopher William of Ockham.

If the signal is historical, switch it off. If it's contemporary, uncover the intent of the signal and respond.

Was the right answer:

a. Only fools rush in.
b. Be decisive. Right or wrong, make a decision.
c. The road of life is paved with flat squirrels who couldn't make a decision.

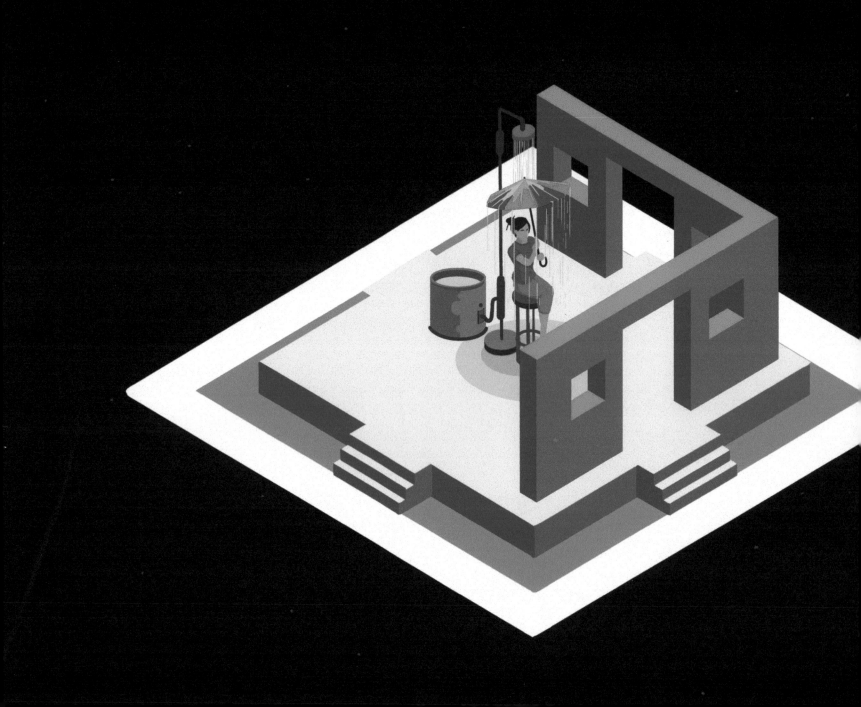

INTENTIONS

LESSONS FROM ALICE

Alice: *"Would you tell me, please, which way I ought to go from here?"*

The Cheshire Cat: *"That depends a good deal on where you want to get to."*

Alice: *"I don't much care where."*

The Cheshire Cat: *"Then it doesn't matter which way you go."*

— Lewis Carroll[1]

The key to making sense of Alice's wish for direction is hidden in her unstated intentions. She asks for direction and, moments later, she tells the Cheshire Cat that she doesn't care where she goes. Perhaps it's more about the nature of the journey for her, time to take it all in, appreciating being present in the moment, or simply enjoying who she travels with.

If we focus too much on goals or the destination, we can easily end up striving through life in an unpleasant state. What if the destination turns out to be less satisfying than we imagined? What if we spend decades chasing a dream without ever catching it? What if we change or the context changes without us even noticing?

Traveling through life without a plan, or not considering future optionality can also leave us vulnerable or fragile to change. Ignoring problems can leave us vulnerable too, although an overemphasis on problems or problem-solving can lead us to miss opportunities.

Action or inaction, planning, or even a random walk through curiosity space all have upsides and downsides often with intentions that are rarely explicit. Like Alice, our intentions are commonly unclear, unstated, and unconscious.

Mission and vision, purpose, strategy, plans, goals, outcomes, KPIs, solutions . . . there's a bewildering array of signposts and maps that can be applied to help define and design for a resilient future, provided we involve our unconscious and accommodate intentions that might be strongly held and deeply hidden. These concepts are all useful approaches to solving problems and managing future risks and opportunities, provided they are applied in the correct context and deployed over appropriate time frames.

WHAT WOULD YOU LIKE TO HAVE HAPPEN?

There are many advantages to an outcome-orientation, even if, like Alice, it is enough knowing that directionless travel is an outcome in itself, not a problem.

People often have a more resourceful relationship with their problem from the perspective of a well-formed outcome. We find that people need little additional help to explore the nature of problems. Those who can articulate what they would like to have happen tend to find that problems simply disappear when attention is placed on *what to do*, rather than *what not to do*.

Often, the problem is not the problem; rather, it's our relationship to the problem.

The Problem-Remedy-Outcome (PRO) model was developed by Penny Tompkins and James Lawley as an effective way of moving people from problems toward desired outcomes. It does this by tracking and leading attention using a simple set of questions. PRO can be self-applied, used in coaching, or to help teams or organizations identify an agreed-upon outcome.[2,3]

Without a focus on a desired outcome, we can find ourselves stuck in a problem-remedy loop. Take the dieting industry for example. Their marketing amplifies the problem, then switches immediately to a focus on their (branded) remedy. If the remedy they are selling actually addressed the problem once and for all, they'd quickly go out of business.

The Problem: I am overweight.

The Remedy: I need to lose weight.

By contrast, a Desired Outcome could involve a sustainable, life-long change to someone's relationship to food and movement. Their actions might be as simple as eating well and moving daily.

The Outcome: I want to be fit and healthy.

In coaching and therapy, it is well established that questions focused on solutions or outcomes are generally more effective than problem-focused ones.[3-8] This is not to say that problems should be avoided or ignored; rather, place emphasis on the bridge between the problem and a relevant desired outcome.

A problem can be identified in language through the following attributes:

PROBLEM STATEMENT

A dislike for a current or future situation is stated or implied

It does not contain any words of desire, for example, want, need or would like

The ideal question for a problem is to ask what someone would like.

I'm inundated with paperwork   **My boss is a bully**

WHAT KIND OF OUTCOME?

A remedy is a means of counteracting or eliminating something undesirable.

If you listen carefully to yourself or others, most proposed remedies describe, in metaphor, how they expect the problem to be solved, for example: stop, less, away from, not have.

A proposed remedy does not describe what the situation will be like after the remedy has been applied.

The end result of a remedy, linguistically, is an absence — or *not the problem*.

If someone wants less paperwork, and they get what they want, what do they have?

With no paperwork, they might not be overwhelmed, but they might not know what's going on. They might not even have a job at all.

A remedy eliminates the problem, but it does not set a direction for action once the remedy has been successfully applied.

The features of a remedy statement are that it:

> **REMEDY STATEMENT**
>
> Has not yet happened
>
> Contains a description of the problem
>
> Contains a desire for the problem to not exist or to be reduced

I want less paperwork

Ideal questions for those using remedy statements include:

And then what would happen?

Or

What happens next?

I want my boss to go away

Desired outcomes describe how the world will be when someone has what they want. They differ from remedies because they are not a solution to a problem. Instead, they set a goal and a specific trajectory.

The features of a desired outcome statement are that it:

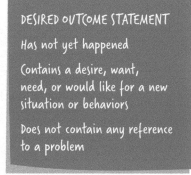

DESIRED OUTCOME STATEMENT

Has not yet happened

Contains a desire, want, need, or would like for a new situation or behaviors

Does not contain any reference to a problem

I want a way to organize my paperwork

Once you have their focus on an outcome, uncover more detail:

Is there anything else about?

Or

What kind of?

I want a boss who can communicate with respect

229

SMARTER OUTCOMES

Once a desired outcome is identified, the next step is to develop it. Is it well formed? Is it coherent with the context? This might involve asking explicit questions of a metaphor to bring intangible or abstract desires into a more literal evidence-based realm.

We often use a checklist that is similar to the SMART goals commonly used in business.

SMART is an acronym for Specific, Measurable, Achievable, Realistic, and Time bound.

We have expanded the original acronym here to include elements that test for context and for the possibility of unforeseen risks or feedback loops.

Rather than create a whole new set of criteria, we have tweaked the SMART goals and added in Ecology and Risk to make SMARTER Outcomes.

SPECIFIC

Sensory-specific evidence to identify what the outcome is. This must involve criteria that you or another person can see, feel, hear, taste, and/or smell.

MEASURABLE

Projects or outcomes should have criteria that can be measured.

A surprising number of Key Performance Indicators (KPIs) in business are used to reference outcomes that are not well formed. Often, those who set KPIs like "improved corporate governance" or worse "strive to improve corporate governance" do so without providing any sensory-specific, measurable criteria to identify outcomes.

Vague KPIs like this merely create further questions: How will improvement be measured? How much striving is enough? Is striving an outcome at all?

This sort of ambiguity sits at the center of a lot of poor management practices and is commonly associated with bullying and stress.

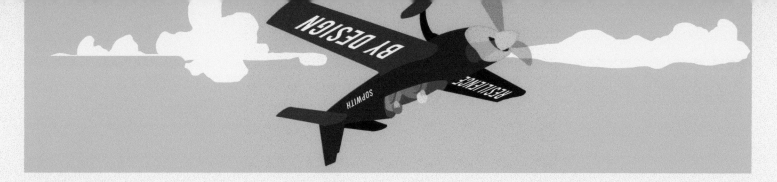

ACHIEVABLE

Has a similar outcome been achieved by someone else? If it has, it is quite possible that you too could achieve this outcome. If you are the first, find out if it is possible, perhaps by having a go in a way that is safe to fail.

Also consider whether every aspect of the outcome is within your control or influence. If an outcome depends on someone else's permission or participation, it is not well formed. It will only be well formed when all third-party agreements are in place.

REALISTIC

Are the resources required to achieve the outcome accessible? For example, if you want to build a $500K house, will the bank lend you the money? And if they do, is it realistic that you could and would meet the mortgage repayments?

TIME BOUND

Time is one of the most poorly considered criteria for outcomes. It is much more common to hear that a project has overrun than to hear that it was delivered on time.

ECOLOGY

Ecology describes whether an outcome has acceptable costs, time frames, and consequences, including benefits, when considered in the broadest frame. Ecology also questions the fit between the outcome and the context.

RISK

Risk is a critical element to consider when launching out toward a desired outcome. The key question is *what if*? The most common approach to risk is to balance the likelihood of the event occurring against the consequences. Sometimes, though, the likelihood of an event happening is incalculable. Some disruptive events come out of left field, like the Black Swan events we described earlier. All we can do is prepare for *plausible* downsides.

Ok, so we have a well-formed outcome, we know:

☑ **S,** what criteria would tell us we had it

☑ **M,** we could measure it in some way

☑ **A,** it's achievable

☑ **R,** it's realistic and resourced

☑ **T,** we've considered time

☑ **E,** we know what sort of system it is, and we've thought about relationships and impacts

☑ **R,** the risk has been considered and is deemed acceptable

WAIT JUST A MINUTE. There's one more question.

What's

it for?

NOT, BUT WHY?
INSTEAD, AND WHAT FOR?

If you've ever been interrogated by a four-year-old, you've dealt with an endless string of *but why?* questions. At a certain point along the chain, you just end up shrugging your shoulders. When you reach this point, the answer is usually "just because" or some variation of this, as we resort to a simple cause-effect justification.

A *why?* questioning pattern tends to take attention down in logical levels into more and more detailed justifications. It doesn't help us understand or elicit broader intentions.

A great question to ask of ourselves or others is: and when I/you have that, what's it for? When placed in the context of possible consequences, this question offers a simple, highly effective decision-making process that considers outcome, intentions, and consequences (OIC) as a connected whole.

The OIC process, identified by psychotherapists Jules and Chris Coillingwood, encourages people to consider desired outcomes in a broad context, acknowledging high-level intentions and likely consequences before investing resources. It also considers the potential that the outcome will produce direct and cascading impacts.[9]

Just like other forms of scenario testing, the OIC process is best done in a fully associated and embodied way. Through vivid and detailed imaginings, we can experience each step as though it's happening right now.

Outcomes, intentions, and consequences can be mapped out spatially on the floor, which allows the whole body to move through space to make the most of different perspectives. They can also be drawn on a whiteboard to help visualize the thinking process or to share concepts with others; or they can be scribbled on the back of a napkin at a cafe.

Step 1.

Associate into the desired outcome, checking that all the senses are involved in the created experience. What will you see, hear, feel, taste, and even smell when this outcome is achieved?

Is the outcome SMARTER?

Step 2.

Step backwards while asking yourself, *What is this outcome for?*

Similar questions include, *What is its purpose?* Or *What does having this outcome then give me?*

Step 2n.

This process can be repeated until the answers either become recursive or it's apparent that there is nothing else. Phases like "It's just happiness" are a giveaway.

There are many variations on this pattern, and it is common for there to be multiple intentions or a chain of linked intentions.

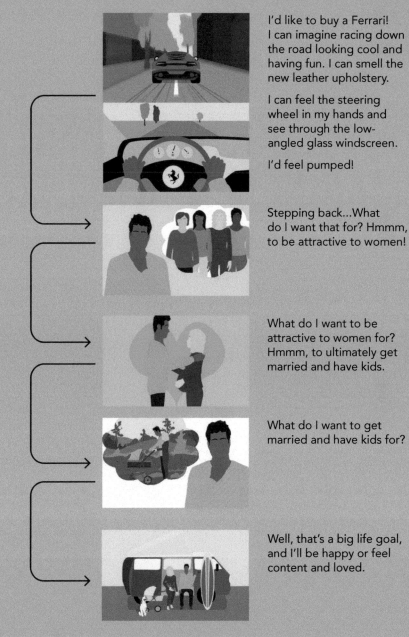

I'd like to buy a Ferrari! I can imagine racing down the road looking cool and having fun. I can smell the new leather upholstery.

I can feel the steering wheel in my hands and see through the low-angled glass windscreen.

I'd feel pumped!

Stepping back...What do I want that for? Hmmm, to be attractive to women!

What do I want to be attractive to women for? Hmmm, to ultimately get married and have kids.

What do I want to get married and have kids for?

Well, that's a big life goal, and I'll be happy or feel content and loved.

ACTIVITY

CONSEQUENCES: REAL, IMAGINED, AND UNINTENDED

Once the intention chain is established, it is important to consider the consequences of having the desired outcome. What will happen when those intentions are met?

Step 3.

Having explored intentions, step back into the outcome. Briefly reconnect with the sense of having that outcome, then step to the side while asking yourself, *What are the upsides and downsides of having this outcome?*

Consider consequences such as time, money, and how having the outcome might affect other people.

Step 3n.

Consequences can also be considered for all of the intentions in the chain. You can explore these by stepping into each intention, briefly reconnecting with having that intention met, then stepping to the side to consider the upsides and downsides.

It is useful to shake out between steps as you consider the consequences of having the outcome and meeting the intentions. They can be reintegrated as a whole in Step 5.

Step 4.

Step into a third position, away from the outcome, intention, and consequences pattern on the floor. Consider the alignment or coherence as a whole.

Does the outcome deliver or meet its intentions with acceptable consequences?

Let's return to the outcome, intentions, and consequences of having a Ferrari...

Mmm, well, it does go fast and I do look cool, but it costs $350K, the insurance is high, there is no room for kids or a pram, I won't be able to resist hitting the throttle, and I'll almost certainly lose my license for speeding!

Observing the higher intentions, there are probably much better ways of attracting a partner and having a family.

Maybe this is not the best outcome as a means to meet my previously unconscious intentions of a family and happiness, contentment, and love.

When you have built an intention chain that includes examination of both upside and downside consequences, it is important to make sure that you still want the outcome.

The process can also be run backwards from a high-level intention to compare alternatives of possible outcomes and associated consequences that might meet the intention. This is especially useful if you realize that after running this process you no longer want the outcome and you want to find a different way to meet that higher-level intention that's important to you.

In this example an alternative outcome could be a camper van...

Sometimes, we explore an outcome and intention chain in this way and the internal signal says, Yes, let's do this!

Even then, it's sometimes worth exploring several different outcomes, or even testing a few things out. For example, you might consider hiring a Ferrari for a day to see what it's really like.

Step 5.

Once an outcome seems promising, and as a final check just before committing to pursuing it, imagine a more distant future. Consider what life might be like having had that outcome for some time. This is called a future pace. To do this, start at the outcome. Step forward, imagining that three, six, or twelve months have passed (the appropriate duration will depend on the circumstances). Now consider what has changed with the passage of time.

Is the ecology of the decision still ok given what you have learned from this future perspective?

The basic Outcome-Intention-Consequenes pattern looks like this.

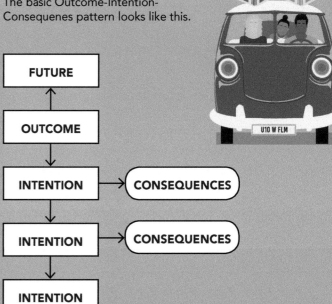

```
        ┌──────────────┐
        │   FUTURE     │
        └──────┬───────┘
               ↑
        ┌──────────────┐
        │   OUTCOME    │
        └──────┬───────┘
               ↓
        ┌──────────────┐        ╭──────────────╮
        │  INTENTION   │───────▶│ CONSEQUENCES │
        └──────┬───────┘        ╰──────────────╯
               ↓
        ┌──────────────┐        ╭──────────────╮
        │  INTENTION   │───────▶│ CONSEQUENCES │
        └──────┬───────┘        ╰──────────────╯
               ↓
        ┌──────────────┐
        │  INTENTION   │
        └──────────────┘
```

WHAT'S YOUR RAISON D'ETRE?

One special example of an intention chain involves outcomes that are strongly linked to a compelling sense of purpose. Sense of purpose is also sometimes referred to as mission, raison d'etre (reason for being), or intrinsic motivation.

Our sense of purpose can be any activity: a project or hobby, all the way through to a whole-of-life commitment. It often describes a situation where someone associates what they do with their sense of identity. Instead of playing golf or making music, they *are* a golfer or a musician.

When asked what it's like operating at this highest level of intention, people often struggle to express the experience adequately. Words like happiness, contentment, or satisfaction just don't do justice to the states they are trying to describe.

"I'm a little pencil in the hand of a writing God, who is sending a love letter to the world." — Mother Teresa

"Here's to the crazy ones, the misfits, the rebels, the troublemakers, the round pegs in the square holes. The ones who see things differently; they're not fond of rules. You can quote them, disagree with them, glorify or vilify them, but the only thing you can't do is ignore them because they change things.

They push the human race forward, and while some may see them as the crazy ones, we see genius, because the ones who are crazy enough to think that they can change the world, are the ones who do." — Steve Jobs/Apple

Mother Teresa and Steve Jobs couldn't be further apart in terms of the spheres they operated in, but they both discovered and lived their purpose. They clearly shared a common pattern for achieving successful outcomes. When they knew what they were here to do, they set about changing the world.

We wonder just how far either of them, or any changemaker, could have gone without first identifying their purpose?

A number of personal stories of survival, such as *Man's Search for Meaning* by Holocaust survivor Victor Frankl, describe the importance of intrinsic motivation or sense of purpose as a key attribute of personal resilience.[10]

Intrinsic motivation or sense of purpose is also recognized in several of the dozen or so resilience scales that are documented in the scientific literature[11-15]

IDENTIFYING YOUR OWN SENSE OF PURPOSE IS RESILIENT

A small number of published research papers describe the importance of motivation and sense of purpose for resilience. More common are studies that describe the impact of loss of purpose through retirement, burnout, or some form of enforced change.[16,17] For example, several papers have documented the struggles of elite athletes and military frontline professionals who must transition to a new career or retirement. The studies show an increased prevalence

of depression following previously healthy or even superhuman states of well-being.[18-22]

As reflected in the published literature, the importance of being engaged at the level of intention becomes more apparent when someone becomes disconnected from purpose in an occupational, social/relational, familial, or sporting context. For example, there is a big difference between working long, hard hours when you are passionate about your work, compared with when you're being driven to deliver a project that you think is pointless.

The relationship between sense of purpose or meaning and other motivating or rewarding facets of life or career is typically interwoven with other elements of resilience, like flow, social connection, and "coherence." Coherence is a sense of belonging within an identifiable reference frame.

As an example of coherence, let's consider guests at a wedding. Most people go to weddings with the intention to support and celebrate the newly married couple. Sometimes, that shared intention is all that connects the guests. Even when Uncle Roy embarrasses everyone after too many drinks and appalling dancing, the wedding party is still coherent thanks to this shared intention.

However, change the intention of just one guest, maybe a jilted ex or a jealous brother who wants revenge, and all of a sudden the occasion can be undermined and even ruined for everybody.

Coherence doesn't have to mean that we all want the same things in the same form, or that we all go about achieving outcomes in the same way. However, if we want to collaborate effectively, we do need to have shared intentions at some level. We rarely benefit from forcing behaviors that "align" everyone. Whereas the concept of coherence acknowledges the benefits of diversity and difference, providing that families, partnerships, teams or organizations operate within a shared intention frame.

When designing for transition to a new career or lifestyle, it often pays to remain coherent with any sense of purpose, or mission, that is still viewed as being important. The idea is not for exact replication with the new job, for example. It is more important to find alternative outcomes that are coherent with the higher intention. Like switching out a Ferrari in favor of a camper van, in our earlier example.

SAM

served as a Royal Marine for seven years and a police officer for fourteen years, eight of which he served in SO19, the special firearms command.

Since retiring from the police, he's led hundreds of high-risk security operations in Syria, Afghanistan, Iraq, Libya, Kurdistan, Lebanon, Congo, Namibia, Mozambique, Uganda, Tanzania, and Egypt.

He is a special advisor and trainer to various law enforcement programs.

MANAGING DELIRIUM

"Am I going to die today?" asked our cameraman tentatively.

"No, I scheduled it for tomorrow," I said with a laugh.

He nodded, and then went back to his spot near the correspondent who was sleeping soundly, as he had been for most of the last two days.

The cameraman's way of dealing with our life-and-death situation was to seek certainty; the correspondent's was to sleep excessively; mine has always been to joke about it.

I'm leading security for a small but very high-profile news crew, reporting on the fighting and atrocities in Syria. It's early 2012, and the civil war is tearing the country apart, causing one of the largest humanitarian disasters of our age. This is our fifth day of being relentlessly shelled by over a hundred Syrian army tanks and artillery. The tanks have surrounded a rebel stronghold that we were unfortunate enough to have entered whilst seeking out our story. And now we must move, be captured, or get hit.

As the tanks inch closer to us I know it's time to make a break for the border while we still can.

Between the edge of a rebel-held town and the forest that may provide us cover on route to the Lebanese border, there is a wide-open field of some 1km in length.

That field area is flanked by Syrian army on both sides — the same army that has been shelling us for the past five days and is intent on ensuring we don't make it out of the country with news footage.

For US$200, I am able to buy the services of a Syrian rebel medic and his fiberglass-topped pickup truck. This is our only way across the open range to freedom, and I silently pray he doesn't double-cross us, trading us in for a lot more than we are paying him. Our team of five flattens into the bloodstained cargo bed of the truck, and without a second's hesitation, our driver begins racing through the streets and out across the open field area.

For a few alluring moments everything is eerily quiet, and false hope arises. Then that hope is shattered like the ground exploding all around us. In what is the longest, most time-distorted minute of my life, artillery explodes all around and shrapnel sprays our vehicle as the ground shudders and convulses.

We all attempt to stay prone in the truck but get bounced into the fiberglass roof, as a form of delirium takes hold. A paralyzing mix of expectancy, doom, and acceptance all compete for the attention of our senses.

"In my experience, everyone responds to high-pressure environments differently."

Time has no meaning for us as the truck takes more small shrapnel hits.

"Did I leave it too late to exit the town? Will I see my family again? Was this operation worth it? Did I really need to come here again? This has to be my last crossing" — these are my thoughts before I have no thoughts at all and the whole experience becomes a moment that is intensely beyond words.

With fear replaced by flow, we skid into the forest and are screamed at to exit the vehicle. Three boys, barely old enough to shave, await us with engines revving on their cheap Chinese motorbikes. These are our escorts, sent by the smugglers we paid, to get us in and out of the country.

What follows is too similar to an Indiana Jones movie to credibly write about. Suffice to say that we are shot at by the Syrian army, pursuing us in jeeps, and our group becomes separated as the teenage bike riders split along narrow trails, racing at high speed through endless lines of unfarmed olive trees.

After an hour of weaving and barely staying on the back of the 150cc bikes, we somehow all arrive within minutes of each other at the last hurdle before we can cross the Lebanese border.

One hundred meters of landmines and two forty-meter-high banks separate us from freedom. The smugglers have cleared a narrow path through the minefield and run confidently in front of us to the base of the banks. This is where we part company with our guides — with no thanks or ceremony. As our news crew begins a final manic sprint up the hills to the crossing point, we hear gunshots.

I turn and then scream at the crew to keep looking forward, no looking back. There is no benefit to be had in them seeing one of the smuggler boys who is now lying lifeless in the dirt.

I have crossed back and forth into Syria sixteen times since the civil war started. In every single crossing I've been shelled or shot at.

It gets harder each time and I do my best to avoid calculating the odds of taking another team into the territory. However, I would be a liar if I did not admit that the intensity of the moment, the feeling of aliveness, and the total disconnect from mundane life was not... completely compelling. I can even laugh about my near misses as I talk about them now.

WHERE AM I... GOING?

Like using any kind of map, the first step is to understand where you are presently. Only from there can you start to plot a course to get to where you want to be. Of course, it's also ok to wander around directionless like Alice, for a time at least.

Critically, how we might move or respond depends on the terrain. The type of system we are in and its level of unpredictability should inform our approach. Is the context clear to us? Do we understand our intentions, the map and our place in it? Can we predict consequences or downsides reasonably well? If we can answer yes to all these questions, then we can begin to manage future actions with detailed planning and goal-setting. In these situations, the path between A and B is often obvious.

In complex and unfamiliar situations it is especially important to understand intentions because often the map and our place in it are not precisely known. The path ahead is less certain. We can't predict the future with ease, nor can we anticipate all the risks and the consequences of our actions.

If there is no path and a wide stream to cross, your course of action will likely benefit from exploring multiple different ways of moving forward in the general direction you desire. Crossing the stream might require transferring from stepping stone to stepping stone, or it might require backtracking.

As the saying goes:

"If plan A doesn't work, then there are 25 more letters, 204 if you are in Japan."
— Claire Cook, author[23]

The value of planning in complex situations is not to fix the plan; rather, it is the act of considering and preparing for probable, possible, and plausible futures. This being the case, intention becomes the guiding principle. This allows a change of course, while making headway into the wind.

Just like sailing, sometimes the best way to get to our destination involves many changes in direction, visiting a sequence of safe ports along the way.

Linking ports in this way is known in complexity as the adjacent possible. In the ocean, as in life, we can be caught out by the unexpected, and a reversal or moving sideways is the intelligent choice until more information is gathered. There's rarely a critical downside in turning back to port when you've been caught in an unexpected storm, or waiting it out until clearer, long-term weather patterns emerge.

We speak to many people in organizations who report a lack of clarity as to where their organization is headed, or how they fit in to the intended direction. Or worse, they do know where the organization is headed, and it is a different direction to the stated mission and what originally attracted them to the enterprise when they first joined.

It is all too common to find that outcomes, directions for change, or future plans are poorly defined and disconnected from intentions. Even the seemingly innocuous family holiday can be seen as a stressful experience with competing unspoken agendas. This ambiguity often extends into personal financial planning, roles at work, project plans, corporate strategies, planning a wedding, or even a Mad Hatter's tea party.

Always be careful who you invite along on your journey, your wedding, or your tea party. It helps to have shared intentions, even if, like Alice, it's to share a journey with no stated destination.

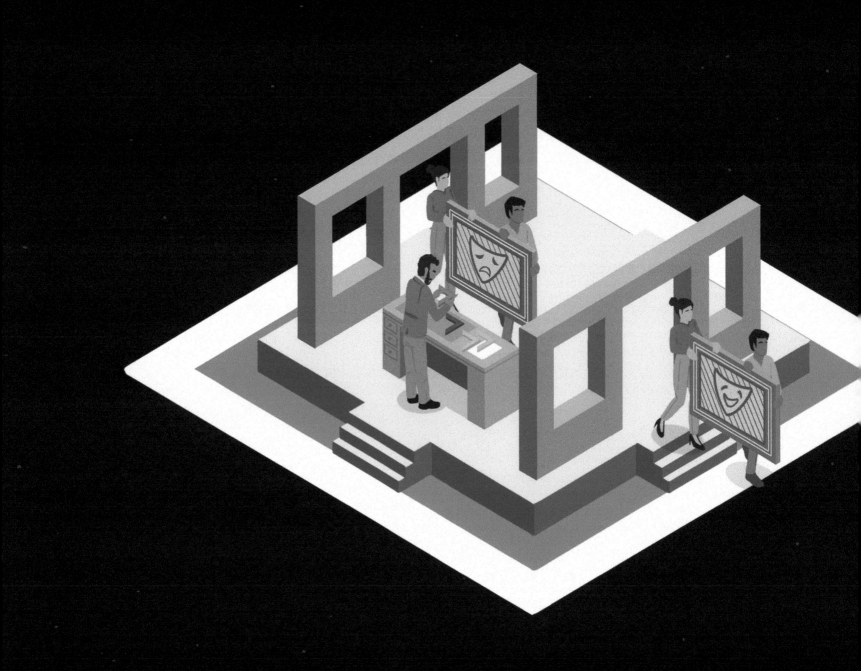

REFRAMING

REFRAMING IS THE ART OF DIRECTING ATTENTION

"Before I speak, I have something important to say."

— Groucho Marx

Framing is both a verbal and a non-verbal pattern that sets the scene and guides attention. A common element in naturally occuring (unconscious) interactions, framing is frequently used as a strategy for dealing with challenging events.

"This chapter is going to be very useful for helping yourself and others develop resilience..."

Framing can expand, contract, or move our attention sideways, possibly setting up for what comes next. It can focus our attention on what we want to keep in frame, or distract attention away from something we'd rather keep out of the frame.

Reframing can be used to help us develop resilience by transforming meaning without hiding the existence of evidence. If improperly applied by others, it can also reduce our resilience when it is used to deceive through redirection, fake news, or denialism. Learning how to use framing and reframing will help us notice when we are being manipulated.

We didn't say (above):

"The reading time for this chapter is 60 minutes."

It will take most people around 60 minutes to digest this chapter and work through the activities in a single sitting. However, as we noted in the introduction, we have designed this book so that you can graze, dipping in-and-out depending on your appetite.

We didn't make explicit — until now — that each double-page spread in this book has a containing frame that stands alone, offering a digestible chunk of useful information or a skill to learn. Each spread is then nested and sequenced in a way that is coherent within a chapter, and each chapter is sequenced and nested within the book as a whole. This is an example of how framing can remain hidden to others. It's not necessary for the reader to know this consciously to appreciate and get practical value from the book. It is important for the writers and editors to appreciate this frame explicitly though.

We could reframe this whole book by noting that every chapter is an example of reframing.

The book is also coherent with a larger frame of what the authors do in their business, Frontline Mind. The book is consistent with their mission:

"To enable individuals, teams, and organizations to survive and thrive in a complex, turbulent world."

This chapter unpacks how to reframe experiences to maximize resilience. The techniques we'll describe in the coming pages will help you survive and thrive in even the most challenging situations. We also make explicit some of the ways that framing and reframing are used to exploit and manipulate.

THE ANSWER IS 1.672 * 10^25 MOLECULES

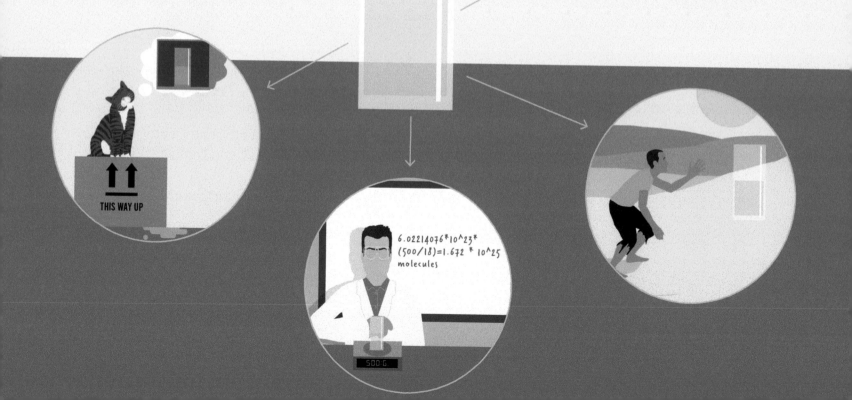

For a curious two-year-old, cigarette butts on the pavement are fascinating.

Obviously, having a two-year-old picking up cigarette butts off the street presents a hygiene problem.

A commonly used remedy might be the instruction to:

Stop!

or worse

Don't pick that up! (with the embedded instruction to *pick that up!*)

Butt (sorry!), what is the child's positive intention?

It could be, "I'm curious about the world, and these things on the ground are interesting!"

The outcome we want is the one that maintains curiosity and interest whilst avoiding the downsides of picking up cigarette butts. The intervention needs to be quick. There's only a split second between reaching for the butt and eating it!

We need to make it clear to the toddler that their curiosity is good, and our instruction needs to take a more constructive form. We might say, "Those are dirty, we have to use our feet and stamp on them, like this. Let's see how many we can stamp on!"

THIS REFRAME:

- Identified a problem behavior
- Guessed what the positive intention might be
- Introduced a safe alternative that met the positive intention
- Amplified the alternative behavior into a compelling game with mutual participation

The same pattern can be used for other hazards to children, like using a stick to poke potentially poisonous wild berries or toadstools, rather than using fingers to explore. This particular reframe used the Problem-Remedy-Outcome and the Outcome, Intentions, and Consequences models we covered previously.

LOOKS LIKE A DUCK

Reframing is an artform that can be developed with practice or learned inductively from others.

To fast-track learning, we use a priority-sequenced structure to help people develop their reframing skills. This involves considering evidence, inference, and intentions to change impact. Often, responses (impact) to challenging situations happen unconsciously, without reference to the sensemaking process and biases (inference) or sensory-based evidence. We usually start by reintroducing or evaluating evidence. We then proceed to the inference given, sometimes with a side trip to intention.

EVIDENCE FIRST

Is there magical thinking under a tinfoil hat? Or does it pass the duck test?

"If it looks like a duck, swims like a duck, and quacks like a duck, then it *probably* is a duck."

INFERENCE IS EVERYTHING

Just like the duck/rabbit illusion, any difference in perspective can change the inference.

One popular way of reframing involves switching context. For example, *who or what could benefit from the current situation?* A switch in attention from *it's bad weather* to *it's great weather for ducks!* is a good example. This keeps the evidence (rain), whilst changing the inference to one of rain is good, and the impact of bad weather is lessened as we smile (or groan) and accept that being wet is not always so bad.

The story or parts that make up a context are what we call content, and content can also be reframed: *Personally, I prefer rabbits*, is a content reframe. Reframing intention also involves content or story. For example, imagine hearing a friend and colleague being criticized at work by their boss.

You respond, *"Wow, I don't know why you tolerate that jerk!"*

They respond: *"It's ok, I know he just wants me to deliver this project on time. He's put me forward for promotion, and he wants me to be successful. His tone and harsh words are like water off a duck's back to me."*

This reframes to a positive intention.

HUMOR CAN BE USED AT ANY STAGE. APPLY LIBERALLY.

What did the duck say to the doctor when he realized that in a random control trial his medication was found to be no better than a placebo?

Quack!

We rarely need to reframe impact directly, so long as we have carefully considered evidence, inference, and intentions.

INTENTION

EVIDENCE

INFERENCE

or Interpretation
or Perspective

IMPACT

or Response
or Meaning
or Consequences

BELIEVING WON'T MAKE IT TRUE

There is a common misconception that disciplines such as science and law are impartial, rational explanations of evidence that are able to prove or uncover "truth."

They are not.

Truth, like reality, might be an aspirational goal, a concept, or metaphor, but the term truth is often used inaccurately and misleadingly.

Lies that are driven by deliberate deceit differ from congruent beliefs and honest accounts of what someone recalls they have experienced. What we believe and remember might not be fully accurate. How we make sense of the world is highly subjective. It is very easy to change memory through narrative, and our sensemaking is confounded by inattentional blindness. We have evolved to detect patterns, and we often see what we expect to see and miss what we aren't looking for. We only get part of the picture, not some sort of objective reality.

Use and abuse of the concept of truth by scientists, lawyers, preachers, or anyone for that matter, have consequences that undermine personal resilience.

To use reframing artfully with integrity, and to protect yourself from deceit or being "framed," it is useful to understand the distinctions between science, belief, faith, and other forms of magical thinking.

THE SCIENTIFIC METHOD (IN 349 WORDS)

Scientific methods have been evolving since before Aristotle brought together concepts ranging from physics and logic to biology and psychology more than 2000 years ago.

"Science, from the Latin *scientia*, meaning 'knowledge,' is a systematic enterprise that builds and organizes knowledge in the form of testable explanations and predictions about the universe." — Wikipedia 2021

One of the great philosophers of science, Karl Popper, argued that a theory can never be proven, but it can be falsified.[1] Theories should be scrutinized and tested with the aim of disproving. No amount of testing can prove a theory, but a single line of evidence can refute it. A well-designed experiment that fails to refute a theory might

improve confidence, but never to the level of "proven" or the unconditional acceptance of "truth."

With reference to earlier work by Thomas Bayes in the 1700s, many philosophers of science argue that while falsification is very strong evidence compared to confirmation, falsification is still probabilistic in nature.[2,3] Falsification is not governed by fundamentally different rules from confirmation, as Popper argued, and it is entirely possible that a theory that has been falsified could have the falsification overturned.[4]

The scientific method can never be absolutely certain that something does or does not occur.

There is also an important distinction between the intent of the scientific method and the subjective application of the scientific method by humans.

Thomas Kuhn argued that appreciation of, and engagement with, the scientific methodology needs to recognize and acknowledge the role of subjectivity.[5] Science, he said, does not evolve gradually toward truth. Instead knowledge amasses within a paradigm that remains constant before going through a paradigm shift, when current theories can't explain some phenomenon, and someone proposes a new theory.

Science, then, is not established solely by objectivity. It is defined subjectively by a consensus of a scientific community.[3] This is especially the case for complex issues.

Ideally, consensus would use some sort of weight-of-evidence approach. This refers to a systematic evaluation of the evidence to assess if the science supports a particular conclusion.[6]

JUDGE THE WEIGHT OF EVIDENCE

Sometimes, the evidence is clear and the conclusions are obvious. In complex, challenging situations or problems, however, there are more likely to be lines of evidence that support contradictory positions. In such cases, our best option is to consider each line of evidence on its merits, weighting some and discounting others, before we draw a conclusion. In particular, we want to consider reliability, which means looking at both accuracy (degree of systematic error or bias) and precision (degree of random error).[7]

We heavily discount any evidence or paradigm that is strongly sponsored by vested interests. There is incredible immunity to changing scientific ideas, especially when one's reputation, profession, or wealth depends on the maintenance of the status quo.

When considering weight-of-evidence, be alert to momentum, which is the tendency for old ideas to rumble along well after they have been discredited. Emerging counterfactual positions are often ignored for a long time due to not matching the narrative we expect. At the same time, don't accept ideas simply because they are new. Question whether new ideas are robust. Are they on the leading edge of a paradigm shift, or is this a one-off study that hasn't been replicated? Is the source a respected scientist, a trusted friend, or a savvy entrepreneur, or are they a crank, a shady acquaintance, or a con artist?

Remember that science is about testing the evidence for beliefs and a belief is only as valid as its evidence.

For any belief, there is always some uncertainty. At one end of the range, there is a high degree of certainty that the hypothesis is either true or false. We are confident one way or the other. At the other end of the range, we are not at all confident about whether something is true or false. In fact, in that situation, the only thing we might be confident of is that we are confused, which is often far better than having a strongly held belief that is incorrect.

We (Ian and Mike) often use the term "temporary operating position" for concepts or ideas that we don't necessarily believe, but find useful. Presenting normalized population data is one example. We very much doubt that populations are truly normally distributed, but the concept helps us discuss the way that people become categorized without opening up a statistical can of worms.

TESTABLE AND FALSIFIABLE

The types of beliefs that form today's scientific body of knowledge can be tested and falsified.

Faith exists outside of this system. It is a very different type of belief that does not require evidence, nor does it seek evidence biased toward falsification.

By definition, faith is the "complete trust or confidence in someone, something, or an idea." The term "blind faith" means to refute evidence even when it is presented in a way that is clear to others, although of course some people "lose faith" when compelling evidence or some counter example to their faith construct suddenly arises.

Blind faith opens us to risk and fragility, as the captain of the "unsinkable" *Titanic* might have realized as the abandon-ship klaxon wailed.

While academics might argue about what we have summarized here in two pages, this distinction between belief and faith helps to distinguish science from religion, fiction, and fantasy.

Belief and faith also strongly influence legal systems and the subjective application of laws. Many legal systems are intimately related to faith-based doctrine, *and* they use evidential processes to a greater or lesser extent. Regardless of the paradoxical nature of the dominant culture you might inhabit, it's useful to be situationally aware, especially if you are to be judged.

In many Western legal systems there is a deliberate bias toward innocence, and the onus is on the prosecution to demonstrate their case. This is similar to science, where there is a bias in favor of rejecting rather than supporting an idea or hypothesis. There are two important clauses required for conviction:

In criminal cases, the evidence must be "beyond all reasonable doubt." The term "reasonable" is a critically important subjective term.

Or for civil cases, where the consequences are less onerous, the evidential basis must be "on the balance of probabilities."

Even with a legal burden of proof biased toward the presumption of innocence, there are countless examples of wrongful conviction. Even for the most heinous crimes that warrant the death sentence in the United States, researchers estimate that if all death-sentenced defendants remained under sentence of death indefinitely, at least 4.1% would be exonerated. The implications of wrongful execution are not limited to the United States.[8]

Humans just don't have access to truth, either in science, law, or any other mode of thinking. So what does an absence of truth mean for resilience? We believe we have some ideas!

THE DANGER OF HAVING FAITH IN SCIENCE OR RELIGION

Faith-based thinking, distinguished by an absence of falsifiability, testing, or the search for evidence, is central to religion, including extreme groups that we classify as cults.

However, to make sense of both science and religion, it is better to consider them as socio-cultural systems rather than simply modes of thinking. Like addiction, religion and cults confer certain benefits through constraints and loss of choice. Having unquestioning faith in science is no less perilous.

As we previously wrote, for perception, there is an argument that fitness beats truth. This position essentially means you can believe/have faith in whatever you desire, just so long as it conveys a benefit to you and your offspring.[9-11]

Resilient beliefs and faith-based constructs don't need to be grounded in more accurate, evidence-based versions of reality. Of course, you might need an evidence-based approach to determine if something is resilient or not, but let's not go down that rabbit hole.

As an example of reframing survival with faith, saying, "I was spared by God," after an illness or accident, can be a highly resilient position. However, saying, "God will protect me," whilst hurling yourself into dangerous situations without preparation, can get you killed in any one of a million-and-one dumb ways to die. Those who have developed resilience take personal responsibility for their actions regardless of what they believe or have faith in.

After the 9/11 terrorist attacks, Americans found very different ways to cope and come to grips with what had happened. Many Americans turned to their faith:

- 98% of them said that they coped by talking with others.
- 90% of them turned to religion.
- 60% of them participated in group activities.
- 36% of them made donations to charitable causes.[12]

Unfortunately, from these statistics, we cannot determine which of these strategies were the most resilient or which worked the best. We suspect that all of them were helpful to some extent.

So-called evidence-based medicine is another example of where faith is taken to extremes. There is no question that modern evidence-based medicine has mostly improved health, well-being, and longevity. However, this doesn't mean we should place our complete faith in modern medicine. Medical error is one of the top three causes of mortality. There are also multiple medical procedures that are advertised as evidence-based, and they *are* evidence based. Unfortunately, the evidence indicates that they are not very good, and that is omitted from the marketing. Blind faith in doctors and science, like blind faith in anything else, leaves you vulnerable to a host of risks (death among them).[13-15]

Having faith or a very strong belief that you can heal yourself offers the best opportunity to activate your innate placebo. We suspect that having faith, or a very strong belief, in an external supernatural or magical agent, could also be a useful way to maximize the placebo effect, provided there is some form of internal activation of the body's natural healing system and the belief is fully congruent. For example, imagined imagery and voices and feeling the effect of God's intervention could be an effective way to activate the neuroplastic potential for remapping the brain's experience of pain. Extrapolating what we know from recent neuroscience studies of pain, we speculate that passively waiting for help with no embodied engagement would be less effective.

Importantly, being coherent in beliefs and faith seems an unlikely prerequisite for resilience. There are plenty of religious practitioners and leaders who somehow manage to operate effectively in a scientific domain and keep their faith.

We have met a number of people who attribute their resilience to their faith, and they successfully reframe potentially traumatic experiences with God in mind. While many credit their survival to God, we note how they also demonstrate remarkable agency and personal responsibility. As an example, we interviewed one senior ranking U.S. military officer who was the recipient of the Silver Star (an American medal for exceptional bravery). He attributed his survival against the odds to God. We also note that he made every effort to move fast and keep his head down whilst rescuing his compatriots from a barrage of bullets.

The big danger of adopting a position of faith is that more vulnerable people become open to manipulation and exploitation: 51.6% of cults involve faith in supernatural, paranormal, or magical thinking.[16]

JUST IN CASE YOU WERE THINKING OF JOINING A CULT

Cults use framing and reframing to trap people in ways that create advantage for the leader(s) of the cult. Using the Evidence, Inference, Impact model, we offer the following advice on how to avoid becoming a cult member:

Does a religion, cult, or organization demand unquestioning belief (faith) in something that conveys an asymmetric advantage to the elite? (impact)

Men advantaged at the expense of women is the most common asymmetry (evidence and impact). Sex abuse, for example, is common in religious organizations and cults where faith and magical thinking or the threat of divine retribution (inference) is used to perpetrate sex crimes.[17-22]

Membership involves you giving money to support a wealthy guru or cadre of leaders (impact).

If your guru has a collection of 93 Rolls Royce cars, a string of court cases for fraud or theft, or personal wealth running into hundreds of millions of dollars, you might want to question, who paid for that wealth (evidence)? [23,24]

We're not judging anyone for owning car collections (inference), just drawing attention to the incongruence between many spiritual teachings and the upward (rather than outward) flow of capital (evidence, inference, and impact).

Does your participation in a faith-based organization result in more or less choice for you (evidence and impact)?

Many faith-based organizations offer relief from initial distress of some sort (impact), in a way that is similar to addictive disorders. In return, they demand loyalty, subservience to an established order or hierarchy, often followed by exploitation (inference and impact).[16,23]

Are you being steered into a political, religious or scientific, or medical extreme that could pose risks (evidence and impact)?

Social media and content algorithms are creating increasingly polarized societies.

Reflecting on a paper in the *American Journal of Political Science* in 2014 by Eric Oliver and Thomas Wood, Eric Levitz proposes a link between belief in the supernatural and conspiracy theories such as QAnon:

"Conspiracy theories, like fundamentalist theologies, posit that behind the maddening ambiguity and complexity of observed reality lies a straightforward conflict between the good and the wicked."[25]

Like so many religions and cults, "truth" is presented as something that can only be found inside.

"QAnon is a movement of people who interpret as a kind of gospel the online messages of an anonymous figure – 'Q' – who claims knowledge of a secret cabal of powerful pedophiles and sex traffickers."

— J. C. Wong[26]

Cult-like political manipulation is not simply a problem on the right end of the political spectrum. Dr. Alexandra Stein is a survivor of a left-wing cult, The O. Now an academic and practitioner who helps people escape and recover from cults, Stein spent 10 years as a young woman in a political cult, an experience she described in her book, *Inside Out*.[27] Her later book *Terror, Love and Brainwashing: Attachment in Cults and Totalitarian Systems* offers practical advice that can be applied even to the not-so-extreme examples of being framed.[28]

"Conspiracy theories connect the dots of random events into meaningful patterns (patternicity), and then infuse those patterns with intentional agency (agenticity). Add to this the confirmation bias (the tendency to look for and find confirmatory evidence for what we already believe) and the hindsight bias (after the fact explanation for what you already know happened), and we have the foundation for conspiratorial cognition."

— Michael Shermer[29]

YOU'VE BEEN FRAMED

"By drawing attention to certain details or facts, a headline can affect what existing knowledge is activated in your head [brain and nervous system]. By its choice of phrasing, a headline can influence your mindset as you read so that you later recall details that coincide with what you were expecting."

— Maria Konnikova "How Headlines Change the Way We Think"[32]

We don't have far to look to find examples of disingenuous framing. News organizations, depending on the political bent of their owners or the political leanings of their readers/viewers, can cast the same event in very different lights.

For example, let's look at some of the reporting surrounding the response in America and abroad to the death of George Floyd.

We searched the following two sentences online, with the purposeful use of the word "riots":

"Fox news report George Floyd riots"

And

"CNN news report George Floyd riots"

On one channel, we had the following:

"Thousands around the world protest George Floyd's death in global display of solidarity."

"Over the weekend, demonstrators gathered in London, Berlin and Auckland, among other cities, to protest against police brutality in solidarity with the US crowds."[30]

Over on the other channel, the protests were being framed very differently:

"American cities are spending Monday morning digging out from scenes of destruction after demonstrations against the police-involved death of George Floyd gave way to a fifth straight night of looting and rioting, resulting in another wave of arrests."[31]

If you have even the slightest experience of American news, you'll know which report belongs to which channel.

Media professionals exploit the difference between "demonstrating" and "rioting," between "mob" and "crowd." Rather than attempting to communicate facts objectively, the event is framed subjectively to line up with the viewer's or reader's expectations. If news were objective, we would only require one news channel for everyone on the planet. The reporting would be a delivery of facts rather than a narrative that supports the socio-political position of the media platform.

Headlines act as frames to the content in a report and can guide our attention to what is spoken about thereafter. Dramatic headlines trigger a felt response, and people return for more content following responses of this kind.[33]

Nearly two-thirds of Americans report fatigue from news reports.[34] In part, this is an unconscious response to a continuous stream of overly dramatic hype. The fear response is generally stronger than the feel-good response, so news media exploit this in much the same way that some politicians do to get votes.

In addition to regularly switching off, we encourage people to identify the patterns in what is being offered to them as news. By doing this, we can start to tell the difference between factual content and disingenuous framing. The more we can recognize this framing and identify the patterns it is reinforcing, the more we can navigate with agency.

We don't have to swallow what the media presents to us. Instead, we can seek to detect the underlying patterns and intentions. Broaden your access to different perspectives as well. Some news agencies are more balanced politically than others. If you start seeing references to evidence and sources, you're probably on the right track. If they present alternative facts, run away.

Next time you read a headline or watch the opening segment of a news program, ask yourself what kind of frame is being applied and for what purpose. How is the factual content being manipulated and shaped by this frame? Is it being framed to draw our attention to the evidence or away from it? This line of questioning can provide clarity and help prevent the spread of false information.[35]

This skeptical approach can be applied to advertisers and influencers, preachers and giants of the personal development world, gurus, filmmakers, and authors.

SCIENCE HAS AN UNDESERVED REPUTATION ISSUE

"The great tragedy of science is the slaying of a beautiful hypothesis by an ugly fact."

— Thomas Huxley

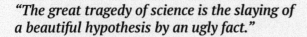

The scientific method might not be perfect or even universally agreed upon, but it is the best approach we have for understanding the natural world. Where we get into trouble is the subjectivity and unfortunate effect that distorting drivers within the "business" of science has on that. The presentation of science is also very much prone to framing and reframing.[36]

"Scientifically proven" is an example of a term that is either used to misrepresent scientific evidence as being true for the purposes of selling you something or because someone has faith in science in a way that misses the whole benefit of the scientific approach — to question, test, and refute based upon evidence.

Another over-hyped term that we've previously addressed is "evidence-based." There are plenty of health treatments that claim to be evidence-based, but when you look at that evidence, the positive benefits are often no better than the placebo. Or the evidence is simply not very good, and vested interests mean there's little enthusiasm to chase down anything that could provide counterevidence.

BEWARE VESTED INTERESTS

As an example of vested interest, if you watched a documentary promoting the benefits of eating only plants, and:

- The executive producer owns an organic pea protein company.
- The celebrities and medical "professionals" all have side hustles selling plant-based supplements.
- Athletes who are prominent vegans are chosen to create the impression that you too can be an elite athlete if you stop eating meat (no training required).
- Scientific articles are presented that represent only one small part of the scientific body of evidence.

Be on your guard. You are being framed. To be clear, we have nothing against vegans. We would have the same reservations when watching a documentary discussing the benefits of a carnivorous diet if it were produced by the owner of a cattle ranch and supported by famous carnivores and medical doctors with shares in a fried chicken franchise!

*"There are three kinds of lies:
lies, damned lies, and statistics."*

— Mark Twain

SCIENTIFIC BIAS BY DESIGN

There is a well-reported "crisis in science" that concerns the widespread inability to replicate scientific findings, especially in the social sciences.[37-41] There are many "innocent" reasons for this, including perverse incentives in academia and disproportionate recognition for publishing new ideas rather than refuting old ones.[40,42-44] However, bias by design can occur through a variety of means:

- Theory can be framed or reframed in such a way as to allow a favorable inference.[45]
- Subjects can be chosen to maximize the treatment effect with respect to placebo.[46,47]
- Statistical risk and benefit can be presented in a way that maximizes apparent benefit and downplays risk.[48]
- Data can be "tortured" to yield a positive result.[49]
- Lots of trials can be conducted and only the positive ones reported.[49]

To illustrate how science can be biased by careful framing, consider the findings of a 2008 American study. Researchers tracked 74 antidepressant trials involving 12,564 patients: 38 trials had positive results; 36 of the trials had negative results, showing no benefit. Of the positive trials, 37 out of 38 were published. Of the negative trials, only 14 out of 36 saw the light of day, and 11 of these were spun into a positive light. Only 3 of the negative trials were presented as evidence against the drugs' efficacy.[50]

BEWARE CELEBRITY EXPERTISE

Just because you can judge a family cooking competition to determine who makes the best meatballs, doesn't qualify you as an epidemiologist.

Beware celebrity or influencer endorsements. If a background in fringe conspiracy theories is not a sufficient red flag, follow the money. What are they getting in return for their endorsement? What are they selling? If it's meatballs, fine. If it's a treatment for Covid-19 using a $15,000 (untested) "BioCharger subtle energy light revitalization platform," that's a different story. It shouldn't take court action by the Therapeutic Goods Administration to alert you to potential exploitation (you couldn't make this up if you tried).[51]

If you're ever in doubt, follow the money.

ROLL OUT THE DISCREDITED SCIENTIST

Whether they're making a case for or against something, those with an axe to grind or a dollar to pocket will go out of their way to present discredited scientists who have been "silenced" by the establishment. These subject experts are rolled out as whistleblowers who are, so we are told, here to tell us an inconvenient truth. Behind this, you'll often find a long track record of problematic and debunked claims, court cases, and retracted or discredited papers.[52-55] Sitting on the board of companies that benefit from an extreme view which denies the weight of scientific evidence is another giveaway. Always beware when personal benefit has biased the interpretation of factual information. Even if they are sermonizing the benefits of science, they might have their own benefits in mind.[56-58]

Again, follow the money, and also the fame.

265

EVIDENCE OFTEN NEEDS RESCUE

When attempting to make sense of information, it is often important to RESCUE evidence from the forces of vagueness, obfuscation, and alternative facts (i.e., deliberate bullshit that demonstrates contempt for the audience's ability to discern fact from fiction).

R

ROBUST?

Is the evidence of high quality?

E

EXCEPTIONAL?

Is the evidence exceptional, or does it support a consensus view? Exceptional claims demand exceptional evidence, so look for multiple and diverse lines of evidence that stack up. However, remain alert to exceptions.

S

SOURCE?

Do you have access to the source? Is this a second-hand, mysterious, or anecdotal account? Does the publication have a long history of accurate reporting?

C

COHERENT?

Is the evidence coherent with the wider body of general knowledge, or is it at odds with fundamental ideas? If there are divergences, how are they explained?

U

UNBIASED?

Does the evidence fit your own bias (beware confirmation bias)? Do those endorsing the claims have something to gain from the endorsement? Follow the money!

E

ENOUGH?

Do you have enough evidence? Before you decide or act, look for contrary evidence.

FEEDFORWARD FROM FAILURE

He's not helped with cooking, cleaning or the kid's bed time in fourteen years!...

"There is no failure, only feedback"

— Anonymous

Point a microphone at a speaker, and the high-pitched tone that fills the room will have most people covering their ears. Nobody likes this kind of feedback, and not many people like the form of feedback used in the workplace. In this context, feedback is an attempt at framing criticism as insights that are good for you.

To effectively give and receive feedback requires more than superficial reframing. Simply criticizing under the banner of "feedback" does little to build trust or improve performance or relationships.

In *From Contempt to Curiosity*, Caitlin Walker offers a clean feedback process that can be adapted more broadly for resilience and decision-making. With the addition of considering intention, we use the same process of considering *evidence*, *inference*, and *impact* as a guide to reframing more generally.[59]

Evidence: observable behavior.

What did you see and hear?

Inference: our subjective interpretation of that behavior.

What meaning did you attribute to the behavior?

Impact: Your response to the inference (not the evidence).

What were the consequences of the inference?

Let's look at a few examples of how we might give feedback using this model (after Walker):

A POST-PRESENTATION REVIEW:

Evidence: I saw and heard you subtly ask me questions about points I had forgotten to mention in the presentation.

Inference: You care about how the company perceives me within our team.

Impact: We all celebrated a successful presentation and my gratitude for our work relationship increased.

A STRUGGLING RELATIONSHIP:

Evidence: I overheard you describing my shortcomings to your friends.

Inference: You don't respect me.

Impact: I am planning ways to separate.

It's essential in the sequence to separate inference from evidence. Value-attribution terms such as "good" and "bad" are too subjective, too loaded with personal meaning and interpretation. Be specific with your evidence.

For ambiguous evidence, the simplest challenges are specifier questions, though without careful attention to rapport they can appear a bit abrupt. Remember to soften their delivery with packaging.[60]

For unspecified nouns, ask:

What specifically?

For unspecified verbs, ask:

How specifically?

"You asked good questions" is not the same as the more specific "You asked three questions to remind me of what I had forgotten."

Or:

"You criticized me" is not the same as "You told me that I sit on the sofa drinking alcohol in the evenings, whilst you make dinner and put the kids to bed."

The specificity of the evidence and how it is described is key to communicating in any feedback process.

One useful reframe for unhelpful criticism is to set up a blah-blah-blah filter. This filter converts all criticism into the sound of blah-blah-blah until something is said that is based on evidence and is useful. That evidence-based feedback is then taken into account when considering what to do differently in the future.

The next stage of reframing failure into future success is to establish a feedforward loop for "do differently." Feedforward can then be designed to be explicit or implicit, depending on how new knowledge is integrated into the OODA loop(s) we described previously.

ACTIVITY

REFRAMING INFERENCE USING EVIDENCE

Here are five brief narratives from coaching clients. Identify the three key components of these exchanges: the evidence, the inference, and the impact. Once you've identified these components, rewrite the narrative reframing the *inference* and thereby changing the impact. There are additional evidential clues in the illustrations.

Authentic client reframes for these events are presented on the next double page.

My boss is a bully. He shouted at me and threw his papers across the room in a fit of rage. I'm so stressed I can't face going back to the office.

Evidence

_____

_____

_____

_____

Inference

_____

_____

_____

_____

Impact

_____

_____

_____

_____

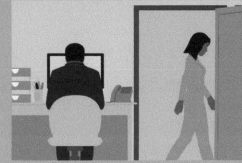

Our team culture is terrible. There's no respect. They never say good morning to me. They just walk straight past my office door. I'd rather work somewhere else.

Evidence

_____

_____

_____

_____

Inference

_____

_____

_____

_____

Impact

_____

_____

_____

_____

I confessed to my manager that I was anxious about meeting expectations. She sent me to see you, to work on improving my confidence and self-esteem.

I'm struggling to cope with my kids constantly wanting my attention. They rarely pester their dad.

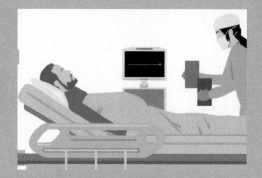

I lost one today. They were flat-lined when I arrived.

Evidence
_____
_____
_____
_____

Evidence
_____
_____
_____
_____

Evidence
_____
_____
_____
_____

Inference
_____
_____
_____
_____

Inference
_____
_____
_____
_____

Inference
_____
_____
_____
_____

Impact
_____
_____
_____
_____

Impact
_____
_____
_____
_____

Impact
_____
_____
_____
_____

EXAMPLES OF REFRAMING INFERENCE

These examples of reframing are from our coaching clients.

My boss is a baby! He's having a tantrum like a four-year-old. I realize that I am the adult in the room, and I can manage this.

Oh, they just think I don't want to be disturbed! I'll say good morning and see what happens.

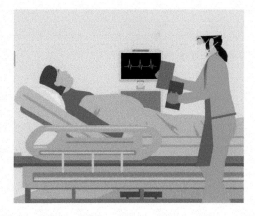

Ah, I see that a bit of "anxious" is serving me well in the context of this project. I don't have all the resources I need to confidently deliver what was originally presented. I have been set up to fail. I need to take action and manage expectations.

I can view my children's attention as a sign that they love spending time with me. It's a sign I am a good mum. I wonder if their father feels that he has enough time to play with the kids as much as he would like?

They were already dead when I arrived. I didn't lose them. I was simply unable to perform a miracle and bring them back from death. I did all I could, and I know that every now and again miracles do happen when we get to a patient just in time to save them.

> *"I've been known to tell people that my favorite dish is goat. Preferably fried in a hubcap, over a burning tire with a drizzle of motor oil, served with anything except the local water.*
>
> *Admittedly I've never actually consumed such a meal, only seen it cooked and served this way; though luckily not the goat I met in Haiti right after the 2010 earthquake."*

RECALLING A GOAT

CHRIS TOMPKINS

A professional firefighter, paramedic and technical rescue technician with 30 years of experience in emergency response, Chris Tompkins once held a volunteer role as an NGO executive. He now consults for global humanitarian organizations.

Chris has worked as operations leader in Haiti, Chile, Pakistan, Japan, The Philippines, Kashmir, Gaza, Jordan, Greece, Nepal, Iraq, Sudan, and several other countries.

The air in those first days after the quake was heavy with the presence of death, made worse by sweltering temperatures and 230,000 lost souls. Some 3 million people were affected and desperate. From those 3 million, traumatic injuries flowed with no end to the scant medical providers who were first in the country.

Through unbidden tears and anger, time was distorted, and most days crawled into nighttime like a week of purgatory holding us tight.

Standing in the dark at the open flaps of a tent not designed for medical work, the canvas walls allowing just enough room to fit a patient litter perched atop stacked cinder blocks, I witnessed yet another leg amputation. This night my observer position felt like respite from a brutal day. Minding my headlamp etiquette so as not to interfere with the headlamps responsible for removing the leg, I noticed a rooster under the operating table; it was pecking up the offerings falling, much to its delight.

Sensing a new presence to my left and expecting a medical companion, I turned, speaking my distaste, only to find a male goat also watching the rooster. Rather than wasting the moment, I continued speaking what was on my mind and the goat courteously gave me his full attention, with something of an apologetic look on his face. As if to say, "I'm sorry for the ill manners of my chicken friend, but you have to pull yourself together now and stop speaking aloud to me."

The goat and I turned our attention back to the feeding rooster before re-engaging in silent concurrence that the rooster had taken things too far, even for this situation. My horned companion then returned to the shadows and I went back to work, strangely refreshed.

I realized upon returning home how that rooster represented the often-surreal desperation we were faced with in Haiti. However, the goat became a resource to me, providing a memory that allowed me to smile, for a moment at least.

Years later and the horned, hooved Billy has been exchanged for a far more precise and effective approach. My colleagues and I have remained healthy and resilient through some of the most extreme experiences by way of the resilience training we undergo. I firmly believe that resilience training should be considered a standard for emergency responders in all fields. It's also considerably more convenient than relying on a goat.

FROM DARK HUMOR COMES LIGHT

"Things can't be that bad if I can still laugh."
— Carmen Moran and Margaret Massam[63]

Humor, especially gallows humor or black humor, has long been recognized as a resilient strategy. It helps us cope with challenging or potentially traumatic events. It is no surprise that this type of humor is commonly used by emergency services personnel.[61–63]

Humor is also recognized in several scales that aim to measure resilience.[64–66]

To the uninitiated, dark humor may appear callous, uncaring, politically incorrect, or just plain offensive. For those new to frontline or high-pressure work, such humor can be shocking, and comments and gestures can often seem as though they cross the line.[67,68]

The question is, what defines the line?

On one side of the line we have humor as an important part of a portfolio of resilient strategies; on the other side of the line we have what some perceive as highly inappropriate behavior.

Intention makes a lot of difference, though perception makes all the difference. When humor is used to harm others, or others perceive it to be offensive, then it is inappropriate. When we use it to change our perception of events unfolding around us, and in a culturally appropriate context, it can be a powerful technique.

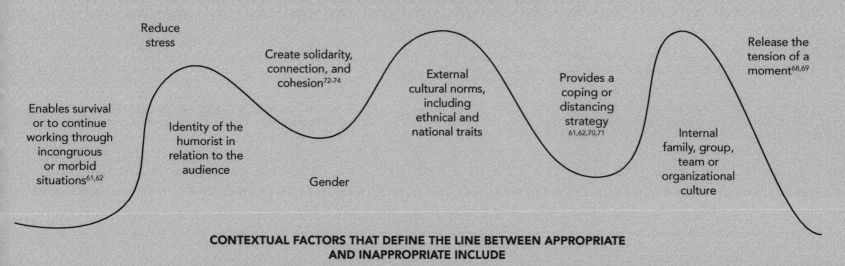

DESCRIPTIONS OF RESILIENCE BENEFITS INCLUDE

Reduce stress

Create solidarity, connection, and cohesion[72-74]

External cultural norms, including ethnical and national traits

Provides a coping or distancing strategy[61,62,70,71]

Release the tension of a moment[68,69]

Enables survival or to continue working through incongruous or morbid situations[61,62]

Identity of the humorist in relation to the audience

Gender

Internal family, group, team or organizational culture

CONTEXTUAL FACTORS THAT DEFINE THE LINE BETWEEN APPROPRIATE AND INAPPROPRIATE INCLUDE

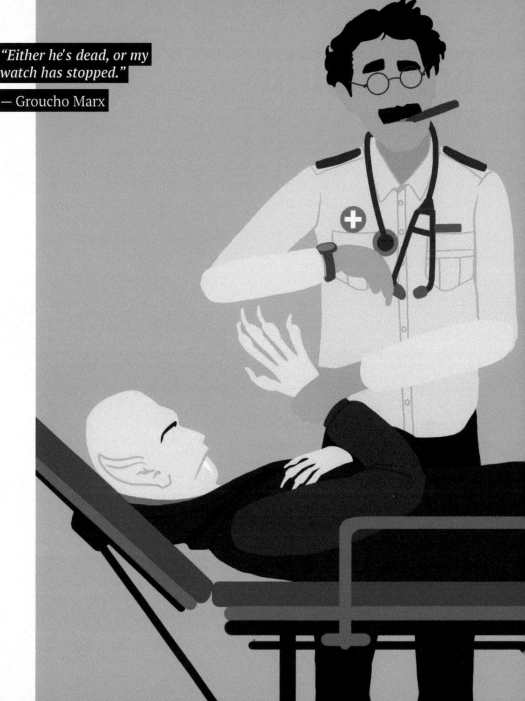

In her review of the use of humor for preparing paramedic students, Sarah Christopher from the University of Lincoln notes that black humor is informally passed along like a trait from experienced emergency personnel to those who are new in their role.

Christopher builds on earlier work that notes the benefits of deliberate efforts to inject humor into the workplace.[69,70] These earlier studies found that humor also benefits patients: it can distract from pain and anxiety, and it can help create a stronger team dynamic.[71,72]

Like any resilience strategy, context matters enormously, and, unlike in the movies, humor cannot be scripted. It is quirky, creative, and of course wickedly good fun. We can't think of any situation where a well-timed comedic response is not a great resilient strategy.

Just like any efforts to change culture, if there is a need to make explicit the line between ok and not ok, subtle verbal and non-verbal encouragement for "more like this" and "less like that" can be highly effective. Subtle clues like cocking your head and raising your eyebrows when a joke is poorly timed might help you make that blurry line between appropriate and inappropriate humor a little clearer. Or simply explain that a line has been crossed.

REFRAMING WITH INTENT

The following conversation is paraphrased from a coaching session during which we used reframing, in combination with a number of techniques described in this book, to create more choice for a client who was experiencing work-related stress.

Client: I'm stressed and being bullied at work. I have been off work now for six weeks, and I can't face going back.

Coach: Imagine for a moment going to an entirely new workplace, one that is safe and rewarding.

(Coach observes client's non-verbal patterns).

If you were offered a job in a workplace like that, would you take it?

Client: Yes!

Coach: And how did you know that the answer was "yes"? (coach helps client discover how she knows "yes")

Coach: And if you were invited to return to your old workplace…(coach observes strong "no" signal, is interrupted)…

Client: No!…(narrative objection; coach helps client discover how she knows "no")

Coach: Just step back for a moment and observe stressed-out (client name) over there. What is the positive intention for stress in the context of work?

Client: To keep me safe and away from my manager who is bullying me.

Coach: You can keep the state of stress if it is serving you well. What other states or strategies could potentially serve you better?

There followed two sessions discovering different states and strategies.

Client: If I sit like this (shows upright posture, breathing) and to the side, I can argue my case with Human Resources.

I have spoken with my family, and I have decided to get a lawyer to represent me. We can commit $80K to this case before I need to concede defeat and walk away.

Any more than $80K, and my stress signal returns.

After some very assertive negotiating and help from a lawyer, the client successfully won a transfer within the organization. She has been happy and productive in this new role for a number years now. In this case, the approach and outcome are unusual. Most people choose to just leave the workplace.

N-STEP REFRAMING

Six or n-step (n meaning there could be any number here) reframing is an effective behavior-change format that can be adapted and expanded to include change for any situation that needs improving. Additional steps can be added, some steps can be used recursively, and there are various ways to meet the intention of each of the original six steps.

The original six steps as coded and presented by Bostic St. Clair and Grinder are shown in **bold,** and our adaptations are shown alongside.[73] The most common additional or recursive steps are indicated.

You can apply the process to yourself, or you can use it to coach others or teams. The applications and adaptations are limitless.

Step 1.

Identify the behavior(s) to be changed.

Behavior can be extended to include the present state more generally.

It is possible to reframe right here in Step 1 to identify a desired outcome, but it is better to wait until after you've identified the positive intentions in Step 4.

Step 2.

Establish a reliable involuntary signal system with the unconscious.

The intention here is to ensure deeper engagement, beyond conscious narrative from the left brain interpreter. This step could also include induced flow, or it could include working with metaphors and symbols, either embodied or through the arts.

Step 3.

Confirm the positive intention(s) behind the behaviors to be changed.

There are often additional intentions (sometimes a chain of them).

This step can be as simple and elegant as an unconscious "yes" signal, or it could involve a metaphor, a narrative, or even a discussion with your family or team at work.

Step 6.

Ecological check

This is best done by embodied visualization of a future situation or scenario.

Especially for complex situations, it often pays to introduce one or more challenges or pressure tests to help develop general resilience that can handle the unforeseen.

Step 5.

Get the unconscious to accept responsibility for implementation.

As with Step 3, there are many ways to ensure that the unconscious is involved and accepts responsibility for action.

It's usually easy to calibrate that a hesitant "yes" means no!

You might need to repeat Steps 5 and 6 a number of times.

Step 4.

Generate a set of desirable alternative behaviors that satisfy the positive intention(s) of those being changed.

These could remain unconscious, or they could be discovered consciously. They might also emerge from flow with the aid of a flowstate game.

BE SKEPTICAL OF PESSIMISM AND OPTIMISM

Skepticism is a useful operating position for scientists and anyone concerned with evidence-based decision-making. There is a big difference, though, between skepticism and denialism. Denialism takes skepticism to an extreme position by refusing to accept reasonable evidence. Denialism is often motivated by personal gain or fear.

Being in denial also often results in blaming others for our emotional responses (cause/effect myths) or for pretty much anything (or everything). It is a particularly fragile strategy. Just about the only coaching clients who have failed to benefit from the methods in this book are those who prefer to externalize their own responses upon someone or something else, refusing to accept personal responsibility.

Equally, reframing events into the positive can be overdone at the expense of grounding in evidence. Positive psychology and mindfulness are effective resilience strategies when applied in an appropriate context while maintaining situational awareness.

Reframing a challenging situation with platitudes, like *All things come to those who wait* or *If it's meant to be, it's meant to be*, creates a passive acceptance. This is not resilient if action is the required response.

Instead of reframing with platitudes, use humor. Rather than falling further and further into passivity, humor will allow us to activate resourceful states, strengthening our resolve and preparing us for the challenges we face.

Even the most pessimistic of creatures can summon at least some form of reframe every so often...

"It's snowing still," said Eeyore, gloomily.

"And freezing."

"However," he said, brightening up a little, "we haven't had an earthquake lately."

How would it be to translate this pattern throughout life? This simple three-part reframe can be used on the frontline, in business, at home, or even on a freezing-cold building site, where an earthquake really would be bad.

LET'S KEEP A LOW PROFILE...

Imagine you are the fly on the wall for a conversation in an alien galaxy far, far away.

Boss: Welcome back, Zog! How was your trip to Earth? Tell us, what did you discover?

Zog: It was warm and sunny. It was perfect. I didn't want to leave! I had the time of my life sunbathing.

Boss: Did you find intelligent life?

Zog: Err, no...

Boss: Did you look thoroughly, Zog? Remember: "Absence of evidence is not evidence of absence."

Zog: Hmm, I'll go back and have another look.

Some time later

Boss: Welcome back again, Zog! Tell us, what did you discover this time?

Zog: It was cold! I went back to the place I visited last time. The first time I visited, the temperature was 30°C. This time it was 4°C! I traveled to the top and bottom of the planet, and it was even colder there! The bottom was −50 °C.

Boss: And did you find intelligent civilized life?

Zog: Hmm. It was so cold, my crew thought it unlikely that anything could still live there.

Boss: Zog, did you personally check the WHOLE planet?

Zog: Hmm. I'll go back and have another look.

Some time later

Boss: Welcome back again Zog! So... lifeforms?

Zog: Boss! It's incredible. There are so many forms of life. The apex predators are bipedal and can communicate quite adequately. In fact, they never seem to shut up. Something about the left brain interpreter.

Boss: And are they intelligent and civilized?

Zog: Well...they are still tribal. Mostly they compete with each other and many tribes are at war. Most don't even have enough to eat.

Boss: Oh, good...Do they have a God?

Zog: Err...err...I'll go back and have another look.

Some time later

Boss: Welcome back, again Zog! Tell us, do they have a God?

Zog: Well, after interviewing many earthlings, we discovered more than 10,000 religions and many more gods![74] Here's the weird part, though. We couldn't find evidence for any of them.

They have gods, but zero evidence for any of them. They are a tribal people after all.

Boss: This is critical Zog. We need to know if they are intelligent, and civilized.

Are they aware of our intentions Zog?

Zog: No! I spoke to dozens of them, and when they told others in their tribe, they were laughed at and locked up.

Boss: Good, Zog!

I think we have enough evidence to decide. It's clear that they are not intelligent or civilized.

So, Zog, are they tasty?

Zog: Err...I forgot to taste them!

Boss: ZOG! Your mission was to hunt and gather. You have two simple criteria to determine whether they are suitable for harvesting: 1) Do they display civilized intelligence? 2) Are they tasty?

How hard is it, Zog? (shuffles clipboard marked "Performance Review").

The evidence I have before me is that you made four incredibly expensive trips to this planet, and you still do not have the critically important answers we need. You have not met the intention for your trip.

I infer from this that you, Zog, are not intelligent.

The impact is…

GULP…

BURP!

Sometimes it pays to keep a low profile.[75]

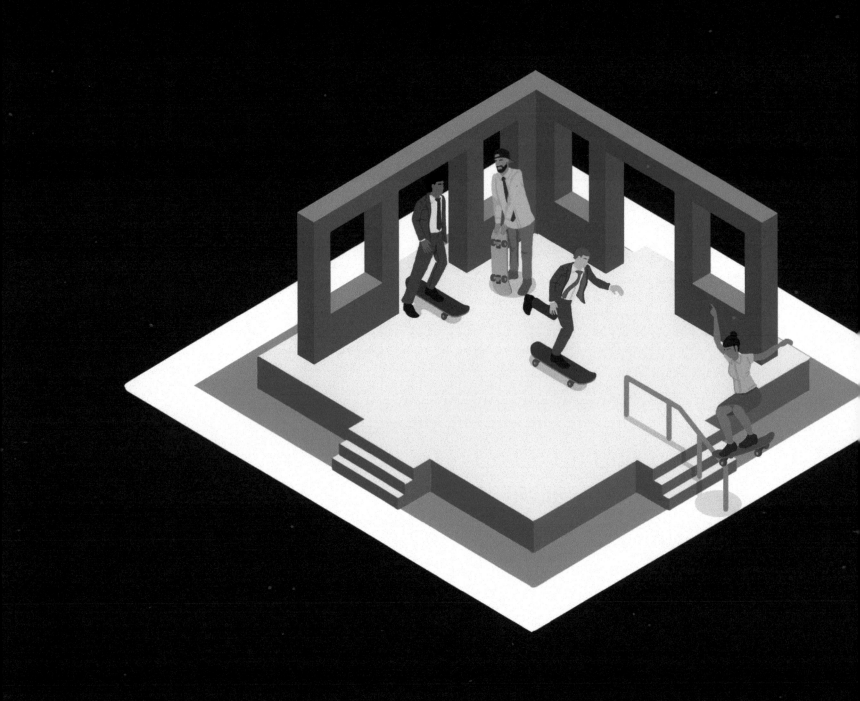

FLOW

"Decision making in flow is effortless, spontaneous and nonlinear."

"It's a sense of oneness with my surroundings."

"MY BODY JUST DOES THE WORK"

"I DON'T THINK ABOUT ANYTHING, I JUST AM"

DESCRIBING THE INDESCRIBABLE

Until recently, the highly focused states of elite athletes, prolific authors, inspiring musicians, and great scientists have mostly remained a mystery. Their intense passion seems to be combined with a magical ingredient. It can seem as if elite performers have a gift or calling, outside of their control and supposedly beyond the rest of us.

Hungarian-American psychiatrist Mihaly Csikszentmihalyi (pronounced muh-hei-lee chik-sent-mee-hai) first named and introduced the concept of *flow* after interviews with exceptional performers who described their experiences as "like being in water carried along."[1-3]

Also described as "being in the zone," flow is a state of full immersion, energized focus, and complete absorption. It's in this state that we can operate at the peak of our abilities.[4-7] When asked to explain what they're experiencing when in flow, high performers often struggle

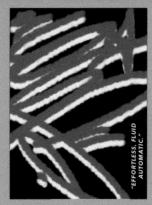

"EFFORTLESS, FLUID AUTOMATIC."

"Profound clarity"

"A voice just tells me what to do, and it's not my usual voice."

"My peripheral vision fades away......"

" M y p e r i p h e r a l v i s i o n o p e n s u p . "

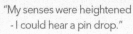

"It's such a peaceful state of mind."

"My senses were heightened - I could hear a pin drop."

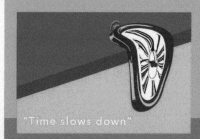

"Time slows down"

None of these descriptions of flow are sufficient for others to replicate the state.

to find the words, like it's some sort of supernatural state of being.

High-performance states vary according to the individual, activity, and context, and they can vary in intensity, stability, and duration.

Flow is often both a prerequisite for expert performance and a desired outcome in itself. By entering into flow, we can call up meditative-like states that provide release from the complexities and cognitive overload so common in modern living.

Regardless of what we call them, high-performance flow states become relatively easy to access when there is an appropriately high level of connectivity between the hemispheres of the brain — when we've activated our whole embodied neurology, when we are thinking without apparently thinking at all.

THE NEUROSCIENCE OF FLOW

Where exceptional people are often at a loss for words when trying to describe what being in flow feels like, science offers a rich, though no less opaque, articulation of what constitutes this privileged state.

Flow states have been studied in a variety of immersive and challenging settings, such as playing the piano, exercise, software development, rock climbing, and playing video games.[8-13] The scientific results support what the practitioners already know:

- Flow promotes risk-taking in activities like mountaineering or extreme water sports.
- Productivity increases when people are able to focus intensely.
- Flow enhances creativity.
- We can accelerate learning by incorporating flow into education or training.

When we coach teams and networks of teams in organizations, exponential benefit arises when those teams act in flow. Flow brings an unconscious ability to detect patterns, and this accelerates anticipation of the needs of others, allowing faster and higher-quality interactions between members. The sum becomes far greater than the parts. The emergence of collective intelligence leads to innovation and a step-change in performance, opportunity, and resilience.

"Flow state emergence requires transient hypo-frontality to momentarily suppress the analytical meta-conscious abilities of the explicit system, in favor of the implicit system mainly localised in the basal ganglia circuit."[14,15]

The experience of flow was associated with relative increases in neural activity in the left anterior inferior frontal gyrus and the left putamen. Relative decreases in neural activity were observed in the medial prefrontal cortex and the amygdala.[9]

Cathodal and anodal transcranial direct current stimulation (tDCS) over, respectively, the left dorsolateral prefrontal cortex and right parietal areas, may encourage flow experiences in complex real-life motor tasks that occur during sports, games, and everyday life.[16]

Smoothness perception seems to be at the root of the flow sensation and, among the different EEG rhythms, beta oscillation (13–30 Hz) is probably another relevant candidate for indexing flow.[8]

Electroencephalogram (EEG) readings taken in the midst of flow state show a combination of increased frontal theta and moderate frontocentral alpha rhythm.[17]

Flow is characterized by specific neural activation patterns and distinguishable brain activation patterns, encompassing reward-related midbrain structures, as well as cognitive and sensorimotor networks.[10]

DESIGNING GAMES TO INDUCE FLOW

Flow occupies the zone between understimulated and overwhelmed. It doesn't matter what level you start at, where you get on the stairs, or how high you ascend. Your intention is to enter the flow zone and then stabilize the flowstate.

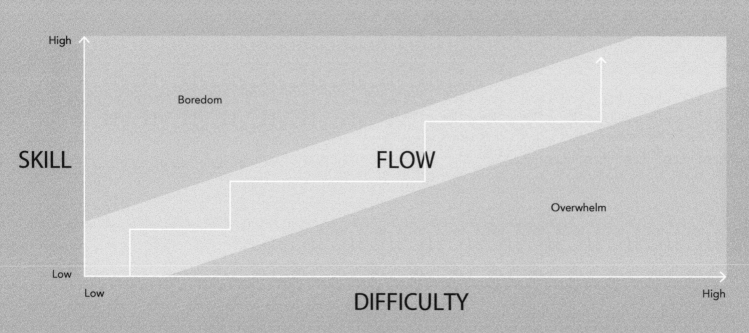

For some people flow is easy to find and stabilize through high-pressure activities. For others, flow is more elusive.

Fortunately, it is possible to induce flow and practice activating and stabilizing the state by playing flowstate games. With practice, many people report that even remembering the experience of playing a flow game is enough to trigger a state change.

Flowstate games use design principles that mimic the conditions in many sports. Most importantly, the game must accommodate activity that offers a range of difficulty (a scale). As you develop skills or mastery, the game ramps up in difficulty so that you have to continually rise to the challenge.

In addition to scalable difficulty, flow games should involve simultaneous use of both sides of the body. This requires cross-hemispherical activity in the head brain, which seems to be an important pre-condition for flow states.

Games should be performed with an even rhythm and a tempo (a rate) that is just fast enough to prevent consciously thinking your way through the challenge.

Games that verbalize externally by speaking aloud or singing help to eliminate internal self-talk. When people describe flow, they often reference the absence of internal dialogue. When you are flowing, the left brain interpreter takes a break.

Games are best played with a coach who monitors performance. The coach's job is to also calibrate for a change in state. With the coach, not the player, tracking for mistakes, the player can fully immerse themselves in the activity.

For many people, when they first start to play, "trying" to get to the end of a particular challenge or task creates problems. Peer pressure, internal dialogue, and competitiveness get in the way. Remember that completing the task is not important. The only measure of success with the game is the quality of state, and that means letting go and simply being in the moment.

With enough practice of entering flow, many people can just use subtle muscle movements to activate the state at will. Flow, like any state, can be activated and stabilized through any of the senses, using a variety of anchors or triggers.

ACTIVITY

THE ALPHABET GAME

A quick and effective way to get into flowstate is by playing the Alphabet Game. The version we present here is modified after original work by John Grinder, Roger Taub, and Judith DeLozier.[18]

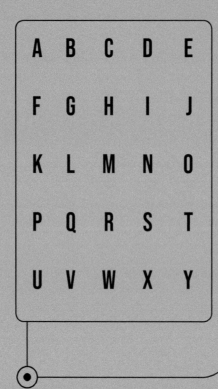

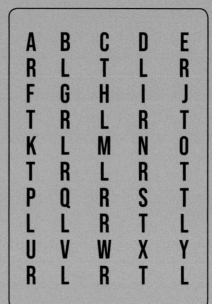

Step 1.

ALPHABET

Write the alphabet on a large sheet of paper using letters A-Y, with 5 letters on each line and enough space under each letter to add another letter of the same size.

Step 2.

INSTRUCTIONS

Beneath each alphabet letter, mostly at random, write either L (left), R (right), and T (together). We say "mostly" because beneath the letter T, use T (together); beneath L use R (right), and beneath R use L (left). This will make the game a little more difficult.

Ensure there are no more than 2 L's, R's, or T's next to each other either reading across the page or reading down the page.

The intention is to make the chart difficult. Colors, lines, or other aids are not helpful. Remember, the aim here is to create a game that meets the condition of scalar difficulty.

Charts only last for one use before they become too familiar and they need to be replaced.

Step 3.

SET UP

Set up and get yourself ready to play.

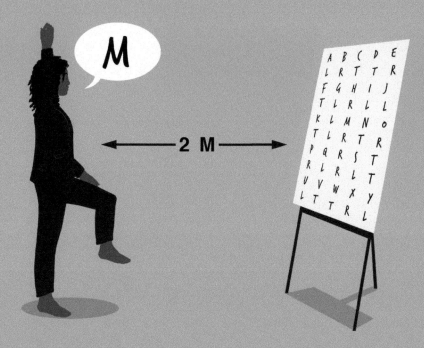

If you are coaching someone to play the game and develop flow, we recommend that you and the players stand so that the whole chart is visible and legible within your field of vision.

If you are coaching, your role is to establish rapport and frame the experience. Stand off to one side, forming a triangle with you, the player, and chart. Observe and monitor quality of action and changes in state, whilst also tracking for errors in performance.

Steady rhythm is important, and the player needs to progress through the game quickly enough to prevent conscious recovery from mistakes.

As the coach, you can also include instructions for making mistakes. Whenever a player makes a mistake, you can instruct them to shake off the state, relax, and start again at the beginning of that condition.

If you are coaching, you need to find the right balance between the frequency of correcting the player with the downside of interrupting flow.

ACTIVITY

LETTING GO TO FLOW

PLAYING THE GAME

First condition

Beginning at A, the player reads out loud the letters of the alphabet and simultaneously lifts the arm that correlates to the letter. If there is an L, the player lifts their left arm; if there is an R, they lift their right; if there is a T, they lift both arms at the same time.

Second condition

Begin bottom right at Y and work backwards to A following the same instructions as for the first condition using arms and calling the alphabet out aloud.

We suggest playing at this stage for at least two or more rounds.

Most people spend about 2–5 minutes in the first and second conditions.

Third condition

Beginning from A, and keeping the same arm-lifting pattern, add a further layer of difficulty. Whenever you lift your left arm, also lift your right leg; when you lift your right arm, also lift your left leg; when you lift both arms, bend both your knees. The pattern continues until you finish at Y.

Even if someone struggles with the first and second conditions, we find there is benefit to having a go at the

third condition. This might need careful framing and reassurance from the coach.

The third condition is typically used for about ten minutes. This is how long it takes most people to get a noticeable state change from the game. Calibration by the coach for a shift in physiology and a change in flow performance is more important than timed duration. However, when playing alone, we've found that a ten-minute time limit for the third condition works well. You can set a timer.

Ideally, you should progress through the various conditions so that you're always challenged. If you find the third condition too difficult, go back to the second condition.

Elite athletes and people who regularly tap into flow state and the unconscious might move extremely quickly through the flowgame to these more advanced conditions.

Fourth condition

Snake your way up and down the alphabet chart. Beginning from A, go down to U, then across to V, up to B, across to C and so on.

Fifth condition

Letters are randomly chosen by the coach. We use a pointing stick to identify letters and set the rhythm.

Sixth condition

Start to scrub out letters of the alphabet (but not the letter indicating which arm to raise) until there are progressively no letters left, with the client working backwards holding the alphabet in their memory. Going forwards is relatively easy, of course; most people find it quite difficult to go backwards through the alphabet. It's rare that anyone can hold the spatial distribution of the whole chart unconsciously for random choices led by a coach.

We have found the Alphabet Game to be one of the fastest and most effective ways to enter into a state of flow. It allows people to enhance their performance abilities, which can then be applied in a wide range of contexts. We use it to help prepare ourselves for high-pressure situations, or to get more resourceful perspectives of an event that has already occurred.

It's possible to modify the game for solo use. Ideally, you want something that can act like the coach to alert you if you make a mistake because it's more difficult to be in flow if you are simultaneously tracking for mistakes.

An advanced option for solo use is to modify the leg movements and play the game whilst balancing on a fitness ball wobble board.

When using a stopwatch for solo use, set the timer for ten minutes. You can progress through the levels whilst forgetting all about the timer. Ideally you will forget all about any other factor except the game itself. When you start to notice that you're getting into flow more quickly, lower the time limit.

We have clients who keep a laminated alphabet chart in their office, with empty space under each letter of the alphabet. This makes it easy to use a whiteboard marker to change the letter sequences below the alphabet, which ensures the player never gets too used to the sequence.

Flowstate can be applied throughout life. Examples include:

- When struggling to stay focused on a unit of work.
- Before going on stage to perform or speak.
- When playing sport.
- In conjunction with embodied visualization to work through a challenging context.
- When struggling to make a decision.
- For improving resilience in a challenging context.

We provide a handrail for applying flow in challenging situations in the next section.

WARNING!

The following pages are heavy with text and process descriptions. You may feel as though you're about to overload your noggin, just like the conditions for flow! However, engaging with these games could profoundly change your life.

ACTIVITY

FLOWSTATE CHANGE FORMAT

"Your problem is rarely the problem. Your problem is the state you approach the problem context with."

— John Grinder

To discover new perspectives or find new solutions to longstanding problems, we can induce a flowstate and then apply that state in either a remembered or imagined context.

The following six-step process can be mapped out on the floor using Post-It notes.

Step 1a.

IDENTIFY CONTEXT

From a third position (that of the curious observer), choose a physical space you can visualise yourself inhabiting.

Choose a context or an event to re-create "over there" in that space. It can be a memory that you are struggling to make sense of, it can be a current problem, or it can be a future event you are concerned about.

In your imagination, build a rich and detailed version of this event or context. This might be a bit like watching a hologram, seeing and hearing a projection of real life, including people, objects, and interactions, and, most importantly, yourself.

Step 1b.

SWITCH TO FIRST

From third position, move directly into first position (yourself) in the space you just developed. You should now be fully experiencing the situation with all your senses. Pay particularly close attention to felt sensations, states/emotions, and how you are breathing in this simulation.

This is an optional step with the advantage of a felt sensation of the situation. If the experience threatens to become at all overwhelming, you can step back out to third position and continue from there.

Step 2.

BREAK STATE

Step out of the immersed state. Shake your arms and move your body for at least a few seconds to shift the sensations you just experienced.

This "break and shake" helps to prevent you from taking the sensations from the context into the flowstate.

Step 3.

ACCESS FLOW

Using a different location, access flow. You can use the Alphabet Game, or you can go for a bike ride, juggle, or balance on a slackline — whatever helps you enter flow.

Step 4.

RETURN TO CONTEXT

Return to the context in location 1b (marked by a Post-It note). This would be 1a if your experience became overwhelming at any point. Carry the new embodied state of flow with you. Be sure to maintain the posture and the breathing as you walk into the location where you experienced the context. Ideally, re-enter the context maintaining the peak state of flow.

Notice how, when you carry the flowstate back into the context with you, your experience of that context changes. At first, experience this with a sense of curiosity, without consciously trying to change any part of the context you imagined.

At this step, many people describe that problems simply disappear or cease to be significant.

Step 6.

ECOLOGY CHECK

At a different location, imagine a context in the future in which what you discovered has come to pass.

What are the consequences for you and others? Consider cascading effects.

There are often downside consequences for taking action, and of course for not taking action.

There are even downsides to entering flow.

Step 5.

DISCOVERY

Sometimes, it is enough to detect that there is a new opportunity, even if we don't consciously understand what kind of opportunity it is.

When discovering, questions can help clarify:

- What would I like to have happen?
- What are my intentions?
- What state or resources will help me in this context?

THE DARK SIDE OF FLOW

While flow delivers performance, resilience, and enhanced survival abilities in extreme situations, it also has a dark side.[4]

When outlining flow, Csikszentmihalyi noted that it can be addictive. Flow is autotelic, meaning that it is an end or purpose in itself. The state of flow releases a host of neurochemicals that produce a feel-good hit that many describe as being better than drugs, alcohol, or even sex.

"The brain produces a giant cascade of neurochemistry. You get norepinephrine, dopamine, anandamide, serotonin and endorphins. All five of these seem to be performance enhancing neurochemicals."
— Steven Kotler[19]

In addition to the performance-enhancing benefits of flow, the compulsion to seek out more and more flow is also driven by the release from mundane responsibilities. For many, flow produces a catharsis — a dissociation or transcendence from self-induced anxiety or worry.[20-22] Flow has been implicated in online game and internet addiction, where obsessive use is associated with a breakdown in social connections or a drop in school or work focus.[23-25] Extensive research and development funding goes into crafting user interfaces and video games in order to capture the attention of gamers to have them enter immersive flowstates for extended periods of time. There are even a number of specialized treatment programs for online flow addiction.

The impact of overdoing flow is most immediately and dramatically apparent in extreme sports, where there is the potential for severe injury or even death. In sports as diverse as skateboarding, snowboarding, skiing, big wave surfing, or wingsuit flying, the neurochemical cocktail that accompanies flow propels flow junkies to pursue greater and greater risks.[19,26]

Flow distorts our ability to evaluate risks and consequences. Inexperienced participants in high-risk activities are easily seduced by flow. Where they should be cautious, they rush in, acting as though they were invincible, often with fatal consequences.[27]

Not being able to access flow can also lead to anti-social behavior.[28] Flow is central to motivation for many frontline service professionals. They thrive under pressure. When the lights are flashing and the sirens blaring, and when the crisis demands immediate and consequential action, they are at their best. The challenge comes when they start to consider a career change, or when they are forced (either by trauma or burnout) to step away from their frontline roles. For these high performers, finding alternative access to flow is an important part of the recovery from trauma and the transition from frontline service.

Switching from having a regular experience of flow in frontline work to a sedate job is like going cold turkey. For some, this transition is extremely abrupt. Soldiers returning from active duty are an important example. When engaged in combat, "one's entire awareness is absorbed in the present moment."[29] Soldiers lose a sense of self-awareness when completely absorbed in combat, with a "heightened sense of being alive," a loss of self-awareness, concentration, and a distortion in time.[28] Julia Schüler, a researcher at the University of Konstanz, suggested that this loss of self-reflective awareness is what allows soldiers to kill without guilt.[28]

Regardless of how people access flow, whether work, sports, or deep immersion in a hobby, transitioning to other contexts and managing the addictive nature of the experience can take deliberate effort and design.

I started BASE jumping as a way to extend the experience of being in the mountains. It was a dream of mine to climb up a big mountain or wall and then fly back down to the ground. I BASE jumped for four years, and there is almost no way to describe the feeling of wingsuit flying through mountain valleys at 100mph.

In the minutes leading up to a launch, my attention is 100% on the smallest details: the wind speed and direction, the state of my equipment, obstacles at the launch area. The adrenaline is building, but it also has to be controlled so that I make good decisions.

Check, check, check...

Then the world narrows down to become a single flowing moment. Step, step, launch...

The chambers in the wings of the suit fill with air and expand, then the initial drop slows, and you begin to glide. Even though there are many small parts in a sequence, in one second it all becomes the moment — one so intense that you can feel it in every cell of your body.

You become like a bird. For a very short duration you can twist, turn, and glide at high speed fully free of gravity's restrictions.

Pulling the chute always comes with a moment of trust and hope and as the flight slows under the canopy, the focus becomes landing safely, often amongst rocks and trees. Once you land, the world opens wide again. All the focus and inner attention moves over to your jump partners and friends, what you just did and the euphoria coursing through your body, often for many hours afterwards.

And then you want to do it all over again.

BASE jumping is ADDICTIVE. There's nothing else like it. It's also really, really dangerous. I've lost too many friends in the peak of their lives. There's no room for error, which is what makes the attention requirement so intense. If it wasn't so dangerous, I doubt we'd experience such flow in the moment.

Six years ago my son was born, and I had recently lost another close friend to base jumping and one whose partner was pregnant. It was time to hang up my wings. There are other ways to experience intense flow, though maybe not as all-consuming as wingsuit base jumping.

At least my son knows his dad is coming home.

NO ROOM FOR ERROR

Photo by Matt Robertson

TIM EMMETT

is a professional adventurer and climber. One of the world's top all-around climbers, he's attained world renown in ice, mixed, rock, deep-water solo, traditional, alpine, and para-alpinism. He lives in Squamish, Canada, with his wife and son.

THE LAST BARRIER TO FLOW

Recent advances in neuroscience, real-time sensing, and machine learning are only just beginning to characterize the patterns underlying flow states. In the near future, we might be able to elicit and stabilize flow states with the assistance of technologies such as virtual or augmented reality. We might also soon be able to model the flow of genius or elite performers and transfer those states to others by matching brainwaves and movement patterns. Technologies like qEEG are already helping athletes and soldiers access flow so they can learn faster and perform better.[30-32]

Flowstate games such as the Alphabet Game can be used for developing content-free high-performance states that can be applied to just about anything. In our practice, we've used flowstate games to train athletes, assist with neurological recovery from traumatic brain injuries, help clients discover solutions to challenging problems, help professionals access creative business solutions, and manage interpersonal relationships.

Paradoxically, we've found that flow games help people sleep. Quieting the left brain conscious chatter produces just the sort of high-performance state needed for deep sleep.

Practice, practice, practice. Then develop skills to access, stabilize, and apply the state. In time, you'll be able to do this without using games. Flow is quite possibly the ultimate resilience hack.

Remember, though, that flow is about letting go. As Yoda famously said to Luke, "Do or do not, there is no try." Any sense of trying, apprehension, or concern for success is inconsistent with flow.

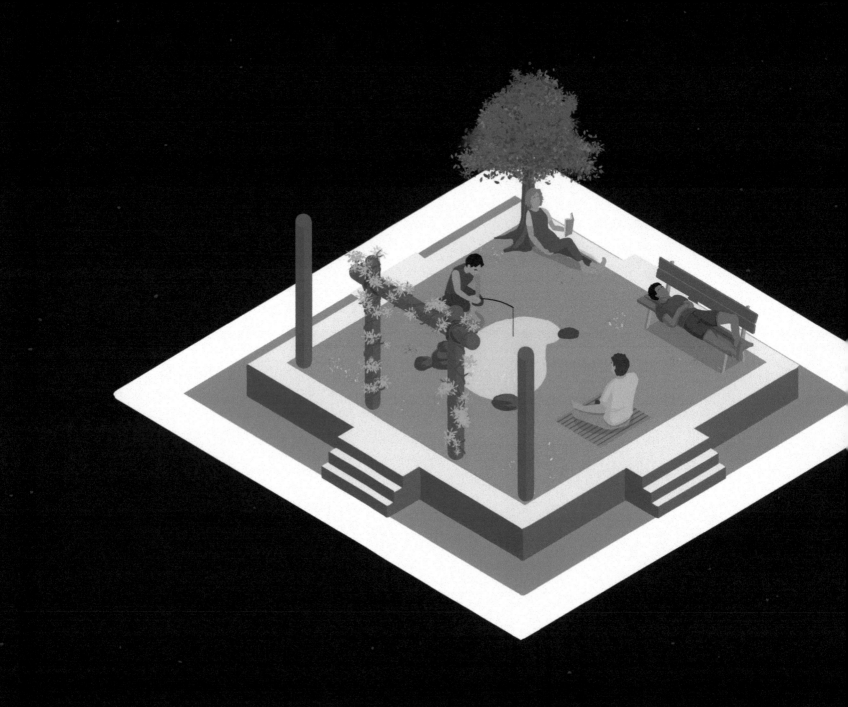

REST

3 MINUTES 59 AND 4/10 OF A SECOND

In *Peak Performance*, Brad Stulberg and Steve Magness describe their early days as prodigies. Steve was a world class middle-distance runner, Brad a high-level consultant in the high-stakes world of health care analysis. They describe the abrupt crash back to earth they experienced after suffering burnout. One minute they were soaring high above the clouds in the domain of the gods; the next minute they found themselves plummeting back to earth.

The experiences of exceptional early performance followed by burnout are extremely common in fields as diverse as sports, music, and business.

Burnout is not a failure to perform in a chosen field of endeavor; it is a failure to design and implement an effective recovery strategy.

In the 1940s and 1950s, The Mile was the running world's most prestigious event. Yesteryear's running community was obsessed with the quest for a sub-four-minute mile. The record had been progressively lowered from four minutes and fourteen seconds (1913) to four minutes and one second (1945). The record sat, seemingly unmovable, for more than a decade. Nobody could trim that extra second off. The world's best runners tailored their training to break the elusive barrier, but nobody was able to break the record — not until Roger Bannister became the first man to run a sub-four-minute mile in 1954.

Up until the moment that Bannister crossed the finish line, the four minute barrier was viewed as a physiological limitation on human capability. Accounts of Bannister's success overwhelmingly focused on his intense interval

Icarus is not a story about the limits of human performance. It is a story about the perils of poor design.

training and the immaculate teamwork of his pacemakers, Christopher Chataway and Chris Brasher.

Guided by their own experience of burnout, Stulberg and Magness identified an equally critical and often-overlooked aspect of Bannister's training: Bannister rested, possibly like no other athlete at the time who was competing at his standard.

"Before taking on history, Bannister made what seemed like a very questionable decision. He abandoned his training plan of intense intervals on the track and instead drove off to the mountains of Scotland, only a mere 2 weeks before the race. For days, he and a few buddies didn't speak of, let alone see a track. Instead they hiked and climbed in the mountains. They completely checked out of running psychologically and, to a great extent, physically.

Upon returning to England, Bannister once again shocked everyone in the running community. Instead of immediately hopping on a track in a fit of compulsion to do some "panic training" in the hopes of making up for lost time, he continued to rest. For 3 more days, Bannister let his body recuperate from the demands of

the training he'd put in during the months prior. With just a couple days to go before the record attempt, Bannister completed a few short workouts to tune his body up, but that was it.

When the bell rang signifying the final lap, Bannister burst into a maddening drive. As he slowly pulled away from the field, everyone in the crowd rose to their feet: 3:40, 3:41, 3:42…. Down the final straightaway, the energy was palpable. fans screaming at the top of their lungs … 3:54, 3:55…

As Bannister crossed the finish line, unaware of anything other than how hard he was pushing himself, the crowd roared. In 3 minutes, 59 and 4/10 of a second, Roger Bannister had broken one of the greatest barriers in history.

As Stulberg and Magness conclude, Bannister's remarkable achievement was in no small part due to his courage to rest.

THERE ARE NO MAGIC METRICS FOR WHEN OR HOW TO REST

Given the well-known anecdotal evidence for the importance of periodic rest, and the widespread use of macrocycle planning in sport, there is surprisingly very little peer-reviewed literature on the benefits of periodization in sport or any aspect of life.

One reason that quantitative studies of sleep and rest are under-represented is that so much attention is placed on the "doing" of performance. As Diana Renner and Steven D'Souza explore in *Not Doing: The Art of Turning Struggle into Ease*, there is a pervasive fixation on excessive activity that often occurs at the expense of well-being.

Also, the signals alerting us to burnout and fatigue are generally idiosyncratic. This is highlighted in a systematic review of burnout in physicians published in the *Journal of the American Medical Association*:[1]

"In this systematic review, there was substantial variability in prevalence estimates of burnout among physicians, ranging from 0% to 80.5%, and marked variation in burnout definitions, assessment methods, and study quality. Associations between burnout and sex, age, geography, time, specialty, and depressive symptoms could not be reliably determined."

— Lisa Rotenstein

In addition to marked variations in burnout definitions, descriptions of burnout in the literature are vastly different to the descriptions of felt experiences of burnout, or the signals or warning signs to take a break or rest just before burnout occurs. Compare this page from scientific accounts with the next one from people we have interviewed.

The so-called Maslach Burnout Inventory describes burnout as a prolonged response to chronic emotional and interpersonal stressors on the job. Burnout is characterized by **emotional exhaustion, depersonalization, and a low sense of personal accomplishment.**[2]

For athletes, burnout is a
psychosocial construct[3]

In much the same way that signs and symptoms of burnout are idiosyncratic, so too is the path to recovery.[8]

Unsurprisingly, researchers note that the path to burnout recovery becomes easier to navigate when personal agency is strong and other life areas support the recovery process.[8]

The key to avoiding burnout is to recognize and respond to the signal to rest before crossing the tipping point.

For nurses, burnout is a form of **moral distress.**[4]

For teachers, burnout usually involves **exhaustion, cynicism, and substantially reduced professional efficacy.**[5]

Burnout amongst police officers usually includes **emotional exhaustion and depersonalization.**[6]

For paramedics, burnout is linked to **poor job retention, poor patient care, and decreased emotional and physical well-being.**[7]

SIGNALS TO REST AND SLEEP

For busy people, it's all too easy to ignore the signal to rest or to let sleep pressure build to the point of exhaustion.

Compare the following descriptions of burnout signals from the people we interviewed for this book with the previous descriptions of burnout from academic researchers.

"I felt a crushing load on my shoulders."

— Domenic Baker,
  CEO Cricket Tasmania

"My legs usually 'bonk,' and the first sign is they begin to shake."

— Tim McCartney-Snape AOM,
  Extreme Mountaineer, Founder
  Sea-to-Summit outdoor gear

"It's time for me to take a full week of rest and recovery when I become jaded with people and lose my optimism in them."

— Nick Mitchell, Global CEO
  UP Fitness

"When I go past my limit, I cut my fingers. I would be cooking and I'd slip. That's when I knew I was beyond exhausted. I got better at reading myself before this point and I set up strategies and people I trusted to help me with this."

— Lauren Burns, Olympic
  Gold Medalist, Taekwondo

"My mood is a good signal of fatigue. I'm aware that when I get a little negative, my self-talk turns more to worry about the past/future, instead of being in the present. I want to feel energetic, present, and optimistic, so when I don't, it's time for rest."

— Anthony Hudson,
  International Football Coach

"I used to get wired and tired, a sense of running on empty, squeezing out the last drops of energy before having no control over falling to sleep. I don't allow myself to get that tired anymore and schedule multiple short and mid-term breaks."

— Linzi Boyd, Author and Founder
  of BoB Earth

SET ALARM:
07:59

THE MYTH OF 8 HOURS

If you've ignored your sleep and rest signals for months and years rather than a few days, it can be useful to know how much sleep other people report they need, as you reconnect to your own internal clock.

The National Sleep Foundation (NSF) provides an ideal number of sleep hours to attain each day and night, as a rule of thumb. Notice the wide range by age group.

Age Group	Hours
Newborns (0–3 months)	14–17 hrs
Infants (4–11 months)	12–15 hrs
Toddlers (1–2 years)	11–14 hrs
Preschoolers (3–5)	10–13 hrs
School Age Children (6–13)	9–11 hrs
Young Adults (14–17)	8–10 hrs
Adults (26–64)	7–9 hrs
Older Adults (65+)	7–8 hrs

It is important to respond to rest signals on a variety of time frames: within each day, day to day, weekly, and throughout the year. Look for opportunities to relax during gaps in busy days, schedule restful moments during the week, and plan recuperation periods into your yearly calendar.

In elite sports, this is called periodization. The best coaches now appreciate that constantly pushing hard for peak performance can lead to fatigue and burnout, so they meticulously plan to peak at benchmark events whilst allowing time for rest and recovery in between.[9,10]

On even longer time frames (decades), consider taking a longer break or a sabbatical. Countries and companies that support long service leave, with several months out of the workplace, offer a smart approach to sustainable retention of employees.

Rest and recuperation can involve different activities, a reduction in intensity, or simply a period of deliberate focus on well-being and enhanced sleep. Most importantly, establish what works best for you throughout life. Be flexible. Change your life tempo and sleep cycle to match the needs of the moment, rather than attempting to get a fixed eight hours sleep that has no basis in your personal needs.

I FEEL THE NEED FOR SLEEEEP

"Tonight, I'll go to bed early." We've all said it after a long day that started early, followed by struggling all day to stay awake in a state of sleep-deprivation.

If you binge on TV shows until you can't keep your eyes open, or if you consistently get less sleep than you need, do you know how much harm you are doing?

Lack of sleep degrades our state in a dose-response way. Just like drinking alcohol, the more you drink, or the less you sleep, the bigger the effect. In fact, foregoing sleep for 24 hours will create the same level of cognitive impairment as having a blood alcohol content of 0.1 percent, more than the drink-drive limit in most countries.[11,12]

Sleep is regulated by two systems: our circadian clock modulates our urge to sleep, and homeostatic sleep pressure drives the need for sleep.[13] The circadian clock is a biochemical cycle that synchronizes our sleep cycle with the 24-hour solar cycle. Sleep drive or homeostatic sleep pressure reflects adenosine build-up in our brain the longer we stay awake, which signals us to sleep.[14]

UC Berkeley sleep researcher Matthew Walker says that: "After 16 hours [of not sleeping] it should be at a screaming level." He continues, "When you do sleep, the [adenosine] pressure valve is released."[15]

Ideally, the circadian clock and sleep pressure would also be synchronized. However, for most people they are out of sync. One of the most common reasons is biochemical stimulation. Either through our activities or through our diets, we create states of biochemical confusion within ourselves. Caffeine, for example, blocks sleep urges by inhibiting adenosine receptors in the brain. The effects of overriding the sleep drive with chemical stimulants soon reveal themselves. The end result is a paradoxical state of agitated fatigue.[16]

Chronic lack of sleep takes a profound toll on health. Sleeping just four hours a night for six nights in a row leads to higher blood pressure, increased levels of the stress hormone cortisol, and insulin resistance, a precursor to type two diabetes.[17] Cognitive decline, obesity, diabetes, premature death, and a wide range of other undesired effects are all linked to poor sleep.[18-22]

We can't *just* power nap our way out of this. Brief fragmented sleep has little recuperative value and is similar to total sleep deprivation in its effects on performance.[23] Medical professionals such as nurses, emergency physicians, and surgeons, who work long shifts punctuated with short naps, are more prone to error as their sleep deficit builds and cognitive function declines.[24-26]

Lack of sleep impairs working memory, innovative thinking, and flexible decision-making. It impacts employee performance and can even make us more likely to engage in unethical behaviors.[27-31]

If your sleep pressure is in the red, the simple solution is to ease off the throttle and repay the debt as soon as you can. This starts with recognizing that you need to catch up on lost sleep in the first place. There is evidence to suggest that the more sleep deprived we are, the harder it is to recognize that we're running on fumes. Even one night of sleep loss can dramatically impair judgment.[23] Learning to listen to signals, especially those directing us to rest, is critically important.

Having a lazy Sunday morning might be one way to reduce the sleep deficit, but there are more effective ways to design for optimal sleep and rest.

R90 SLEEP PLANNING

Like so many other facets of resilience, successful sleeping is a natural process that many people have lost touch with. If you are not sleeping well, or would like to benefit from exceptional sleep and rest, the good news is that everyone can develop a personalized approach — by design.

The approach we take is best explained by elite sleep coach Nick Littlehales, who says it's best to think about sleeping in cycles rather than hours. We should be considering the whole day, and the whole week, not just how many hours of sleep you are getting each night.[13]

Our nighttime sleep cycle is where we can start the design process, assuming that you have typical daytime working hours. If you are a shift worker on nights, the principles are the same, but you might need next-level planning and discipline, especially when it comes to managing your circadian rhythms.

It is well established that most people go through four or five stages of sleep in a sleep cycle lasting roughly ninety minutes. Within a cycle, there is a mix of dozing off, light sleep, deep sleep, and a dreaming stage characterized by rapid-eye movement or REM sleep. Finally, there is the wake-up stage.

Each stage is important in different ways. The idea is to maximize access to all the stages whilst minimizing wasted time in inefficient attempts to catch up if we're in a sleep deficit.

Littlehales suggests that, rather than aiming for eight hours a night and creating states of anxiety when we don't hit our numbers, we should take a broader view of the week with a concept he calls Recovery in ninety minutes (R90).

In the R90 planner, the basic assumption is that different people need a different number of ninety-minute cycles over the course of a week. For most people, this means somewhere between four and six cycles per night (six to nine hours of sleep). Over the course of the week, this means between twenty-eight and forty-two cycles.

Rather than thinking of eight hours per night, start by aiming for around thirty-five sleep cycles over the course of the week. Experiment with your sleep cycles, adding and subtracting until you find the ideal plan for you. Use self-calibration as a guide to develop this personalized plan.

Remember that your ideal number of cycles will vary depending on the seasons, macro-periodization of training regimes, or even intense periods of learning or creative writing.

SLEEP PLANNING

Here we can see an example of a sleep plan. Whilst writing this book, Ian knew that he would be tempted to stay up late. He needed to make sure that his writing didn't have a negative impact on his resilience and well-being. He set an ambitious weekly target of forty R90 sleep cycles.

Like many people, Ian normally gets a little drowsy after lunch, and he knows that the best time to take a power nap is in the early afternoon. Ideally, he would sleep every day for between eight and twenty-two minutes at that time. The reality is that this is an inconvenient time to be napping, and demands of work and family often get in the way. Although consistency never happens, he averages three power naps a week, and he sometimes grabs a quick bonus nap in a cab or on a plane.

In this example week, Cycles R90-4, 10, 21, 26, and 31 were broken with young kids waking in the night. R90-34 is a bonus Sunday afternoon full sleep cycle. Quite often, the whole family, tired after a big week, manic Saturday in town, and a social Sunday morning, uses this opportunity to catch up on sleep.

Using the R90 and R30 planner during the week allows for a considerable amount of flexibility. The sleep plan can be adjusted to fit the opportunities and demands of modern life. Logging what you actually do against the plan provides you with a way to adjust. If, for example, you pushed it a bit hard for a few days and are feeling a little sluggish, schedule time in the plan to go to bed early for an extra R90, or make some space for a bonus afternoon R90 or a quick afternoon R30.

Read on if you are still awake!

	Mon	Tue	Wed	Thur	Fri	Sat	Sun
☼ **Midday**							
13:00							
14:00	R30 Powernap			R30	R30		Bonus R90-34
15:00							
16:00							
17:00							
18:00							
19:00							
20:00	Pre-sleep routine						
21:00							
22:00	Be asleep target R90-1	R90-7	R90-13				R90-35
23:00	R90-2	R90-8	R90-14	R90-19	R90-24	R90-29	R90-36
☾ **Midnight**							
01:00	R90-3	R90-9	R90-15	R90-20	R90-25	R90-30	R90-37
02:00	R90-4	R90-10	R90-16	R90-21	R90-26	R90-31	R90-38
03:00							
04:00	R90-5	R90-11	R90-17	R90-22	R90-27	R90-32	R90-39
05:00	R90-6	R90-12	R90-18	R90-23	R90-28	R90-33	R90-40
06:00							
07:00	Wake up target						
08:00							
09:00							
10:00							
11:00							

USE YOUR SIGNALS TO GUIDE YOUR POWER NAPS

A power nap is a short revitalizing sleep intended to supplement normal sleep, especially when there is an accumulated deficit.

The key to a high-performance power nap is in the duration. It is best to exit the power nap before entering deep sleep so as to prevent sleep inertia (the feeling of grogginess or being even more fatigued than before taking the nap). Based on a number of studies, the ideal length for a power nap is anywhere from ten to thirty minutes.

Short-duration naps of this kind can reduce the impact of poor nighttime sleep, restore alertness, reduce the effect of overwhelm, and improve performance, memory, and learning ability.[32–36]

One large clinical study in Greece also found that people who took a midday siesta of any duration were less likely to die from coronary illnesses than those not napping. Those who occasionally siesta had a 12% lower risk, whereas more regular napping had a 37% reduction in risk.[37]

In another study of the benefits of napping, Amber Brooks and Leon Lack of Flinders University compared sleep latency, subjective sleepiness, fatigue, vigor, and cognitive performance across different nap durations.[38] They concluded that the ideal nap duration was 10 minutes:

- A 5-minute nap produced few benefits in comparison with the no-nap control.
- A 10-minute nap produced immediate improvements in all outcome measures, with some of these benefits maintained for as long as 155 minutes.
- The 20-minute nap was associated with improvements emerging 35 minutes after napping and lasting until 125 minutes after napping.
- The 30-minute nap produced a period of impaired alertness and performance immediately after napping, indicative of sleep inertia. This was followed by improvements lasting up to 155 minutes after the nap.

While we don't dispute the evidence Brooks and Lack collected, we prefer a more flexible approach to napping. Our preferred way to power nap taps into your internal signal system.

Step 1.

Find a quiet, comfortable place — ideally somewhere you can stretch out other than the bedroom.

We acknowledge that quiet, comfortable, and stretched out are relative conditions, so if all you have is a 30-minute cab ride through a busy city, decide if you trust the driver (using more signal detection), make your apologies, stick in your earplugs or earphones, and get ready to switch off.

Step 3.

Scroll up and down between 8 minutes and 30 minutes until you settle on a number that *feels* right for that moment.

Step 4.

Enjoy your nap. You might feel a little sleep inertia upon waking. That is normal. If there is too much inertia, you may need to train yourself to recalibrate your duration to ensure that you don't enter deep sleep. You might also want to consider lifestyle changes that will help you get more rest at night.

For a short-term hack, you might like to frontload your nap with a coffee.

Step 2.

Open your mobile phone to the countdown timer.

NAPPUCCINO TIME

Caffeine in coffee generally takes around 30 minutes to kick in, so the idea is to drink coffee just before taking a nap: enjoy the benefits of sleep, and use the stimulant to bypass any sleep inertia and sustain alertness afterwards. The so-called nappuccino has been shown to be more effective than napping or drinking coffee alone.[39-41]

There are downsides, though. The half-life of caffeine (the time it takes to reduce by half in the body) varies a lot from person to person. Studies document a range between 1.5 and 9.5 hours.[36] This means that, if you enjoy a nappuccino during that afternoon lull in your circadian rhythm, boosting your short-term performance might cost you some of your quality night-time sleep, depending on how quickly you metabolize caffeine.

As a professional athlete, training was so gruelling that most days I trained (requiring consistent effort) for seven hours at different times of the day. It's not possible to expend that much energy without rest, and I had conditioned myself to nap in between sessions, completely turning off when needed. Early morning training sessions would start at 5:30 a.m., and I would often sleep in the car for an hour afterwards and then go into work.

For deep relaxation and recovery, I used progressive muscle relaxation (PMR) techniques via audio recordings from my sports psychologist. His voice would guide a whole-of-body relaxation through PMR techniques, and I would often fall asleep whilst listening.

Entirely sleepless nights are common before a competition. It's not just nerves. Many places have too much noise, bright lights, and less than ideal living conditions. When I entered a competition after a sleepless night, I'd remind myself that my competitors were also likely to have gone without much sleep and were feeling equally as tired and wired.

One missed night of sleep is manageable, and I knew I could rise above the fatigue, but if I had weeks of poor sleep, it would be an entirely different story.

As a professional competitor we're often on lots of flights, traveling from one event to the next, so we had to be able to take sleep and rest at any opportunity on the road and make space for it.

I'd always ensure that my kit bag had all my soft, lumpy stuff, such as tracksuits and any other clothes. That was my emergency pillow. I could just lie down anywhere and get some rest. I trained myself to drop off as I found a comfortable position in places where not many people would.

Even before a semi-final or final, I could lie down, grab a quick nap, and wake up ready to start warming up for my fight. I was so connected to process, and I had so much experience as a competitor that I knew when to "switch off" and when to "switch on." I didn't want to waste time and energy being "on" when I could be recharging and resting.

It's really important to know how and when to be switched on and off. In the ring and when training, I would be totally on, 100% focused and ready. Outside of these, I worked, I laughed, I got inspired, and I planned. Placing rest and recovery in that plan is just as important as everything else. It's impossible to improve if you can't recover effectively.

FIGHTING SLEEP

"It's really important to know how and when to be switched on and off."

LAUREN BURNS

OAM won Olympic gold in taekwondo at the 2000 Olympics in Sydney. She is a motivational speaker, author, naturopath (BHSc), and PhD at RMIT, where she looked at the factors that influence elite athlete performance.

HARMONIZING PERFORMANCE

REST AND SLEEP WITH CIRCADIAN RHYTHMS

Humans have evolved as a consequence of environmental factors, such as temperature, caloric availability, terrain, and the cycles of night and day. Each of us still carries the evolutionary programming developed over millions of years that (artificial light notwithstanding) mostly dictates that when it's dark we rest, and when it's light, we are more active.[41]

Circadian rhythms are light-driven changes in our biochemical system that follow a 24-hour cycle. They often have more effect on us than we realize, and the clock is bidirectional, meaning that we can influence or disturb our natural diurnal biochemical changes through the timing of activities such as exercise, eating, working, or exposure to artificial light.[42-44]

Knowing the basics of circadian rhythms can help us get the most out of each day if we match activities to the times that are best suited to them. We repeat our caveat that there's no such thing as an "average person." Individuals invariably differ from generalized observations. Use population observations as optional insights, not a constraint.

Exposure to early-morning sunlight has been shown to normalize the circadian rhythm, so this is a good place to start.[42] This is also consistent with Nick Littlehales's approach: begin with an ideal wake-up time and work backwards from there with your nighttime sleep planning.[13]

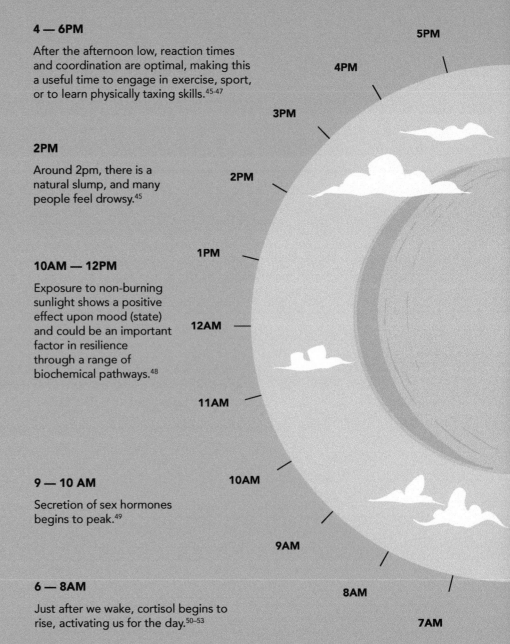

4 — 6PM

After the afternoon low, reaction times and coordination are optimal, making this a useful time to engage in exercise, sport, or to learn physically taxing skills.[45-47]

2PM

Around 2pm, there is a natural slump, and many people feel drowsy.[45]

10AM — 12PM

Exposure to non-burning sunlight shows a positive effect upon mood (state) and could be an important factor in resilience through a range of biochemical pathways.[48]

9 — 10 AM

Secretion of sex hormones begins to peak.[49]

6 — 8AM

Just after we wake, cortisol begins to rise, activating us for the day.[50–53]

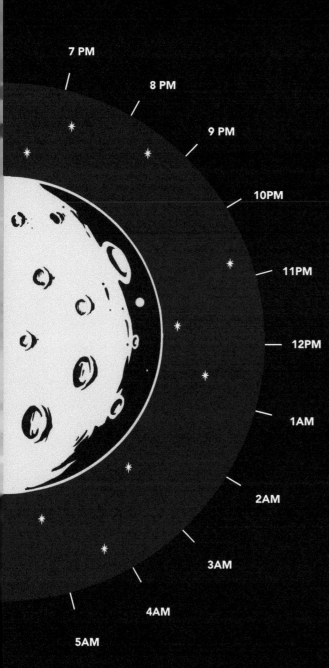

7 PM

8 PM

9 PM

10PM

11PM

12PM

1AM

2AM

3AM

4AM

5AM

7 — 9PM

As natural sunlight decreases (typically) artificial blue light is turned on, which interferes with insulin sensitivity. This may be a factor in evening snacking and weight gain.[54]

9 — 11PM

Around late evening, we begin secreting the hormone melatonin, which triggers feelings of tiredness. This is ideal lights-out time — and we do mean out. Even low light can interfere with melatonin release.[55]

12PM — 2AM

Melatonin peaks and metabolic rate decreases, allowing our nervous system to recover, heal, and consolidate conscious experiences.[55]

2 — 6AM

Metabolism continues to decrease and body temperature falls. The decreased metabolic rate signals the increase in cortisol, which starts the cycle all over again.[56]

LARK OR OWL?

As we've seen in many population studies, when we look at circadian rhythms in fine detail, we find idiosyncracies. Two well-studied variations involve preferences for mornings or evenings according to so-called lark or owl chronotypes. Larks and owls have been shown to vary greatly in their diurnal performance. Harmonizing with our circadian rhythm can also improve treatment of disease.[43, 44, 57, 58]

Of course, humans also modify their sleep patterns for personal preference, social or work reasons, or inadvertently disrupt their natural rhythms through use of light and stimulants. Often this comes at a personal cost to performance, health, or longevity.[54,59]

11.00PM

LET THERE BE...DARK

In recent years, mounting evidence reveals the negative consequences from exposure to devices that emit artificial light in the blue spectrum.[60-63]

Throughout the vast majority of our evolution, humans have adapted to constant light wave spectrums from three sources: sunshine, moonlight, and fire. At sunrise, red-light spectrums dominate. As the sun rises higher in the sky, blue light becomes more concentrated, before reducing again as red light increases and peaks at sunset.

In *Lights Out: Sleep, Sugar and Survival*, T.S. Wiley and Bent Formby draw together evidence that diabetes, heart disease, cancer, and depression are all increasing thanks to one seemingly innocuous invention: the light bulb.[64]

Artificial light interrupts the ancient light cycles, and our in-built light-sensing systems haven't had enough time to adapt. Light bulbs and screens stimulate us to a near constant state of daytime activation, with increased neurotransmitter and hormonal production that accompanies the presence of blue light at times when it would naturally be dark.[65, 66]

If your home is fitted with regular light bulbs, or worse yet, fluorescent strip lights, it may be worth investing in incandescent bulbs or warm LEDs. You might even consider wearing blue-light-blocking glasses in your home after sunset.

Most smartphones have features that disable blue light. If you use a laptop, apps like F-Lux (used for writing these very words in the evening) and Twilight can be set to automatically block blue light at times, syncing your laptop's and the sun's light spectrums.

However, light might not be the only phone-related factor that could be affecting your sleep. Some people fear that low-frequency electromagnetic waves (EMF) from phone towers, Wi-Fi boxes, and the phones under our pillows provide a constant disruption to the cells in our bodies, with changes to brain activity being observed even after low-dose exposure to home Wi-Fi.[67]

In response to growing public health concerns over possible health effects from exposure to electromagnetic field sources, the World Health Organization launched the International EMF Project in 1996. The WHO website currently notes that approximately 25,000 articles have been published over the past 30 years. Based on the weight of the collected evidence, they conclude that there are no measurable health consequences from exposure to low-level electromagnetic fields.[68]

A recent double-blind random control trial conducted in a sleep laboratory confirmed the findings of several other neurophysiological studies. The researchers concluded that "acute RF-EMF exposure has no effect on the macrostructure of sleep."[69]

Having noted that the weight of evidence for risk from domestic Wi-Fi is low, it is important to acknowledge that some people report hypersensitivity to EMF. More importantly, if you believe that your sleep could be impacted by proximity to your phone or router, then it likely will be! Simply take a precautionary approach: move or turn off your devices at night.

For a good night's sleep, we suggest that you do more than put your phone in a drawer or turn it off. Make the bedroom a screen-free zone. Your notifications will be waiting for you in the morning.

SLEEP LIKE A VAMPIRE

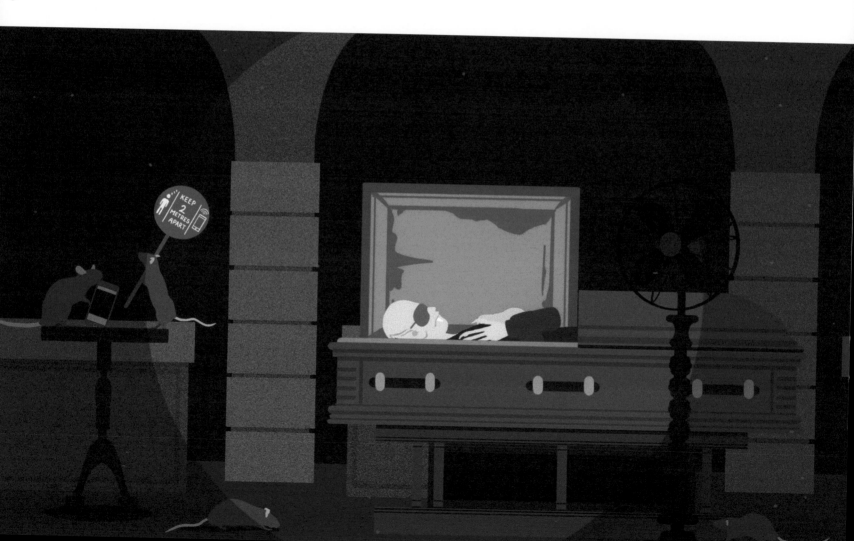

**No, we're not proposing that you sleep in a coffin —
just that you consider a few vampire-like behaviors
to improve your sleep environment.**

Whilst we might imagine that the circadian rhythm of a vampire is the opposite of ours, it seems likely the principles apply — perhaps even more so, given the same devastating consequences of exposure to sunlight for vampires.

In the movies, vampires spend their days sleeping in the depths of ancient buildings with barely a creak or pin drop to disturb them. They are, of course, shut off from light and we would assume, have a cool (as in temp cool) resting place.

We might benefit from a similarly blacked-out sleeping environment. A number of studies raise concerns that light pollution in the form of street lighting or LEDs in the home can disturb sleep. Many experts say that, if we want high-performance sleep, we need total blackout conditions.[13,70]

Crypts are quiet places. The city, not so much. Nocturnal noise pollution has been shown to reduce both quality and quantity of sleep. The World Health Organization recognizes that night-time noise pollution leads to adverse health effects and impacts daytime performance in a range of activities.[71] If traffic noise or other forms of urban racket are disrupting your sleep, we suggest buying the very best earplugs that you can afford or using noise-canceling earphones. This will also give you more freedom to leave a window open. The fresh air circulating through the room will help make sleep deep and restful, and with the sounds blocked out you'll be in la-la-land before you know it.[72]

Temperature has a clear effect upon sleep quality, duration, and access of REM (rapid eye movement) cycles. Unlike Dracula, who clearly likes icy cold, our optimal sleep temperature is a relatively balmy 23°C (73.4°F).[73] At this temperature, onset of sleep takes the least amount of time compared to lower or higher temps, and slow-wave sleep lasts the longest.

Evidence noted, we find that people vary considerably in how warm they like to be while they sleep, and a number of companies make quilts that have different fill ratings on the left and the right for couples who prefer different temperatures. Some even prefer a weighted cover.

Finally, if you're tossing and turning, the problem might not be the temperature, the light, or the noise. If you've been sleeping on the same mattress for a decade or more, it's probably due for a refresh. Given that we spend almost a third of our lives in bed, investing in a quality mattress might be like the difference between night and day. Combine the right sleep conditions with the right sleep surface and you'll sleep like the living dead.

BEATING INSOMNIA

STILL STRUGGLING TO GET TO SLEEP?

Check:

- ☑ Paying attention to your signals to rest and sleep

- ☑ Using your R90 sleep planner to prioritize time to sleep

- ☑ Taking power naps when you can

- ☑ Harmonizing activities with your circadian rhythms

- ☑ Managing your pre-sleep routine to avoid blue light and stimulants such as caffeine and illuminated screens

- ☑ Room is dark

- ☑ Room is quiet (or ears are plugged)

- ☑ Bed and covers are optimal for you

**Dum, dum, dum du dum...
STILL WIDE AWAKE!**

MIND STILL HYPERACTIVE?

You might consider practicing the tongue drop to decrease your self-talk or, as we suggested in Chapter 10, you could also play a flowstate game before bed. We find that the net effect of flow is to reduce conscious involvement in thinking in a way that can help access high-performance sleep.

If your mind is still racing, or if there's a signal clamoring for attention, it might be time to make a contract with yourself to get things done. Write a list of all of the tasks and/or problems that you are ruminating on. Make some decisions and commit to action.

WAKING IN THE NIGHT?

If you wake in the middle of the night, perhaps with your attention back on your to-do list, you probably neglected to be specific about when you will take action on those tasks. Alternatively, you could be awake for some other significant concern that your unconscious would like to have resolved.

You might consider creating a contract with yourself. Building on the framing and rapport between conscious and unconscious we developed in Chapter 7, address your unconscious mind: "Unconscious Mind, I am putting aside all of these tasks/problems/to-dos until the morning, so that I can experience a deep and relaxed sleep with no interruption. I WILL get to them most efficiently if you will kindly support me to sleep."

A similar frame can be used if you are hyper-alert to risk. This is where you wake worrying about every creak or sound. The watchman function can be retrained by framing with phrases directed to the unconscious like this: "Please reserve waking me for sounds or other conditions that pose a threat."

HMMM... STILL AWAKE?

Time for some straight talk with your unconscious:

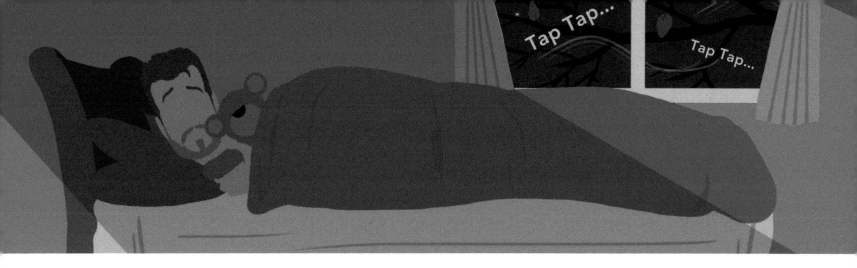

"Unconscious, you have my attention at this horribly unsociable hour. What for? What is your intention for waking me?"

What signals do you get in response? It might be that something does genuinely require your attention then and there. You might have forgotten something crucial, or you may be on the verge of a breakthrough.

RECURRING NIGHTMARES?

Recurring nightmares are a complex issue. The techniques we've covered here might help, and you may need professional help or a more comprehensive approach. Often, our unconscious is attempting to process a past experience into memory in a way that meets a positive intention, usually for safety in the future. There is usually a clue to the solution in the content or metaphor of the nightmare. The process to approach these sorts of disturbances is beyond the scope of this book.

WAKING TOO EARLY?

For some people, the crossover into consciousness in the morning is driven by an overly enthusiastic unconscious.

The concept of sleeping on a problem is not new. History is full of anecdotal stories of discoveries and creativity during sleep.[74]

Researchers have demonstrated that we are each capable of directed thinking in our sleep using stimuli such as sound or smell to activate unconscious creativity.[75,76] The same is possible using careful framing before entering sleep, or we can also do this inadvertently with nothing more than curious attention.

There is a small amount of research on so-called creative insomnia, most of it suggesting that creativity can be a by-product of poor sleep.[77] We also find the reverse to be true, though. People sometimes wake earlier than they would like to with a solution to a problem they had been mulling over for a while. They were processing the problem while they

slept, and the eureka moment pulled them out of sleep and into consciousness. As with contracting to get to sleep or stay asleep during the night, be explicit when you address your unconscious about waking time.

YOU'RE STILL NOT GETTING ENOUGH QUALITY SLEEP?

It might be time to visit your medical practitioner. You may have sleep apnea or some other sleep disorder.

Sleep apnea is a potentially serious sleep disorder in which breathing repeatedly stops and starts. If you snore and feel tired even after a full night's sleep, you might have sleep apnea and related medical conditions. It can be caused by upper airway dysfunction, obesity, or respiratory disease, and is associated with high risk for cardiovascular disease and functional impairment during waking hours.[78,79]

SLEEP TALK

We established in Chapter 2 that the words we use and the stories we tell can shape our experience and even our memories. This is commonly the case regarding our perceptions of sleep and rest. We can either convince ourselves that we have had poor sleep when in fact it was good, or that we don't need to sleep or rest when we do!

Objective data on sleep quality and duration can also help or hinder our experience of sleep. In cases where our story is about poor sleep and the data show the opposite (i.e., when sleep was actually better than reported), an updated narrative can make a difference to subsequent sleep.[80,81] In other words, just telling ourselves that we are poor sleepers can be a self-fulfilling prophecy. By simply changing the story, we can change the recalled experience of sleep.

Conversely, in the quest of improved sleep, sleep trackers are becoming more and more popular. Paradoxically, their use can make sleep worse as people become anxious about or even obsessed with their performance data in the pursuit of perfection. In much the same way that a focus on problems can lead to more problems or we find ourselves trapped in a problem-remedy loop, so too can an obsession with poor sleep exacerbate insomnia.[80–83]

We began this chapter by noting that there are no magic metrics. People are idiosyncratic, and attempting to design your lifestyle for rest and sleep according to an inflexible template is fraught with difficulties. The challenge is to integrate evidence in a useful way, whilst working with our own unique signals and desires for resilience, performance, and well-being.

Remember, you are the expert on yourself, and, like all experts, you can also be wildly wrong.

We recommend a weight-of-evidence approach to designing optimal rest and sleep on a range of timescales through the day, during the week, and throughout different chapters of your life.

We also need to have a coherent narrative that supports our needs while also reflecting the evidence. Framing how we approach sleep is important, and by changing how we describe sleep and our nighttime routines, we may very well improve the quality of our sleep.

Throughout this book, we present evidence, both empirical and perceived, that few if any of our behavioral patterns are so strongly inherited or entrenched as to be unchangeable. Nothing is cast in stone, and there are no curses sent from on high.

The same, of course, goes for sleep and rest. If you are someone who defines yourself as a poor sleeper or, worse yet, if you are a self-diagnosed insomniac, we'd like to whisper gentle soothing words in your ear to reassure you that you can learn to sleep as well as you once learned to walk, eat, ride a bike, or any other activity that makes up a valuable part of your lifestyle.

Sleep provides us with a platform to engage in our waking activities. It is an absolutely essential piece in the quality of our overall lifestyle — one in which all the parts can be improved — by design.

Achieving great sleep and rest could be as straightforward as simply nodding off on a warm lazy afternoon, or it might be a complex issue that requires discipline and trial and error. If your sleep and rest will benefit from this kind of deliberate design, be curious enough to trial different approaches, and track what works well for you. All the while, be mindful of the paradox that your self-talk and sleep metric-tracking could be getting in the way of doing what comes naturally to each of us.

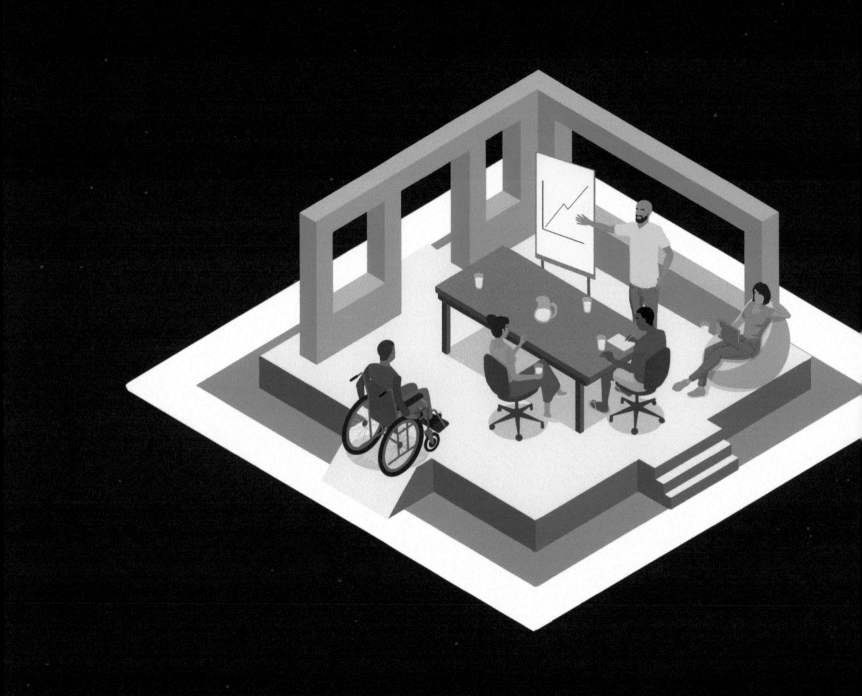

LIFESTYLE

A RESILIENT LIFESTYLE IS ONE WITH AGENCY

Lifestyle, like life itself, is a continually evolving outcome of our interactions with others and the external environment that we inhabit and co-create.

A lifestyle by design maximizes individual agency. It builds on our ability to reflect on the past and present, and to imagine the future. Ultimately it is about taking action to shape our course through life.

Unless you're an extreme stoic or Buddhist, surviving and thriving in a complex, turbulent world requires more than simply drifting through life being in the now. When we say "by design," we mean an ongoing creative process that can help us prepare, plan, and take action in resourceful and resilient ways.

Much of the need for recovery after burnout, or having to cope with extreme challenges and hardship in the now, can be avoided with a little preparation for life's potential downsides ahead of time.

Importantly, having a design is not the point of lifestyle by design. The chief

benefits come from the process of reflecting and learning from the past, on being situationally aware of the present, and on our deliberate and thoughtful engagement with the present and future.

Some elements of a lifestyle by design might lend themselves to detailed planning; others might be more complex and require an agile approach; and some yet-to-be-discovered aspects of life might benefit from immersion in different environments in a state of flow.

Although there are common themes and dozens of psychometric criteria for "quality of life," there is no ideal, one-size-fits-all lifestyle blueprint. We caution against scoring your lifestyle against someone else's indicators. Later in this chapter, we provide a template that will guide you through your own design process.

One more cautionary note: For some, there is an almost obsessive focus on work-life balance. The term implies that work is somehow separate from life, and that quality of life somehow depends on finding the ideal balance between them.

Lifestyle by design is much more than simply divvying up time and resources to create a neatly balanced ledger. It includes questioning our values and how we assign meaning to what's important in life. It's about allocating attention to best reflect our highest priorities. This sort of prioritization and re-prioritization is often more akin to triage than to balance.

TRIAGE

Triage is the sorting and allocation of treatment to patients according to a system of priorities designed to maximize the number of survivors. Triage is also the assigning of priority order to projects on the basis of where funds and other resources can best be used, are most needed, or are most likely to achieve success.[1]

Triage is undoubtedly a useful skill. Although constantly having to triage in a crisis can be exhausting, it can improve outcomes and even save lives. Triage principles can be applied across the portfolio of activities that define lifestyle. In times of overwhelm, triage is essential.

Most people, at some point or another, accept or even plan for a deliberate imbalance for a period of time. This allows them to get ahead in one facet of life at the expense of another. They triage, allocating time and resources to specific needs and outcomes. Examples include working long unsocial hours for six months to deliver a project with the view of winning a promotion; or taking a year out of education to travel and discover what your passion is, before committing to a university course; or taking time out of elite competition to have children; or quitting your nightly jaunts at the pub so you can save money for a deposit on a house.

Lifestyle by design encourages you to question assumptions, identify lifestyle traps, renegotiate expectations, and challenge accepted norms.

Lifestyle by design brings together all the resilience skills presented in this book. Throughout, we have deliberately moved attention from the "whole," considering mind as embodied and embedded in context; to "parts," human subsystems, small chunks of relevant neuroscience information, and discrete skills; and then of course, back up again. We have deliberately taken an ecosystems approach to personal resilience, recognizing that we are all part of, and intimately connected to, many evolving systems (environmental, organizational, cultural, etc.). Our focus on the "by design" process involves ensuring that important aspects of lifestyle, especially work, health, wealth, and relationships, coevolve with awareness of context in ways that are rewarding and enhance resilience.

However, if your version of nirvana is being holed up in a remote cave with just your dog for company, we get that — we love our dogs too! Please consider the outcome, your intentions for the outcome, and the consequences of your choice, and ensure that you can cover future mortgage payments on the cave. If that's your well-considered outcome, go ahead and enjoy the solitude!

Our point is that everyone is different, and everyone's ideal lifestyle is different.

Just get real about where your time and resources are going.

If, late in your years, you are struck by a startling realization that you've blown your one shot at life, stop right there! Savor every moment; it's never too late to start living the life you want.

Life can only be truly lived moment to moment, not in hours, days, weeks, or months.

WORK-IN(G) LIFE

Nobody on their deathbed has ever said
"I wish I had spent more time at the office."

— Rabbi Harold Kushner

EQUALLY, THERE ARE FOLKS WHO:

- Worked hard and retired to happiness
- Worked hard and retired only to die
  shortly afterwards
- Worked hard, played hard, and are still having a blast
- Prioritized having fun, and struggled later in life with
  poor health and wealth
- Prioritized career in a way that led to
  broken relationships
- Prioritized relationships only to get divorced and find
  themselves struggling financially

There really is no ideal or right answer to the questions
of how much work is the right amount, and how you
seamlessly integrate work with the rest of life.

We do, however, invest vast amounts of time and
resources in activities that are not productive, efficient,
rewarding, or even purposeful.

The answer isn't doing more. Paradoxically, the answer is
"not doing.'[2] Strategy, in the business sense, often fails to
effectively guide company activities because it becomes
little more than an overwhelming to-do list. The same
is true of lifestyle design. By applying triage principles
to lifestyle design, we can learn to accept that only the

highest-priority activities will get done. We can learn to
accept that some things simply cannot be saved with the
resources at hand.

In another paradox, studies have shown that productivity
often increases when workers shorten their workday from
eight to five or six hours.[3,4] You see a similar productivity
boost when they switch from a five-day workweek to
a four-day one.[5,6] When allowed or forced to work in
a compressed time frame, people seem to spend less
time on useless projects, unproductive meetings, and
busywork. They stop wasting time and get the important
activities done.

In his Four-Hour series of books, Tim Ferris challenges
much of the contemporary thinking surrounding work,
time, and purpose. He argues for a form of hyper-efficiency
that focuses on doing no more than is absolutely necessary
to achieve your goals — financial, lifestyle, fitness, or any
other goals you can think of.[7-9] It goes without saying that
working only fours hours a week frees up a lot of spare
time to do...whatever you want.

Whilst most people do not have the personal
circumstances or entrepreneurial flair to make a living in
only four hours a week, there is still much we can learn
from Ferris. From a list of literally hundreds of useful
lifestyle hacks, three principles stand out:

1. Take personal responsibility for your life.

2. Relentlessly question the intention for what you
   are doing.

3. Use evidence to evaluate what works best.

Globally, only 15% of employees are engaged at work. This means that 85% of employees either aren't engaged, or worse, they are actively disengaged — ruining workplaces, societies, and general world productivity.

— Jim Clifton[10]

For resilience at work, this means precisely identifying what you are working for. Consider the benefits, the constraints, and, of course, the risks. Then check that the decisions you have made are working for you.

Most people consider the obvious benefits and constraints of work, such as money and fringe rewards, location, working conditions and hours, and role and opportunities for promotion.

Have you also considered the risks?

For extreme jobs, such as deep sea fishing, underground mining, or frontline military work, the risk of physical harm is well known and usually accepted. Physical risks are by no means the only risks that make workplaces dangerous places.

Few people take time to consider workplace risk factors until they are exposed to them, especially if the risks involve a sense of threat from their teammates or their manager. Personal resilience can be greatly helped by carefully choosing where you work or who you work for and with.

This includes you!

If you are the boss or you are self-employed, and you are a particularly poor manager, consider lifting your game or firing yourself! Seriously, being self-employed is not for everyone. The key point, whether self-employed or working for others, is one of fit.

A Gallup poll of more than 1 million employed American workers concluded that the top reason people quit their jobs is a bad boss or immediate supervisor; 75% of workers who voluntarily left their jobs didn't have issues with the position itself. The problem was how they were being managed.

Leaders set the scene for psychological safety in workplaces, and all safety flows from psychological safety. If workers can't speak up, the organization's most effective risk control mechanism, its people, will fail to function.

Being disengaged and operating from a position of constant threat in the workplace is not resilient. Remember, in addition to putting up with poor working conditions, you can also engage constructively to change the nature of your workplace, or you can leave — especially if there is a strong work-related stress signal telling you to get out.

We recently asked experts in disability services, neurodiversity, human rights, and human-centered workspace design the following question: *What is needed for people with diverse needs to thrive at work?*

The answers surprised us. It turns out that demographic groups across the board don't need anything specifically to thrive at work. The fundamentals of effective people skills and leadership are universal. Applied with the right intention, they can enable resilient and high-performing individuals, teams, and organizations.

There are two key ingredients to create psychologically safe working environments that meet everyone's needs: involvement in decision-making and reasonable adjustment.

INVOLVEMENT AND REASONABLE ADJUSTMENT

The concept of reasonable adjustment is well articulated by the Human Rights Commission. Workplaces, they say, should make reasonable adjustments to working conditions so that people with physical, neurological, or cultural differences are not discriminated against.

This might mean allowing for more flexible work arrangements, or perhaps helping someone with auditory sensitivity find a quiet space to work; it might mean providing uninterrupted time and space for people to work in flow, or it might mean removing barriers so that someone living with a disability is able to do their job.

Reasonable adjustment also provides a frame for high-quality conversations between employees and employers, as both co-create an agreed-upon way of working.

This sort of conversation, where employees are involved in decision-making, can improve many of the strategic decisions, goals, KPIs, and performance measures that characterize modern organizations. Communication becomes less about top-down command and control, and more about ground-up involvement and co-ownership.

In their book *Overload: How Good Jobs Went Bad and What to Do About It*, Erin Kelly and Phyllis Moen document how they measured burnout and retention in a Fortune 500 company. With one group they focused on work redesigns that gave employees more flexibility over how and where they worked. They also changed performance management. Another group continued to operate without change.[11]

Employees in the redesign group reported less stress and burnout, and job retention over a four-year period was 40% higher. Those people who chose to leave did so at great expense to the company, which had to pay the cost of employee churn.

A CRISIS IS A CRUCIBLE FOR CHANGE

As one of the consequences of the Covid-19 pandemic, the global trend of working from home, or indeed working from anywhere, has accelerated. Initially, there were concerns about how this would affect productivity, but many employers discovered that employees are often more productive when not distracted by office life or struggling with long commutes.

Often in management, less is more; less managing, fewer meetings, and less direction lead to more productivity. Of course, this is not true in all cases. Some people like or need clear and precise direction. The de-centered workplace has been extremely challenging and isolating for some. Some people have a closed-door office at home where they can work uninterrupted, while others have had to set up a makeshift workstation at the kitchen table with the kids bouncing off the walls all around them.

Another upside to the Covid-19 pandemic is that it has prompted conversations between managers and staff about reasonable adjustment. Everyone was forced to be flexible, to find ways to work through adversity together. Some organizations are now considerably more productive than before the pandemic.

In addition to the pressure to innovate, there was a sense of urgency that stimulated conversations and helped develop trusting relationships. Rather than sapping productivity, these new and more flexible arrangements have helped optimize performance and enable resilience at team and organizational levels. Through open dialogue, employers and employees have found ways to create or add value while safeguarding the health and well-being of employees.

Sadly, some organizations went the other way in their response to Covid-19. The pressure to adapt exacerbated existing cultural and strategic weaknesses, and those companies saw increased tensions between management and employees, or they folded under the pressure.

TRIBALISM

Belonging to a tribe is resilient in the right context; after all, tribalism has been a part of human evolution since at least prehistoric times, so it clearly confers benefits.[12]

We surround ourselves with people who think and act in similar ways, and we are attracted to those who are loyal to a shared identity frame, precisely because this is, or rather was, a resilient strategy. What we need to remember is that strong tribal boundaries are a form of insulation. They are a protective barrier, and they can also isolate us from different perspectives and fresh ideas. In modern, complex, interconnected or even hyper-mobile organizations and societies, it is more important than ever to ensure that tribal boundaries are porous, open to newcomers and the ideas they bring with them.

For personal resilience, it's important to find out what kind of tribes dominate your culture or workplace. What are the membership rules and assumptions? Is there sufficient exchange of people and knowledge between tribes, or are the tribes at war? Is there an opportunity to be genuinely included in the culture at work, or in other social settings?

We're learning that this doesn't have to mean sharing a physical workplace. Extensive studies by global companies like Google and Atlassian have found that virtual teams are just as productive as those that are co-located — provided that the conditions are right to form strong relationships and social connections.

Social isolation has been described as the emerging plague of the twenty-first century. Cut off from our tribes, there is often a sense of feeling adrift in a digital sea. Creating inclusive communities is the antidote, and, whether we are working online or together in the workplace, inclusion is the key to productive workplace culture.

We can do this with the aid of reasonable adjustment. Many people are able to create a near seamless integration of work, family, and social activities. When evaluating the benefits, constraints, and risks of joining a workplace, or a social group, ask yourself, what are the tribal rules of membership? What value do you place on inclusive decision-making and reasonable adjustment?

RELATIONSHIP MATTERS

We established in previous chapters that context, which includes place, people, and systems, can influence us in subtle ways.

Through mirror neurons, we can experience the actions and felt states of others without even realizing it. This offers an important advantage for perceiving and learning. It comes with a downside, though. We can inadvertently experience other people's states, like anxiety or distress, as a form of vicarious ill health. In a similar way, the beliefs we hold, whether perceived as our own or adopted from others, can activate the natural placebo we all have inside of us, giving us the ability to heal and to be well. At the same time, our beliefs can trigger placebo's evil twin: the nocebo.

CHOOSE YOUR ASSOCIATES WISELY

If you spend a considerable amount of time exposed to others' trauma or people experiencing pain and illness, it is advisable to have filters in place. This could be as simple as operating from third position, or it might mean calibrating using a body scan to check that you are not picking up other people's states or behaviors.

When choosing how to live your life, consider if those around you are helping amplify your innate placebo. Are they

perhaps doing the opposite? Do they draw your attention to ill health in a fatalistic way, rather than helping you focus on health and healing?

An important factor for personal resilience is support from others. Resilient people are often buttressed by resilient relationships. Are your relationships supportive or destructive?

In a study of factors that influence the performance of elite level athletes, lead author and Olympic gold medalist Lauren Burns describes the important role that supportive interpersonal relationships play in high performance. She argues that quality relationships can induce positive physiological changes that improve adaptation to stress and enhanced performance. Support from friends and loved ones can help build resilience to the lows of competition loss, injury, illness, and the grueling demands of high-performance sport, such as travel, securing funding, or juggling a dual-career.

Importantly, Burns notes, poor relationships and social structures, such as bullying, harassment, and ostracism, or sexual and physical violence, can all lead to a host of negative outcomes.[13]

Relationship quality is especially important for those in high-stakes roles or challenging frontline jobs. Depending on

their quality, relationships can either build resilience or contribute to burnout.[14]

We are in the midst of an epidemic of social isolation that was already well under way before Covid-19 came along and made the figurative distance between us literal. Researchers have found direct links between social isolation and poor levels of life satisfaction, high levels of work-related stress, and increased risk of substance abuse. Social networks are especially important for those who are vulnerable, and intimate partner violence has escalated as a consequence of stay-at-home orders.[15-18]

We can never know what the future holds, but a resilient lifestyle will prepare us for whatever life brings. For vulnerable people at risk of intimate partner violence, disasters like the Covid-19 pandemic can make the situation unexpectedly worse in a matter of hours or days.

It is often very difficult to escape toxic relationships, even at the best of times. Women are particularly vulnerable. In Australia, a country of under 26 million people:[19]

- One woman is murdered by her current or former partner every week.[20]
- One in three women have experienced physical and/or sexual violence perpetrated by a man.[21]

Our rule of thumb is, *if in doubt, get out.*

And get help to manage the exit risk.

Changing context (moving away) is often important to manage the risk of recurring domestic violence.

In some cases, moving is also the best way to manage environmental factors that are negatively influencing your well-being. For example, if you work in a building that has a high-chemical offgas load, or where the job requires the use of toxic chemicals, then relationship risk factors on the job might be the least of your worries.[22-27]

Very commonly, buildings, systems, and structures block access to flow. In many places, it seems as though the modern workplace has been designed to make work difficult or joyless. Some people report experiencing such an endless interruption of noise, meetings, and emails that they literally never do what they are paid to do.

Meetings, like vampires, suck the life from otherwise productive employees.

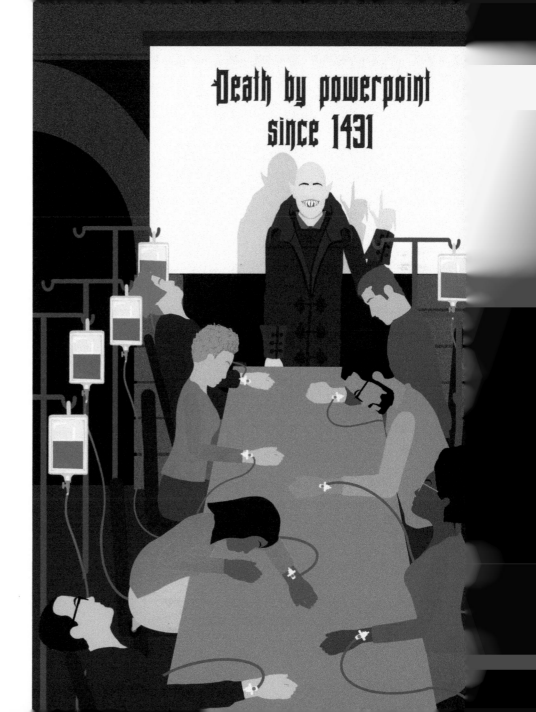

THE COST OF A THING

"The cost of a thing is the amount of what I will call life which is required to be exchanged for it, immediately or in the long run."

— Henry David Thoreau

When Thoreau wrote these words, life expectancy was much lower than it is today. The author died in 1862, when he was only 44 years old, and we assume he spent many moments of his life as though they were a precious thing. We have extended our life expectancy to almost 80 years, but do we live life as if it were a precious thing? Over a lifetime, our usage of time can be radically different from what we might assume. Here are some estimates for the time-cost of a thing:

If you watched an average of 2.5 hours of TV each day (a low estimate), you'll spend 7.9 full, around-the-clock years of your life staring at a box of moving pictures.[28,29]

Spending 8 hours a week in a bar, starting when you turn 21, will mean you spend 2.8 years at the local watering hole.

We hope these statistics challenge you to reconsider how much of life you are prepared to spend to pay for a thing.

Being employed full-time (with four weeks annual holiday) from the age of 21 means it will cost you at least 11 continuous years at work (even if you're less than fully present most of that time).

In those 11 continuous years, how much time will you spend in meetings? As the saying goes, "A meeting is indispensable when you don't want to get anything done."[30]

There are an estimated 11 million meetings every day in the United States alone with an estimated cost of $37b annually in wasted time due to unproductive time spent gasbagging.[31,32]

Commuting to and from work for 1 hour each day potentially consumes another 1.3 years of cumulative life.

Based on typical usage patterns, you will probably spend at least 4 years of your life using your smartphone.

One 2018 estimate suggested that Americans spend an average of 9 hours looking at screens each day. In 2019, this jumped to 10 hours. Since the introduction of Covid lockdowns, that number has grown. In 2020, the average adult in America spent over 13 hours a day consuming digital media.[33]

Seven hours of sleep per night means that you will spend 23 years of your life between the sheets.

A FACTFUL PERSPECTIVE ABOUT WEALTH AND HEALTH

In *Factfulness: Ten Reasons We're Wrong About the World and Why Things Are Better Than You Think,* Hans Rosling presents a sobering yet hopeful account of global poverty.[34]

Rosling says the world is a much better place today than at any other time in history. Many perceptions of global poverty are based on an outdated world view that has carried on unchanged since the 1960s, when academics grouped countries into two categories: developed or developing.

Countries like the UK, America, and Canada fell into the developed category; Africa, South America, and southern Asia tended to fall into the developing category. Today, most of the countries that were originally labeled as developing meet all the 1965 criteria for developed nations, and most countries are on an upward trajectory in wealth and health.[35] Rosling goes on to challenge the rich and poor gap myth by breaking down wealth into four income groups.

Four income levels and associated lifestyles based on world population in 2017 (modified after Rosling 2019). Income per person in US$ per day. Each figure represents 1 billion people.

LEVEL 1. LESS THAN $2 PER DAY

- Four to seven children.
- Walk barefoot to collect water more than one hour away.
- Spend time gathering firewood.
- Prepare a simple meal if not drought affected.
- Child mortality is high because health care is beyond reach.
- Roughly 1 billion people live like this.
- If crops are good, perhaps you earn more than $2 per day, moving you into the next income bracket.

LEVEL 2. BETWEEN $2 AND $8 PER DAY

- Two to four children.
- Can buy sandals, a bike, and collecting water now takes <30 minutes.
- Can now cook on a gas stove.
- Can now buy food, own chickens, and eat eggs.
- Health care remains precarious, and illness can wipe out savings.
- Roughly 3 billion people live like this.
- If you can land a job locally, you will be the first to bring home a salary, moving you up into the next income bracket.

LEVEL 3. BETWEEN $8 AND $32 PER DAY

- Around two children, and both will be educated.
- Can install a water tap.
- Electricity is stable and children's education improves.
- A motorcycle means you can travel to better paid work.
- Health care and paying for children's education are priorities, and income and saving are enough to provide some resilience.
- Roughly 3 billion people live like this.
- Your better job means that you can save and invest in education and you could move up into the next income bracket.

LEVEL 4. MORE THAN $32 PER DAY

- One or two children who will be educated for twelve years or more.
- You have access to clean drinking water and power.
- You eat out once a month or more, and you have a car.
- Your savings and access to health care provide considerable resilience.
- Roughly 1 billion people live like this.
- People on Level 4 struggle to understand the reality of the other 6 billion people in the world.

If you are reading this book, you almost certainly receive Level 4 income and have access to the top levels of health. Of course, there is a large range of incomes above $32 per day, and wealth is relative.

Apart from reframing wealth and health into a global context, we have included this spread to illustrate a pattern: when used wisely, even a small amount of capital can enable resilience. This could mean a small but growing savings account; it could mean investments in education either for yourself or for your children; it could even mean purchasing a bike to help you collect the water or raising chickens to get eggs and meat for next to nothing.

Rosling argues that a fact-based world view "creates less stress and hopelessness than a dramatic world view, simply because the dramatic one is so negative and terrifying." Factfulness is the antidote to what he calls "devastating ignorance."

Remember, too, it only takes someone $3 a day to move from average Level 1 to average Level 2.

SHOW ME THE MONEY

For some, thinking about money is literally thinking about the essentials of life: food and shelter.

It's not surprising to find poor finances are associated with stress, depression, anxiety, and lower quality of life. For some people, money worries are so profound that sensations of pain are increased alongside the struggles to meet financial needs.[36-39]

A RECENT SURVEY BY AMERICAN LENDER CAPITAL ONE FOUND THAT:[40]

77%

of Americans feel anxious about their financial situation.

58%

feel that finances control their lives.

52%

have difficulty controlling their money-related worries.

43%

are fatigued from money-related stress.

42%

have difficulty concentrating at work because of money-related stress.

When it comes to money, the trick is to always have some (of course!) — preferably more than you need, with a reserve for emergencies.

There are many paths to this level of financial resilience. Being in the right place at the right time and recognizing and seizing opportunities is important. However, be cautious if the path to riches appears almost too good to be true. It probably is too good to be true. Frauds and scams permeate society and social media, exploiting people's desire for easy money. Scammers use a number of linguistic tricks and feed off our cognitive biases. Older people are particularly vulnerable, with fraudsters exploiting loneliness and social isolation. Of elderly people living independently in the United States, around 5.6% or 1 in 18 have been scammed.[41,42]

One of the heuristics or patterns we've identified from those who have made it rich (being born rich doesn't count) is to spend less than you earn, invest some of the remainder, and save the rest.

Spending less is more efficient than earning more, because you have to pay taxes on every dollar you earn.

For those billion or so lucky wealthy folks in Rosling's Level 4 (earning more than $32 per day), the online financial guru

Mr. Money Moustache has some sound practical advice for living frugally and becoming financially independent:[43]

- Prioritize getting rid of all debt.
- Live close to your work or work from home.
- Refrain from borrowing money for cars. Use a bicycle wherever you can.
- Cancel TV subscriptions.
- Stop wasting money on groceries.
- Refrain from pampering your kids too much.
- Avoid overpriced cell phones.
- Beware of reliance on convenience.
- Create a side hustle to generate extra income.

As with all general advice, ignore it if it doesn't suit your personal circumstances or values.

If saving or living frugally is one-half of the wealth equation, increasing income is the other. We can do this in one of two ways: either we get a better-paying job or we invest in some financial instrument that has a high likelihood of return.

One approach we use in our business is the "investment barbell" described in Nassim Nicholas Taleb's *Antifragile*.[44] The metaphor of a barbell represents the distribution of risk and reward across a portfolio of investments or business ventures. This approach invests in the extremes of very low risk (low returns) and very high risk (high returns), skipping all the average-risk options in the middle.

It's also important to recognize that Taleb is a professional trader with a PhD in the mathematics of this kind of investing. He is qualified to assess opportunities at both ends of his barbell approach in a way that many of us are not, so approach your investment decisions carefully.

Think of investment the same way you think of gambling (unless, of course, you have a gambling problem):

- Never play with more than you are prepared to lose.
- Spread the risk. Don't put all your eggs in one basket.

If you have no trading experience, you might hope that professional financial advice is the way forward. *A Random Walk Down Wall Street* by Burton Malkiel is a popular book that has sold more than 1.5 million copies. Malkiel's central message: most financial advisors fare no better, on average, than a blindfolded chimpanzee throwing darts at stocks.[45,46] As with stocks, don't bet it all on one horse (trader). Seek out a range of opinions, and always remember, there are no sure bets. Investing is always a gamble.

If you're determined to trade yourself rich, the following sobering statistics might help:[47]

- 100% of traders start with the same dream: to get rich quick (ok, we made that statistic up).
- Around 1% of traders make a profit from the other 99% who lose money (we didn't make that up).
- Only 7% remain trading after five years.
- 40% trade for only one month.
- 80% quit within two years.

We also caution against trusting anyone who is selling trading systems, software, or know-how. If someone has THE system to make money, why would they be marketing it to you when they could be spending all that wealth and having a good time?

However you decide to manage your money, it goes without saying that an empty bank account or a debt that cannot be paid off are not conditions for resilience. Weekly budgeting and keeping track of incomings and outgoings may be boring, but boredom is often preferable to sleepless nights.

WATCH OUT FOR LIFESTYLE TRAPS

Lifestyle traps limit freedom and choice. Some traps are obvious to us, like having to pay a mortgage and service debts that we have taken out to pay for cars, boats, and holidays. Other traps are often hidden from conscious awareness, such as beliefs about our obligations to family, or accepting cultural norms.

Sometimes these traps creep up on us. For example, as our income grows, we tend to increase our expectations of what material wealth we want or think we deserve. We take on more and more commitments to support a lifestyle that becomes fragile. When we want to change or need an exit from the way we currently fund our lifestyle, we find that we are trapped.

MONEY TRAPS

- Poor provision for tax.
- Increasing expectations for lifestyle based on credit, not income.
- Recurring subscriptions continue to extract money long after we finish using the service.
- Spending out of habit, not necessity.
- Spending out of boredom.
- Spending on convenience and becoming habituated to instant gratification.

GUILT AND DUTY TRAPS

- Committing to a company, team, or relationship out of a sense of loyalty, duty, or guilt.

- Staying with a poor lifestyle choice to avoid someone else having an unpleasant emotional response that they blame us for (e.g., postponing quitting a terrible but well-paying job for fear their partner will become upset).

FAMILY OR FAMILY BUSINESS TRAPS

These usually occur when we believe we are indispensable or that we have no choice. Harper Lee said, "You can choose your friends, but not your family."

They might always be family in the formal sense, but many people disown their family and have nothing to do with them. Take the extreme case of Omar bin Laden as an example. Brought up with Al Qaeda as a child, Omar broke free of radicalization. He repeatedly condems the September 11 attacks, denounces terrorism, his father's actions, and violent ideaologies, and seeks to bring peace to the world through art.[48]

If Omar could break free from Al Qaeda and his family to choose his own path, anyone can.

TRIBAL TRAPS

Tribal or cultural traps are often subtle expectations or beliefs that we hold and accept as necessary for belonging to a group. These tribal frames range from relatively benign shared cultural identities to expectations of violence in gangs and complete submission to authority in cults.

Gang membership is particularly risky for young people who are working out their own sense of identity as they grow into adulthood. In America, around 20% of homicides in cities are gang related, and many young people looking for somewhere to belong end up trapped in a lifestyle of crime and imprisonment.[49]

It is very easy to accept the tribal customs we all live by without questioning or challenging them. We can always exercise our choice to leave, even if we have to manage exit risks.

A QUICK GUIDE TO HEALTH LITERACY

In much the same way that financial management is concerned with decisions of risk and reward, making informed decisions about health involves weighing potential benefits against potential harms and overall quality of life.

Unfortunately, there is no simple way to determine where the weight of evidence lands for many health interventions. Each person's values and situation are different. Additionally, the scientific evaluation of medicine is difficult to understand even for experts. Examples of misleading health advice abound in everything from prescription medications and alternative medicine to therapy and witchcraft of all persuasions.

One of the most studied examples, and the boogeyman of Bad Pharma, are statins. Statins are marketed as medicines that reduce cholesterol and the incidence of cardiovascular disease. They are amongst the most commonly prescribed drugs in the world, with global market sales reaching approximately $28.5 billion

in 2014. This is despite independent research that has highlighted the ways in which statistics have been misused to exaggerate the benefits of statin use. We present an in-depth profile of statin marketing here to showcase how statistics can be manipulated in the service of medical marketing. We hope this will motivate you to become more involved in the decisions surrounding your health.[50-52]

BEWARE "RELATIVE RISK"

Relative risk reduction tends to exaggerate the benefit of a treatment because the benefit of treatment versus a control is greatest where there is a low or rare chance of an adverse event. Even a very small absolute change can have a very large relative change.[50,53,54] Compare the two labels below. The first shows relative risk, the second one absolute risk. Absolute risk is a less persuasive statistic, and what does 1% reduction in the risk of a heart attack mean anyway?

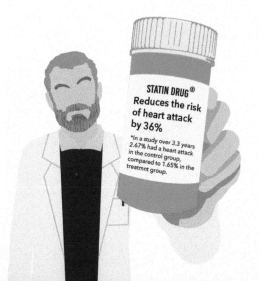

STATIN DRUG®
Reduces the risk of heart attack by 36%

*In a study over 3.3 years 2.67% had a heart attack in the control group, compared to 1.65% in the treatmnt group.

STATIN DRUG®
Reduces the risk of heart attack by 1%

*In a study over 3.3 years 2.67% had a heart attack in the control group, compared to 1.65% in the treatmnt group.

WHO'S THE LUCKY WINNER?

Another statistic to watch for is the number of people who need to be treated (or NNT) for just one person to *probably* benefit. It's a bit like a lottery. When you take the meds, you don't know if you will be that lucky person. The bigger the number, the less likely it is that you would benefit. An NNT of 1 would be perfect (everybody taking the medication would benefit). Look again at our label. It's not as compelling as a 36% reduction in risk of heart attack, and it's still not clear what the benefits and risks might be.

A team of researchers led by Christopher Chong in the Department of Medicine at the University of Toronto found a significant negative correlation between NNT and a measure they called "quality-adjusted life years." Using this, they created a rule: If NNT is greater than 15, then the therapy should be ruled out; if less than 5 it should be considered. Between 5 and 15 is less clear. Statins are typically in the range 31-250, except when they have a negative NNT, meaning that people in the placebo control group were statistically better off![55,56]

Instead of a lottery, Marlene Kristensen from the Department of Clinical Pharmacology, University of Southern Denmark, considered the benefits of statins differently. They shared the benefit across the whole population measured as postponement of death from taking the drug. They calculated a "benefit" between -10 and +27 extra days of life in exchange for taking a drug every day for between 2 and 6.1 years.[56] How compelling is our label now?

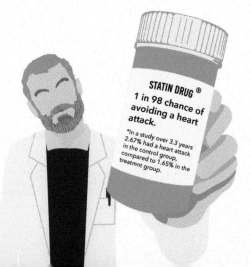

STATIN DRUG ®
1 in 98 chance of avoiding a heart attack.
*In a study over 3.3 years 2.67% had a heart attack in the control group, compared to 1.65% in the treatmnt group.

STATIN DRUG ®
Could increase your lifespan by 2 days.
*In a study over 3.3 years 2.67% had a heart attack in the control group, compared to 1.65% in the treatmnt group.

WARNING: THE PHARMACEUTICAL INDUSTRY HAS SERIOUS SIDE EFFECTS

The tag line (above) from Ben Goldacre's book *Bad Pharma* says it all. The possibility of those extra years, or mere days that we might buy for ourselves, comes at a cost. There are the obvious financial costs, and there are also lifestyle sacrifices and adverse side effects to consider.

Statistics like NNT are not intuitive to understand and they are widely criticized in the science communication literature for that reason.[57]

SO WHO LIVES AND WHO DIES?

In a follow-up to the statin study we have profiled in the previous pages, eight years later the original authors looked to see who lived and who died. They found a small statistically significant drop in all cause mortality in those originally prescribed the drug, but **no significant drop in death from cardiovascular events**. For a drug marketed and sold globally as reducing cholesterol to prevent heart attacks and cardiovascular disease, they could not explain the small significant drop in non-cardiovascular deaths.[58]

Statins also come with a wide range of side effects. The prevalence and severity of these effects are not well known for statins, partly because people who tolerate statins poorly are often excluded from trial results (you read that correctly).

Dr. Paul Mason estimates that adverse outcomes might occur in as many as 1 in 4 people.[59] Well-known side effects include new-onset diabetes, brain fogginess, and acute muscle pain.[59-61]

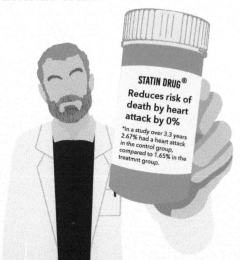

STATIN DRUG®
Reduces risk of death by heart attack by 0%

*In a study over 3.3 years 2.67% had a heart attack in the control group, compared to 1.65% in the treatmnt group.

STATIN DRUG®
Increases risk of making you sick by 25%

*In a study over 3.3 years 2.67% had a heart attack in the control group, compared to 1.65% in the treatmnt group.

WHAT DOES THIS ALL MEAN?

Firstly, as we demonstrate for statins, it's easy to go:

- Reduces the risk of heart attack by 36%
- Reduces the risk of heart attack by 1%
- 1 in 98 chance of avoiding a heart attack
- Increase your lifespan by two days
- Reduces risk of death by heart attack by 0%
- Increases risk of making you sick by 25%

Look closely at the evidence for both benefit and harm. How might each affect your overall quality of life?

Population statistics serve as a guide but, ultimately, we rarely know where we fit in the population. To understand both your own cardiovascular risk associated with cholesterol and the potential for statins to offer you a net benefit will require a nuanced evidence-based conversation with an informed medical practitioner or specialist. The same is true of any medical treatment.

Our rule-of-thumb is to carefully calibrate your own response to treatment. Be alert to potential side effects, and if you start to feel unwell or something changes, go back to your medical practitioner and ensure that you are being listened to.

Also consider changes to your lifestyle as a form of treatment. For heart attacks, there is abundant evidence that eating nutritious whole food, moving well and regularly, eliminating bad stress (you have the solution in your hands), stopping smoking, and consuming alcohol in moderation can all reduce risk factors for cardiovascular disease and death, with very few if any adverse side effects.[62-68] Though, of course, quality-of-life is a matter of personal perception.

More broadly, ask yourself how healthier lifestyle choices might improve your well-being and resilience. Often, even small changes can flow on throughout life.

Your relationship with your doctor and other medical professionals is an important consideration. Many people consult Doctor Google before taking action or seeing their doctor. There are upsides and downsides to this approach. Being informed is a great place to start, and it can help you ask specific questions of your doctor. However, it's easy to get misled on the internet. Remember that doctors spend many years in medical training.

In the words of Dr Greg Swartz:

"Be that difficult patient who asks lots of questions and seeks to be involved in your own well-being."

There is a current trend in medicine toward shared decision-making.[69]

Ultimately, you are responsible for your own health and well-being.

HEALTHCARE RULES TO LIVE BY

HEALTH RULES:

- What is my outcome?
- Is there a low-risk and evidenced-based option I can try?
- What support do I need?
- What evidence would inform me that what I am doing is working?

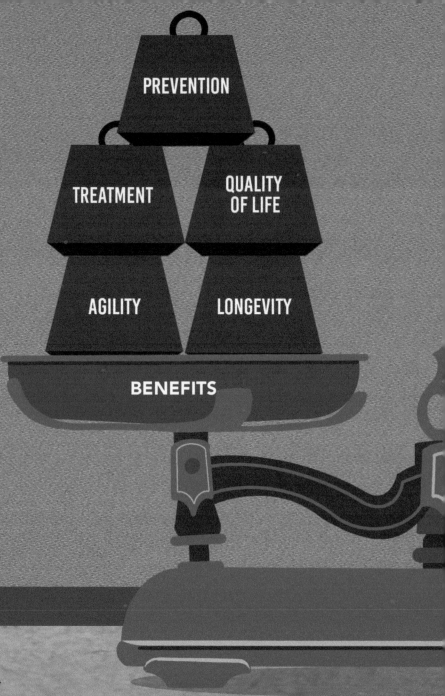

354

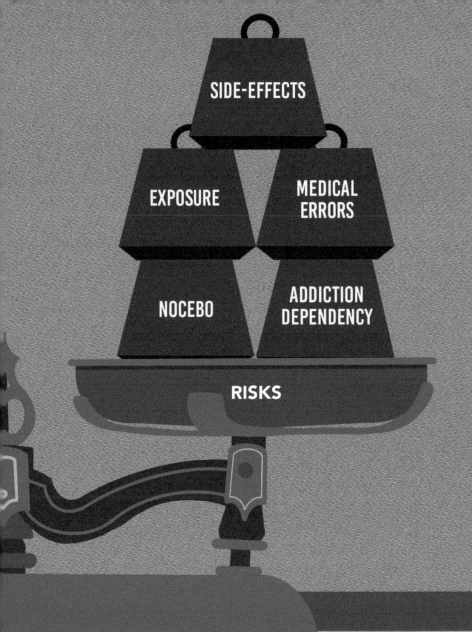

HEALTH RULES:

- Is the treatment working well for me?
- Am I taking an active role in my well-being?
- Do I have a health-supporting lifestyle?
- What would my doctor do in this situation?[44,54,70]

EBBS AND FLOWS

VINAY NAIR

is the co founder, CEO, and chairman of Tifin Group, which has ten operating companies and 120 staff across four time zones. He also has a professor role at Wharton, and advises JP Morgan. He's married with three young children, ages four, six, and eight. When not running businesses, he skis and fly fishes.

It's true to say that I often struggle to manage all my workload. Though if it feels like a struggle, I'm not thinking clearly about managing it. I hesitate to use the term "manage" because that makes all of life seem like work. Undeniably there are some less exciting days than others, but I mostly find great satisfaction in the number of roles I have.

To stay on top of everything, as a general rule, I try to seek moments of fun and excitement each day, whilst also putting my focus on three principles: purpose, relationships, and ideas.

For purpose, the question is, am I being of service, having humility and "not thinking less of myself, but thinking of myself less?"

Are my relationships meaningful, whether they're for work or social?

Does the task or activity drain or energize me? If it energizes me, I aim to do more of it. If it drains me, then I find better ways to engage, or I pass it to someone who would appreciate it.

It's obvious that we put more time into what we enjoy doing, rather than what we don't. On a day I've fought with my spouse, I mostly avoid family time! (laughs)

In our companies, we will often work on as many as six projects with the same people from different parts of the business. The important factor is always the relationship, not the particular project. We use the metaphor of putting more and more logs into the same fire rather than burning a lot of fires.

I previously ran the business from our home city of New York. Over time, I realized that New York was draining me of energy for far too long, and that I should try a change of scenery by moving to the mountain town of Boulder, Colorado. Some people thought it was an extreme move, but I assessed the downside and worse case, concluding that we could always move back to NYC, and if we did, it would be with a new appreciation for our life there.

Many times, it's the fear of change that is worse than the reality of it. As you get older, more inertia can arise and it takes a conscious effort to let new things into your life

Taking a family or a firm to a new city can be difficult because people dig their heals in. What I realized with our move is that I was so busy convincing others of the move, I forget to notice or find issue with my own changes!

"The best we can do is work on the present and plan for downsides. And always be prepared for the unexpected!"

At the end of the day, a move is reversible and you can always go back.

When it comes to my kids, my priority is not how much time I am with them, but more the consistency that they can rely on. When I'm with them I'm really with them and not splitting attention. Family time is dedicated time and my wife and I get in a one-on-ones every two weeks, with a rule of no discussion of admin or kids.

My work volume ebbs and flows between busy or very busy and my team religiously apply the approach from the book *Measure What Matters.*

As a rule, our staff are allowed no more than five objectives and no more than three key results in a week. Focusing on one to three tasks every week is enough, especially if at least one high-value task is completed every week. We're also trialing a new rule of no work (including calls or messages) after 5:30 p.m. It's important that people are able to make the most of their work and nonwork time equally.

My personal schedule includes at least two one-on-one dinners in the week, with a member of our team. These meals improve relationships and have become an essential part of each week.

Three mornings per week I take physical activity, such as a hike, tennis, or chi gong. I meditate every morning and also use a journal regularly. I recently wrote in my journal, "how can I simplify my life some more?" The answer that arose was, "to reduce the quantity of people in my life, with more attention for those who matter."

I also realized that some meals can be a takeaway pizza, and don't have to be a fancy, sit-down affair every time. I think it all comes down to appreciating the basics, such as quality relationships.

If you look back on your life in five years' time, it's highly likely you will be in a position that was impossible to predict. The best we can do is work on the present and plan for downsides. And always be prepared for the unexpected!

Maybe in five years I will have moved to my dream lifestyle, which will involve lots more travel and time with friends. I'll no longer be involved with hiring and firing and I will have stopped taking life so seriously!

Until then, it's always a work in progress.

CREATE A LIFESTYLE BY DESIGN

Knowing what is most important to you as an individual, and understanding how various aspects of life can be linked in mutually supporting ways, can help you prioritize allocation of time and resources.

The information on this page and the activity on the next one are intended to help you develop a holistic approach for living the life you want. The template is designed to evaluate your current life, identify actions and a way to track your progress, and help you triage if you are overwhelmed.

Element: Wife   Score: 5/10

Intention(s): Love and happiness

Action: Commit to finish work on friday
evening. Book morning breakfast(s) with
my wife on Saturday, instead of responding
to emails.

GETTING STARTED

To begin, choose up to ten elements of lifestyle that are most important to you.

An element could be a relationship, your job, a hobby or leisure activity, or anything in your life that you think is important.

Be specific.

It is ok to choose an element that you already have a lot of in your life, and it is ok to choose an element that you currently have none of. This is an opportunity to deeply reflect on what is important to you.

For each element you have chosen, ask the following questions:

When I have this:

- What would I see?
- What would I hear?
- What would I feel?
- What would I taste and smell?

Once you have answers to the above, ask yourself an intention question:

- When I have this element in my life, what will the benefit be?

These questions will help you to associate into the state of having this outcome. They will also help you identify the positive intention for having that element prioritized in your life.

For example:

"My wife is the most important aspect in my life. I love seeing her smiling face and hearing her laughter. When I am with her, I feel light in the chest. I experience being with her as joy and happiness."

Repeat this embodied visualization process for each element you previously identified. Check, is anything missing?

If you have dozens of elements and you are struggling to reduce it to less than ten, you might need to combine items together. For example, you might go from "spending time with [each child]" to "spending time with children."

Next, score how satisfied you currently are with each of the elements you have identified: 0 is not at all satisfied, and 10 is completely satisfied.

Check that 10 is achievable and realistic even if it's a highly ambitious goal.

Move between each topic you have chosen, associating into those elements of your life as you go. Identify intentions, and score each element on your list like this.

When completed, this is like a map that identifies where your lifestyle is today, and it identifies where you would like to get to.

Next, look at the satisfaction scores. For each element of your life that scores low, perhaps 7 or less, identify one action you can do in the next three days that will improve that score. Be specific. "Spend more time with my wife" is not the same as arranging to walk together in the park on Saturday or to go out for dinner and a movie on Friday.

Are there any consequences for those actions?

Project into the future to a time when you have taken those actions. Experience this future in an associated state — feel, hear, and see the action, the outcome, and the consequences. This is essentially the outcome, intention, and consequences pattern we described previously, now applied to each element in your lifestyle.

When you are satisfied with that one course of action, write it down.

Repeat this same process for every low-scoring element.

Next, identify one action or change you could make in the next three months or so that could have the most impact on multiple elements of your lifestyle. Importantly, what can you do immediately to set that plan of action in motion?

For example, if you scored low on time with friends, outdoor sports, and travel, a good approach might be a camping trip with your best friend and your family. You might increase your score even more if you widen the circle further by inviting a few extra families to join you.

For the next step, make sure this happens. Get in touch with your best friend, right now. Don't plan to make plans. Take action, now.

When you have considered the changes you want to make, you may find the need to do less of some elements in your life to make space for new ones that have a higher priority. Remember that lifestyle by design is more about triage than balance, and at the heart of triage is the decision about what to not do. Remember too the importance of rest and sleep and "not doing" more generally.

The last and most important step is to make a commitment to live the lifestyle that

you have designed for yourself. Revisit and revise your plan as necessary.

It is important to be aware that the elements you have chosen can change over time. Priorities change as our lifestyles change. Our template provides a guide that you can revisit and revise whenever you like.

ACTIVITY

TEMPLATE

What action could I take to impact multiple of these elements?

Element: Score:

Intention(s):

Action:

Element: Score:

Intention(s):

Action:

Element: Score:

Intention(s):

Action:

Element: _____ **Score:** _____

Intention(s): _____

Action: _____

_____

_____

_____

_____

_____

Element: _____ **Score:** _____

Intention(s): _____

Action: _____

_____

_____

_____

_____

_____

Element: _____ **Score:** _____

Intention(s): _____

Action: _____

_____

_____

_____

_____

_____

LIFESTYLE BY DESIGN

Element: _____ **Score:** _____

Intention(s): _____

Action: _____

_____

_____

_____

_____

_____

Element: _____ **Score:** _____

Intention(s): _____

Action: _____

_____

_____

_____

_____

_____

Element: _____ **Score:** _____

Intention(s): _____

Action: _____

_____

_____

_____

_____

_____

Element: _____ **Score:** _____

Intention(s): _____

Action: _____

_____

_____

_____

_____

_____

NUDGE YOURSELF TO TAKE A STEP

In a study that compared strategies of expert and novice orienteers, a team of researchers led by David Eccles found that more experienced orienteers looked at their maps more often whilst moving. They spent significantly less time stationary than their less-experienced counterparts.[71]

This study provides an important crossover for creating a lifestyle by design. Knowing where you are is always a critical place to begin. We need to orient ourselves before we can establish a direction and pathway, and we need to *keep on orienting ourselves* whilst moving. Unlike competitive orienteering, it's ok to pause as well, provided that you don't lose momentum on something that is important to you.

Two common challenges to enacting change involve getting started and maintaining momentum.

Sometimes there is a perceived barrier to beginning. Check that:

☑ The first step is small enough.

☑ Secondary gains have been considered.

☑ The change is sufficiently important and not a distraction from a more pressing issue.

☑ You have support in place or have managed context to allow you to take the first step.

How many people buy a gym membership and a new pair of training shoes for January, only to revert to old habits by February? If you are finding it difficult to maintain momentum, check that:

☑ You have introduced small, manageable changes rather than aiming for perfection.

☑ The outcome is backed by a compelling intention.

☑ The outcome is self-generated and not someone else's desire to change you.

Another concept that can help navigate change is to relate your map and preferred direction to what Dave Snowden calls the adjacent possibles.[72]

Let's say you want to start hitting the gym four times a week. You find that this hurts too much, costs too much, or is simply unmanageable with your busy schedule. An adjacent possible might be to swim three times a week at lunch time. Get going on something that is possible. In time, you can move to an activity that is closer to what you really want.

In *Nudge: Improving Decisions About Health, Wealth, and Happiness*, Richard Thaler and Cass Sunstein note important differences between ideal, rational humans and the quirky reality of what it is to be human. We don't all save wisely for our futures, exercise daily, or even surround ourselves with people who have our best interests at heart.

Thaler and Sunstein focus on changing habits by nudging, taking small, manageable steps, and the aid of what they call choice architecture.

Choice architecture is a term that was originally used to describe how choices can be presented to consumers to influence or nudge them in a particular

direction, such as buying a particular item from a menu. The same patterns can be applied to personal choice to make certain actions easier or harder. The idea is to organize your situation to create barriers for the habits you want to change, and to make the desired choice the easy default. For example, if you find yourself snacking on sweets whilst trying (and failing) to maintain a natural food diet, you might do the following:

- Eat well before shopping. This will make it easier not to buy junk foods. Manage the intervention at the supermarket, not your fridge door.
- Get the whole family to join your nutrition regime.
- Take some time to plan and even pre-cook meals and healthy snacks. Make them easier and tastier than junk food.

Nudging can be applied to any facet of life. For example, for saving, consider the Save More Tomorrow nudge. The idea is to commit to saving when your wages rise. This makes the impact less noticeable.[73]

Another tactic to help you stay committed is to tell everyone your plan. Posting your progress and confessing publicly to any transgressions can provide the combination of encouraging good behavior and disincentivizing bad behavior to help you stick to the plan.

On a final note of caution, beware fools' choices.

Fools' errand: a task or activity that has no hope of success.

Fools' gold: all that glitters is not gold.

One of the problems with goal setting is that too much emphasis is placed on the shiny goal, and not enough on the journey or the very act of living.

There is also risk in attempting to be extraordinary or "normal."

We wish you luck if you want to create an extraordinary life for yourself. We aspire to that for ourselves. We also recognize that we must make these aspirations fit within the conditions of the ecosystem we inhabit and co-create. At the extremes of any endeavor, there is a risk that resilience

can be diminished, like the flow junkie pushing to their limit in extreme sports.

Fools' normal: trying to fit in based on statistics.

If striving for the extraordinary has risks, trying to be "normal" or fitting into some sort of population statistic is possibly even more dangerous. Far too many people are either put or put themselves under unnecessary pressure to conform or fit in. Some societies and cultures have come a long way in accepting neurodiversity, gender fluidity, and a respect for differences of all sorts. Thankfully.

Trying to fit a round peg into a square hole is always a challenge (and usually an impossibility), though we acknowledge that fitting in might be resilient, for a short time at least.

LIFE IS LIKE A BOX OF CHOCOLATES

Depending on which perspective you take, life is just like a box of chocolates, nothing like a box of chocolates at all, or a little bit like a box of chocolates depending on the chocolates in the box and the life context the chocolates are being compared to.

Most boxes of chocolate come with a menu that shows which ones are which. The menu describes something of the experience you might have. Equally, if you choose to dip into the box without reading the menu, don't be surprised if you're hoping for a chocolate-coated hazelnut and find yourself gagging on something that looks like it belongs on a Carmen Miranda fruit hat. The description of "orange delight" on the menu would have warned you what to expect.

What matters more for resilience, though, is:

Do you have enough agency to choose to eat the chocolates or not?

And

If you chose a chocolate that's not to your taste, are you able to learn from this and not reach in for more of the same?

Who knows, maybe all the chocolates in the box are fruit horrors. Do you keep on dipping in anyway, hoping for something different when all the evidence suggests that you'll keep getting the same experience over and over again?

When *Forrest Gump* hit the box office, it received widespread acclaim, winning many accolades including Academy Awards and Golden Globes. It also received something of a backlash for its portrayal of Forrest, an intellectually challenged young man from 1950s Alabama.

His naive, kind-hearted nature, almost color-blind response to racial issues in America, and impossibly resilient and lucky life intersects with many of the iconic turbulent moments in American history.

Critics argue that Gump presents a dangerous fantasy in which hard questions of race, politics, institutionalization, and war don't matter. Movie critic Eric Kohn describes the movie as "fake news on an epic scale." The movie, he says, "presents a grinning idiot savant as epitomizing everything about America, suggesting that he could catapult to fame and fortune he doesn't really earn, while people enduring genuine struggles to make a difference in the world struggle all the way to the grave."[74]

For others, it's an inspirational endearing story of resilience and love carried by incredible acting.

From our perspective, the story is a metaphor for one way of living life, or approaching certain aspects of life.

Wandering through our complex and, at times, turbulent world with a resourceful flowstate of not consciously being aware of our thinking, guided by a few principles or heuristics, just like Forrest, is one of several highly resilient approaches to life. It also often benefits us to take multiple perspectives on context; sometimes to apply a careful blend of the rational and the intuitive, along with a mix of planned, ordered responses and more tentative probes into uncertain situations.

Expressed in terms of chocolates, living a lifestyle by design sometimes means dipping into the box without looking, remaining open to a pleasant surprise; other times it might mean reading the menu and making our choices carefully. Whether we are designing for predictability or uncertainty, we need to be prepared for both sweet surprises and bitter disappointments.

We (Ian and Mike) prefer a mixed box of chocolates that offers choice. If life was like an endless supply of chocolate-coated hazelnuts, how dull it would be. As for decorations from a Carmen Miranda fruit hat masquerading as chocolates... each to their own!

Momma always said, "Life is like a box of chocolates.
You never know what you're gonna get."

— Forrest Gump

01. RESILIENCE

A delicious nutty center that delights with a sense a freedom.

02. SENSEMAKING

A beautiful blend of tasty flavors, that sounds as good as it smells.

03. THINKING

A perfect fusion to soothe your digestion, stimulate the mind, and connect the heart.

04. STATE

A shockingly tasty morsel that is sure to make you gasp with joy.

05. PERSPECTIVE

Is it a nut wrapped in a soft center, or a soft center with a nutty inclusion?

06. CONTEXT

A simple chocolate outer that gives way to a complex creamy center.

07. SIGNALS

Simply moreish, every nerve in your body will be clamoring for attention.

08. INTENTIONS

Hot chilli flames, tears, and of course joy.

09. REFRAMING

No need for a cup of concrete; this chewy delight will keep you going further.

10. FLOW

Oozing with yumminess to take you to a quiet place where time stands still.

11. REST

A soothing blend of deliciousness for the afternoon and early evening.

12. LIFESTYLE

Is that from a Carmen Miranda fruit hat?

REFERENCES

CHAPTER 1

1. Szabo, S. *et al.* 2012. The legacy of Hans Selye and the origins of stress research: A retrospective 75 years after his landmark brief "Letter" to the Editor of Nature. *Stress* 15, 472–478.

2. Selye, H. 1936. A syndrome produced by diverse nocuous agents. *Nature* 138, 32–32.

3. Fink, G. 2016. Eighty years of stress. *Nature* 539, 175–176.

4. Selye, H. 1976. Stress without distress. In *Psychopathology of Human Adaptation*. Springer US. 137–146.

5. Selye, H. 1979. *Stress of My Life: A Scientist's Memoirs.* Van Nostrand Reinhold Company.

6. World Health Organization. WHO | Stress at the workplace. *WHO Website.* https://www.who.int/occupational_health/topics/stressatwp/en/.

7. Medibank. 2008. The cost of workplace stress in Australia Medibank private and workplace health. *Econtech.* http://www.medibank.com.au/.

8. Berninger, A. *et al.* 2010. Trends of elevated PTSD risk in firefighters exposed to the World Trade Center disaster: 2001–2005. *Public Health Rep.* 125, 556–566.

9. Chuang, C. H. *et al.* 2016. Burnout in the intensive care unit professionals. *Medicine (Baltimore).* 95, 1–12.

10. Monsalve-Reyes, C. S. *et al.* 2018. Burnout syndrome and its prevalence in primary care nursing: A systematic review and meta-analysis. *BMC Fam. Pract.* 19, 59-65.

11. Reynolds, C. A. & Wagner, S. L. 2007. Stress and first responders: The need for a multidimensional approach to stress management. *Int. J. Disabil. Manag.* 2, 27–36.

12. Ganster, D. C. & Rosen, C. C. 2013. Work stress and employee health. *J. Manage.* 39, 1085–1122.

13. Heads up. Workplace Stress. https://www.headsup.org.au/healthy-workplaces/workplace-stressors.

14. Bhui, K. *et al.* 2016. Perceptions of work stress causes and effective interventions in employees working in public, private and non-governmental organizations: A qualitative study. *BJPsych Bull.* 40, 318–325.

15. Selye, H. 1952. physiology and pathology of exposure to stress. A treatise based on the concept of the general adaptation syndrome and the diseases of adaptation. *Ind. Med. Gaz.* 87, 431.

16. Carroll, D. *et al.* 2012. Systolic blood pressure reactions to acute stress are associated with future hypertension status in the Dutch Famine Birth Cohort Study. *Int. J. Psychophysiol.* 85, 270–273.

17. Guimont, C. *et al.* 2006. Effects of job strain on blood pressure: A prospective study of male and female white collar workers. *Am. J. Public Health* 96, 1436–1443.

18. Markovitz, J. H. *et al.* 2004. Increases in job strain are associated with incident hypertension in the CARDIA study. *Ann. Behav. Med.* 28, 4–9.

19. Steptoe, A. & Kivimäki, M. 2012. Stress and cardiovascular disease. *Nat. Rev. Cardiol.* 9, 360–370.

20. Nabi, H. *et al.* 2013. Increased risk of coronary heart disease among individuals reporting adverse impact of stress on their health: The Whitehall II prospective cohort study. *Eur. Heart J.* 34, 2697–2705.

21. Rosengren, A. *et al.* 2004. Association of psychosocial risk factors with risk of acute myocardial infarction in 11 119 cases and 13 648 controls from 52 countries (the INTERHEART study): Case-control study. *Lancet* 364, 953–962.

22. Kivimaki, M. 2002. Work stress and risk of cardiovascular mortality: Prospective cohort study of industrial employees. *BMJ* 325, 857–857.

23. Sheps, D. S. *et al.* 2002. Mental stress-induced ischemia and all-cause mortality in patients with coronary artery disease. *Circulation* 105, 1780–1784.

24. Stewart, R. A. H. *et al.* 2017. Persistent psychological distress and mortality in patients with stable coronary artery disease. *Heart* 103, 1860–1866.

25. Kivimäki, M. *et al.* 2018. Work stress and risk of death in men and women with and without cardiometabolic disease: A multicohort study. *Lancet Diabetes Endocrinol.* 6, 705–713.

26. Karasek, R. A. J. 1979. Job demands, job decision latitude, and mental strain: Implications for job redesign. *Adm. Sci. Q.* 24, 285–308.

27. Monroy, V. 2020. Overwhelmed at the bedside. *Am. J. Nurs.* 120, 1–13.

28. Bakker, A. B. & Demerouti, E. 2007. The Job Demands-Resources model: State of the art. *J. Manag. Psychol.* 22, 309–328.

29. Huang, J. *et al.* 2016. The Job Demands-Resources model and jobs burnout: The mediating role of personal resources. *Curr. Psychol.* 35, 562–569.

30. Nielsen, M. B. & Einarsen, S. 2012. Outcomes of exposure to workplace bullying: A meta-analytic review. *Work Stress* 26, 309–332.

31. Kivimaki, M. 2003. Workplace bullying and the risk of cardiovascular disease and depression. *Occup. Environ. Med.* 60, 779–783.

32. Kendra, M. A. *et al.* 1996. Safety concerns affecting delivery of home health care. *Public Health Nurs.* 13, 83–89.

33. Keegan, A. E. & Den Hartog, D. N. 2004. Transformational leadership in a project-based

environment: A comparative study of the leadership styles of project managers and line managers. *Int. J. Proj. Manag.* 22, 609–617.

34. Bond, S. A. *et al.* 2010. Psychosocial safety climate, workplace bullying, and symptoms of posttraumatic stress. *Organ. Dev. J.* 28, 38–56.

35. Idris, M. A. *et al.* 2012. Psychosocial safety climate: Conceptual distinctiveness and effect on job demands and worker psychological health. *Saf. Sci.* 50, 19–28.

36. de Menezes, L. M. & Kelliher, C. 2011. Flexible working and performance: A systematic review of the evidence for a business case. *Int. J. Manag. Rev.* 13, 452–474.

37. Frone, M. R. 2000. Work–family conflict and employee psychiatric disorders: The national comorbidity survey. *J. Appl. Psychol.* 85, 888–895.

38. Kivimäki, M. *et al.* 2015. Long working hours and risk of coronary heart disease and stroke: A systematic review and meta-analysis of published and unpublished data for 603 838 individuals. *Lancet* 386, 1739–1746.

39. Fulton, J. J. *et al.* 2015. The prevalence of posttraumatic stress disorder in Operation Enduring Freedom/Operation Iraqi Freedom (OEF/OIF) Veterans: A meta-analysis. *J. Anxiety Disord.* 31, 98–107.

40. Griffin, M. L. *et al.* 2010. Job involvement, job stress, job satisfaction, and organizational commitment and the burnout of correctional staff. *Crim. Justice Behav.* 37, 239–255.

41. Doody, C. B. *et al.* 2019. Pre-deployment programmes for building resilience in military and frontline emergency service personnel. *Cochrane Database Syst.* Rev. 2019, 1–15.

42. Waegemakers Schiff, J. & Lane, A. M. 2019. PTSD symptoms, vicarious traumatization, and burnout in front line workers in the homeless sector. *Community Ment. Health J.* 55, 454–462.

43. Mason, S. *et al.* 2016. A longitudinal study of well-being, confidence and competence in junior doctors and the impact of emergency medicine placements. *Emerg. Med. J.* 33, 91–98.

44. Shanafelt, T. D. *et al.* 2012. Burnout and satisfaction with work life balance among US physicians relative the to the general US population. *Arch. Intern. Med.* 172, 1377–1385.

45. Taouk, Y. *et al.* 2020. Psychosocial work stressors and risk of mortality in Australia: Analysis of data from the Household, Income and Labour Dynamics in Australia survey. *Occup. Environ. Med.* 77, 256–264.

46. Salleh, M. R. 2008. Life event, stress and illness. *Malaysian J. Med. Sci.* 15, 9–18.

47. Stephen Covey acknowledged that he was not the originator of this quote, and does not recall where he got it from.

CHAPTER 2

1. Partanen, E. *et al.* 2013. Learning-induced neural plasticity of speech processing before birth. *Proc. Natl. Acad. Sci.* 110, 15145–15150.

2. Hoffman, D. D. 2000. *Visual Intelligence: How We Create What We See*. W. W. Norton & Company.

3. Bateson, G. 1972. Form, substance and difference. In *Steps to an Ecology of Mind*. Chandler Publishing Company.

4. Hoffman, D. D. 2019. *The Case Against Reality*. W. W. Norton & Company.

5. Primary source unknown. A version of this psychological illusion is widely circulating on the internet and in numerous blogs and reviews. We cannot confirm if this is an urban myth or confirm provenance.

6. Chabris, C. & Simons, D. 2010. *The Invisible Gorilla: And Other Ways Our Intuitions Deceive Us*. Random House.

7. Drew, T. *et al.* 2013. The invisible gorilla strike again. *Psychol. Sci.* 24, 1848–1853.

8. Chabris, C. F. *et al.* 2011. You do not talk about fight club if you do not notice fight club: Inattentional blindness for a simulated real-world assault. *i-Perception.* 2, 150–153.

9. Moseley, G. L. & Butler, D. S. 2015. Fifteen years of explaining pain: The past, present, and future. *J. Pain* 16, 807–813.

10. Ramachandran, V. S. & Rodgers-Ramachandran, D. 1996. Synaesthesia in phantom limbs induced with mirrors. *Proc. R. Soc. London. Ser. B Biol. Sci.* 263, 377–386.

11. Butler, D. S. & Moseley, G. L. 2003. *Explain Pain*. Noigroup Publications.

12. Butler, D. S. *et al.* 2012. *The Graded Motor Imagery Handbook*. Noigroup Publications.

13. Flor, H. 2003. Cortical reorganisation and chronic pain: Implications for rehabilitation. *J. Rehabil. Med.* 35, 66–72.

14. Kuner, R. & Flor, H. 2017. Structural plasticity and reorganisation in chronic pain. *Nat. Rev. Neurosci.* 18, 20–30.

15. Keci, A. *et al.* 2019. Role of rehabilitation in neural plasticity. *Open Access Maced. J. Med. Sci.* 7, 1540–1547.

16. Hazeley, J. & Morris, J. 2015. *The Ladybird Book of Mindfulness*. Penguin.

17. Tolle, E. 2004. *The Power of Now: A Guide to Spiritual Enlightenment*. New World Library.

18. Rovelli, C. 2018. *The Order of Time*. Riverhead Books.

19. Herzog, M. H. *et al.* 2016. Time slices: What is the duration of a precept? *PLOS Biol.* 14, 1-12.

20. Toso, A. *et al.* 2021. A sensory integration account for time perception. *PLOS Comput. Biol.* 17, 1-25.

21. Kirk, U. & Axelsen, J. L. 2020. Heart rate variability is enhanced during mindfulness practice: A randomized controlled trial involving a 10-day online based mindfulness intervention. *PLoS One* 15, 1–23.

22. Zaccaro, A. *et al.* 2018. How breath control can change your life: A systematic review on psycho-physiological correlates of slow breathing. *Front. Hum. Neurosci.* 12, 1–16.

23. Maymin, P. Z. & Langer, E. J. 2021. Cognitive biases and mindfulness. *Humanit. Soc. Sci. Commun.* 8, 40–50.

24. feelSpace. 2021. feelSpace - taktile Information. https://www.feelspace.de/?lang=en.

25. Bostic St. Clair, C. & Grinder, J. 2001. *Whispering in the Wind*. J & C Enterprises.

26. Tosey, P. *et al.* 2013. *Clean Sources: Six Metaphors a Minute?* University of Surrey.

27. Lakoff, G. & Johnson, M. 2003. *Metaphors We Live By*. University of Chicago Press.

28. Williams, L. E. & Bargh, J. A. 2008. Experiencing physical warmth promotes interpersonal warmth. 322, 606–607.

29. Boulenger, V. & Nazir, T. A. 2010. Interwoven functionality of the brain's action and language systems. *Ment. Lex.* 5, 231–254.

30. Albro, R. 2014. Troping the Enemy: Culture, Metaphor Programs, and Notional Publics of National Security. *ethnography.com*. http://www.ethnography.com/2014/01/troping-the-enemy-culture-metaphor-programs-and-notional-publics-of-national-security/.

31. Lawley, J. & Tompkins, P. 2000. *Metaphors in Mind: Transformation Through Symbolic Modelling*. The Developing Company Press.

32. Gazzaniga, M. S. 2000. Cerebral specialization and interhemispheric communication: Does the corpus callosum enable the human condition? *Brain* 123, 1293–1326.

33. Volz, L. J. & Gazzaniga, M. S. 2017. Interaction in isolation: 50 years of insights from split-brain research. Brain 140, 2051–2060.

34. Boroditsky, L. & Schmidt, L. A. 2018. 9. Syntax and semantic. In *Syntactic Structures after 60 Years*. De Gruyter Mouton. 92–105.

35. Loftus, E. F. & Palmer, J. C. 1974. Reconstruction of automobile destruction: An example of the interaction between language and memory. *J. Verbal Learning Verbal Behav.* 13, 585–589.

CHAPTER 3

1. Merriam-Webster. 2020. Dictionary by Merriam-Webster. https://www.merriam-webster.com/.

2. Logan, R. K. & Tandoc, M. 2018. Thinking in patterns and the pattern of human thought as contrasted with AI data processing. *Inf.* 9, 1–15.

3. Fedorenko, E. & Varley, R. 2016. Language and thought are not the same thing: Evidence from neuroimaging and neurological patients. *Ann. N. Y. Acad. Sci.* 1369, 132–153.

4. Mahoney, M. 2003. The Subconscious Mind of the Consumer (And How to Reach It). *Harvard Business School*. https://hbswk.hbs.edu/item/the-subconscious-mind-of-the-consumer-and-how-to-reach-it.

5. Ayan, S. 2018. There Is No Such Thing as Conscious Thought. *Scientific American*. https://www.scientificamerican.com/article/there-is-no-such-thing-as-conscious-thought/.

6. Oka, M. 2012. *mBraining*. Createspace Independent Publishing Platform.

7. Kulkarni, S. *et al.* 2018. Advances in enteric neurobiology: The "brain" in the gut in health and disease. *J. Neurosci.* 38, 9346–9354.

8. Sender, R. *et al.* 2016. Revised estimates for the number of human and bacteria cells in the body. *PLoS Biol.* 14, 1-14.

9. Merzenich, M. 2013. *Soft-wired: How the New Science of Brain Plasticity Can Change Your Life*. Parnassus Publishing.

10. Pattanayak, R. *et al.* 2014. The study of patient Henry Molaison and what it taught us over past 50 years: Contributions to neuroscience. *J. Ment. Heal. Hum. Behav.* 19, 91-93.

11. Dossani, R. H. *et al.* 2015. The legacy of Henry Molaison (1926–2008) and the impact of his bilateral mesial temporal lobe surgery on the study of human memory. *World Neurosurg.* 84, 1127–1135.

12. Scoville, W. B. & Milner, B. 1957. Loss of recent memory after bilateral hippocampal lesions. *J. Neurol. Neurosurg. Psychiatry* 20, 11–21.

13. Squire, L. R. & Wixted, J. T. 2011. The cognitive neuroscience of human memory since H.M. *Annu. Rev. Neurosci.* 34, 259–288.

14. Corkin, S. 1968. Acquisition of motor skill after bilateral medial temporal-lobe excision. *Neuropsychologia* 6, 255–265.

15. Corkin, S. 2013. *Permanent Present Tense: The Unforgettable Life of the Amnesiac Patient, H. M.* Basic Books.

16. Corkin, S. 2002. What's new with the amnesic patient H.M.? *Nat. Rev. Neurosci.* 3, 153–160.

17. Milner, B. 1962. Physiologie de l'Hippocampe: Colloque International. Ed. du Cent. Natl. la Rech. Sci. 107, 512.

18. Carey, B. 2008. H. M., an Unforgettable Amnesiac, Dies at 82. *The New York Times*. https://www.nytimes.com/2008/12/05/us/05hm.html.

19. Rizzolatti, G. *et al.* 2014. Cortical mechanisms underlying the organization of goal-directed actions and mirror neuron-based action understanding. *Physiol. Rev.* 94, 655–706.

20. Rizzolatti, G. & Sinigaglia, C. 2016. The mirror mechanism: A basic principle of brain function. *Nat. Rev. Neurosci.* 17, 757–765.

21. Rizzolatti, G. *et al.* 1996. Premotor cortex and the recognition of motor actions. *Cogn. Brain Res.* 3, 131–141.

22. di Pellegrino, G. *et al.* 1992. Understanding motor events: A neurophysiological study. *Exp. Brain Res.* 91, 176–180.

23. Lu, J. S. *et al.* 2019. Contagious itch can be induced in humans but not in rodents. *Mol. Brain* 12, 12–38.

24. Ramachandran, V. S. 2012. The neurons that shaped civilization. In *The Tell-Tale Brain: Unlocking the Mystery of Human Nature*. Random House.

25. McGilchrist, I. 2012. *The Master and His Emissary: The Divided Brain and the Making of the Western World*. Yale University Press.

26. Gazzaniga, M. S. 2000. Cerebral specialization and interhemispheric communication: Does the corpus callosum enable the human condition? *Brain* 123, 1293–1326.

27. Volz, L. J. & Gazzaniga, M. S. 2017. Interaction in isolation: 50 years of insights from split-brain research. *Brain* 140, 2051–2060.

28. Gazzaniga, M. S. & LeDoux, J. E. 1978. The split brain and the integrated mind. In *The Integrated Mind*. Springer.

29. Gazzaniga, M. S. 2005. Forty-five years of split-brain research and still going strong. *Nat. Rev. Neurosci.* 6, 653–659.

30. Erskine, L. & Herrera, E. 2014. Connecting the retina to the brain. *ASN Neuro* 6, 1–26.

31. Taylor, L. 2011. Leon Taylor 5255 - Athens 2004 Prelim. *YouTube*. https://www.youtube.com/watch?v=kYZIWnvATEI&ab_channel=LeonTaylor.

32. Schmidt, J. E. *et al.* 2009. Effects of tongue position on mandibular muscle activity and heart rate function. *Oral Surgery, Oral Med. Oral Pathol. Oral Radiol. Endodontology* 108, 881–888.

33. Kim, H. G. *et al.* 2018. Stress and heart rate variability: A meta-analysis and review of the literature. *Psychiatry Investig.* 15, 235–245.

34. Soosalu, G. *et al.* 2018. mBIT as an experiential coaching and therapeutic approach, a series of case studies and scientific background. *J. Exp. Psychother.* 21, 24-33.

35. von Bartheld, C. S. *et al.* 2016. The search for true numbers of neurons and glial cells in the human brain: A review of 150 years of cell counting. *J. Comp. Neurol.* 524, 3865–3895.

36. Cognigni, P. *et al.* 2011. Enteric neurons and systemic signals couple nutritional and reproductive status with intestinal homeostasis. *Cell Metab.* 13, 92–104.

37. Durães Campos, I. *et al.* 2018. A brain within the heart: A review on the intracardiac nervous system. *J. Mol. Cell. Cardiol.* 119, 1–9.

38. Armour, J. A. 2007. The little brain on the heart. *Cleve. Clin. J. Med.* 74, S48–S48.

39. Bechara, A. & Damasio, A. R. 2005. The somatic marker hypothesis: A neural theory of economic decision. *Games Econ. Behav.* 52, 336–372.

40. Lent, J. 2017. *The Patterning Instinct.* Prometheus Books.

41. McGilchrist, I. 2011. The divided brain. *RSA Animate.* https://www.ted.com/talks/iain_mcgilchrist_the_divided_brain.

42. Goldie, J. 2016. The implications of brain lateralisation for modern general practice. *Br. J. Gen. Pract.* 66, 44–45.

43. McGilchrist, I. 2012. *The Master and His Emissary: The Divided Brain and the Making of the Western World.* Yale University Press. p437.

44. Heyes, C. 2012. New thinking: The evolution of human cognition. *Philos. Trans. R. Soc. B Biol. Sci.* 367, 2091–2096.

45. Snowden, D. J. & Boone, M. E. 2007. A leader's framework for decision making. *Harv. Bus. Rev.* 85, 68–76.

46. Snowden, D. J. 2017. Liminal Cynefin. *Cognitive Edge.* https://www.cognitive-edge.com/liminal-cynefin/.

47. World Health Organization. 2018. World health statistics 2018: Monitoring health for the SDGs, sustainable development goals.

48. Woollett, K. & Maguire, E. A. 2011. Acquiring "the knowledge" of London's layout drives structural brain changes. *Curr. Biol.* 21, 2109–2114.

49. Doidge, N. 2010. *The Brain That Changes Itself.* Scribe Publications.

50. Doidge, N. 2015. *Brain's Way of Healing: Remarkable Discoveries and Recoveries from the Frontiers of Neuroplasticity.* Viking.

51. Robinson, K. 2006. Do schools kill creativity? *TED.* https://www.ted.com/talks/sir_ken_robinson_do_schools_kill_creativity?language=en.

52. Moseley, G. L. & Butler, D. S. 2015. *The Explain Pain Handbook: Protectometer.* Noigroup Publications.

53. Arrowsmith-Young, B. 2013. *Woman Who Changed Her Brain: How I Left My Learning Disability Behind and Other Stories of Cognitive Transformation.* Simon & Schuster.

54. Carey, L. *et al.* 2019. Finding the intersection of neuroplasticity, stroke recovery, and learning: Scope and contributions to stroke rehabilitation. *Neural Plast.* 2019, 1–15.

55. Taub, E. *et al.* 1999. induced movement therapy: A new family of techniques with broad application to physical rehabilitation — a clinical review. *J. Rehabil. Res. Dev.* 36, 237–251.

56. Kunkel, A. *et al.* 1999. Constraint-induced movement therapy for motor recovery in chronic stroke patients. *Arch. Phys. Med. Rehabil.* 80, 624–628.

57. Frank, M. G. & Benington, J. H. 2006. The role of sleep in memory consolidation and brain plasticity: Dream or reality? *Neurosci.* 12, 477–488.

58. Connor, K. M. & Davidson, J. R. T. 2003. Development of a new resilience scale: The Connor-Davidson Resilience Scale (CD-RISC). *Depress. Anxiety* 18, 76–82. (See Table 2: Content of the Connor-Davidson Resilience Scale Item 21).

59. Boyd, J. 2018. The OODA loop. In *A Discourse on Winning and Losing.* Air University Press. (ed. Hammond, G. T.) 383–385.

60. U.S. Government. 2012. Col John Boyd.

61. Richards, C. 2012. Boyd's OODA loop. *Necesse* 5, 127–136.

62. Olsen, J. A. 2016. Boyd revisited. *Air Power Hist.* 63, 7–16.

63. Ullman, D. G. 2007. "OO-OO-OO!" The sound of a broken OODA loop. *CrossTalk* 20, 22–25.

64. Bostic St. Clair, C. & Grinder, J. 2001. *Whispering in the Wind.* J & C Enterprises.

65. Taleb, N. N. 2012. *Antifragile: Things That Gain from Disorder.* Random House.

66. Low, T. 2016. Black swan: The impossible bird. *Australian Geographic.* https://www.australiangeographic.com.au/topics/wildlife/2016/07/black-swan-the-impossible-bird/.

67. Taleb, N. N. 2012. *Antifragile: Things That Gain from Disorder.* Random House. (After original ideas by Francis Bacon in 1620).

68. Gigerenzer, G. 2008. *Gut Feelings: The Intelligence of the Unconscious.* Penguin Group.

69. Gladwell, M. 2005. *Blink: The Power of Thinking Without Thinking.* Little, Brown and Company.

CHAPTER 4

1. Zhao, S. *et al.* 2017. Continuous probability distribution prediction of image emotions via multitask shared sparse regression. *IEEE Trans. Multimed.* 19, 632–645.

2. Nummenmaa, L. *et al.* 2018. Maps of subjective feelings. *Proc. Natl. Acad. Sci. U. S. A.* 115, 9198–9203.

3. Mirams, L. *et al.* 2013. Brief body-scan meditation practice improves somatosensory perceptual decision making. *Conscious. Cogn.* 22, 348–359.

4. Whitaker, R. 2010. *Anatomy of an Epidemic: Magic Bullets, Psychiatric Drugs, and the Astonishing Rise of Mental Illness in America.* Crown Publishers.

5. Moncrieff, J. & Cohen, D. 2006. Do antidepressants cure or create abnormal brain states? *PLoS Med.* 3, 961–965.

6. This drill is modified after original activities designed and named by Carmen Bostic St. Clair.

7. Keller, A. *et al.* 2012. Does the perception that stress affects health matter? The association with health and mortality. *Heal. Psychol.* 31, 677–684.

8. McGonigal, K. 2013. Kelly McGonigal: How to make stress your friend. *TEDGlobal.* https://www.ted.com/talks/kelly_mcgonigal _how_ to_make_stress_your_friend /discussion? nolanguage=en. Kelly+McGonigal%3A+ Controlling+ Our+WillpowerWe.

9. Cuddy, A. 2012. Amy Cuddy: Your body language may shape who you are. *TEDGlobal.* https://www. ted.com/talks/amy_cuddy_your_body_language_ may_shape_who_you_are.

10. Carney, D. R. *et al.* 2010. Power posing: Brief Nonverbal displays affect neuroendocrine levels and risk tolerance. *Psychol. Sci.* 21, 1363–1368.

11. Gronau, Q. F. *et al.* 2017. A Bayesian model-averaged meta-analysis of the power pose effect with informed and default priors: The case of felt power. *Compr. Results Soc. Psychol.* 2, 123–138.

12. Cuddy, A. J. C. *et al.* 2018. P-curving: A more comprehensive body of research on postural feedback reveals clear evidential value for power-posing effects: Reply to Simmons and Simonsohn (2017). *Psychol. Sci.* 29, 656–666.

13. Ranehill, E. *et al.* 2015. Assessing the robustness of power posing: No effect on hormones and risk tolerance in a large sample of men and women. *Psychol. Sci.* 26, 653–656.

14. Simmons, J. P. & Simonsohn, U. 2017. Power posing: P-curing the evidence. *Psychol. Sci.* 28, 687–693.

15. Bostic St. Clair, C. & Grinder, J. 2001. *Whispering in the Wind.* J & C Enterprises.

16. Divine, M. 2016. *Kokoro Yoga: Maximize Your Human Potential and Develop the Spirit.* Griffin.

17. McKeown, P. & Shah, M. 2004. *Close Your Mouth: Buteyko Clinic Handbook for Perfect Health.* Asthma Care.

18. Barth, J. *et al.* 2017. Hyperventilation reduces the decrease of power output in a repeated sprint training in cyclists. *Rev. Andaluza Med. del Deport.* 3–7.

19. Durand, F. *et al.* 2000. Evidence for an inadequate hyperventilation inducing arterial. *Med. Sci. Sports Exerc.* 32, 926–932.

20. Hassan, Z. M. *et al.* 2012. Effect of Buteyko breathing technique on patients with bronchial asthma. *Egypt. J. Chest Dis. Tuberc.* 61, 235–241.

21. Santino, T. A. *et al.* 2020. Breathing exercises for adults with asthma. *Cochrane Database Syst. Rev.* 3, 1–3.

22. Hof, I. 2016. The Wim Hof Method Explained.

23. Kox, M. *et al.* 2014. Voluntary activation of the sympathetic nervous system and attenuation of the innate immune response in humans. *Proc. Natl. Acad. Sci. U. S. A.* 111, 7379–7384.

24. Zwaag, J. *et al.* 2020. Involvement of lactate and pyruvate in the anti-inflammatory effects exerted by voluntary activation of the sympathetic nervous system. *Metabolites* 10, 1–18.

25. Frontline Mind. 2018. Frontline Mind USMC Camp Pendleton. *Vimeo.* https://vimeo.com/280441552.

26. Oka, M. 2012. *mBraining.* Createspace Independent Publishing Platform.

27. Kulkarni, S. *et al.* 2018. Advances in enteric neurobiology: The "brain" in the gut in health and disease. *J. Neurosci.* 38, 9346–9354.

28. Armour, J. A. 1991. Intrinsic cardiac neurons. *J. Cardiovasc. Electrophysiol.* 2, 331–341.

29. McCraty, R. *et al.* 2009. The coherent heart: Heart-brain interactions, psychophysiological coherence, and the emergence of system-wide order. *Integr. Rev.* 5, 10–115.

30. Alshami, A. M. 2019. Pain: Is it all in the brain or the heart? *Curr. Pain Headache Rep.* 23, 1–4.

31. Avena, N. M. *et al.* 2008. Evidence for sugar addiction: Behavioral and neurochemical effects of intermittent, excessive sugar intake. *Neurosci. Biobehav. Rev.* 32, 20–39.

32. Noakes, T. *et al.* 2015. *The Real Meal Revolution.* Little, Brown Book Group.

33. Volk, B. M. *et al.* 2014. Effects of step-wise increases in dietary carbohydrate on circulating saturated fatty acids and palmitoleic acid in adults with metabolic syndrome. *PLoS One* 9, 1–16.

34. Lowden, A. *et al.* 2004. Performance and sleepiness during a 24 h wake in constant conditions are affected by diet. *Biol. Psychol.* 65, 251–263.

35. Nowson, C. A. *et al.* 2012. Vitamin D and health in adults in Australia and New Zealand: A position statement. *Med. J. Aust.* 196, 686–687.

36. Norman, A. W. *et al.* 2009. 13th Workshop Consensus for Vitamin D Nutritional Guidelines. 27, 417–428.

37. Black, H. & Rhodes, L. 2016. Potential benefits of omega-3 fatty acids in non-melanoma skin cancer. *J. Clin. Med.* 5, 1-10.

38. Noel, S. E. *et al.* 2014. Consumption of omega-3 fatty acids and the risk of skin cancers: A systematic review and meta-analysis. *Int. J. Cancer* 135, 149–156.

39. Schöttker, B. *et al.* 2013. Strong associations of 25-hydroxyvitamin D concentrations with all-cause, cardiovascular, cancer, and respiratory disease mortality in a large cohort study. *Am. J. Clin. Nutr.* 97, 782–793.

40. Lindqvist, P. G. 2018. The winding path towards an inverse relationship between sun exposure and all-cause mortality. *Anticancer Res.* 38, 1173–1178.

41. Grant, W. 2009. In defense of the sun: An estimate of changes in mortality rates in the United States if mean serum 25-hydroxyvitamin D levels were raised to 45 ng/mL by solar ultraviolet-B irradiance. *Dermatoendocrinol.* 1, 207–214.

42. Liu, D. *et al.* 2014. UVA irradiation of human skin vasodilates arterial vasculature and lowers blood pressure independently of nitric oxide synthase. *J. Invest. Dermatol.* 134, 1839–1846.

43. Sharovsky, R. & Cé sar, L. A. M. 2002. Increase in mortality due to myocardial infarction in the Brazilian city of São Paulo during winter. *Arq. Bras. Cardiol.* 78, 106–109.

44. Pereira, M. T. R. e. P. *et al.* 2015. Seasonal variation of haemoglobin A1c in a Portuguese adult population. *Arch. Endocrinol. Metab.* 59, 231–235.

45. Halliday, G. M. & Byrne, S. N. 2014. An unexpected role: UVA-induced release of nitric oxide from skin may have unexpected health benefits. *J. Invest. Dermatol.* 134, 1791–1794.

46. Avenell, A. *et al.* 2012. Long-term follow-up for mortality and cancer in a randomized placebo-controlled trial of vitamin D3 and/or calcium (RECORD Trial). *J. Clin. Endocrinol. Metab.* 97, 614–622.

47. Pittas, A. G. *et al.* 2011. Vitamin D and

cardiometabollic outcomes: A systematic review anastassios. *Ann Intern Med* 152, 307–314.

48. Autier, P. *et al.* 2014. Vitamin D status and ill health: A systematic review. *Lancet Diabetes Endocrinol.* 2, 76–89.

49. Kollias, N. *et al.* 2011. The value of the ratio of UVA to UVB in sunlight. *Photochem. Photobiol.* 87, 1474–1475.

50. Mason, P. 2011. Dr. Paul Mason - "Sunlight and health - from Vitamin D to Fish oil". https://www.youtube.com/watch?v=mFlITzqRBWY.

51. Gillings, M. R. *et al.* 2015. Ecology and evolution of the human microbiota: Fire, farming and antibiotics. *Genes (Basel).* 6, 841–857.

52. Martin, C. R. *et al.* 2018. The brain-gut microbiome axis. *Cmgh* 6, 133–148.

53. Valdes, A. M. *et al.* 2018. Role of the gut microbiota in nutrition and health. *BMJ* 361, 36-44.

54. Sudo, N. 2019. Role of gut microbiota in brain function and stress-related pathology. *Biosci. Microbiota, Food Heal.* 38, 75–80.

55. Liu, R. T. 2017. The microbiome as a novel paradigm in studying stress and mental health. *Am. Psychol.* 72, 655–667.

56. Foster, J. A. *et al.* 2017. Stress & the gut-brain axis: Regulation by the microbiome. *Neurobiol. Stress* 7, 124–136.

57. Carpenter, S. 2012. That gut feeling. *Monit. Psychol.* 43, 50.

58. Maenner, M. J. *et al.* 2020. Prevalence of autism spectrum disorder among children aged 8 years — Autism and Developmental Disabilities Monitoring Network, 11 sites, United States, 2016. *MMWR. Surveill. Summ.* 69, 1–12.

59. Kang, D. W. *et al.* 2019. Long-term benefit of Microbiota Transfer Therapy on autism symptoms and gut microbiota. *Sci. Rep.* 9, 1–9.

60. Łukasik, J. *et al.* 2019. Early life exposure to antibiotics and autism spectrum disorders: A systematic review. *J. Autism Dev. Disord.* 49, 3866–3876.

61. Xu, M. *et al.* 2019. Association between gut microbiota and autism spectrum disorder: A systematic review and meta-analysis. *Front. Psychiatry* 10, 1–11.

62. Queen, J. *et al.* 2020. Oral antibiotic use and chronic disease: Long-term health impact beyond antimicrobial resistance and Clostridioides difficile. *Gut Microbes* 11, 1092–1103.

63. Valdes, A. M. *et al.* 2018. Role of the gut microbiota in nutrition and health. *BMJ* 361, 36–44.

64. Holmes, R. & Snape, I. 2019. Effectiveness of treatment of veterans with PTSD: A critical review. *J. Exp. Psychother.* 22, 3–14.

65. Abbott, A. *et al.* 1998. Part V: Psychology. Consumer expectations of sport psychology. *J. Sports Sci.* 16, 68–110.

66. Frank, C. *et al.* 2014. Mental representation and mental practice: Experimental investigation on the functional links between motor memory and motor imagery. *PLoS One* 9, 1-12.

67. Bernier, M. & Fournier, J. F. 2010. Functions of mental imagery in expert golfers. *Psychol. Sport Exerc.* 11, 444–452.

68. Immonen, O. *et al.* 2012. Elements of mental training in music. *Procedia - Soc. Behav. Sci.* 45, 588–594.

69. Rekik, G. *et al.* 2019. The effect of visualization format and content complexity on acquisition of tactical actions in basketball. *Learn. Motiv.* 65, 10–19.

70. Crede, M. 2018. A negative effect of a contractive pose is not evidence for the positive effect of an expansive pose: Commentary on Cuddy, Schultz, and Fosse (2018). *SSRN Electron. J.* 3, 1–5.

CHAPTER 5

1. Borke, H. 1971. Interpersonal perception of young children: Egocentrism or empathy? *Dev. Psychol.* 5, 263–269.

2. Kross, E. & Ayduk, O. 2011. Making meaning out of negative experiences by self-distancing. *Curr. Dir. Psychol. Sci.* 20, 187–191.

3. Kesselring, T. & Müller, U. 2011. The concept of egocentrism in the context of Piaget's theory. *New Ideas Psychol.* 29, 327–345.

4. Lagattuta, K. H. *et al.* 2015. Beyond Sally's missing marble. In *Advances in Child Development and Behavior.* Elsevier Inc. vol. 48, 185–217.

5. Long, M. R. *et al.* 2018. Individual differences in switching and inhibition predict perspective-taking across the lifespan. *Cognition* 170, 25–30.

6. Garfinkel, S. N. *et al.* 2015. Knowing your own heart: Distinguishing interoceptive accuracy from interoceptive awareness. *Biol. Psychol.* 104, 65–74.

7. Gibson, J. 2019. Mindfulness, interoception, and the body: A contemporary perspective. *Front. Psychol.* 10, 1-18.

8. Christensen, J. F. *et al.* 2016. Dance expertise modulates behavioral and psychophysiological responses to affective body movement. *J. Exp. Psychol. Hum. Percept. Perform.* 42, 1139–1147.

9. Bock, A. S. *et al.* 2013. Visual callosal topography in the absence of retinal input. *Neuroimage* 81, 325–334.

10. Haller, J. *et al.* 1997. Catecholaminergic involvement in the control of aggression: Hormones, the peripheral sympathetic, and central noradrenergic systems. *Neurosci. Biobehav. Rev.* 22, 85–97.

11. Kiss, O. *et al.* 2016. Detailed heart rate variability analysis in athletes. *Clin. Auton. Res.* 26, 245–252.

12. Christoforidi, V. *et al.* 2012. Heart rate variability in free diving athletes. *Clin. Physiol. Funct. Imaging* 32, 162–166.

13. Oelz, O. *et al.* 1986. Physiological profile of world-class high-altitude climbers. *J. Appl. Physiol.* 60, 1734–1742.

14. Meißner, M. & Oll, J. 2019. The promise of eye-tracking methodology in organizational research: A taxonomy, review, and future avenues. *Organ. Res. Methods* 22, 590–617.

15. Al Aïn, S. *et al.* 2019. Smell training improves olfactory function and alters brain structure. *Neuroimage* 189, 45–54.

16. Wyatt, T. D. 2009. Fifty years of pheromones. *Nature* 457, 262–263.

17. Wyatt, T. D. 2015. The search for human pheromones: The lost decades and the necessity of returning to first principles. *Proc. R. Soc. B Biol. Sci.* 282, 1-9.

18. Epley, N. *et al.* 2004. Perspective taking as egocentric anchoring and adjustment. *J. Pers. Soc. Psychol.* 87, 327–339.

19. Evans, A. M. & Krueger, J. I. 2011. Elements of trust: Risk and perspective-taking. *J. Exp. Soc. Psychol.* 47, 171–177.

20. Royzman, E. B. *et al.* 2003. "I know, you know": Epistemic egocentrism in children and adults. *Rev. Gen. Psychol.* 7, 38–65.

21. Bostic St. Clair, C. & Grinder, J. 2001. *Whispering in the Wind.* J & C Enterprises.

22. Gallese, V. & Goldman, A. 1998. Mirror neurons and the theory of mind reading. *Trends Cogn. Sci.* 2, 493–501.

23. Ruby, P. & Decety, J. 2001. Effect of subjective perspective taking during simulation of action: A PET investigation of agency. *Nat. Neurosci.* 4, 546–550.

24. Prince, M. J. & Felder, R. M. 2006. Inductive teaching and learning methods: Definitions, comparisons, and research bases. *J. Eng. Educ.* 95, 123–138.

25. Corradini, A. & Antonietti, A. 2013. Mirror neurons and their function in cognitively understood empathy. *Conscious. Cogn.* 22, 1152–1161.

26. Bechara, A. *et al.* 2001. Decision-making deficits, linked to a dysfunctional ventromedial prefrontal cortex, revealed in alcohol and stimulant abusers. *Neuropsychologia* 39, 376–389.

27. Howarth, J. 1987. Science education in late-Victorian Oxford: A curious case of failure? *Engl. Hist. Rev.* CII, 334–371.

28. Robinson, K. 2006. Do schools kill creativity? TED. https://www.ted.com/talks/sir_ken_robinson_do_schools_kill_creativity?language=en.

29. Smith, E. R. 2008. Social relationships and groups: New insights on embodied and distributed cognition. *Cogn. Syst. Res.* 9, 24–32.

30. Kim, H. Y. *et al.* 2018. Social perspective-taking performance: Construct, measurement, and relations with academic performance and engagement. *J. Appl. Dev. Psychol.* 57, 24–41.

31. Frith, C. D. & Frith, U. 2006. The neural basis of mentalizing. *Neuron* 50, 531–534.

32. Grèzes, J. *et al.* 2009. A failure to grasp the affective meaning of actions in autism spectrum disorder subjects. *Neuropsychologia* 47, 1816–1825.

33. Perkins, T. *et al.* 2010. Mirror neuron dysfunction in autism spectrum disorders. *J. Clin. Neurosci.* 17, 1239–1243.

34. Ramachandran, V. S. & Seckel, E. L. 2011. Synchronized dance therapy to stimulate mirror neurons in autism. *Med. Hypotheses* 76, 150–151.

35. BBC. 2018. - Daniel Day-Lewis: 10 defining roles from the method master. https://www.bbc.co.uk/programmes/articles/3YyMsjqxVBMgJDfvPRFZtpb/daniel-day-lewis-10-defining-roles-from-the-method-master.

36. Elshaer, N. S. M. *et al.* 2018. Job stress and burnout syndrome among critical care healthcare workers. *Alexandria J. Med.* 54, 273–277.

37. Milligan-Saville, J. *et al.* 2018. The impact of trauma exposure on the development of PTSD and psychological distress in a volunteer fire service. *Psychiatry Res.* 270, 1110–1115.

38. Pines, A. M. & Keinan, G. 2005. Stress and burnout: The significant difference. *Pers. Individ. Dif.* 39, 625–635.

39. Williams, B. *et al.* 2017. The relationship between empathy and burnout – Lessons for paramedics: A scoping review. *Psychol. Res. Behav. Manag.* 10, 329–337.

40. Schilpp, P. A. 1970. *Albert Einstein, Philosopher-Scientist: The Library of Living Philosophers Volume VII.* Open Court.

41. Miranda, J. C. *et al.* 2011. Interactive technology: Teaching people with autism to recognize facial emotions. In *Autism Spectrum Disorders - From Genes to Environment.* InTech.

42. Tsangouri, C. *et al.* 2016. An interactive facial-expression training platform for individuals with autism spectrum disorder. In *2016 IEEE MIT Undergraduate Research Technology Conference (URTC).* IEEE. 1–3.

43. House of Hoops. 2016. Identical Plays: Kobe Bryant vs Michael Jordan. YouTube. https://www.youtube.com/watch?v=mFlITzqRBWY.

44. Ayduk, Ö. & Kross, E. 2008. Enhancing the pace of recovery. *Psychol. Sci.* 19, 229–231.

45. Leitão-Gonçalves, R. *et al.* 2017. Commensal bacteria and essential amino acids control food choice behavior and reproduction. *PLOS Biol.* 15, 1-29.

46. Reed, D. R. & Knaapila, A. 2010. Genetics of taste and smell. In *Genes and Obesity.* Academic Press. (ed. Bouchard, C.) vol. 94, 213–240.

47. Breslin, P. A. S. 2013. An evolutionary perspective on food and human taste. *Curr. Biol.* 23, R409–R418.

48. Nagaoka, C. & Komori, M. 2008. Body movement synchrony in psychotherapeutic counseling: A study using the video-based quantification method. *IEICE Trans. Inf. Syst.* E91-D, 1634–1640.

49. Lake, J. 2015. The integrative management of PTSD: A review of conventional and CAM approaches used to prevent and treat PTSD with emphasis on military personnel. *Adv. Integr. Med.* 2, 13–23.

50. Pereira, T. *et al.* 2017. Heart rate variability metrics for fine-grained stress level assessment. *Comput. Methods Programs Biomed.* 148, 71–80.

51. Pirrone, F. *et al.* 2017. Measuring social synchrony and stress in the handler-dog dyad during animal-assisted activities: A pilot study. *J. Vet. Behav.* 21, 45–52.

CHAPTER 6

1. Karinthy, F. 1929. Chains (Láncszemek).

2. Bhagat, S. *et al.* 2016. Three and a half degrees of separation. *Facebook Research.* https://research.fb.com/blog/2016/02/three-and-a-half-degrees-of-separation/.

3. Snowden, D. J. & Boone, M. E. 2007. A leader's framework for decision making. *Harv. Bus. Rev.* 85, 68–76.

4. Snowden, D. J. & Friends. 2020. *Cynefin: Weaving Sense-Making into the Fabric of Our World.* Cognitive Edge Pte Ltd.

5. Drew, T. *et al.* 2013. The invisible gorilla strikes again. *Psychol. Sci.* 24, 1848–1853.

6. Karasek, R. A. J. 1979. Job demands, job decision latitude, and mental strain: Implications for job redesign. *Adm. Sci. Q.* 24, 285–308.

7. Bakker, A. B. & Demerouti, E. 2007. The job demands resources model: State of the art. *J. Manag. Psychol.* 22, 309–328.

8. Huang, J. *et al.* 2016. The job demands resources model and job burnout: The mediating role of personal resources. *Curr. Psychol.* 35, 562–569.

9. Ophir, E. *et al.* 2009. Cognitive control in media multitaskers. *Proc. Natl. Acad. Sci.* 106, 15583–15587.

10. Lin, L. *et al.* 2016. Task speed and accuracy decrease when multitasking. *Technol. Knowl. Learn.* 21, 307–323.

11. Skaugset, L. M. *et al.* 2016. Can you multitask? Evidence and limitations of task switching and multitasking in emergency medicine. *Ann. Emerg. Med.* 68, 189–195.

12. Snyder, A. 2009. Explaining and inducing savant skills: Privileged access to lower level, less-processed information. *Philos. Trans. R. Soc. B Biol. Sci.* 364, 1399–1405.

13. Snyder, A. *et al.* 2004. Concept formation: "Object" attributes dynamically inhibited from conscious awareness. *J. Integr. Neurosci.* 3, 31–46.

14. Brady, J. V. 1991. Rat AA-26: Behavioral pharmacology science pioneer. *J. Exp. Anal. Behav.* 56, 171–172.

15. Heilig, M. *et al.* 2016. Time to connect: Bringing social context into addiction neuroscience. *Nat. Rev. Neurosci.* 17, 592–599.

16. Alexander, B. K. *et al.* 1978. The effect of housing and gender on morphine self-administration in rats. *Psychopharmacology (Berl).* 58, 175–179.

17. Coambs, R. B. *et al.* 1980. A drug dispenser to measure individual drinking in rat colonies. *Pharmacol. Biochem. Behav.* 13, 593–595.

18. Alexander, B. K. *et al.* 1981. Effect of early and later colony housing on oral ingestion of morphine in rats. *Pharmacol. Biochem. Behav.* 15, 571–576.

19. Hadaway, P. F. *et al.* 1979. The effect of housing and gender on preference for morphine-sucrose solutions in rats. *Psychopharmacology (Berl).* 66, 87–91.

20. Alexander, B. K. & Hadaway, P. F. 1982. Opiate addiction: The case for an adaptive orientation. *Psychol. Bull.* 92, 367–381.

21. Alexander, B. K. 2001. The Myth of Drug-Induced Addiction. *Senate of Canada.* https://sencanada.ca/content/sen/committee/371/ille/presentation/alexander-e.htm.

22. Gage, S. H. & Sumnall, H. R. 2019. Rat Park: How a rat paradise changed the narrative of addiction. *Addiction* 114, 917–922.

23. Khoo, S. Y. S. 2020. Have we reproduced Rat Park? Conceptual but not direct replication of the protective effects of social and environmental enrichment in addiction. *J. Reprod. Neurosci.* 1, 1–9.

24. Bozarth, M. A. *et al.* 1989. Influence of housing conditions on the acquisition of intravenous heroin and cocaine self-administration in rats. *Pharmacol. Biochem. Behav.* 33, 903–907.

25. Hofford, R. S. *et al.* 2017. Effects of environmental enrichment on self-administration of the short-acting opioid remifentanil in male rats. *Psychopharmacology (Berl).* 234, 3499–3506.

26. Imperio, C. G. *et al.* 2018. Exposure to environmental enrichment attenuates addiction-like behavior and alters molecular effects of heroin self-administration in rats. *Neuropharmacology* 139, 26–40.

27. Venniro, M. & Shaham, Y. 2020. An operant social self-administration and choice model in rats. *Nat. Protoc.* 15, 1542–1559.

28. Venniro, M. *et al.* 2020. Abstinence-dependent dissociable central amygdala microcircuits control drug craving. *Proc. Natl. Acad. Sci.* 117, 8126–8134.

29. Venniro, M. *et al.* 2019. Operant social reward decreases incubation of heroin craving in male and female rats. *Biol. Psychiatry* 86, 848–856.

30. Venniro, M. *et al.* 2018. Volitional social interaction prevents drug addiction in rat models. *Nat. Neurosci.* 21, 1520–1529.

31. Sinha, R. *et al.* 2011. Translational and reverse translational research on the role of stress in drug craving and relapse. *Psychopharmacology (Berl).* 218, 69–82.

32. Wilson, N. *et al.* 2020. Drug and opioid-involved overdose deaths — United States, 2017–2018. *Morb. Mortal. Wkly. Rep.* 69, 290–297.

33. Peacock, A. *et al.* 2018. Global statistics on alcohol, tobacco and illicit drug use: 2017 status report. *Addiction* 113, 1905–1926.

34. Kinner, S. A. & Rich, J. D. 2018. Drug use in prisoners: Epidemiology, implications, and policy responses. In *Drug Use in Prisoners: Epidemiology, Implications, and Policy Responses.* Oxford University Press. (eds. Kinner, S. A. & Rich, J.).

35. Walmsley, R. 2013. World Prison Population List. International Center for Prison Studies.

36. Carpentier, C. *et al.* 2018. The global epidemiology of drug use in prison. In *Drug Use in Prisoners: Epidemiology, Implications, and Policy Responses.* Oxford University Press. (eds. Kinner, S. A. & Rich, J.).

37. Taxman, F. S. & Mun, M. 2018. Recidivism: The impact of substance abuse on continued involvement in the justice system. In *Drug Use in Prisoners: Epidemiology, Implications, and Policy Responses.* Oxford University Press. (eds. Kinner, S. A. & Rich, J.).

38. Drug Policy Alliance. 2018. Drug Decriminalization in Portugal: Learning from a Health and Human-Centered Approach. http://www.drugpolicy.org/sites/default/files/dpa-drug-decriminalization-portugal-health-human-centered-approach_0.pdf.

39. Rudd, R. A. *et al.* 2016. Increases in drug and opioid-involved overdose deaths - United States, 2010-2015. *Morb. Mortal. Wkly. Rep.* 65, 1445–1452.

40. Bakker, A. B. & Demerouti, E. 2013. The spillover crossover model. In *New Frontiers in Work and Family Research.* Psychology Press. (eds. Grzywacz, J. G. & Demerouti, E.) 54–70.

41. Demerouti, E. *et al.* 2005. Spillover and crossover of exhaustion and life satisfaction among dual-earner parents. *J. Vocat. Behav.* 67, 266–289.

42. Westman, M. *et al.* 2001. Job insecurity and crossover of burnout in married couples. *J. Organ. Behav.* 22, 467–481.

43. Westman, M. *et al.* 2004. The toll of unemployment does not stop with the unemployed. *Hum. Relations* 57, 823–844.

44. Bakker, A. B. *et al.* 2005. The crossover of burnout and work engagement among working couples. *Hum. Relations* 58, 661–689.

45. Bakker, A. B. & Demerouti, E. 2009. The crossover of work engagement between working couples. *J. Manag. Psychol.* 24, 220–236.

46. Westman, M. *et al.* 2009. Expert commentary on work-life balance and crossover of emotions

and experiences: Theoretical and practice advancements. *J. Organ. Behav.* 30, 587–595.

47. Demerouti, E. *et al.* 2004. Positive and negative work-home interaction: Prevalence and correlates. *Equal Oppor. Int.* 23, 6–35.

48. Bakker, A. B. & Schaufeli, W. B. 2000. Burnout contagion processes among teachers. *J. Appl. Soc. Psychol.* 30, 2289–2308.

49. Barnett, R. C. *et al.* 1995. Change in job and marital experiences and change in psychological distress: A longitudinal study of dual-earner couples. *J. Pers. Soc. Psychol.* 69, 839–850.

50. World Economic Forum. 2020. The Global Risks Report 2020. http://wef.ch/risks2019.

51. Taleb, N. N. 2010. *The Black Swan: Second Edition: The Impact of the Highly Improbable: With a new section: "On Robustness and Fragility."* Random House.

52. Darwin, C. 1859. *On the Origin of Species.* John Murray.

53. Lenton, T. M. *et al.* 2021. Survival of the systems. *Trends Ecol. Evol.* 36, 333–344.

54. Low, T. 2016. Black swan: The impossible bird. *Australian Geographic.* https://www.australiangeographic.com.au/topics/wildlife/2016/07/black-swan-the-impossible-bird/.

55. Wucker, M. 2016. *The Gray Rhino: How to Recognize and Act on the Obvious Dangers We Ignore.* St. Martin's Press.

56. Tappe, A. 2019. 5 questions with the woman who coined the term "gray rhino." *MarketWatch.* https://www.marketwatch.com/story/what-is-a-gray-rhino-and-why-are-they-so-dangerous-to-investors-5-questions-for-michele-wucker-2019-01-23.

CHAPTER 7

1. Doidge, N. 2015. *Brain's Way of Healing: Remarkable Discoveries and Recoveries from the Frontiers of Neuroplasticity.* Viking.

2. Carney, J. 2020. Thinking avant la lettre: A review of 4E cognition. *Evol. Stud. Imaginative Cult.* 4, 77-90.

3. Meloni, M. & Reynolds, J. 2020. Thinking embodiment with genetics: Epigenetics and postgenomic biology in embodied cognition and enactivism. *Synthese* 1–41.

4. McGonigal, K. 2013. Kelly McGonigal: How to make stress your friend. *TEDGlobal.* https://www.ted.com/talks/kelly_mcgonigal_how_to_make_stress_your_friend/ discussion?nolanguage=en.Kelly+McGonigal %3A+Controlling +Our+Willpower We.

5. Keller, A. *et al.* 2012. Does the perception that stress affects health matter? The association with health and mortality. *Heal. Psychol.* 31, 677–684.

6. Tracey, I. 2010. Getting the pain you expect: Mechanisms of placebo, nocebo and reappraisal effects in humans. *Nat. Med.* 16, 1277–1283.

7. Benedetti, F. 2008. Mechanisms of placebo and placebo-related effects across diseases and treatments. *Annu. Rev. Pharmacol. Toxicol.* 48, 33–60.

8. Turi, Z. *et al.* 2018. Evidence for cognitive placebo and nocebo effects in healthy individuals. *Sci. Rep.* 8, 1-14.

9. Eknoyan, D. *et al.* 2013. The neurobiology of placebo and nocebo: How expectations influence treatment outcomes. *J. Neuropsychiatry Clin. Neurosci.* 25, 250–254.

10. Wager, T. D. & Atlas, L. Y. 2015. The neuroscience of placebo effects: Connecting context, learning and health. *Nat. Rev. Neurosci.* 16, 403–418.

11. Kanherkar, R. R. *et al.* 2017. Epigenetic mechanisms of integrative medicine. *Evidence-Based Complement. Altern. Med.* 2017, 1–19.

12. Cai, L. & He, L. 2019. Placebo effects and the molecular biological components involved. *Gen. Psychiatry* 32, 1-10.

13. Avins, A. L. *et al.* 2010. Placebo adherence and its association with morbidity and mortality in the studies of left ventricular dysfunction. *J. Gen. Intern. Med.* 25, 1275–1281.

14. Broelz, E. K. *et al.* 2019. The neurobiology of placebo effects in sports: EEG frontal alpha asymmetry increases in response to a placebo ergogenic aid. *Sci. Rep.* 9, 2381.

15. Kirchhof, J. *et al.* 2018. Learned immunosuppressive placebo responses in renal transplant patients. *Proc. Natl. Acad. Sci.* 115, 4223–4227.

16. Benedetti, F. *et al.* 2014. Nocebo and placebo modulation of hypobaric hypoxia headache involves the cyclooxygenase-prostaglandins pathway. *Pain* 155, 921–928.

17. Darragh, M. *et al.* 2015. Placebo "serotonin" increases heart rate variability in recovery from psychosocial stress. *Physiol. Behav.* 145, 45–49.

18. Stewart, R. A. H. *et al.* 2017. Persistent psychological distress and mortality in patients with stable coronary artery disease. *Heart* 103, 1860–1866.

19. Steptoe, A. & Kivimäki, M. 2012. Stress and cardiovascular disease. *Nat. Rev. Cardiol.* 9, 360–370.

20. Osborne, M. T. *et al.* 2020. Disentangling the links between psychosocial stress and cardiovascular disease. *Circ. Cardiovasc. Imaging* 13, 1–13.

21. Goldacre, B. 2013. *Bad Pharma.* Farrar Straus & Giroux.

22. *Whitaker, R. 2010. Anatomy of an Epidemic: Magic Bullets, Psychiatric Drugs, and the Astonishing Rise of Mental Illness in America.* Crown Publishers.

23. Gibbons, R. *et al.* 2019. Medications and suicide: High Dimensional Empirical Bayes Screening (iDEAS). *Harvard Data Sci. Rev.* 1, 1-33.

24. Lenzer, J. & Brownlee, S. 2008. An untold story? *BMJ* 336, 532–534.

25. Keaveney, A. *et al.* 2020. Effects of acetaminophen on risk taking. *Soc. Cogn. Affect. Neurosci.* 15, 725–732.

26. Arria, A. M. *et al.* 2014. Evidence and knowledge gaps for the association between energy drink use and high-risk behaviors among adolescents and young adults. *Nutr. Rev.* 72, 87–97.

27. Giles, G. E. *et al.* 2017. Cautiously caffeinated: Does caffeine modulate inhibitory, impulsive, or risky behavior? *J. Caffeine Res.* 7, 7–17.

28. Slovic, P. *et al.* 2004. Risk as analysis and risks as feelings: Some thoughts about affect, reason, risks, and rationality. *Risk Anal.* 24, 311–322.

29. Ait-Daoud, N. *et al.* 2018. A Review of alprazolam use, misuse, and withdrawal. *J. Addict. Med.* 12, 4–10.

30. Risse, S. C. *et al.* 1990. Severe withdrawal symptoms after discontinuation of alprazolam in eight patients with combat-induced posttraumatic stress disorder. *J. Clin. Psychiatry* 51, 206–209.

31. Fava, G. A. & Cosci, F. 2019. Understanding and managing withdrawal syndromes after discontinuation of antidepressant drugs. *J. Clin. Psychiatry* 80, e1-e6.

32. Henssler, J. *et al.* 2019. Antidepressant withdrawal and rebound phenomena. *Dtsch. Aerzteblatt Online* 116, 355–361.

33. Loewenstein, G. F. *et al.* 2001. Risk as feelings. *Psychol. Bull.* 127, 267–286.

34. Popovici, I. *et al.* 2012. Alcohol use and crime: Findings from a longitudinal sample of U.S. adolescents and young adults. *Alcohol. Clin. Exp. Res.* 36, 532–543.

35. George, S. *et al.* 2005. The acute effect of alcohol on decision making in social drinkers. *Psychopharmacology (Berl).* 182, 160–169.

36. Brevers, D. *et al.* 2014. Impaired decision-making under risk in individuals with alcohol dependence. *Alcohol. Clin. Exp. Res.* 38, 1924–1931.

37. Bechara, A. *et al.* 2001. Decision-making deficits, linked to a dysfunctional ventromedial prefrontal cortex, revealed in alcohol and stimulant abusers. *Neuropsychologia* 39, 376–389.

38. Gigerenzer, G. 2008. *Gut Feelings: The Intelligence of the Unconscious.* Penguin Group.

39. Moseley, G. L. & Butler, D. S. 2015. *The Explain Pain Handbook: Protectometer.* Noigroup Publications.

40. Bourke, J. 2013. Emotions affect how pain feels, as soldiers know only too well. *The Conversation.* https://theconversation.com/emotions-affect-how-pain-feels-as-soldiers-know-only-too-well-25889.

41. Harris, I. 2016. *Surgery, The Ultimate Placebo: A Surgeon Cuts Through the Evidence.* NewSouth.

42. Wartolowska, K. *et al.* 2014. Use of placebo controls in the evaluation of surgery: Systematic review. *BMJ* 348, 1-15.

43. Moskowitz, M. & Golden, M. 2013. *Neuroplastic Transformation Workbook.* Neuroplastic Partners, LLC.

44. Moseley, G. L. *et al.* 2008. Visual distortion of a limb modulates the pain and swelling evoked by movement. *Curr. Biol.* 18, R1047–R1048.

45. Ramachandran, V. S. & Rodgers-Ramachandran, D. 1996. Synaesthesia in phantom limbs induced with mirrors. *Proc. R. Soc. London. Ser. B Biol. Sci.* 263, 377–386.

46. Flor, H. 2002. Phantom-limb pain: characteristics, causes, and treatment. *Lancet Neurol.* 1, 182–189.

47. Kaur, A. & Guan, Y. 2018. Phantom limb pain: A literature review. *Chinese J. Traumatol. - English Ed.* 21, 366–368.

48. Merzenich, M. 2013. *Soft-wired: How the New Science of Brain Plasticity Can Change Your Life.* Parnassus Publishing.

49. Holmes, R. & Snape, I. 2019. Effectiveness of treatment of veterans with PTSD: A critical review. *J. Exp. Psychother.* 22, 3–14.

50. Neilson, S. 2016. Pain as metaphor: Metaphor and medicine. *Med. Humanit.* 42, 3–10.

51. Scarry, E. 1987. *The Body in Pain: The Making and Unmaking of the World.* Oxford University Press.

52. Way, M. 2009. Metaphors for Aches and Pains. *CleanLearning.* https://cleanlearning.co.uk/blog/discuss/metaphors-for-aches-and-pains.

53. Tompkins, P. & Lawley, J. 1997. *Less Is More ... The Art of Clean Language. Rapport.*

54. Lawley, J. & Tompkins, P. 2000. *Metaphors in Mind: Transformation Through Symbolic Modelling.* The Developing Company Press.

55. Walker, C. 2014. *From Contempt to Curiosity: Creating the Conditions for Groups to Collaborate Using Clean Language and Systemic Modelling.* Clean Publishing.

56. Doyle, N. *et al.* 2011. Systemic modelling: Installing coaching as a catalyst for organizational learning. *e-Organizations and People* 17, 13–22.

57. Pincus, D. & Sheikh, A. A. 2011. David Grove's metaphor therapy. *Imagin. Cogn. Pers.* 30, 259–287.

58. Schredl, M. & Bulkeley, K. 2020. Dreaming and the COVID-19 pandemic: A survey in a U.S. sample. *Dreaming* 30, 189–198.

59. Barrett, D. 2020. Dreams about COVID-19 versus normative dreams: Trends by gender. *Dreaming* 30, 216–221.

60. Iorio, I. *et al.* 2020. Dreaming in the time of COVID-19: A quali-quantitative Italian study. *Dreaming* 30, 199–215.

61. MacKay, C. & DeCicco, T. L. 2020. Pandemic dreaming: The effect of COVID-19 on dream imagery, a pilot study. *Dreaming* 30, 222–234.

62. Muzur, A. *et al.* 2002. The prefrontal cortex in sleep. *Trends Cogn. Sci.* 6, 475–481.

63. Van den Bulck, J. *et al.* 2016. Violence, sex, and dreams: Violent and sexual media content infiltrate our dreams at night. *Dreaming* 26, 271–279.

64. Barrett, D. 1993. The "committee of sleep": A study of dream incubation for problem solving. *Dreaming* 3, 115–122.

65. Mowbray, D. 2020. Greatest Scientific Discoveries That Were Made in Dreams. *Mattress Online.* https://www.mattressonline.co.uk/blog/sleep-science/greatest-scientific-discoveries-that-were-made-in-dreams/.

CHAPTER 8

1. Carroll, L. 1865. *Alice's Adventures in Wonderland.* Macmillan.

2. Tompkins, P. & Lawley, J. 2006. Coaching for P.R.O.'s. *The Clean Collection.* https://cleanlanguage.co.uk/articles/articles/31/1/Coaching-for-PROs/Page1.html.

3. Lawley, J. & Tompkins, P. 2020. The Evolution of the Problem-Remedy-Outcome (PRO) Model. *The Clean Collection.* https://cleanlanguage.co.uk/articles/blogs/104/The-Evolution-of-the-Problem-Remedy-Outcome-PRO-Model.html.

4. O'Connell, B. & Palmer, S. 2007. Solution focused coaching. In *Handbook of Coaching Psychology: A Guide for Practitioners.* Routledge. (eds. Palmer, S. & Whybrow, A.) 278–292.

5. Nagel, R. 2008. Coaching with a solutions focus - Focusing on the solution not the problem. *Dev. Learn. Organ.* 22, 11–14.

6. Neipp, M. C. *et al.* 2016. The effect of solution-focused versus problem-focused questions: A replication. *J. Marital Fam. Ther.* 42, 525–535.

7. Grant, A. M. 2012. Making positive change: A Randomized study comparing solution focused vs. problem-focused coaching questions. *J. Syst. Ther.* 31, 21–35.

8. Grant, A. M. & Gerrard, B. 2020. Comparing problem-focused, solution-focused and combined problem-focused/solution-focused coaching approach: Solution-focused coaching questions mitigate the negative impact of dysfunctional attitudes. *Coach. An Int. J. Theory, Res. Pract.* 13, 61–77.

9. Collingwood, J. 2016. *Aegis: Patterns for Extending Your Reach in Life, Work and Leisure.* Emergent Publications.

10. Frankl, V. E. 2006. *Man's Search for Meaning.* Beacon Press.

11. Connor, K. M. & Davidson, J. R. T. 2003. Development of a new resilience scale: The Connor-Davidson Resilience Scale (CD-RISC). *Depress. Anxiety* 18, 76–82.

12. Hamby, S. et al. 2018. Resilience portfolios and poly-strengths: Identifying protective factors associated with thriving after adversity. *Psychol. Violence* 8, 172–183.

13. Hamby, S. et al. 2020. Poly-victimization, trauma, and resilience: Exploring strengths that promote thriving after adversity. *J. Trauma Dissociation* 21, 376–395.

14. Wagnild, G. M. & Young, H. M. 1993. Development and psychometric evaluation of the resilience scale. *J. Nurs. Meas.* 1, 165–178.

15. Rossouw, P. & Rossouw, J. 2016. The Predictive 6-Factor Resilience Scale: Neurobiological fundamentals and The Predictive 6-Factor Resilience Scale: Neurobiological fundamentals and organizational application. *Int. J. Neuropsychother.* 4, 31–45.

16. Nygren, B. et al. 2005. Resilience, sense of coherence, purpose in life and self-transcendence in relation to perceived physical and mental health among the oldest old. *Aging Ment. Heal.* 9, 354–362.

17. Shiba, K. et al. 2017. Retirement and mental health: Does social participation mitigate the association? A fixed-effects longitudinal analysis. *BMC Public Health* 17, 526–535.

18. Taylor, J. & Ogilvie, B. C. 1994. A conceptual model of adaptation to retirement among athletes. *J. Appl. Sport Psychol.* 6, 1–20.

19. Lavallee, D. et al. 1997. Retirement from sport and the loss of athletic identity. *J. Pers. Interpers. Loss* 2, 129–147.

20. Schwenk, T. L. et al. 2007. Depression and pain in retired professional football players. *Med. Sci. Sports Exerc.* 39, 599–605.

21. Stambulova, N. et al. 2009. ISSP Position stand: Career development and transitions of athletes. *Int. J. Sport Exerc. Psychol.* 7, 395–412.

22. Williams, R. et al. 2018. "You're just chopped off at the end": Retired servicemen's identity work struggles in the military to civilian transition. *Sociol. Res. Online* 23, 812–829.

23. Cook, C. 2010. *Seven Year Switch.* Voice.

CHAPTER 9

1. Popper, K. 1959. *The Logic of Scientific Discovery.* Basic Books.

2. Howson, C. & Urbach, P. 1989. *Scientific Reasoning: The Bayesian Approach.* Open Court Publishing Company.

3. Press, S. J. & Tanur, J. M. 2016. *The Subjectivity of Scientists and the Bayesian Approach.* Dover Publications.

4. Yudkowsky, E. S. 2006. An Intuitive Explanation of Bayes' Theorem. https://www.yudkowsky.net/rational/bayes.

5. Kuhn, T. 1962. *The Structure of Scientific Revolutions.* University of Chicago Press.

6. World Health Organization. 2009. Risk Characterization. *Principles and Methods for the Risk Assessment of Chemicals in Food.*

7. Hardy, A. et al. 2017. Guidance on the use of the weight of evidence approach in scientific assessments. *EFSA J.* 15, 1-69.

8. Gross, S. R. et al. 2014. Rate of false conviction of criminal defendants who are sentenced to death. *Proc. Natl. Acad. Sci.* 111, 7230–7235.

9. Hoffman, D. D. 2019. *The Case Against Reality.* W. W. Norton & Company.

10. Prakash, C. et al. 2020. Fact, fiction, and fitness. *Entropy* 22, 1–23.

11. Prakash, C. et al. 2020. Fitness beats truth in the evolution of perception. *Acta Biotheor.*

12. Schuster, M. A. et al. 2001. A national survey of stress reactions after the September 11, 2001, terrorist attacks. *N. Engl. J. Med.* 345, 1507–1512.

13. Wilmoth, J. R. 2000. Demography of longevity: Past, present, and future trends. *Exp. Gerontol.* 35, 1111–1129.

14. Makary, M. A. & Daniel, M. 2016. Medical error — the third leading cause of death in the US. *BMJ* 353, 1–5.

15. Panagioti, M. et al. 2019. Prevalence, severity, and nature of preventable patient harm across medical care settings: Systematic review and meta-analysis. *BMJ* 366, 1-11.

16. Rousselet, M. et al. 2017. Cult membership: What factors contribute to joining or leaving? *Psychiatry Res.* 257, 27–33.

17. Lalich, J. 1996. Dominance and submission. *Women Ther.* 19, 37–52.

18. Dayan, H. 2018. Sexual abuse and charismatic cults. *Aggress. Violent Behav.* 41, 25–31.

19. Raine, S. & Kent, S. A. 2019. The grooming of children for sexual abuse in religious settings: Unique characteristics and select case studies. *Aggress. Violent Behav.* 48, 180–189.

20. Denney, A. et al. 2018. Child sexual abuse in Protestant Christian congregations: A descriptive analysis of offense and offender characteristics. *Religions* 9, 1-13.

21. Royal Commission into Institutional Responses to Child Sexual Abuse. 2021. Religious Institutions. *Commonwealth of Australia.* https://www.childabuseroyalcommission.gov.au/religious-institutions.

22. Hong, N. 2020. Nxivm "Sex Cult" Was Also a Huge Pyramid Scheme, Lawsuit Says. *The New York Times.* https://www.nytimes.com/2020/01/29/nyregion/nxivm-lawsuit-keith-raniere.html.

23. *carsales.* 2018. Old School: Sex, drugs and Rajneesh's 93 Rolls-Royces. https://www.carsales.com.au/editorial/details/old-school-sex-drugs-and-rajneeshs-93-rolls-royces-114002.

24. Way, C. & Way, M. 2018. *Wild Wild Country.*

25. Levitz, E. 2020. QAnon Is Madness. But Believing in It Can Be Rational. *Intelligencer.* https://nymag.com/intelligencer/2020/09/why-qanon-pandemic-popular-trump.html.

26. Wong, J. C. 2020. Down the rabbit hole: How QAnon conspiracies thrive on Facebook. *The Guardian.* https://www.theguardian.com/technology/2020/jun/25/qanon-facebook-conspiracy-theories-algorithm.

27. Stein, A. 2002. *Inside Out: A Memoir of Entering and Breaking Out of a Minneapolis Political Cult.* North Star Press of St. Cloud.

28. Stein, A. 2016. *Terror, Love and Brainwashing: Attachment in Cults and Totalitarian Systems.* Routledge.

29. Shermer, M. & Linse, P. 2014. Conspiracy Theories. *The Skeptics Society.* https://www.skeptic.com/downloads/conspiracy-theories-who-why-and-how.pdf.

30. Yeung, J. *et al.* 2020. June 2 George Floyd protest news. *CNN.* https://edition.cnn.com/us/live-news/george-floyd-protests-06-02-20/index.html.

31. Norman, G. 2020. Rioting, looting linked to George Floyd protests leaves trail of destruction across American cities. *Fox News.* https://www.foxnews.com/us/george-floyd-protests-aftermath.

32. Konnikova, M. 2014. How Headlines Change the Way We Think. *The New Yorker.* https://www.newyorker.com/science/maria-konnikova/headlines-change-way-think.

33. Yoon, S. *et al.* 2019. Detecting incongruity between news headline and body text via a deep hierarchical encoder. *Proc. AAAI Conf. Artif. Intell.* 33, 791–800.

34. Gottfried, J. 2020. Americans' news fatigue isn't going away – about two-thirds still feel worn out. *Pew Research Center.* https://www.pewresearch.org/fact-tank/2020/02/26/almost-seven-in-ten-americans-have-news-fatigue-more-among-republicans/.

35. Fazio, L. 2020. Pausing to consider why a headline is true or false can help reduce the sharing of false news. *Harvard Kennedy Sch. Misinformation* Rev. 1, 1–8.

36. Fanelli, D. *et al.* 2017. Meta-assessment of bias in science. *Proc. Natl. Acad. Sci.* 114, 3714–3719.

37. Simmons, J. P. *et al.* 2011. False-positive psychology. *Psychol. Sci.* 22, 1359–1366.

38. Begley, C. G. & Ellis, L. M. 2012. Raise standards for preclinical cancer research. *Nature* 483, 531–533.

39. Aarts, A. A. *et al.* 2015. Estimating the reproducibility of psychological science. *Science* 349, aac4716–aac4716.

40. Baker, M. & Penny, D. 2016. Is there a reproducibility crisis? *Nature* 533, 452–454.

41. Gelman, A. & Geurts, H. M. 2017. The statistical crisis in science: How is it relevant to clinical neuropsychology? *Clin. Neuropsychol.* 31, 1000–1014.

42. Harris, R. 2017. *Rigor Mortis: How Sloppy Science Creates Worthless Cures, Crushes Hope, and Wastes Billions.* Basic Books.

43. Goldacre, B. 2013. *Bad Pharma.* Farrar Straus & Giroux.

44. Whitaker, R. 2010. *Anatomy of an Epidemic: Magic Bullets, Psychiatric Drugs, and the Astonishing Rise of Mental Illness in America.* Crown Publishers.

45. Gelman, A. & Loken, E. 2016. The statistical crisis in science. In *The Best Writing on Mathematics* 2015. Princeton University Press. (ed. Pitici, M.) 305–318.

46. Wired Staff. 2009. Placebos Are Getting More Effective. Drugmakers Are Desperate to Know Why. *WIRED.* https://www.wired.com/2009/08/ff-placebo-effect/.

47. Gul, M. 2016. Bias in a randomized controlled trial and how these can be minimised. *J. Psychiatry* 19, 2–4.

48. Gigerenzer, G. 2015. *Risk Savvy: How to Make Good Decisions.* Penguin Books.

49. Harris, I. 2016. *Surgery, The Ultimate Placebo: A Surgeon Cuts Through the Evidence.* NewSouth.

50. Turner, E. H. *et al.* 2008. Selective publication of antidepressant trials and its influence on apparent efficacy. *N. Engl. J. Med.* 358, 252–260.

51. The Therapeutic Goods Administration. 2020. Pete Evans' company fined for alleged COVID-19 advertising breaches. *Australian Government.* https://www.tga.gov.au/media-release/pete-evans-company-fined-alleged-covid-19-advertising-breaches.

52. Fichera, A. *et al.* 2020. The Falsehoods of the "Plandemic" Video. *FactCheck.org.* https://www.factcheck.org/2020/05/the-falsehoods-of-the-plandemic-video/.

53. Enserink, M. & Cohen, J. 2020. Fact-checking Judy Mikovits, the controversial virologist attacking Anthony Fauci in a viral conspiracy video. *Science.* https://www.sciencemag.org/news/2020/05/fact-checking-judy-mikovits-controversial-virologist-attacking-anthony-fauci-viral.

54. Omer, S. B. 2020. The discredited doctor hailed by the anti-vaccine movement. *Nature* 586, 668–669.

55. The Editors of The Lancet. 2010. Retraction — Ileal-lymphoid-nodular hyperplasia, non-specific colitis, and pervasive developmental disorder in children. *Lancet* 375, 445.

56. Pilmer, I. 1994. *Telling Lies For God: Reason Vs Creationism.* Random House Australia.

57. Pilmer, I. 2009. *Heaven and Earth: Global Warming, the Missing Science.* Taylor Trade Publishing.

58. Monbiot, G. 2009. Spectator recycles climate rubbish published by sceptic. *The Guardian.* https://www.theguardian.com/environment/georgemonbiot/2009/jul/09/george-monbiot-ian-plimer.

59. Walker, C. 2014. *From Contempt to Curiosity: Creating the Conditions for Groups to Collaborate Using Clean Language and Systemic Modelling.* Clean Publishing.

60. Bostic St. Clair, C. & Grinder, J. 2001. *Whispering in the Wind.* J & C Enterprises.

61. Morreall, J. 1997. Humor in the Holocaust: Its Critical, Cohesive, and Coping Functions. *Holocaust Teacher Resource Center.* http://www.holocaust-trc.org/humor-in-the-holocaust/.

62. Christopher, S. 2015. An introduction to black humor as a coping mechanism for student paramedics. *J. Paramed. Pract.* 7, 610–617.

63. Moran, C. & Massam, M. 1997. An evaluation of humor in emergency work. *Australas. J. Disaster Trauma Stud.* 3, 1–11.

64. Connor, K. M. & Davidson, J. R. T. 2003. Development of a new resilience scale: The Connor-

Davidson Resilience Scale (CD-RISC). *Depress. Anxiety* 18, 76–82.

65. Hurtes, K. P. & Allen, L. R. 2001. Measuring resiliency in youth: The resiliency attitudes and skills profile. *Ther. Recreation J.* 35, 333–347.

66. Kuipera, N. A. 2012. Humor and resiliency: Towards a process model of coping and growth. *Eur. J. Psychol.* 8, 475–491.

67. Sultanoff, S. M. 1995. Levity defies gravity; Using humor in crisis situations. *Ther. Humor* 9, 1–2.

68. Dean, R. A. K. & Major, J. E. 2008. From critical care to comfort care: The sustaining value of humor. *J. Clin. Nurs.* 17, 1088–1095.

69. Wooten, P. 1996. Humor: An antidote for stress. *Holist. Nurs. Pract.* 10, 49–56.

70. Berk, R. A. 2004. Coping with the daily stressors of an academic career: Try Mirthium ®. *Acad. Physician Sci.* 1–4.

71. Kuhlman, T. L. 1988. Gallows humor for a scaffold setting: Managing aggressive patients on a maximum security forensic unit. *Psychiatr. Serv.* 39, 1085–1090

72. Salzberg, R. F. 2000. *How to "Keep On Laughing!" - A Guide to Coping Humor.* Ruth F. Salzberg.

73. Bostic St. Clair, C. & Grinder, J. 2001. *Whispering in the Wind.* J & C Enterprises. p216.

74. Barrett, D. B. *et al.* 2001. *World Christian Encyclopedia: A Comparative Survey of Churches and Religions in The Modern World.* Oxford University Press. vol. 2.

75. Memmott, M. 2010. Don't Tell The Aliens We're Here, Stephen Hawking Says; They Might Not Be Friendly. NRP. https://www.npr.org/sections/thetwo-way/2010/04/aliens_stephen_hawking.html.

CHAPTER 10

1. Csikszentmihalyi, M. 1975. *Beyond Boredom and Anxiety.* Jossey-Bass Publishers.

2. Csikszentmihalyi, M. 1985. Reflections on enjoyment. *Perspect. Biol. Med.* 28, 489–497.

3. Csikszentmihalyi, M. 1990. *Flow: The Psychology of Optimal Experience.* Harper and Row.

4. Nakamura, J. & Csikszentmihalyi, M. 2002. The concept of flow. In *Handbook of Positive Psychology.* Oxford University Press. 89–105.

5. Cheron, G. 2016. How to measure the psychological "flow"? A neuroscience perspective. *Front. Psychol.* 7, 1–6.

6. Engeser, S. & Rheinberg, F. 2008. Flow, performance and moderators of challenge-skill balance. *Motiv. Emot.* 32, 158–172.

7. Mao, Y. *et al.* 2016. Optimal experience and optimal identity: A multinational study of the associations between flow and social identity. *Front. Psychol.* 7, 1–13.

8. Cheron, G. *et al.* 2016. Brain oscillations in sport: Toward EEG biomarkers of performance. *Front. Psychol.* 7, 1-25.

9. Ulrich, M. *et al.* 2014. Neural correlates of experimentally induced flow experiences. *Neuroimage* 86, 194–202.

10. Klasen, M. *et al.* 2012. Neural contributions to flow experience during video game playing. *Soc. Cogn. Affect. Neurosci.* 7, 485–495.

11. Fave, A. D. *et al.* 2003. Quality of experience and risk perception in high-altitude rock climbing. *J. Appl. Sport Psychol.* 15, 82–98.

12. MacDonald, R. *et al.* 2006. Creativity and flow in musical composition: an empirical investigation. *Psychol. Music* 34, 292–306.

13. Gray, J. & Rumpe, B. 2017. The importance of flow in software development. *Softw. Syst. Model.* 16, 927–928.

14. Leroy, A. & Cheron, G. 2020. EEG dynamics and neural generators of psychological flow during one tightrope performance. *Sci. Rep.* 10, 1–13.

15. Dietrich, A. 2004. Neurocognitive mechanisms underlying the experience of flow. *Conscious. Cogn.* 13, 746–761.

16. Gold, J. & Ciorciari, J. 2019. A transcranial stimulation intervention to support flow state induction. *Front. Hum. Neurosci.* 13, 1-23.

17. Katahira, K. *et al.* 2018. EEG correlates of the flow state: A combination of increased frontal theta and moderate frontocentral alpha rhythm in the mental arithmetic task. *Front. Psychol.* 9, 1–11.

18. Grinder, J. & DeLozier, J. 1987. *Turtles All the Way Down: Prerequisites to Personal Genius.* Grinder & Associates.

19. Kotler, S. 2015. The Neurochemistry of Flow States, with Steven Kotler. YouTube. https://www.youtube.com/watch?v=aHp2hkue8RQ.

20. Jackson, S. A. 1992. Athletes in flow: A qualitative investigation of flow states in elite figure skaters. *J. Appl. Sport Psychol.* 4, 161–180.

21. Stranger, M. 1999. The aesthetics of risk. *Int. Rev. Sociol. Sport* 34, 265–276.

22. Celsi, R. L. *et al.* 1993. An exploration of high-risk leisure consumption through skydiving. *J. Consum. Res.* 20, 1-23.

23. Thatcher, A. *et al.* 2008. Online flow experiences, problematic Internet use and Internet procrastination. *Comput. Human Behav.* 24, 2236–2254.

24. Beard, K. W. & Wolf, E. M. 2001. Modification in the proposed diagnosti criteria for internet addiction. *CyberPsychology Behav.* 4, 377–383.

25. Kim, H. K. & Davis, K. E. 2009. Toward a comprehensive theory of problematic Internet use: Evaluating the role of self-esteem, anxiety, flow, and the self-rated importance of Internet activities. *Comput. Human Behav.* 25, 490–500.

26. Partington, S. *et al.* 2009. The dark side of flow: A qualitative study of dependence in big wave surfing. *Sport Psychol.* 23, 170–185.

27. Schüler, J. & Nakamura, J. 2013. Does flow experience lead to risk? How and for whom. *Appl. Psychol. Heal. Well-Being* 5, 311–331.

28. Schüler, J. 2012. The dark side of the moon. In *Advances in Flow Research.* Springer New York. 123–137.

29. Harari, Y. N. 2008. Combat flow: Military, political and ethical dimensions of subjective well-being in war. *Rev. Gen. Psychol.* 12, 253–264.

30. Park, J. L. *et al.* 2015. Making the case for mobile cognition: EEG and sports performance. *Neurosci. Biobehav. Rev.* 52, 117–130.

31. Bertollo, M. *et al.* 2016. Proficient brain for optimal performance: The MAP model perspective. *PeerJ* 4, 1-26.

32. Gong, A. *et al.* 2020. Efficacy, Trainability, and Neuroplasticity of SMR vs. Alpha Rhythm Shooting Performance Neurofeedback Training. *Front. Hum. Neurosci.* 14, 1–14.

CHAPTER 11

1. Rotenstein, L. S. *et al.* 2018. Prevalence of burnout among physicians. *JAMA* 320, 1131–1150.

2. Maslach, C. & Leiter, M. P. 2016. Understanding the burnout experience: Recent research and its implications for psychiatry. *World Psychiatry* 15, 103–111.

3. Eklund, R. C. & DeFreese, J. D. 2020. Athlete burnout. *Handb. Sport Psychol.* II, 1220–1240.

4. Chae, Y. *et al.* 2017. The Relation among moral distress, physical symptoms and burnout of hospital nurses. *J. Korean Acad. Soc. Nurs. Educ.* 23, 430–440.

5. Gluschkoff, K. *et al.* 2016. Work stress, poor recovery and burnout in teachers. *Occup. Med. (Chic. Ill).* 66, 564–570.

6. Padyab, M. *et al.* 2016. Burnout, coping, stress of conscience and psychosocial work environment among patrolling police officers. *J. Police Crim. Psychol.* 31, 229–237.

7. Thyer, L. *et al.* 2018. Burnout in Australian paramedics. *Int. Paramed. Pract.* 8, 48–55.

8. Salminen, S. *et al.* 2017. Narratives of burnout and recovery from an agency perspective: A two-year longitudinal study. *Burn. Res.* 7, 1–9.

9. Naclerio Ayllón, F. *et al.* 2013. Applied periodization: A methodological approach. *J. Hum. Sport Exerc.* 8, 350–366.

10. Krasilshchikov, O. 2010. Application of periodisation in various sports. *Br. J. Sports Med.* 44, i47–i47.

11. Frenda, S. J. & Fenn, K. M. 2016. Sleep less, think worse: The effect of sleep deprivation on working memory. *J. Appl. Res. Mem. Cogn.* 5, 463–469.

12. Williamson, A. M. & Feyer, A. M. 2000. Moderate sleep deprivation produces impairments in cognitive and motor performance equivalent to legally prescribed levels of alcohol intoxication. *Occup. Environ. Med.* 57, 649–655.

13. Littlehales, N. 2016. *Sleep: Change the Way You Sleep with This 90 Minute Read.* Penguin Life.

14. Bjorness, T. E. *et al.* 2009. Control and function of the homeostatic sleep response by adenosine A 1 receptors. *J. Neurosci.* 29, 1267–1276.

15. De Lange, C. 2016. Can you catch up on missed sleep? *New Scientist.* https://www.newscientist.com/article/mg23030750-400-can-i-catch-up-on-what-i-miss/.

16. Ribeiro, J. A. & Sebastião, A. M. 2010. Caffeine and Adenosine. *J. Alzheimer's Dis.* 20, S3–S15.

17. Colten, H. R. & Altevogt, B. M. 2006. *Sleep Disorders and Sleep Deprivation. Sleep Disorders and Sleep Deprivation: An Unmet Public Health Problem.* National Academies Press.

18. Alhola, P. & Polo-Kantola, P. 2007. Sleep deprivation: Impact on cognitive performance. *Neuropsychiatr. Dis. Treat.* 3, 553–567.

19. Chaput, J. P. *et al.* 2010. Do all sedentary activities lead to weight gain: Sleep does not. *Curr. Opin. Clin. Nutr. Metab. Care* 13, 601–607.

20. Beccuti, G. & Pannain, S. 2011. Sleep and obesity. *Curr. Opin. Clin. Nutr. Metab. Care* 14, 402–412.

21. Shan, Z. *et al.* 2015. Sleep duration and risk of type 2 diabetes: A meta-analysis of prospective studies. *Diabetes Care* 38, 529–537.

22. Kim, Y. *et al.* 2013. Insufficient and excessive amounts of sleep increase the risk of premature death from cardiovascular and other diseases: The Multiethnic Cohort Study. *Prev. Med. (Baltim).* 57, 377–385.

23. Belenky, G. *et al.* 1994. The effects of sleep deprivation on performance during continuous combat operations. In *Food Components to Enhance Performance.* National Academy Press. (ed. Marriott, B. M.).

24. Kaliyaperumal, D. 2017. Effects of sleep deprivation on the cognitive performance of nurses working in shift. *J. Clin. Diagnositc Res.* 11, CC01–CC03.

25. Dula, D. J. *et al.* 2001. The effect of working serial night shifts on the cognitive functioning of emergency physicians. *Ann. Emerg. Med.* 38, 152–155.

26. Ramadanov, N. *et al.* 2019. Influence of time of mission on correct diagnosis by the prehospital emergency physician: A retrospective study. *Emerg. Med. Int.* 2019, 1–6.

27. Harrison, Y. & Horne, J. A. 1999. One night of sleep loss impairs innovative thinking and flexible decision making. *Organ. Behav. Hum. Decis. Process.* 78, 128–145.

28. Barnes, C. M. *et al.* 2011. Lack of sleep and unethical conduct. *Organ. Behav. Hum. Decis. Process.* 115, 169–180.

29. Rosekind, M. R. *et al.* 2010. The cost of poor sleep: Workplace productivity loss and associated costs. *J. Occup. Environ. Med.* 52, 91–98.

30. Boivin, D. B. & Boudreau, P. 2014. Impacts of shift work on sleep and circadian rhythms. *Pathol. Biol.* 62, 292–301.

31. Barnes, C. M. & Watson, N. F. 2019. Why healthy sleep is good for business. *Sleep Med. Rev.* 47, 112–118.

32. Dhand, R. & Sohal, H. 2006. Good sleep, bad sleep! The role of daytime naps in healthy adults. *Curr. Opin. Pulm. Med.* 12, 379–382.

33. Lahl, O. *et al.* 2008. An ultra short episode of sleep is sufficient to promote declarative memory performance. *J. Sleep Res.* 17, 3–10.

34. MacDonald, F. 2005. Napping May Be Able to Reverse The Damage of Sleep Deprivation. *ScienceAlert.* https://www.sciencealert.com/napping-may-be-able-to-reverse-the-damage-of-sleep-deprivation.

35. Mollicone, D. J. *et al.* 2007. Optimizing sleep/wake schedules in space: Sleep during chronic nocturnal sleep restriction with and without diurnal naps. *Acta Astronaut.* 60, 354–361.

36. Somani, S. M. & Gupta, P. 1988. Caffeine: A new look at an age-old drug. *Int. J. Clin. Pharmacol. Ther. Toxicol.* 26, 521–33.

37. Naska, A. *et al.* 2007. Siesta in healthy adults and coronary mortality in the general population. *Arch. Intern. Med.* 167, 296–301.

38. Brooks, A. & Lack, L. 2006. A brief afternoon nap following nocturnal sleep restriction: Which nap duration is most recuperative? *Sleep* 29, 831–840.

39. Santos, R. M. & Lima, D. R. 2009. *An Unashamed Defense of Coffee.* Xlibris.

40. Horne, J. A. & Reyner, L. A. 1996. Counteracting driver sleepiness: Effects of napping, caffeine, and placebo. *Psychophysiology* 33, 306–309.

41. Walker, W. H. *et al.* 2020. Circadian rhythm disruption and mental health. *Transl. Psychiatry* 10, 28–45.

42. Farhud, D. & Aryan, Z. 2018. Circadian rhythm, lifestyle and health: A narrative review. *Iran. J. Public Health* 47, 1068–1076.

43. Serin, Y. & Acar Tek, N. 2019. Effect of circadian rhythm on metabolic processes and the regulation of energy balance. *Ann. Nutr. Metab.* 74, 322–330.

44. Valdez, P. 2019. Circadian rhythms in attention. *Yale J. Biol. Med.* 92, 81–92.

45. Byrne, J. E. M. *et al.* 2017. Time of day differences in neural reward functioning in healthy young men. *J. Neurosci.* 37, 8895–8900.

46. Bes, F. *et al.* 2009. Modeling napping, post-lunch dip, and other variations in human sleep propensity. *Sleep* 32, 392–398.

47. National Sleep Foundation. 2020. Sleep Drive and Your Body Clock. https://www.sleepfoundation.org/articles/sleep-drive-and-your-body-clock.

48. Blume, C. *et al.* 2019. Effects of light on human circadian rhythms, sleep and mood. *Somnologie* 23, 147–156.

49. Gall, H. *et al.* 1979. Circadian rhythm of testosterone level in plasma. *Andrologia* 11, 287–293.

50. Law, R. *et al.* 2015. The cortisol awakening response predicts same morning executive function: Results from a 50-day case study. *Stress* 18, 616–621.

51. Wüst, S. *et al.* 2000. The cortisol awakening response - normal values and confounds. *Noise Health* 2, 79–88.

52. Chan, S. & Debono, M. 2010. Review: Replication of cortisol circadian rhythm: New advances in hydrocortisone replacement therapy. *Ther. Adv. Endocrinol. Metab.* 1, 129–138.

53. Elder, G. J. *et al.* 2014. The cortisol awakening response – Applications and implications for sleep medicine. *Sleep Med. Rev.* 18, 215–224.

54. Cheung, I. N. *et al.* 2016. Morning and evening blue enriched light exposure alters metabolic function in normal weight adults. *PLoS One* 11, 1–18.

55. Grivas, T. B. & Savvidou, O. D. 2007. Melatonin the "light of night" in human biology and adolescent idiopathic scoliosis. *Scoliosis* 2, 1–14.

56. Sharma, S. & Kavuru, M. 2010. Sleep and metabolism: An overview. *Int. J. Endocrinol.* 2010, 1–12.

57. Facer-Childs, E. R. *et al.* 2018. The effects of time of day and chronotype on cognitive and physical performance in healthy volunteers. *Sport. Med. - Open* 4, 47-58.

58. Martin, J. S. *et al.* 2016. Chronotype, light exposure, sleep, and daytime functioning in high school students attending morning or afternoon school shifts. *J. Biol. Rhythms* 31, 205–217.

59. Van Dongen, H. P. A. & Dinges, D. F. 2005. Sleep, circadian rhythms, and psychomotor vigilance. *Clin. Sports Med.* 24, 237–249.

60. Janků, K. *et al.* 2020. Block the light and sleep well: Evening blue light filtration as a part of cognitive behavioral therapy for insomnia. *Chronobiol. Int.* 37, 248–259.

61. Shechter, A. *et al.* 2018. Blocking nocturnal blue light for insomnia: A randomized controlled trial. *J. Psychiatr. Res.* 96, 196–202.

62. Tähkämö, L. *et al.* 2019. Systematic review of light exposure impact on human circadian rhythm. *Chronobiol. Int.* 36, 151–170.

63. Cho, Y. *et al.* 2015. Effects of artificial light at night on human health: A literature review of observational and experimental studies applied to exposure assessment. *Chronobiol. Int.* 32, 1294–1310.

64. Wiley, T. S. & Formby, B. 2000. *Lights Out: Sleep, Sugar, and Survival.* Atria.

65. Figueiro, M. G. & Rea, M. S. 2010. The Effects of red and blue lights on circadian variations in cortisol, alpha amylase, and melatonin. *Int. J. Endocrinol.* 2010, 1–9.

66. Figueiro, M. G. 2017. Disruption of circadian rhythms by light during day and night. *Curr. Sleep Med. Reports* 3, 76–84.

67. Pall, M. L. 2016. Microwave frequency electromagnetic fields (EMFs) produce widespread neuropsychiatric effects including depression. *J. Chem. Neuroanat.* 75, 43–51.

68. World Health Organization. 2014. The International EMF Project Progress Report.

69. Danker-Hopfe, H. *et al.* 2020. Spending the night next to a router – Results from the first human experimental study investigating the impact of Wi-Fi exposure on sleep. *Int. J. Hyg. Environ. Health* 228, 1-11.

70. Chepesiuk, R. 2009. Missing the dark: Health effects of light pollution. *Environ. Health Perspect.* 117, 20–27.

71. World Health Organization. 2020. Noise. http://www.euro.who.int/en/health-topics/environment-and-health/noise/noise.

72. Halperin, D. 2014. Environmental noise and sleep disturbances: A threat to health? *Sleep Sci.* 7, 209–212.

73. Pan, L. *et al.* 2012. Investigation of sleep quality under different temperatures based on subjective and physiological measurements. *HVAC R Res.* 18, 1030–1043.

74. Wagner, U. *et al.* 2004. Sleep inspires insight. *Nature* 427, 352–355.

75. Sanders, K. E. G. *et al.* 2019. Targeted memory reactivation during sleep improves next day problem solving. *Psychol. Sci.* 30, 1616–1624.

76. Hu, X. *et al.* 2020. Promoting memory consolidation during sleep: A meta-analysis of targeted memory reactivation. *Psychol. Bull.* 146, 218–244.

77. Healey, D. & Runco, M. A. 2006. Could creativity be associated with insomnia? *Creat. Res. J.* 18, 39–43.

78. Javaheri, S. *et al.* 2017. Sleep apnea. *J. Am. Coll. Cardiol.* 69, 841–858.

79. Senaratna, C. V. *et al.* 2017. Prevalence of obstructive sleep apnea in the general population: A systematic review. *Sleep Med. Rev.* 34, 70–81.

80. Thakral, M. *et al.* 2020. Changes in dysfunctional beliefs about sleep after cognitive behavioral therapy for insomnia: A systematic literature review and meta-analysis. *Sleep Med. Rev.* 49, 1-9.

81. Sabot, D. L. & Hicks, R. E. 2020. Does psychological capital mediate the impact of dysfunctional sleep beliefs on well-being? *Heliyon* 6, 1-10.

82. Baron, K. G. *et al.* 2017. Orthosomnia: Are some patients taking the quantified self too far? *J. Clin. Sleep Med.* 13, 351–354.

83. Morin, C. M. *et al.* 2007. Dysfunctional beliefs and attitudes about sleep (DBAS): Validation of a brief version (DBAS-16). *Sleep* 30, 1547–1554.

CHAPTER 12

1. Merriam-Webster. 2020. Dictionary by Merriam-Webster. https://www.merriam-webster.com/.

2. D'Souza, S. & Renner, D. 2018. *Not Doing: The Art of Effortless Action*. LID Publishing.

3. Aarstol, S. 2016. *The Five-Hour Workday: Live Differently, Unlock Productivity, and Find Happiness*. Lioncrest.

4. Glaveski, S. 2018. The Case for the 6-Hour Workday. *Harvard Business Review*. https://hbr.org/2018/12/the-case-for-the-6-hour-workday.

5. Barnes, A. 2020. *The 4 Day Week: How the Flexible Work Revolution Can Increase Productivity, Profitability and Well-being, and Create a Sustainable Future*. Piatkus.

6. Nicola, S. 2021. Tell Your Boss the Four-Day Week Is Coming Soon. *Bloomberg Businessweek*. https://www.bloomberg.com/news/articles/2021-03-02/four-day-work-week-gains-popularity-around-the-world.

7. Ferriss, T. 2009. *The 4-Hour Workweek: Escape 9-5, Live Anywhere, and Join the New Rich*. Harmony Books.

8. Ferriss, T. 2012. *The 4-Hour Chef: The Simple Path to Cooking Like a Pro, Learning Anything, and Living the Good Life*. New Harvest.

9. Ferriss, T. 2010. *4-Hour Body: An Uncommon Guide to Rapid Fat-Loss, Incredible Sex, and Becoming Superhuman*. Harmony Books.

10. Clifton, J. 2019. It's the Manager. *Gallup*. https://www.gallup.com/workplace/251642/manager.aspx.

11. Kelly, E. L. & Moen, P. 2020. *Overload: How Good Jobs Went Bad and What We Can Do About It*. Princeton University Press.

12. Clark, C. J. et al. 2019. Tribalism is human nature. *Curr. Dir. Psychol. Sci.* 28, 587–592.

13. Burns, L. et al. 2019. Supportive interpersonal relationships: a key component to high-performance sport. *Br. J. Sports Med.* 53, 1386–1389.

14. McFadden, P. 2018. Two sides of one coin? Relationships build resilience or contribute to burnout in child protection social work: Shared perspectives from Leavers and Stayers in Northern Ireland. *Int. Soc. Work* 63, 164–176.

15. Clair, R. et al. 2021. The effects of social isolation on well-being and life satisfaction during pandemic. *Humanit. Soc. Sci. Commun.* 8, 28-35.

16. Kofman, Y. B. & Garfin, D. R. 2020. Home is not always a haven: The domestic violence crisis amid the COVID-19 pandemic. *Psychol. Trauma Theory, Res. Pract. Policy* 12, S199–S201.

17. Evans, M. L. et al. 2020. A Pandemic within a pandemic — Intimate partner violence during Covid-19. *N. Engl. J. Med.* 383, 2302–2304.

18. Anurudran, A. et al. 2020. Domestic violence amid COVID-19. *Int. J. Gynecol. Obstet.* 150, 255–256.

19. Our Watch. 2021. Quick Facts. https://www.ourwatch.org.au/quick-facts/.

20. Bryant, W. & Bricknell, S. 2017. Homicide in Australia 2012–13 to 2013–14: National Homicide Monitoring Program report. *Australian Institute of Criminology*.

21. Australian Bureau of Statistics. 2017. Personal Safety, Australia. https://www.abs.gov.au/statistics/people/population/national-state-and-territory-population/latest-release.

22. Joshi, S. 2008. The sick building syndrome. *Indian J. Occup. Environ. Med.* 12, 61-64.

23. Ghaffarianhoseini, A. et al. 2018. Sick building syndrome: Are we doing enough? *Archit. Sci. Rev.* 61, 99–121.

24. Pigatto, P. D. et al. 2020. Chemical exposure, risk of multiple chemical sensitivity, and occupational safety. *Saf. Health Work* 11, 383–384.

25. Rea, W. J. et al. 1992. Considerations for the diagnosis of chemical sensitivity. In *Multiple Chemical Sensitivities: A Workshop*. National Academies Press.

26. Azuma, K. et al. 2019. Chemical intolerance: Involvement of brain function and networks after exposure to extrinsic stimuli perceived as hazardous. *Environ. Health Prev. Med.* 24, 61-71.

27. Genuis, S. J. 2010. Sensitivity-related illness: The escalating pandemic of allergy, food intolerance and chemical sensitivity. *Sci. Total Environ.* 408, 6047–6061.

28. Hawkey, E. 2019. Media use in childhood: Evidence-based recommendations for caregivers. *American Psychological Association*. https://www.apa.org/pi/families/resources/newsletter/2019/05/media-use-childhood.

29. Stoll, J. 2021. Average daily time spent watching TV per capita in the United States in 2009 and 2019, by age group. *Statista*. https://www.statista.com/statistics/411775/average-daily-time-watching-tv-us-by-age/.

30. Kayser, T. 2010. *Mining Group Gold: How to Cash in on the Collaborative Brain Power of a Team for Innovation and Results*. McGraw-Hill Education.

31. Kim, B. & Rudin, C. 2013. Learning about meetings. *Data Min. Knowl. Discov.* 28, 1134–1157.

32. Jarrett, C. 2013. The scourge of meeting late-comers. *BPS Research Digest*. https://digest.bps.org.uk/2013/03/20/the-scourge-of-meeting-late-comers/.

33. Eyesafe. 2020. COVID-19: Screen Time Spikes to Over 13 Hours Per Day According to Eyesafe Nielsen Estimates. https://eyesafe.com/covid-19-screen-time-spike-to-over-13-hours-per-day/.

34. Rosling, H. et al. 2018. *Factfulness: Ten Reasons We're Wrong About the World — and Why Things Are Better Than You Think*. Flatiron Books.

35. Paprotny, D. 2021. Convergence betweem developed and developing countries: A centennial perspective. *Soc. Indic. Res.* 153, 193–225.

36. Rios, R. & Zautra, A. J. 2011. Socioeconomic disparities in pain: The role of economic hardship and daily financial worry. *Heal. Psychol.* 30, 58–66.

37. Friedline, T. et al. 2020. Families' financial stress & well-being: The importance of the economy and economic environments. *J. Fam. Econ. Issues* 1–18.

38. Taylor, M. et al. 2017. The Impacts of household financial stress, resilience, social support, and other adversities on the psychological distress of Western Sydney parents. *Int. J. Popul. Res.* 2017, 1–12.

39. Huang, R. et al. 2020. Effect of financial stress on self-rereported health and quality of life among

older adults in five developing countries: A cross sectional analysis of WHO-SAGE survey. *BMC Geriatr.* 20, 1–12.

40. Capital One. 2020. Big-Picture Thinking Leads to the Right Money Mindset. https://www.capitalone.com/about/newsroom/mind-over-money-survey/.

41. Burnes, D. *et al.* 2017. Prevalence of financial fraud and scams among older adults in the United States: A systematic review and meta-analysis. *Am. J. Public Health* 107, e13–e21.

42. Williams, E. J. *et al.* 2017. Individual differences in susceptibility to online influence: A theoretical review. *Comput. Human Behav.* 72, 412–421.

43. Mr. Money Mustache. 2021. Mr. Money Mustache - Early Retirement through Badassity. https://www.mrmoneymustache.com/.

44. Taleb, N. N. 2012. *Antifragile: Things That Gain from Disorder.* Random House.

45. Malkiel, B. G. 2019. *A Random Walk Down Wall Street: The Time-Tested Strategy For Successful Investing.* W. W. Norton & Company.

46. Flood, C. 2013. Monkey beats man on stock market picks. *Financial TImes.* https://www.ft.com/content/abd15744-9793-11e2-b7ef-00144feabdc0.

47. Barber, B. M. *et al.* 2014. Do day traders rationally learn about their ability? *SSRN Electron. J.*

48. Butler, G. & Fazal, M. 2021. Osama bin Laden's Son Is a Painter. America Is His Muse. *Vice.* https://www.vice.com/en/article/jgq3gd/osama-bin-laden-son-omar-artwork-trauma-america.

49. McDaniel, D. D. 2012. Risk and protective factors associated with gang affiliation among high-risk youth: A public health approach. *Inj. Prev.* 18, 253–258.

50. Goldacre, B. 2013. *Bad Pharma.* Farrar Straus & Giroux.

51. Goldacre, B. & Smeeth, L. 2014. Mass treatment with statins. *BMJ* 349, g4745–g4745.

52. ClinCalc. 2018. Atorvastatin - Drug Usage Statistics. https://clincalc.com/DrugStats/Drugs/Atorvastatin.

53. Noordzij, M. *et al.* 2017. Relative risk versus absolute risk: One cannot be interpreted without the other. *Nephrol. Dial. Transplant.* 32, ii13–ii18.

54. Gigerenzer, G. 2015. *Risk Savvy: How to Make Good Decisions.* Penguin Books.

55. Chong, C. A. K. Y. *et al.* 2006. An unadjusted NNT was a moderately good predictor of health benefit. *J. Clin. Epidemiol.* 59, 224–233.

56. Kristensen, M. L. *et al.* 2015. The effect of statins on average survival in randomised trials, an analysis of end point postponement: Table 1. *BMJ Open* 5, 1-5.

57. Bastian, H. 2015. The NNT: An Overhyped and Confusing Statistic. *MedPage Today.* https://www.medpagetoday.com/blogs/thirdopinion/50273.

58. Sever, P. S. *et al.* 2011. The Anglo-Scandinavian Cardiac Outcomes Trial: 11-year mortality follow-up of the lipid-lowering arm in the UK. *Eur. Heart J.* 32, 2525–2532.

59. Mason, P. 2019. Dr. Paul Mason - High cholesterol on a ketogenic diet (plus do statins work?) - 2019 update. *YouTube.* https://www.youtube.com/watch?v=mFlITzqRBWY.

60. Beckett, R. D. *et al.* 2015. Risk of new-onset diabetes associated with statin use. *SAGE Open Med.* 3, 1-12.

61. Barry, A. R. *et al.* 2018. Prevention and management of statin adverse effects: A practical approach for pharmacists. *Can. Pharm. J. / Rev. des Pharm. du Canada* 151, 179–188.

62. Hu, Y. *et al.* 2018. Smoking cessation, weight change, type 2 diabetes, and mortality. *N. Engl. J. Med.* 379, 623–632.

63. de Lorgeril, M. *et al.* 1998. Mediterranean dietary pattern in a randomized trial. *Arch. Intern. Med.* 158, 1181.

64. Jha, P. *et al.* 2013. 21st-century hazards of smoking and benefits of cessation in the United States. *N. Engl. J. Med.* 368, 341–350.

65. Dimsdale, J. E. 2008. Psychological stress and cardiovascular disease. *J. Am. Coll. Cardiol.* 51, 1237–1246.

66. Song, H. *et al.* 2019. Stress related disorders and risk of cardiovascular disease: Population based, sibling controlled cohort study. *BMJ* 365, 1-10.

67. Naci, H. *et al.* 2019. How does exercise treatment compare with antihypertensive medications? A network meta-analysis of 391 randomised controlled trials assessing exercise and medication effects on systolic blood pressure. *Br. J. Sports Med.* 53, 859–869.

68. Piano, M. R. 2017. Alcohol's effects on the cardiovascular system. *Alcohol Res.* 38, 219–241.

69. Hoffmann, T. C. *et al.* 2014. Shared decision making: what do clinicians need to know and why should they bother? *Med. J. Aust.* 201, 35–39.

70. Doidge, N. 2015. *Brain's Way of Healing: Remarkable Discoveries and Recoveries from the Frontiers of Neuroplasticity.* Viking.

71. Eccles, D. W. *et al.* 2006. Visual attention in orienteers at different levels of experience. *J. Sports Sci.* 24, 77–87.

72. Butler, N. 2018. Dave Snowden: How to have a lasting impact in a complex world. *Boost.* https://www.boost.co.nz/blog/2018/08/dave-snowden-complex-systems.

73. Thaler, R. H. & Sunstein, C. R. 2009. *Nudge: Improving Decisions About Health, Wealth, and Happiness.* Penguin Books.

74. Kohn, E. 2019. "Forrest Gump," 25 Years Later: A Bad Movie That Gets Worse With Age. *IndieWire.* https://www.indiewire.com/2019/07/forrest-gump-bad-movie-25-anniversary-1202154214/.

INDEX

If stress is the global epidemic, resilience is the cure we create from designing our own experience of the world.